T3-BOW-294

Joint Attention

Its Origins and Role in Development

Joint Attention

Its Origins and Role in Development

Edited by
Chris Moore
Philip J. Dunham
Dalhousie University

With a Foreword by Jerome Bruner

LEA LAWRENCE ERLBAUM ASSOCIATES, PUBLISHERS
1995 Hillsdale, New Jersey   Hove, UK

Lawrence Erlbaum Associates, Inc., Publishers
365 Broadway
Hillsdale, New Jersey 07642

Cover design by Mairav Salomon-Dekel

Library of Congress Cataloging-in-Publication Data

Joint attention : its origins and role in development / edited by
Chris Moore and Philip J. Dunham.
    p.   cm.
    Includes bibliographical references and index.
    ISBN 0-8058-1437-X
    1. Attention in infants. 2. Attention in children.
3. Interpersonal communication in infants. 4. Interpersonal
communication in children. 5. Cognition in infants. 6. Cognition
in children. I. Moore, Chris, 1958–   . II. Dunham, Philip J.
BF720.A85J65 1995
155.42'2—dc20   94-40160
                                                       CIP

Books published by Lawrence Erlbaum Associates are printed on acid-free
paper, and their bindings are chosen for strength and durability.

Printed in the United States of America
10 9 8 7 6 5 4 3 2 1

Contents

Preface

This collection started life as an idea for a symposium at the Society for Research in Child Development in New Orleans, 1993. The idea for the symposium had been to present some of the work that contemporary researchers were conducting in the area of joint attention. The notion that human experience is grounded in its shared nature is one whose significance has long been recognized, and joint attention is a topic that has been on the agenda for developmental psychologists for several years. However, research on joint attention has typically been discussed in isolated subcommunities. The SRCD symposium was supposed to be a first step in bringing together some of these lines of research. In selecting contributors, it quickly became clear that quite a large number of individuals had equally legitimate claims on representation, and that although research on joint attention was spreading in new directions, it was also starting to cohere in an exciting way. A book compiling more of these lines than could be represented in a single symposium seemed the right next step. We therefore explored the potential territory and selected a number of individuals and groups representing the primary domains of interest. It is significant, we believe, that everyone we approached agreed that the project was extremely timely and agreed to participate, in some cases in the face of considerable competing obligations. We are very grateful to the contributors for their promptness.

After the first drafts of the chapters had been collected, Amy Pierce, then our editor at Lawrence Erlbaum Associates, suggested that a foreword might enhance the structure of the book. No one has played a more important role in bringing to our joint attention the shared nature of human experience than

Jerome Bruner. So we asked Bruner to provide a foreword to the collection. To our great satisfaction, he responded with a piece that is much more than just a foreword. It is a personal view that provides both a history and a contemporary perspective on this research topic. Indeed, it contains enough new ideas to be considered a discussion chapter. We have, however, kept to our original intention and included Bruner's piece at the head of the contributions. In a more prosaic and down-to-earth style, we then follow Bruner's foreword with an introductory chapter in which we provide a map to lead the reader through some of the thematic routes that follow in the main contributions.

We would like to thank Imogen Fox who provided invaluable help in the preparation of the final manuscript. Our thanks also to Amy Pierce and Judi Amsel at Lawrence Erlbaum Associates.

—Chris Moore
—Philip J. Dunham

From Joint Attention to the Meeting of Minds: An Introduction

Jerome Bruner
School of Law: New York University

I first became puzzled about the young child's consuming interest in "sharing attention" with others at a symposium at the CIBA Foundation in London in the late 1950s. Discussing the growth of independence in young children, Myriam David (David & Appell, 1961) had reported that after mother and child lost interest in direct eye contact during their first months, they often looked at things around them together as a "substitute." Typically, after one of these joint focus bouts, the two participants would look back at each other as if to confirm shared experience. Still later, it was typical for a toddler, having encountered an unexpected object, say, in an adjoining room, to return with it to show it to his mother, after which he would return, as if requited, to solo explorations. None of this was taken as surprising by any of us: That is how infants and toddlers were. In the discussion that followed the presentation, there was no mention at all of the sheer mystery of mutual knowledge. Or perhaps we simply masked that mystery by plunging into the then standard questions, the ones about "function": "What does sharing visual attention do for the child? Does it reassure her about her mother's presence; is it about attachment, or what?"

Epistemological questions never entered the discussion. How, for example, do infants get from early and simple dyadic eye-to-eye joint attention to the more complex interaction entailed in sharing attentional focus on a common object? Nor did we spend any time brooding about how infants and toddlers come to know about other minds or how they come to realize that other minds knew theirs. And never a whisper about any theories young children might have about "other minds." Or about how the capacity for joint attention got there in the first place

1

or developed subsequently. Had most of us been asked such questions, we would have mumbled something about "learning." For as religion was the opiate of the people, so learning theory in those days was the opiate of developmental psychologists.

Nonetheless, I suspect, with hindsight, that something new must have been in the air those days, for in a few short years new research studies began to appear dealing with early perception and attention. That new interest inevitably created the classic slippery slope into the "other minds" problem. For once one observes infants focusing their attention on virtually anything in the presence of an "other," one is struck by how social or sharing or reciprocal such attentional activity is. Just as in that study by Myriam David. And it was equally inevitable that we grew uncomfortable with learning theory explanations of how eye-to-eye contact came into being, or how it shifted over to shared attention on common objects. With respect to the former, there were even studies indicating that eye-to-eye contact itself was reinforcing in learning tasks (Bower, 1974), and that infants were distressed when adults failed to reciprocate the child's efforts to sustain such contact (Stechler & Latz, 1966).

Once we began losing faith in learning theory as the engine of development, where did things stand? How were we to respond to the logical problems being posed and to the fresh facts being reported? For there were powerful logical *reductios* arguing that from nothing grows nothing, and also puzzling experimental findings about early gaze following. Does a young child naturally "understand" (after a while, anyway) that she and her mother are looking at something together, sharing a common experience? This is the "knowing that" question: Knowing that others are experiencing the world much as you are. Once having grasped that experience is shared, an infant might then routinely learn what another person was looking at by getting to know how to use, say, directional cues (mediated, as we learned years later, by eye-direction detectors in the superior temporal sulcus of the cortex; see Baron-Cohen, this volume). But could any infant, or anybody for that matter, ever learn from scratch, from experience alone, that somebody was looking at something, and that it was the same thing the infant was looking at? You would somehow have to know a priori that somebody was looking at something before it would occur to you to figure out what they were looking at.

And if the child could not at first understand that somebody else was experiencing something or experiencing it in common, but could later acquire such understanding, then that must mean that at the start there must have been some kind of half-baked innate knowledge that could, with some appropriate nurture from experience, be turned into what was needed for full-fledged joint attention later. Some version of an a priori position seemed required in response to the compelling *ex nihilo* argument. What version of a priorism was needed to deal with regard-following data like Scaife and Bruner's (1975) or with theoretical claims like the "protodeclaratives" of Bates and her colleagues (Bates, Benigni, Bretherton, Camaioni, & Volterra, 1977)?

What version indeed. Few psychologists are happy with flat-out nativism, though Chomsky's version (1965) provided a desperate face-saver for some disenchanted empiricists. Nor was the general shape of his argument about language acquisition altogether irrelevant to our issue. In his view, the infant had innately to "know" the deep structure of a language in order to comprehend and learn anything from its degenerate local surface structure, the actual language to which the infant was exposed. Though it was never clear in Chomsky exactly how the infant recognized the "deep structure" of language in general in the surface garbage of some language in particular (how, for example, she figures out the transformation rules by which universal deep structure is converted into a local surface realization), the general idea was intriguing. Never mind that it depended on some sort of minor miracle. Perhaps the Chomskian Language Acquisition Device had some kind of x-ray eye that permitted the growing infant to recognize deep syntactic invariances beneath the fluctuating local surface talk—yet another miraculous "detector" deep in the brain.

Although the Chomsky model did not fit our problem like a glove—how young children know other minds, know that they experience in common—it did at least serve to diminish the thrall of empirical explanations. And besides, is it so altogether farfetched that humans know in some crude way from the start that their conspecifics have in common certain experiences or "inner states," like intending or desiring, and that in time and with the development of sufficient processing capacity, they grow more "expert" in reading these experiences and states? What such a theory would need is some process for getting the young infant from a crude and general grasp of "otherness" and "other-mindedness" to a childhood in which he can grasp such particulars as referring, requesting, and the like. Eventually, with enough experience in "reading the cues," young humans might even reach a Proustian adulthood.

There were theories around that suggested a way around the blatant "all-there-at-the-start" nativism of Chomsky. The most powerful and popular of them was the Piagetian *aliment* solution (1980), a sophisticated version of the classic *maturation* doctrine. In this view, given a certain crude initial endowment, and given some generalized mental feeding on the aliment of sensorimotor experience, the infant's mind gradually blossoms into mastery of such higher-order accomplishments as semiosis, the recognition of invariance, and even possibly the appropriate recognition of other minds. Piaget's theory, faithful to its epistemological intent, proceeded by appealing first to a set of underlying and invariant logical steps required for a logical calculus to increase in power. The empirical task, then, was to demonstrate that there were observable steps in the growing child's actual problem solving acts that corresponded to the formal steps in the underlying logic: that is, actual behavior that improved in correspondence with the "beefing up" of a logical calculus. It would have to be shown that first the child followed a logic dominated by the INRC rules of logic (Identity, Negation, Reciprocity, and the Correlative) and then moved on to the rules embodied in the Sixteen Binary

Propositions, which include the earlier INRC group. It was never clear how the psychological processes conforming to the logical calculus got beefed up on an indifferent diet of unspecified aliment or just plain experience. Yet, for all its vague arguments about aliment, it was an interesting model nonetheless. Besides, it managed to bypass Chomsky's preformist nativism.

Piaget's was surely one of the most ambitious theoretical enterprises in the history of psychology, however premature it might have been, however lacking in sensitivity to cultural aliment, and however abstract it may have been about the generalizability of all experience. Could anything at all like it be made applicable to the unfolding of the child's "theory of mind," beginning with primitive joint attention and ending with a Proustian adult? If we abandoned the formal logical assumption of Piaget's genetic epistemology and characterized the foundational processes of joint attention as substantive processes, could we then come up with a coherent account? What would these foundational processes be like?

Surely a good beginning is to ask what role any possible process, like joint visual attention or pointing, might play in fostering the development of the child's theory of mind. This has the great virtue, at least, of establishing a comprehensive conceptual context within which to impose constraints on how isolated phenomena are to be interpreted. With such constraints, there would be fewer "one-fact theories" cluttering the journals. Michael Tomasello (this volume) is quite right in arguing, for example, that it is unparsimonious to describe early joint visual attention as just a precursor to the child's theory of mind. That would be much like arguing that the child's ballistic reaching is just a precursor of more visually guided reaching, or that the child's grasp of early topic-comment structures in two-word utterances (like Lois Bloom's "Mommy sock," 1973) is just a precursor of the later Noun Phrase-Verb Phrase predicate relationship in fully realized syntax. Might it not be more fruitful to conceive of earlier forms as, say, "constitutive of" or "foundational to" or a "scaffold for" later forms of the child's theory of other minds? With such an initial assumption, one shoulders the responsibility of explaining how early forms combine, are modified, or whatnot, to produce more mature forms.

So what might the underlying processes be that serve as constituents or foundations or scaffolds for the child's (or anybody's) theory of mind? Again, let me use Tomasello's chapter as a takeoff point. He argues that there are at least two "primitives" that might serve as foundational candidates. One is the child's very early construal of people as *agents*—that is to say, the notion that human actions are dedicated to attaining ends. This is not an ontological claim. Whether human beings really act agentively toward preconceived ends, or whether they are really like robots or computers or "goloms" is not the issue. The claim is simply that they are taken to act in that way, toward achieving ends, and that this construal is virtually obligatory, much as in the famous Heider-Simmel film, or in the finding of Poulin-Dubois and Schultz (1988) that year-old children can distinguish between intended and physically caused events.

The second claim is that, perhaps somewhat later along in development, young children grasp that there is a "standing for" relationship between arbitrary signs and things in the world of experience—between, say, words and things, to put it simply. This accomplishment might also go through steps, like C. S. Peirce's progression from ikons through indices to symbols. As many have demonstrated (see Astington, 1993, for a brilliant and comprehensive review), young children cannot distinguish between words or signs that are intended to falsify from those intended as true. It is enough that they grasp the deep notion of standing for, the philosopher's *intentionality*. Just as surely as they have the notion of agency, they also have the notion of intentionality.

And they seem able, soon after or concurrently, to combine the two forms of understanding into the notion that agents are capable of intending their gestures or words to stand for something in the world. Indeed, as several authors in this volume note, mere standing for may be only one way that the acts of agents are construed. We know from related work (Bruner, 1983) that young children construe adult acts as *requestive*: they both request *of* adults and recognize adult requests *to* them, even prelinguistically. And we know as well that they correct their own requests to be better understood, and reinterpret others' misinterpreted requests by appropriate maneuvers, like looking back at the adult to check line of regard or facial expression. To use Halliday's (1975) term, young children seem to have a good grasp of various so-called "pragmatic" functions of language even before they have the lexico-grammatical skills to perform these functions linguistically or to function "mathetically." And as we know from Meltzoff and Gopnik (1993), the parent treats the child's gestural or preverbal signs as intended, treats the child as an agent, and even construes these attributed intentions in quite conventional ways.

And what is particularly interesting is that caretakers of infants in reciprocal exchanges typically provide a helping scaffold for the infant or young child. They "standardize" such occasions of reciprocity in a way to make them easier for the young child to play out her own role as an agent with intentions of different kinds by "formatting" them in certain characteristic, rather stereotyped ways, for example, "book reading" formats for looking at and labelling pictures, "mealtime" formats for negotiating requests and prohibitions concerning food, "greeting" and "farewell" formats, and so on. These not only provide the child with an opportunity for making her own mind known, but also for recognizing what others have on their minds. As I've urged elsewhere, these occasions provide an early entry into the conduct of speech acts, particularly to a grasp of the felicity conditions on such speech acts (see Bruner, 1978; Ryan, 1974; Searle, 1969). By dint of such achievements, the young child is learning not only about communication, but also about the culture, its conventions, and its codes. A considerable amount of this takes place before the child's Mean Length of Utterance (MLU) ever gets to a whole number!

Note, right off, that the child's increasing skill in handling intersubjective encounters is not being fed just on an indifferent Genevan aliment. Rather, the aliment is interaction per se, reciprocal interaction with more adults, more competent members of the culture, adults treating the child as an agent and bent on "teaching" him or her to be more so. It is not teaching in the conventional sense but teaching through the provision of affordances and the imposition of constraints by the adult on the child and, more subtly, in the reverse direction as well. Wood and his colleagues (Wood, 1988; Wood, Bruner, & Ross, 1976), for example, have demonstrated in detail how the adult caretaker provides scaffolding for the young child's intentions, keeps her attention focused, protects her from distractions, reduces the degrees of freedom she must manage. Mother and child are not simply sharing common foci of attention, but are also constructing them, extending them over time by embedding them in task structures, and conventionalizing them in terms of canonical forms in the culture. How different cultures go about this task of formatting the child's expectations and beliefs about adult minds has been particularly well documented in a recent monograph by Rogoff, Mistry, Goncu, and Mosier (1993) that compares the interaction of mothers and children in San Pedro, a Mexican Indian village, and Salt Lake City. Salt Lake City toddlers were encouraged to perceive their parents as "playmates," whereas San Pedro children saw them as "organizers of household duties."

Indeed, so powerful are these reciprocal human patterns of intentional action that they even seem to "humanize" young chimpanzees, at least *Pan paniscus*. But we had better postpone that issue, for we are not quite ready for it yet.

II

Where does "joint attention," more narrowly defined, fit into this emerging foundational picture? The question needs some decomposing before it can be reasonably understood. To begin with, joint attention has to be differentiated in terms of what it consists of, how it is achieved, and by what criteria it is judged. The chapters in this volume provide a rich and valuable guide to these issues. What I want to offer here is a sketch of some relevant points. At its most sophisticated level, joint attention is, in effect, a "meeting of minds." It depends not only on a shared or joint focus, but on shared context and shared presuppositions. Imagine a scenario: A legal scholar in American antebellum jurisprudence says to his equally learned colleague that the Dred Scott decision (1857), after all, at least honored the juridical principle of *stare decisis*. He counts on bringing to his colleague's mind shared knowledge of, say, *Prigg v. Pennsylvania* (1842), or litigations over the Fugitive Slave Law, or various "deals" that eased the ratification of the United States Constitution in a nation then half slave and half free. Now, these are arcana known principally to historians and to law school professors. Such people form an interpretive community based on their being able to evoke a great deal of penumbral "background knowledge" (Clark, 1992; Searle, 1983) around each others' joint attentional focus. This triggering of background knowledge (Levinson, 1983) is done in myriad ways: by emphasizing Justice Taney rather than Justice Storey on Dred Scott, or even by carefully deploying modals of uncertainty in one's speech (words like "might") at just the right junctures. In their company and in that domain of discourse, most of us lack the means for achieving full joint attention. At best, we might simply know we were missing a lot that was going on, a problematic point that will need reconsideration later.

This kind of full attentional sharing is very different from the joint visual attention achieved by simple ostensive signing demonstrated in the old Scaife and Bruner (1975) experiment where young infants followed an adult's line of regard in search of a target out there, particularly after having been in eye to eye contact with the adult who has broken it off with a dramatically intoned "Oh look!", followed by a stagey head turn. All that is needed in this case, beyond a shared knowledge of space (Butterworth, this volume), is knowing that another is looking at and experiencing something in the visual world. Such knowledge is needed, not only to start the infant's action, but also to stop it when the infant finds a visual target out there. In Butterworth and Jarrett's (1991) study, for example, infants were provided a visual target out along the line of regard: If they found it, they stopped searching. If they did not, they turned back to look at the adult's gaze direction again. As the last decade of research has shown, there is a lot more to such joint attention (or secondary intersubjectivity) than Scaife and Bruner recognized back in the 1970s. But this brief account will suffice.

Let me shift now to the studies of Savage-Rumbaugh and her colleagues (1993) to explore some of the perplexities that lurk in the shadows of joint visual attention. These investigators taught a young pygmy chimpanzee, Kanzi, a good deal about the "knowing that" of shared attention, enough so that Kanzi became quite skilled in knowing what his human handlers were referring to. That is to say, by dint of caring human rearing Kanzi knew that both agency and intentionality prevail, that the experimenter as an agent intended to use a word or an arbitrary visual sign on the symbol board to stand for something either in experience or in the world. Without distinctively human rearing, pygmy chimpanzees never exhibit such capacities in the wild or in the laboratory. To be sure, young chimpanzees seem to show some primitive grasp of agency, they learn to follow another animal who has shown on prior trials that it knows where food has been hidden in an open field (Menzel, 1974). But it is primitive, and some seasoned primatologists prefer to explain it as a form of simple conditioning. In any case, it is not in the same league as Kanzi and his foster humans.

We find out how big the difference is from a study by Tomasello, Savage-Rumbaugh, and Kruger (1993). What makes the difference is "enculturation" and its effects. These investigators studied the imitative behavior of mother-reared young pygmy chimpanzees, human-reared ones, and young children, 18 and 30 months of age. Could they learn to imitate novel actions on objects, actions exhibited to them by familiar human caretaker-experimenters? Young subjects, whatever the species or age, were shown an action and then told "Do what I do." Would they perform the act at all, immediately or later, and would they do so by imitating the action or by producing the same outcomes by other means? The findings were clear: Mother-reared chimpanzees were much poorer on immediate imitation than human-reared ones or than human children of both ages, who did not differ from each other. On delayed imitation, the human-reared chimpanzees outperformed all the others. Imitation, particularly delayed imitation when the model is long gone and emulation (achieving the same ends but by means different from the models) is as good an indicator of recognized agency as we have (see Tomasello, Kruger, & Ratner, 1993, for the detailed argument behind this claim).

So how account for the remarkable increase in the "human" quality of the human-reared chimpanzee—Savage-Rumbaugh's Kanzi? Let me take the liberty of quoting from an unpublished communication to me on this query from M. Tomasello (personal communication, January 26, 1994):

> Kanzi and some other "enculturated" apes are different. Why? For precisely the reasons you articulate for children: from an early age Kanzi has spent his ontogeny building up a shared world with humans—much of the time through active negotiation. An essential element in this process is undoubtedly the behavior of other beings—i.e., human beings—who, on a daily basis encourage Kanzi to share attention to objects with them, to perform certain behaviors they have just performed, to take their emotional attitudes toward objects, and so on and so forth. *Apes in the wild have no one who engages them in this way—no one who intends things about their intentional states.*

So let me turn now to the issue of "active negotiation," for I believe it to be crucial. I want to contrast negotiation in chimpanzees (this time *Pan troglodytes*) and in the human case. The observations on the former come from an old study by Meredith Crawford (1937) on "cooperative" behavior in chimpanzees. The task posed to a pair of animals was to pull in a sliding tray baited with food, but too heavy for either to manage by themselves. The animals from the former Yale-Yerkes colony at Orange Park, Florida, and well used to human beings and their experiments, though mother-reared, were not very good at the task. They seemed unable to indicate to each other what they wanted help about. One of them finally hit on a somewhat successful maneuver: getting the task all set up, starting to pull hard on the rope connected with the heavy sliding tray, and then poking the other one to draw attention to its strenuous pulling. It sometimes worked, the other animal grasping the loose end of the rope and joining in. We cannot know, of course, whether there was any recognition of agency. Perhaps it was something more like empathy, or contagion, or even imitation. Certainly there is independent evidence (e.g., Byrne & Whiten, 1991) that higher primates show some "knowledge" of intent in the acts of conspecifics. They even deceitfully signal false intent. But it is a limited capacity. What I want to illustrate, rather, is the impoverished negotiation of the two chimpanzees in Crawford's study with what typically happens in human mother–child negotiation.

Take for comparison a study by Ninio and Bruner (1978) in which a child and mother were book reading, the mother being ostensibly interested in teaching her son, Jonathan, the names of things pictured on the pages of a book. Jonathan and his mother were endlessly negotiating in a fashion that was as conventional as it was affable. At a superficial level, the negotiation was about what a thing should be called (signaled by the mother's typically inflected "What's that?"). More deeply, negotiation was about how things named should be placed, in what context construed. As soon as Jonathan had a passably correct label to offer in reply to the standard "What's that?" question, his mother would begin the "And what's the X doing?" She was trying to get Jonathan to treat their focus of joint attention as imbedded in certain contexts. Just like those law professors might behave with a clever third-year student aspiring to a Supreme Court clerkship: extending his or her presuppositional range about Dred Scott. Indeed, Jonathan's mother (like the lawyers) even used a down-home rule of precedent: She would pose her "What's that?" question with a falling intonation contour to indicate that she knew that Jonathan knew the answer to her question. When she wanted him to extend the context, she reverted to her usual rising intonation.

The affableness of the negotiation inhered, I believe, in the mother's steady adherence to what Sperber and Wilson (1986) call "the principle of relevance." That is to say, she faithfully tried to make sense of everything Jonathan said or did, as in one notable episode when he vetoed her proposal that the lady on the back of an English penny was the Queen in favor of his own that it was his grandmother. To which she replied "Alright, but it's sort of the same thing." They were, so to speak, establishing a corpus of what is to be attended to jointly and what is to be presupposed jointly about it. This strongly suggests that fully developed joint attention is about background knowledge (Searle, 1992) as well as about a target.

It is this close-textured pattern of reciprocity about the intentional states of one's partners that constitutes sociocognitive negotiation at the human, cultural level—human "attunement," to use Stern's (1977) term. It does not exist in the wild even in such extraordinarily intelligent and socially sensitive primates as pygmy chimpanzees and orangs. Now we can return to a point earlier delayed. When we speak of the "humanizing" effect of human culture, it is to this microlevel of mutual expectation that we should refer. It even works on chimpanzees, which is not to deny that there are great genetic and biological differences between man and the great apes, if only in brain size or in corticalization. The point is, rather, that a human cultural microenvironment such as we are describing can even humanize the development of a primate species with only half our human brain weight.

III

On the basis of the foregoing, it seems highly appropriate to propose that "mind reading," our theories of each others' minds, our ways of sharing attention, and so forth, should be viewed not simply as a capacity that gets developed by growing up, but one that also grows out of the nature of the discourse in which we humans engage. This, it seems to me, is to take with proper seriousness the role of negotiation. It is also to take seriously the manner in which context and presuppositions are brought into the picture to assure a joint construal of what lies at the focus of joint attention. It is in conjunction with this latter point that I raised the issue of Sperber and Wilson's "principle of relevance" in discussing Jonathan's mother earlier. Spelled out nakedly, that principle holds that we must always assume that what somebody does or says in a particular context at a particular juncture makes sense. Our task in discourse is to figure out what that sense is. To conform to such a maxim requires that we actively explore possibly relevant contexts and "dig out" all the presupposition that might be presumed to be in play. By the same token, of course, our own acts and utterances must be artificed in such a way as to take account of how our interlocutor might "take" our act or utterance.

It could not be otherwise, given the way joint attention comes to be deployed in speech exchanges. Phrases in ordinary speech spill forth at the average rate of about one per 1.6 second, presumably imposing a monumental load on joint attention. But in fact, it is not so crushing as all that. For there are fairly clear conventions of topic maintenance (Li, 1976), of turn-taking in conversation (Schegloff, Jefferson, & Sacks, 1977), and of repairing joint attention gone off track (see Clark & Anderson, 1979) and children manage all this with little friction or trouble. The conventions for regulating joint attention seem steady enough so that we can safely presume that others are on to the task at hand, on to the referent intended, or, if not, that there are comprehensible extenuating circumstances that can also be conventionally understood. We easily take it for granted that people are accountable for their agency and their intentionality, and that their attention will be under the control of both or either. The only difficulty seems to be with triggering the right background knowledge and the right presuppositions in support of our "surface" attentional focus—T. S. Eliot's famous "That's not what I meant at all."

I suggested elsewhere (1982) that one of the early aids to building up skills in mastering context and presupposition is through the establishment of "formats" that conventionalize the task of construing signifying acts and utterances. These are particularly prominent in the opening years of language use. As the children master displaced reference and the rules of implicature (Grice, 1975), these formats become less necessary for guaranteeing joint attention. After that, the principle of relevance keeps us on track in construing what others do and say. The culture provides us with symbolic formats.

This brings us back to our law professors and their arcane discussion. They plainly know their way around in the twisted "paper trails" that constitute the space of Constitutional jurisprudence. But their untrained fellows are unable to share attention with them in their Constitutional flights. This would lead me to suspect that the knowing that of joint attention is perhaps more dependent upon the knowing what than might first appear to be the case. To say that joint attention is in force seems to some extent to be dependent upon the nature of the domain of discourse in which joint attention is imbedded or contextualized. We say when failures of joint attention occur, "I don't follow." This would seem to imply that we know what it means to follow though we are not following now. But do we really know what it means to follow when we, as layman, get lost in the lawyers' arcana about the domain of stare decisis? Not really. This would suggest, of course, that joint attention is not just joint attention, but joint participation in a common culture. And it is in the light of this anomalous fact that I have always tried to understand what Wittgenstein (1953) meant when he remarked that "to understand a language means to be master of a technique" (p. 81)—a customary way of life.

IV

Circle back finally to the old question to which I referred at the start: What impels children to seek joint attention with others, whether early on through direct eye contact, later by sticking to topics in their worlds of "everyday scripts" (Schank & Abelson, 1977), or finally, by mastering the ways of particular interpretive communities? How does the old question look today?

We know from new research on autism (Baron-Cohen, Tager-Flusberg, & Cohen, 1993) that without a ready ability for joint attention, human beings fall into a grievous state of pathology. Faulty joint attention early on is prognostic of later difficulty in figuring out what might reasonably be on somebody's mind when they do something or say something. Sufferers seem to have difficulty in constructing communally serviceable "intersubjective meanings," difficulty in being able to share presuppositions about how people think and feel, and how they deal with their thoughts and feelings. It is not that normal people are all that accurate in reading the feelings and thoughts of others or in knowing their own. What we are, rather, is conventional: We come up with reasonable, conventional, somewhat corrigible hypotheses about what others deem relevant in their conversations or interactions with us. Autists have great difficulty acquiring these conventions. When they do so—to borrow a phrase from a gifted autist (Temple Grandin, cited in Sacks, 1994)—they manage it by a laborious algorithm rather than by a quick and intuitive heuristic. They have to figure it out rather than knowing it intuitively.

Herbert Clark (1992), discussing the arenas in which language is used, notes that there seem to be four requirements that speech communication imposes: (a) that we have a *common ground* of background knowledge, (b) an awareness of *collaborative processes* involved in interacting, (c) a sense of how to design our messages for our *audiences'* understanding, and (d) a willingness and ability to *coordinate and negotiate meanings.* None of these requirements can be fully met without there first being a coordination of "raw" joint attention. That seems to be the first step toward achieving full joint attention.

If we ask, then, what role is served by joint attention, the answer would be that without it, we cannot construct and coordinate the shared social realities that comprise everyday life. I find it ironic that in all the lists of human instincts that used to be offered by psychologists to explain human nature, nobody ever mentioned "the need to share the objects of our attention with others." Yet, we are the only species that seems driven to do so. The primatologists Chance and Jolly (1970) have shown that the more dominant a simian is in his group, the more attention other members of the group direct toward him. In street slang, they are "watching their wagons," but they are not sharing attention, for they have very little free attention to share that is not tied closely to extrinsic response requirements. Even eye-to-eye contact is tied up in this way. It leads (at least in most baboon species) to the triggering of attack or agonistic behavior.

This freeing of attention from the need for immediate response doubtless reflects the vast increase in the size of the human brain. But it must also be a reflection of the human use of language, or a condition for it. For as already intimated and as linguists note (e.g., Levelt, 1989), language provides the system for framing attention and giving it a continuity that allows for the recruitment of context and background presuppositions—joint visual attention in infancy and early childhood, more ideational joint attention once language becomes established, shared presuppositional attention as we become acculturated into specialized interpretive communities. Joint attention, in this deeper sense, serves not only to form culture but to maintain such coherence as it achieves.

REFERENCES

Astington, J. (1993). *Developing theories of mind.* Cambridge, MA: Harvard University Press.

Baron-Cohen, S., Tager-Flusberg, H., & Cohen, D. J. (Eds.). (1993). *Understanding other minds: Perspectives from autism.* Oxford, England: Oxford University Press.

Bates, E., Benigni, L., Bretherton, I., Camaioni, L., & Volterra, V. (1977). From gesture to the first word: On cognitive and social prerequisites. In M. Lewis & L. Rosenblum (Eds.), *Interaction, conversation, and the development of language* (pp. 247–307). New York: Wiley.

Bloom, L. (1973). *One word at a time: The use of single word utterances before syntax.* The Hague, Netherlands: Mouton.

Bower, T. G. R. (1974). *Development in infancy.* San Francisco: Freeman.

Bruner, J. (1978). Learning how to do things with words. In J. S. Bruner & A. Garton (Eds.), *Human growth and development: The Wolfson Lectures, 1976* (pp. 62–84). Oxford, England: Clarendon Press.

Bruner, J. S. (1982). Formats of language acquisition. *American Journal of Semiotics, 1*(3), 1–16.

Bruner, J. (1983). *Child's talk: Learning to use language.* New York: Norton.

Butterworth, G. E., & Jarrett, N. L. M. (1991). What minds have in common is space: Spatial mechanisms serving joint visual attention in infancy. *British Journal of Developmental Psychology, 9,* 55–72.

Byrne, R. W., & Whiten, A. (1991). Computation and mind reading in primate tactical deception. In A. Whiten (Ed.), *Natural theories of mind* (pp. 127–141). Oxford, England: Blackwell.

Chance, M. R. A., & Jolly, C. J. (1970). *Social groups of monkeys, apes, and men.* New York: Dutton.

Chomsky, N. (1965). *Aspects of the theory of syntax.* Cambridge, MA: MIT Press.

Clark, E. V., & Anderson E. S. (1979). *Spontaneous repairs: Awareness in the process of acquiring language.* Paper presented at the Biennial Meeting of the Society for Research in Child Development, San Francisco.

Clark, H. H. (1992). *Arenas of language use.* Chicago: University of Chicago Press.

Crawford, M. (1937). The cooperative solving of problems by young chimpanzees. *Comparative Psychology Monographs, 14*(2, Serial No. 68).

David, M., & Appell, G. (1961). A study of nursing care and nurse-infant interaction. In B. M. Foss (Ed.), *Determinants of infant behavior: I.* London: Methuen.

Grice, H. P. (1975). Logic and conversation. In P. Cole & J. L. Morgan (Eds.), *Syntax and semantics: Vol 3. Speech acts* (pp. 41–58). New York: Academic Press.

Halliday, M. (1975). *Learning how to mean: Explorations in the development of language.* London: Edward Arnold.

Levelt, W. J. M. (1989). *Speaking: From intention to articulation.* Cambridge, MA: MIT Press.

Levinson, S. C. (1983). *Pragmatics.* Cambridge, England: Cambridge University Press.

Li, C. N. (Ed.). (1976). *Subject and topic.* New York: Academic Press.

Meltzoff, A., & Gopnik, A. (1993). The role of imitation in understanding persons and developing a theory of mind. In S. Baron-Cohen, H. Tager-Flusberg, & D. J. Cohen (Eds.), *Understanding other minds: Perspectives from autism* (pp. 335–366). Oxford, England: Oxford University Press.

Menzel, E. (1974). A group of young chimpanzees in a one-acre field. In M. Schrier & F. Stolnitz (Eds.), *Behavior of nonhuman primates: Vol. 5* (pp. 83–153). New York: Academic Press.

Ninio, A., & Bruner, J. S. (1978). The achievement and antecedents of labelling. *Journal of Child Language, 5,* 1–15.

Piaget, J. (1980). The psychogenesis of knowledge and its epistemological significance. In M. Piatelli-Palmarini (Ed.), *Language and learning* (pp. 23–34). Cambridge, MA: Harvard University Press.

Poulin-Dubois, D., & Schultz, D. R. (1988). The development of the understanding of human behavior: From agency to intentionality. In J. W. Astington, P. L. Harris, & D. R. Olson (Eds.), *Developing theories of mind* (pp. 109–125). Cambridge, England: Cambridge University Press.

Rogoff, B., Mistry, J., Goncu, A., & Mosier, C. (1993). Guided participation in cultural activity by toddlers and caregivers. *Monographs of the Society for Research in Child Development, 58*(8, Serial No. 236).

Ryan, J. (1974). Early language development: A communicational analysis. In M. P. M. Richards (Ed.), *The integration of a child into a social world* (pp. 185–213). Cambridge, England: Cambridge University Press.

Sacks, O. (1994, 3 January). Neurologist's notebook: An anthropologist on Mars. *The New Yorker,* pp. 106–125.

Savage-Rumbaugh, E. S., Murphy, J., Sevcik, R. A., Brakke, K. E., Williams, S. L., & Rumbaugh, D. L. (1993). Language comprehension in ape and child. *Monographs of the Society for Research in Child Development, 58*(3–4, Serial No. 233).

Scaife, M., & Bruner, J. S. (1975). The capacity for joint visual attention in the infant. *Nature, 253,* 265–266.

Schank, R. C., & Abelson, R. P. (1977). *Scripts, plans, goals, and understanding: An inquiry into human knowledge.* Hillsdale, NJ: Lawrence Erlbaum Associates.

Schegloff, E., Jefferson, G., & Sacks, H. (1977). The preference for self-correction in the organization of repair in conversation. *Language, 53,* 361–382.

Searle, J. (1969). *Speech acts.* Cambridge, England: Cambridge University Press.

Searle, J. (1983). *Intentionality: An essay in the philosophy of mind.* Cambridge, England: Cambridge University Press.

Searle, J. (1992). *The rediscovery of the mind.* Cambridge, MA: MIT Press.

Sperber, D., & Wilson, D. (1986). *Relevance: Communication and cognition.* Oxford, England: Blackwell.

Stechler, G., & Latz, E. (1966). Some observations on attention and arousal in the human infant. *Journal of the American Academy of Child Psychiatry, 5*, 517–525.

Stern, D. (1977). *The first relationship: Infant and mother.* Cambridge, MA: Harvard University Press.

Tomasello, M., Kruger, A. C., & Ratner, H. H. (1993). Cultural learning. *Behavioral and Brain Sciences, 16*, 495–552.

Tomasello, M., Savage-Rumbaugh, S., & Kruger, A. C. (1993). Imitative learning of actions on objects by children, chimpanzees, and enculturated chimpanzees. *Child Development, 64*, 1688–1705.

Wittgenstein, L. (1953). *Philosophical investigations.* Oxford, England: Blackwell.

Wood, D. (1988). *How children think and learn.* Oxford, England: Blackwell.

Wood, D. J., Bruner, J. S., & Ross, G. (1976). The role of tutoring in problem solving. *Journal of Child Psychology and Psychiatry, 17*, 89–100.

Chapter 1

Current Themes in Research on Joint Attention

Philip J. Dunham
Chris Moore
Dalhousie University

As infants approach their first birthday, they begin to display an increased interest in various external objects and events during interactions with their caregivers. Previously established dyadic (infant–other) interactional structures are gradually transformed into a triadic (infant–object–other) social system. During this period of development, infants face the difficult task of learning to coordinate their attention and actions on objects in their environment with the attention and actions of their social partners; a task that will continue in increasingly esoteric and complex social endeavors throughout their life. In the contemporary literature concerned with child development, these early coordinated episodes of joint attention are now widely recognized as functionally significant across several basic dimensions of development. Adamson and Bakeman (1991) have argued that ". . . episodes of shared attention are pictured variously as moments for the mutual regulation of affect and of problem solving, for the negotiation of communicative intentions, and for the sharing of cultural meaning" (p. 9).

The present volume was developed to provide the reader with an overview of the rapidly growing literature concerned with the origins of these triadic joint attentional episodes and their potential role in early social, cognitive, and emotional development. The volume has been designed to occupy an important niche in social development libraries that currently exists between texts concerned primarily with early infant–caregiver dyadic interactions (e.g., Field & Fox, 1985; Kaye, 1982; Schaffer, 1977; Stern, 1986), and more recent texts concerned with the preschool child's emerging "theory of mind" (e.g., Astington, 1993; Astington, Harris, & Olson, 1988; Frye & Moore, 1991; Perner, 1991;

Wellman, 1990). In this first chapter, we will place the contents of the present
volume in historical perspective, and then briefly discuss some of the central
themes in the theory and research the reader will encounter in the following
chapters.

A BRIEF HISTORICAL PERSPECTIVE

Although there is obviously a long and rich history of research concerned with the
role of various social structures in early development, psychologists more specifically interested in the origins of early joint attentional episodes generally identify
the work of Bruner and his students as one of the more influential landmarks in
this literature (e.g., Bruner, 1977, 1983; Scaife & Bruner, 1975). In particular, an
early study reported by Scaife and Bruner (1975) is frequently cited as one of the
first cross-sectional descriptions of early joint attentional behavior during adult–
infant social interactions. In this seminal research, they observed an increasing
tendency for infants to "follow the gaze" of adult caregivers during the early and
middle infancy periods, and underlined the potential significance of these episodes
of joint attention during early development. For example, in one particularly
quotable early statement, Bruner (1977) argued: "The joint enterprise sets the
deictic limits that govern joint reference, determines the need for a referential
taxonomy, establishes the need for signaling intent, and eventually provides a
context for the development of explicit predication" (p. 287).

Although hindsight reminds us that this statement ran against the conceptual
tides of the time, the contents of the present volume are a testimony to its
subsequent impact. The current literature reveals that Bruner, working in the
more general theoretical tradition of Jakobson (1960), Werner and Kaplan
(1963), and Vygotsky (1934/1962), provoked a strong and persisting interest in
the developmental role of these early social experiences at a time when Chomsky's deep innate structure and Piagetian egocentrism constituted a formidable
opposing Zietgeist among researchers concerned with early language and social
cognition.

Almost 20 years after making the above statement, Bruner's commitment to
these early arguments has not waned. Indeed, in the Foreword to this volume,
he enthusiastically elaborates on them, now extending his analysis of children's
early joint attentional behaviors to the broader context of social cognition, and
acknowledging the potential role of joint attentional episodes in a more general
cultural psychology (see also Bruner, 1993; Tomasello, Kruger, & Ratner, 1993).

In the following chapters, the reader will discover that the conceptual seeds
planted by Bruner and his students have sprouted into a number of new and
different forms in the current developmental literature. At the empirical level,
a diverse array of joint attentional behaviors have been added to the early
gaze-following phenomenon initially emphasized by Scaife and Bruner. Social

referencing, early protocommunicative gestures, imitation, early productive language, and the emergence of predicative discourse are among the many behaviors that are now accepted as indications of a rapidly emerging, triadic, joint attentional system during infancy. Similarly, at a more theoretical level of analysis, the functional properties of joint attentional experiences, originally emphasized in the context of early language and communicative development, are now implicated in a much broader array of developmental phenomena including, in particular, the infant's incipient understanding of the mental life of others.

CENTRAL THEMES IN CURRENT RESEARCH ON JOINT ATTENTIONAL PHENOMENA

We believe that three basic themes arise consistently enough across the chapters in this book to justify special attention as organizational threads in the fabric of current research on joint attentional episodes. Although these themes are by no means the only interesting issues the reader will encounter, we suspect they will continue to generate a considerable amount of research in the next decade.

First, there is a rapidly growing body of theory and research concerned with the developmental origins of early joint attentional behaviors. Two decades have intervened since Scaife and Bruner first systematically described the emergence of gaze following in the dyadic interactions of infants and their adult caregivers. As noted in the preceding historical overview, the list of functionally significant joint attentional behaviors identified during the infancy period has now increased in number, and different opinions now exist about their antecedents, developmental timing, and nature (see, e.g., Baldwin, chap. 7; Butterworth, chap. 2; Corkum & Moore, chap. 4; Desrochers, Morissette, & Ricard, chap. 5 for overviews).

A substantial amount of interest in the infant's conceptual understanding of their early joint attentional social experiences has also developed in the current literature. As the label "joint attention" implies, some researchers believe that joint attentional behaviors displayed by the infant during their first year betray a rudimentary social understanding of the mental life (attentional states) of others (see Baldwin, chap. 7; and Tomasello, chap. 6). At the other end of the continuum, however, more conservative analyses question the validity of these inferences, placing the emergence of these social-cognitive skills somewhat later in development (e.g., Corkum & Moore, chap. 4).

These contrasting views of the infant's early social insights have, in turn, raised a number of related questions about potential developmental linkages between a presumed rudimentary understanding of the attentional states of others and the subsequent emergence of more sophisticated levels of social cognition observed during the preschool period (i.e., their understanding of desires and beliefs). We call the issues arising in this rapidly expanding area of interest the *social cognition* theme.

A third basic theme in the contemporary literature, developing in parallel with the aforementioned issue, is concerned with the functional properties of early joint attentional episodes. Although much of this research has focused rather narrowly on the role of joint attentional episodes in early language and communicative development (see, for example, Baldwin, chap. 7; and Dunham & Dunham, chap. 8 for overviews), more recent research reveals a rapidly expanding literature concerned with the consequences of individual differences in early joint attentional behaviors across a much wider array of developmental phenomena. Several contributors to the present volume focus, for example, on the functional significance of joint attentional behaviors for various aspects of early social, emotional, and motivational development (see, e.g., Adamson & McArthur, chap. 10; Baldwin, chap. 7; Sigman & Kasari, chap. 9) in both normative and special populations of infants.

Although much of the theory and research presented in this volume reflects a pervasive interest in three general themes, we also want to emphasize that these organizing themes should not be viewed as independent, isolated domains of research activity. In fact, the contents of some chapters cut across all three organizing themes to varying degrees. Regardless of the approach taken or the phenomena considered in any particular chapter, we believe that most contributors are concerned in general with understanding the origins and functional properties of joint attentional structures, and with eventually linking these data to important developmental changes in early social cognition. We turn now to consider each of the chapters in this volume and briefly discuss their relevance to one or more of these basic themes.

An Overview of the *Behavioral Origins* Theme

Much of the research concerned with origins of joint attention has focused specifically on the emergence of the infant's gaze-following behavior. Butterworth's well-known maturational account of this early social behavior (chap. 2) springs perhaps most directly from these conceptual roots. He suggests that infants first reliably follow the gaze of their caregivers when they are about 6 months of age. At this point in development, he discusses an "ecological mechanism" underlying the emergence of gaze-following behavior that presumably predisposes infants to turn their heads in the same direction as their caregivers during social interactions. This natural predisposition to engage in these joint attentional acts is combined with a tendency for infants to fixate on particular objects they encounter in their shifting visual fields. Under natural circumstances, such fixations will of course tend to covary with the adult's perceptual predispositions. Butterworth argues that these two predispositions gradually develop into more precise joint attentional skills with major maturational transitions at about 12 months (a geometric mechanism) and 18 months (a spatial-representational mechanism).

Baron-Cohen (chap. 3) describes similar maturational changes in early gaze following during the infancy period and elaborates on the developmental mechanisms responsible for these descriptive changes in more detail. Specifically, he outlines a maturationally timed modular cognitive architecture assumed to be directly responsible for the developmental changes in joint attention across the first year of life. Using a traditional comparative analysis to argue for a selective advantage enjoyed by gaze following in social species, Baron-Cohen suggests that, in addition to an eye direction detector presumed to exist in many species, humans have evolved a shared attention mechanism specially tuned to situations in which attention to a common object occurs for two interacting individuals. From these selective evolutionary origins, infants are assumed to infer a relatively sophisticated understanding of triadic shared-attentional states by the end of the first year and more sophisticated mental states soon after.

The emphasis on nativistic predispositions toward gaze-following behaviors inherent in the positions outlined by Butterworth and Baron-Cohen contrasts with the kinds of explanations offered by several other contributors (see Corkum & Moore, chap. 4; Desrochers, Morissette, & Ricard, chap. 5; Dunham & Dunham, chap. 8; Tomasello, chap. 6).

After introducing some important methodological precautions that have not typically been used in previous gaze-following research, Corkum and Moore (chap. 4) argue that infant gaze-following behavior is first reliably elicited by adult caregivers near the end of the infant's first year but can be conditioned in the laboratory slightly earlier. In both contexts this behavior is observed somewhat later than reported by Scaife and Bruner, and by Butterworth and his colleagues. Corkum and Moore also observe that infants respond initially to the head movements of a model during episodes of joint attention and appear to be insensitive to changes in eye orientation. In contrast to strictly nativist views, they tentatively argue that the early triadic interactional system might be set up through the infant learning that the head turns of a model indicate the location at which an interesting event will occur.

In chapter 5, Desrochers, Morissette, and Ricard discuss similar issues to those raised by Corkum and Moore, but their focus is on early protocommunicative gestures (pointing) as indicative of the infant's emerging joint attentional skills. Although less explicit than Corkum and Moore, these authors also acknowledge that infants' early pointing behaviors may reflect instrumental or acquired attempts to produce certain desirable reactions from a social partner.

Tomasello (chap. 6) further complicates these diverse views on the origins of joint attentional behaviors like gaze following by suggesting that the label *joint attention* may not be appropriate until the emergence of a constellation of social behaviors near the end of the first year (e.g., communicative gestures, imitation, social referencing). In his model, this particular group of behaviors uniquely defines an underlying change in social cognition—the infant's attribution of intentionality to others—that cannot be assumed during earlier social interactions. Note that we return to this assumption in the next section; in the present context, the point to appreciate is that Tomasello's definition of any joint attentional phenomenon involves an inferred or underlying process that excludes many earlier dyadic interactional behaviors included by others (e.g., gaze following, contingent and reciprocating structures). These differences of opinion will, for various reasons, not be easy to resolve, and they clearly illustrate that answers to presumably straightforward questions about developmental timing will depend very much on one's conceptualization of the term *joint attention*.

In chapter 8, Dunham and Dunham emphasize the role of certain structural characteristics of the infant's early dyadic social environment in the subsequent emergence of triadic (infant–object–other) social structures during the middle infancy period. Their view, which does not focus exclusively on early gaze following, shares much in common with Kaye (1982) by arguing that many kinds of early contingent, reciprocating adult behaviors help to build a basic foundation for the eventual integration of object-oriented behaviors into the social system. In discussing the "infant's representations" of these early dyadic social structures, Dunham and Dunham, unlike Tomasello's social cognition model, describe generalizable changes in underlying perceptual–cognitive mechanisms (e.g., contingency detection) that are assumed to mediate the young infant's attentional state across both social and nonsocial contexts.

Considered together, many of these conceptual issues concerned with the nature, antecedents, and developmental timing of early joint attentional behaviors like gaze following have the familiar ring of the ubiquitous nature–nurture issue. On the nativist side, the comparative evolutionary arguments made by Baron-Cohen mesh well with the systematic maturational analysis of gaze following described by Butterworth. Together these positions represent a strong argument for maturational constraints on the development of early social behaviors, in particular, like gaze following. In addition, the reader should note that some of the data discussed in other chapters can also be viewed as compatible with the explicit emphasis these nativist views place on the infant's precocious ability to detect gaze direction. For example, Baldwin (chap. 7) argues convincingly that the adult's gaze is a dominant cue for infants as they begin to learn new words for novel objects and events.

At the same time, however, the data and arguments discussed by Corkum and Moore (chap. 4), Desrochers, Morissette, & Ricard (chap. 5), Tomasello (chap. 6), and Dunham and Dunham (chap. 8) make it difficult to discount the possibility that the development of early joint attentional behaviors relies to some extent on environmental, and specifically social environmental, conditions. In addition, we should note that these latter explanations find some general support in the apparent differences in joint attentional skills observed between mother-reared and human-reared chimpanzees (see Bruner's discussion in the Foreword to this volume).

An Overview of the *Social Cognition* Theme

In parallel with the questions described previously about the antecedents and developmental timing of joint attentional behaviors, researchers are also now beginning to ask whether these same behaviors are telling us something about the infant's early conceptualizations of self and others. Some of the more specific questions about early social cognition that arise across different chapters are: When does the infant first develop a rudimentary understanding of the attentional state of others? What is the precise nature of this early social understanding and how does it change across the infancy period? Are there developmental linkages between the infant's early understanding of attentional states and the subsequent emergence of a more flexible and sophisticated understanding of the mental life of others during the preschool years? Again, we suspect that much of the research on joint attentional behaviors in the next decade will reflect a strong interest in these very challenging questions.

Of the various contributors to this volume, Tomasello (chap. 6) provides perhaps the most systematic set of answers to each of these questions. On the matter of developmental timing, he describes two milestones in social cognition during the infancy period. Working within the context of his broader cultural learning theory (see Tomasello, Kruger, & Ratner, 1993), he assumes that infants begin to understand a selective sharing of the attentional states and goals with their adult partners near the end of the first year. He describes this initial rudimentary social understanding as an attribution of intentionality to others, and, as we just noted, suggests that the wide range of joint attentional behaviors emerging during this period reflect this understanding of others as intentional agents. Note also, however, that the typical 1-year-old child's social understanding is limited to inferring that the "points of view" of others are similar to their own.

The second important transition in social cognition described by Tomasello occurs near the end of the second year. Around this time infants undergo a "deepening of their understanding of others as intentional agents," including in particular an emerging ability to understand that others may have intentions that differ from their own. The evidence for this more sophisticated level of social insight comes primarily from studies of lexical and communicative development demonstrating that children are sensitive to various subtle changes in their partner's attention during lexical learning, and from research documenting their attention-directing skills in the pragmatic use of language.

Tomasello is also very explicit in discussing the linkage between early joint attentional behaviors and the child's later, more sophisticated "theory of mind." He summarizes his views on this issue as follows:

> Indeed, a good case could be made that the first step in the ontogeny of social cognition—the understanding of other persons as intentional agents—is in an important sense foundational for all the rest. This is true not only in the sense

that the other levels of social cognition including children's theories of mind depend on it, but also in the sense that it is at this level already that we find what is uniquely human. (chap. 6, p. 126)

Other approaches to the social cognition theme in this volume reveal substantial differences of opinion on the timing and nature of the infant's early social understanding of others. When, for example, can we assume that the infant's joint attentional behaviors reflect a rudimentary understanding of a shared attentional state? At one end of the continuum, several contributors suggest that infants engaging in joint attentional behaviors with adults (e.g., early gaze following, communicative gestures, social referencing) are reaping many developmental benefits from participating in these interactive social structures prior to attributing any kind of psychological (attentional) state to their partner. (See, e.g., Baldwin, chap. 7; Corkum & Moore, chap. 4; Desrochers et al., chap. 5; Dunham & Dunham, chap. 8; Moore & Corkum, in press, for variations on this perspective.)

Dunham and Dunham (chap. 8) explicitly argue, for example, that the dyadic contingent, reciprocating structures during early infancy, and triadic reciprocating structures in the middle infancy period have multidimensional effects on development in the absence of any incipient understanding of the mental states of the adult partner. Although their data reveal that infants as young as 3 months of age are influenced across time and context by fundamental differences in the structure of early social interactions, they argue that the first major milestone in social cognition (i.e., attributions of shared visual–perceptual experiences to others) emerges much later in the second year. Following Perner's (1991) analysis of early representational development, they link this milestone to a major transition in the infant's secondary representational skills which are assumed to emerge at this time.

Baldwin's (chap. 7) arguments in the context of early lexical development reflect a similarly conservative view of early social cognition, at least with respect to the role of joint attentional behaviors in early lexical development. In a clever series of experiments manipulating the adult's attentional cues during novel word learning, she demonstrates that it is not until later in the infancy period (18–19 months) that ". . . infants appear to make relatively subtle judgments concerning the speaker's focus and referential intent and establish new mappings only if attention and referential intent toward the relevant object is perceived" (chap. 7, p. 153). She also cautions the reader that additional research is required to determine if the developmental timing of the "shared intersubjective understanding" suggested by her lexical learning data is specific to the domain of lexical development. Indeed, some of the initial data she describes on early social referencing behavior indicate that the question of domain specificity in early social cognition may emerge as an important issue over the next few years.

Baron-Cohen's (chap. 3) account of early social cognition shares much in common with Tomasello's in assuming that the infant understands the partner's attentional states by 1 year of age. He similarly proceeds to discuss this early social understanding of attentional states as the ontogenetic foundation on which a more complex theory of mind can be built, including an understanding of the goals, desires, reference, and beliefs of others. However, in spite of this surface similarity, it is also evident that the mechanisms Baron-Cohen describes as underlying these milestones in social cognition are very different from those outlined by Tomasello. His evolutionary analysis of an early eye direction detector mediating dyadic shared-attentional states during early infant-caregiver interactions, and a shared-attention mechanism mediating the infant's understanding of shared-attentional states in triadic interactional structures definitely has a more modular and nativistic flavor than Tomasello's cultural learning model.

We believe that the issues developing around this social cognition theme are likely to dominate much of the research on joint attentional phenomena in the next decade. Several trends seem to be gathering momentum as researchers begin to focus on these questions. First, as this research expands, we suspect that the current tendency of some researchers to conceptualize early changes in social cognition as all or nothing insights into the mental life of self and others will give way to a more detailed developmental story. Like most complex concepts (e.g., animacy), the child's embryonic concept of mental states like joint attention is probably not unitary and very likely undergoes a number of major transformations during early development. So, instead of asking precisely when the child first attributes an attentional state to self and others, we suspect that future research will eventually undermine this question by decomposing mental concepts like joint attention into the series of transformations that are presumably occurring in social cognition across developmental time. Among the contributors to this volume, Tomasello's model of changes in early social cognition is perhaps most clearly headed in this direction, and we suspect a more detailed analysis of the infancy period is forthcoming. It appears that most contributors to the present volume agree, in general, that the rudimentary understanding of joint attention suspected to emerge during the infancy period is longitudinally linked to a more sophisticated understanding of the mental life of others. It is also clear, however, that the precise nature of these developmental linkages remains to be determined. Work on these longitudinal linkages is just beginning to emerge, particularly in the research with special populations of infants (e.g., Baron-Cohen, chap. 3; Landry, chap. 11; Raver & Leadbeater, chap. 12; and Sigman & Kasari, chap. 9). As we discuss later, it should be particularly interesting to explore associations suspected between individual differences in early joint attentional behaviors and the extensively researched theory of mind phenomena emerging across the preschool years.

An Overview of the *Functional Significance* Theme

As the preceding discussion indicates, most contributors to this volume agree that episodes of joint attention observed during infant-caregiver interactions are functionally significant "social hot spots" influencing many different dimensions of early development. In concert with the questions previously discussed about the origins of joint attentional behaviors, and the rapidly growing interest in the underlying mechanisms of social cognition, a number of contributors to the present volume have also devoted considerable attention to questions about the functional significance of these social hot spots.

Before we consider this research, we should note that evidence for the functional significance of early joint attentional episodes is perhaps most persuasive and ecologically valid when it demonstrates that naturally occurring individual differences in children's joint attentional behaviors are associated with different developmental outcomes across time and context, and that experimental manipulations of the same joint attentional behaviors can induce similar developmental changes in a controlled laboratory setting. For obvious reasons, evidence in the second category is generally in short supply. Although experimental demonstrations are occasionally encountered in the more developed literature concerned with the effects of joint attentional episodes on some aspects of early language development (see Baldwin, chap. 7; and Dunham & Dunham, chap. 8, for overviews), in other domains the individual differences strategy continues to dominate much of this research.

All things considered, we believe that one of the more informative variations on the individual differences approach mentioned earlier has been to explore the developmental consequences of deficits in the joint attentional behaviors suspected to exist in special populations of young children. Several contributors to the present volume have adopted this strategy, and their data collectively support the view that early deficits in joint attentional skills can have serious consequences across several domains of early development.

In chapter 9, for example, Sigman and Kasari explore individual differences in the joint attentional behaviors of both a normative group during infancy and a group of autistic children (developmental age: 18–24 months). These special children have well-documented, unfortunate deficits in their ability to relate to other people. In their work with this group, Sigman and Kasari measured joint attentional behaviors across three different social contexts: the amount of gaze monitoring during natural play with an adult; the likelihood of referencing the affective expressions of an adult in the presence of an ambiguous object; and the duration of attentional responses to an adult expressing distress. Their data indicate that individual differences in these joint attentional behaviors across the three different contexts tend to be consistently correlated during the infancy period in normative development, suggesting that a similar underlying mechanism may be operating across both time and context. In addition, when compared to both normative development and a mentally challenged group of children, the autistic children displayed less joint attentional behavior in each of these three contexts than either comparison group. Although Sigman and Kasari acknowledge that additional work will be necessary to understand this specific deficit, they tentatively suggest that the social behavior of autistic children may reflect not so much an inability to monitor the attentional states of others as an inability to coordinate the convergence of attentional and affective information during their social interactions. If they are correct in this interpretation, the deficit in integrative skills would have serious consequences for the child's subsequent ability to conceptualize more complex mental states (e.g., the desires and beliefs of others). As noted earlier, additional data linking early individual difference measures in joint attentional skills to later individual differences in more advanced theory of mind tasks with this special population should be very informative on these matters.

Adamson and McArthur (chap. 10) reach very similar conclusions based on their comparison of joint attentional behaviors in a group of autistic children (chronological age: 3 to 5 years) and children with severe deficits in expressive language skills. Specifically, they describe interactions in which an adult social partner attempts to elicit interest in object-focused play with the child. In this context, autistic children were significantly less likely to engage in joint attentional behaviors than a language-delayed comparison group. Perhaps of more interest, the adult partners in this object-play context reacted to unsuccessful social encounters with more "literal" (i.e., physical) attempts to engage the autistic child's attention on the objects. These alternative adult strategies remind us once again that early social influences are bidirectional. These changes induced in the adult's behavior by the children suggest that ". . . nonverbal children with autism may have fewer opportunities to experience how symbols may be used exclusively to direct another person's attention toward objects" (chap. 10, p. 216).

Finally, Baron-Cohen (chap. 3) also discusses the growing line of evidence suggesting that autistic children show little interest in joint attentional behaviors. He suggests, in the context of his own theoretical analysis and data, that autistic children may be able to build simple representations of the dyadic interactional system (e.g., self-object, agent-object), but are unable to construct the more complex triadic representations (e.g., agent-object-self) involved in the eventual emergence of a reflective understanding of more complex mental states.

In comparing these three different discussions of joint attentional behavior in autistic children, the reader will note that each of the contributors assumes that the severe social problems known to be associated with this disorder potentially originate with these deficits in early joint attentional behaviors. As Adamson and McArthur suggest: "From a developmental perspective, the reduction of interpersonal processes that interferes with the establishment of episodes of joint attention appears as an ominous prelude to a restricted introduction to cultural conventions" (chap. 10, p. 217).

Note, however, that differences of opinion are also expressed with respect to the nature of these early deficits. Sigman and Kasari (chap. 9) and Adamson and McArthur (chap. 10) both point to problems of integrating attentional and emotional information during interactions. Baron-Cohen (chap. 3) takes a different view, suggesting that the autistic child essentially lacks the general cognitive capacity to construct and participate in triadic joint attentional structures. A number of other researchers are also using these same methods and rationale to explore joint attentional behaviors in other special infant-caregiver groups with interesting results. For example, in chapter 11, Landry describes important individual differences in the joint attentional behaviors of high- and low-risk premature infants, and in chapter 12, Raver and Leadbeater examine the joint attentional episodes observed in interactions between socioeconomically disadvantaged adolescent mothers and their infants. In both of these chapters, the researchers measure the interactional structure from both directions, asking about the characteristics of both the caregiver and the infant.

Landry's (chap. 11) intensive analysis of unconstrained toy play involving caregivers and infants between 6 months and 24 months of age reveals deficits in the joint attentional skills of high-risk preterm infants at 6 months, 12 months, and 24 months of age. The high-risk preterm infants were less able to initiate and direct their mother's attention using gaze, verbalizations, and communicative gestures. In systematic follow-up research at 3 years of age, these same children were also less likely to initiate social interactions or to respond appropriately to parental requests, suggesting that the early deficits may have longer term consequences in this special population. In parallel measures of the mothers' behavior during these early interactions, Landry also observed a negative impact of maternal attention-directing strategies on the amount of joint attentional play that was amplified in the high-risk preterm children. (See also Dunham & Dunham, chap. 8 for similar observations in the context of early lexical development.)

Raver and Leadbeater (chap. 12) focus primarily on characteristics of adolescent mothers and their potential impact on episodes of joint attention between these young mothers and their infants during natural play sessions. Their detailed sequential analysis of collaborative joint attentional behaviors during play sessions at 12 and 20 months of age indicate that both maternal sensitivity and maternal depression are related to the amount of collaborative joint attention observed during interactions. Note, however, that each of these relationships also interacts in some interesting ways with both the age and gender of the infant.

Although the individual differences in these special infant–caregiver populations are obviously not as dramatic as those associated with childhood autism, the data obtained from these special populations described in both chapters 11 and 12 suggest that the infant's participation in early joint attentional episodes can be placed at risk by conditions as common as prematurity, and the emotional status of the primary caregiver. We believe that additional research exploring individual differences in early joint attentional behaviors across a wider range of special populations will eventually increase our understanding of both normative development and the characteristics of special groups that may be at risk.

CONCLUSION

To summarize, we have identified three related, underlying themes characterizing much of the current research on joint attentional phenomena: (a) A theme concerned with the developmental origins of joint attentional behaviors like gaze following; (b) a widespread interest in the infant's early conceptual understanding of joint-attentional experiences; and (c) a theme concerned with various functional consequences of individual differences in early joint-attentional experiences. In concluding this brief overview, we also want to emphasize that our goal in this overview and in designing this book has not been to promote any particular theoretical perspective. On the contrary, we believe these chapters portray the diverse range of opinions and research that characterize the contemporary literature in this area, and will generate the research necessary to expand and resolve the issues arising. We also want to advise the reader that the three general themes we have identified as interesting and pervasive in the present volume are by no means the only important and interesting issues or questions that arise both within and across the various chapters. In more specific contexts, the reader will discover informative discussions on matters ranging from gender differences to measurement issues, and these discussions, in general, are raising many interesting questions for future research.

REFERENCES

Adamson, L., & Bakeman, R. (1991). The development of shared attention during infancy. In R. Vasta (Ed.), *Annals of child development Vol. 8* (pp. 1–41). London: Kingsley.

Astington, J. (1993). *Developing theories of mind.* Cambridge, MA: Harvard University Press.

Astington, J., Harris, P., & Olson, D. (1988). *Developing theories of mind.* Cambridge, England: Cambridge University Press.

Bruner, J. (1977). Early social interaction and language acquisition. In H. R. Schaffer (Ed.), *Studies in mother–infant interaction* (pp. 271–289). New York: Academic Press.

Bruner, J. (1983). *Child's talk: Learning to use language.* New York: Academic Press.

Bruner, J. (1993). Do we "acquire" culture or vice versa? *Behavioral and Brain Sciences, 16*, 515–516.

Field, T., & Fox, N. (1985). *Social perception in infants.* Norwood, NJ: Ablex Press.

Frye, D., & Moore, C. (1991). *Children's theories of mind: Mental states and social understanding.* Hillsdale, NJ: Lawrence Erlbaum Associates.

Jakobson, R. (1960). Linguistics and poetic. In T. Sebeok (Ed.), *Style in language* (pp. 350–357). New York: Wiley.

Kaye, K. (1982). *The mental and social life of babies.* Chicago: University of Chicago Press.

Moore, C., & Corkum, V. (in press). Social understanding at the end of the first year of life. *Developmental Review.*

Perner, J. (1991). *Understanding the representational mind.* Cambridge, MA: MIT Press.

Scaife, M., & Bruner, J. (1975). The capacity for joint visual attention in the infant. *Nature, 253,* 265–266.

Schaffer, H. R. (1977). *Studies in mother-infant interaction.* London: Academic Press.

Stern, D. (1986). *Development of the infant's sense of self.* New York: Basic Books.

Tomasello, M., Kruger, A., & Ratner, H. (1993). Cultural learning. *Behavioral and Brain Sciences,*
    16, 495–552.
Vygotsky, L. S. (1962). *Thought and language.* (E. Hanfmann & G. Vakar, Eds. & Trans.). Cambridge,
    MA: MIT Press. (Original work published 1934)
Wellman, H. (1990). *The child's theory of mind.* Cambridge, MA: MIT Press.
Werner, J., & Kaplan, B. (1963). *Symbol formation.* New York: Wiley.

Chapter 2

Origins of Mind in Perception and Action

George Butterworth
University of Sussex: England

This chapter is concerned with the spatial signaling function of gaze and the associated postures of the human head and hand, which serve as the foundation for human referential communication. Deictic gaze, or joint visual attention as it is often called, may be defined simply as "looking where someone else is looking." Joint attention is thought to pave the way in human development for deictic gestures, such as manual pointing, which draw attention to a particular object by locating it for another person. For humans, joint visual attention and pointing may offer one of the bases in shared experience for the acquisition of language (Bruner, 1983).

A series of studies carried out in our laboratories over nearly 20 years with human infants is reviewed in this chapter. Some of these studies are now published, others have been presented as conference papers, and other work is still in progress. This chapter reviews the whole program in the chronological order in which it was carried out, with special reference to the main concern of this book, namely the origins and role of joint attention in human development. The research program also has implications for theories of childhood egocentrism, for theories of the origins of thought and language, for the phylogeny of visual attention, and for theories of mind. For reviews dealing more specifically with these issues, see Butterworth (1987), Butterworth and Grover (1988), and Butterworth (1991a).

COMPREHENSION OF GAZE

Over the years we have been concerned with three interrelated questions. The first question is: How does a baby know where someone else is looking? This eventually led us to ask whether how a baby knows where someone else is looking is linked to their comprehension of pointing. Pursuing this question naturally led us eventually to ask how the comprehension of pointing is related to the production of pointing and to social communication.

Let us begin with the most basic question in the field of joint attention: How does a baby know where someone else is looking? Perhaps because young babies have traditionally been considered totally egocentric, it has been assumed that they must be incapable of following the gaze of an adult, because this implies taking into account another person's point of view. Furthermore, babies aged below 8 or 9 months are rather distractible and their flightiness may have seemed to preclude shared attention with an adult.

Until fairly recently it was assumed that the adult took responsibility for joint attention by monitoring the infant's gaze and bringing her own attention to the same focus. There is little doubt that adults monitor very closely the focus of the infant's attention and adjust their own gaze to maintain shared experience. Schaffer (1984) reviewed a number of studies that show that the majority of episodes of joint attention do indeed arise as a result of the mother's monitoring the infant's line of gaze. There is, however, a logical problem with any theory that places sole responsibility for joint attention on the adult, because the infant must be capable, in principle, of monitoring the focus of attention of the adult if there is truly to arise any possibility of joint visual experience.

It was therefore a welcome discovery when Scaife and Bruner (1975) showed that infants as young as 2 months would adjust their gaze contingent on a change in the focus of attention of an adult. This observation suggested that the capacity for joint attention may be a reciprocal phenomenon; that the baby may be aware of a spatial objective of the mother's change of gaze.

Butterworth and Cochran (1980) and Butterworth and Jarrett (1991) conducted a series of studies that replicated and extended Scaife and Bruner's observation, with particular focus on the mechanisms serving joint visual attention. These studies established the basic paradigm; they were carried out under strictly controlled conditions in an undistracting environment, with identical targets placed at various positions relative to the mother and infant. In these experiments, the mother was instructed to interact naturally with the infant and then, on a signal, to turn in silence and without pointing manually, to inspect a designated member of a set of targets placed around the room at various positions relative to the mother and baby. Babies between the ages of 6 and 18 months were studied. The interaction was videotaped and subsequently scored by two independent observers who noted the direction and accuracy of the infant's response relative to the mother's line of gaze. These conditions allowed relatively unambiguous conclusions to be drawn concerning how the baby is able to single out the referent of the mother's gaze when distractions and other possible artifacts are eliminated. Of course, the infant always had the opportunity to make use of any available cues, such as the orientation of the adult's head and trunk, because we were not concerned with eliminating the natural postural consequences of the adult's change in visual orientation.

Evidence was obtained for three successive mechanisms of joint visual attention in the age range of 6 to 18 months. At 6 months, babies looked to the correct side of the room, as if to see what the mother was looking at, but they could not tell on the basis of the mother's action alone which of the two identical targets on the same side of the room the mother was attending to, even with angular separations as large as 60° between the targets. The babies were accurate in locating the object referred to by the mother's change of gaze when the correct target was first along their path of scanning from the mother to the target. However, they were at chance level when the correct target was second along the scan path and they had to ignore a distractor before arriving at the correct target. It would appear, therefore, that the change in the adult's orientation conveyed information about the direction in which to look (left or right in the visual field) but the precise location is not specified.

That joint visual attention is limited by the boundaries of the babies' visual space is suggested by the fact that infants only localize the targets within their own visual field and hardly ever locate targets that the mother looks at in the region behind the baby, out of view. If the mother looks at a target behind the baby, the infant either fixates a target in front and within the visual field or does not respond. This phenomenon is not caused by any inability of babies to turn behind them; indeed they often would turn behind them on first being seated in the laboratory or in response to some inadvertent noise.

In fact, it seems possible that the space behind the infant is initially specified auditorily. One conceivable explanation for failure to search behind on a visual signal from the adult may be that the young infant has difficulty comprehending visual reference to auditory space when the mother looks behind the baby. In any event, there is a basic inability to attribute the mother's signal to the space outside the immediate visual field. Failure to search "behind" (first reported in Butterworth & Cochran, 1980) has subsequently been replicated on several occasions in our own laboratories. It is noteworthy that a similar inability to search at locations out of view of the infant has been demonstrated in a manual search task involving rotation of the infant relative to objects that were first hidden in the field of view (Landau & Spelke, 1988). The space behind the infant is inaccessible, whether the task is to search on the basis of joint attention cues or to conduct only a simple manual search.

On the other hand, so long as all the possible locations are within the infants' field of view, babies are capable of correctly locating targets presented one at a time at visual angles that introduce separations between mother and the referent of her gaze of up to 135°. This was shown by rearranging the seating so that mother and infant were in the corner of the room and the targets were presented around the opposite walls. The babies were perfectly capable of noting even very small changes in the mother's head orientation, suggesting that mother and target need not be kept simultaneously in view. Thus, failure to search behind cannot be attributed to failure to perceive the change of the adult's head orientation, or to the fact that changes in head orientation differ in their absolute magnitude depending on the target position. Rather, it seems that joint attention operates within the boundaries specified by the infant's visual field. It is as if the baby perceives its own visual space to be held in common with others and this allows the baby to respond to the adult signaling "there is something interesting there."

For targets within the field of view, accurate localization of the referent among the youngest babies we tested (6 months) seems to depend not only on the adult's signal but also on the intrinsic differentiating properties of the object being attended to by the mother. Grover (1988), for example, showed that adding movement to one or the other of the alternative targets on the same side of the field of view increased not only the probability of a response among 9-month-old babies, but also the accuracy. This earliest mechanism of joint visual attention we have called "ecological," because we believe that it is the differentiated structure of the natural environment that completes for the infant the communicative function of the adult's signal. What initially attracts the mother's attention and leads her to turn is also likely, in the natural environment, to capture the attention of the infant. The ecological mechanism enables a "meeting of minds" in the self-same object. It is as if the change in the mother's gaze serves as an orienting signal specifying the direction for the infant to look while the interesting object completes the communicative link with the adult to specify the position at which to look.

By 12 months, the infant is beginning to localize the targets correctly, even when this requires the baby to ignore the first along the scan path and when the target is stationary in the visual field (Butterworth & Jarrett, 1991). We found that babies from 12 to 18 months of age could localize the correct target of a pair separated by 60° of visual angle, when the correct target was at a distance of approximately 1.3 m. During the trial, the infant fixates intently on the mother while she is turning, then when the mother is still, the infant makes a rapid eye and head movement in the direction of the target. The mean latency of response after the end of the mother's head movement is about 1 sec (Butterworth & Cochran, 1980).

We call this new ability the "geometric" mechanism because it seems to involve extrapolation of an invisible line between the mother and the referent of her gaze, as plotted from the infant's position. That is, the mother's change of gaze now signals both the direction and the location in which to look for the infant. Despite this new-found geometric ability however, babies at 12 months still fail to search for targets located behind them. Again, we have carried out control studies in which the visual field is emptied completely of targets, yet babies of 1 year do not turn behind them at the mother's signal. Instead, they turn to scan to about 40° of visual angle and give up the search when they fail to encounter a target. It seems that the geometric mechanism is still restricted to the infant's perceived space.

By 18 months, babies are as accurate when the correct target is first along their scan path from the mother as when it is the second target they encounter (with a target separation of 60° of visual angle and when the correct target was at a distance of approximately 1.3 m). This suggests the availability of a geometric mechanism that allows discrimination between targets separated by at least 60° of visual angle using head and eye signals alone. However, we found in subsequent studies, with a much larger room, with targets at greater distances, and with smaller angular separations between targets, that changes in head and eye orientation alone are not sufficient to allow the baby to identify the correct target (Butterworth, 1991b). The spatial layout and conditions of testing do make a difference as to whether one observes a geometric ability on the basis of changes in head and eye movements alone. The effects of adding manual pointing are discussed later.

While 18-month-old babies still do not search behind them when there are targets in the field of view, they will do so if the visual field is empty of targets. We found that eye movements alone, or head and eye movements to targets behind the baby would elicit turning to the correct target, so long as there was nothing in front in the field of view. The probability of the infant's making a response was higher if the adult's eye movements were accompanied by head movements but eye movements alone were sufficient. Thus, infants are able to access the invisible portion of space at 18 months (but not at 12 months) so long as there is no competition from locations within the visual field. It seems that the visual field has primacy for joint visual attention at all the ages we studied, but a third "representational" spatial mechanism for controlling joint visual attention, which is based on an understanding of being contained within space, develops between 12 and 18 months. Representational space can be accessed at 18 months, using an adult's eye movement or head and eye movement signal, so long as there is no competition from targets in perceived space.

In summary, as far as the comprehension of gaze is concerned, we have evidence in the first 18 months of life that three successive mechanisms are involved in "looking where someone else is looking." The earliest, the ecological mechanism, depends on completion of joint attention by the intrinsic, attention-capturing properties of objects in the environment, as well as on the change in the mother's direction of gaze. At around 12 months, we have evidence for the beginning of a new mechanism, a geometric process, whereby the infant from its own position extrapolates from the orientation of the mother's head or gaze the intersection of a line with a relatively precise zone of visual space.

Finally, at sometime between 12 and 18 months, there is an extension of joint reference to a represented space, which contains the infant and other objects outside the immediate visual field (see Butterworth & Jarrett, 1991). Demonstrating these subtle developmental changes depends rather a lot on the precise conditions of testing the babies. There is no reason to suppose that these mechanisms replace each other with development. Rather, they become mutually embedded, with the ecological mechanism forming the essential central core.

The Relation Between Comprehension of Gaze and Comprehension of Manual Pointing

In our more recent studies, we have attempted to establish how the infant's comprehension of gaze may be related to comprehension of manual pointing (Butterworth, 1991b). Manual pointing, defined as the use of an outstretched arm and index finger to denote an object in visual space, is species specific to humans, and it is thought to be intimately linked to language acquisition. It is the specialized referential function that is of interest here because it is a particularly human type of social cognition. Could the comprehension of pointing be related to the comprehension of looking?

It is generally agreed that comprehension of manual pointing occurs toward the end of the first year, somewhat in advance of production of the gesture (Schaffer, 1984). Looking where others point is observed in most babies by about 12 months (Guillaume, 1971; Leung & Rheingold, 1981; Schaffer, 1984). Piaget (1945/1952) considered comprehension of manual pointing to arise simultaneously with comprehension of other complex signs between 10 and 12 months.

Grover's (1988) findings on the infant's comprehension of pointing can be readily summarized. She compared the accuracy of response of babies when the mother merely looked at the correct target, with when the mother looked and pointed to the target. She found that the addition of the manual pointing signal by the mother did not make the space outside the field of view more accessible. Infants at 12 months failed to locate targets behind them, whether the mother looked or looked and pointed. They could correctly locate the mother's referent target within their own visual field whether the target was first or second on their scan path. The main effect of adding the manual point was significantly to increase the probability that the infant of 12 months, who comprehends the meaning of the sign, would respond.

We recently showed, using a much larger laboratory than previously, that babies were very much more accurate in locating the target when the adult looked and pointed at it, than when the signal involved only a reorientation of head and eyes (Butterworth, 1991b). Targets separated by as little as 25° of visual angle, at approximately 4 m from the baby, were localized by infants from age 12 months, when the adult simultaneously looked and pointed, as long as the infant comprehended the pointing gesture. Our results are consistent with our previous research in suggesting that pointing becomes effective as a signal redirecting the infant's attention toward the end of the first year of life; we have obtained little evidence that manual pointing by the adult assists babies much below 12 months of age to localize the target.

With the increase in laboratory size there was a significant increase in the accuracy of spatial localization when manual pointing was used to single out the target. Babies who could comprehend pointing were accurate in localizing the target when the adult pointed, but they were at chance level when the signal comprised merely a change of head and eye orientation. One possible explanation is that the extended arm provides a much better differentiation between the identical, alternative targets than do changes in the orientation of head and eyes alone. For any given angular distance between targets, the long "lever" of the arm undergoes a greater lateral displacement between alternative targets than does the head. Pointing with the arm thus assists in disambiguating the referent in the context of joint attention.

In summary, a long apprenticeship in the comprehension of gaze is not sufficient for the comprehension of manual pointing. Cognitive developmental changes that become available to babies from approximately 10–12 months are involved. In particular, the acquisition of a geometric mechanism for localizing the referent of manual pointing as well as other possible cognitive changes involving comprehension of signs and the ability to make part–whole discriminations may be implicated (Piaget, 1952). The geometric process allows the infant to determine not only the correct direction in visual space (a process common to the ecological mechanism) but also the precise location within the visual hemifield. Our evidence on the geometric mechanism is consistent with the hypothesis that infants may extrapolate a straight line along the arm of the adult to intersect with a potential object of joint attention in visual space.

Relation of Pointing to Prehension and to Social Communication

We will now turn to the production of pointing in babies. The use of an outstretched arm and index finger to denote an object in visual space may reflect hominoid evolutionary adaptations of the index finger and thumb, and the precise gesture is species specific to man (Butterworth, 1991a; Hilton, 1986). Theorists do not agree on the ontogeny of pointing. Preyer (1896) considered pointing to be a movement originally expressing a wish to seize. Vygotsky (1926/1962) similarly argued that pointing develops out of the mother's interpretation of the infant's failed attempts at prehension. Shinn (1900, cited in Schaffer, 1984) suggested that manual pointing may develop out of the exploration of objects with the tip of the index finger while the baby is engaged in close visual inspection. Shinn also suggested that pointing may begin with the application of this intersensorimotor coordination to an extended space. All of these hypotheses suppose that pointing, which occurs at the average age of about 14 months, develops out of prehension.

An alternative explanation is that the pointing gesture serves a specialized communicative function from the outset. Fogel and Hannan (1985) showed that index finger extensions occurred reliably in face-to-face interaction in infants as young as 2 months. The index finger did not single out a particular object; it was not correlated with the infant's gaze nor was there any arm extension. However, the point was reliably preceded or succeeded by either vocalization or mouth movement. By 6 months, the hand may have spontaneously adopted the pointing posture when an object attracted the infant's attention in a social context but again, the arm was not extended. Extension of the arm and index finger, in a communicative gesture, was observed at the beginning of the second year of life (at 14 months on average). According to Fogel and Hannan (1985) the specialized function of the index finger in relation to shared attention may be innate, while the progress to instrumental use of the gesture may be explained by successive acquisition of arm control, fine manipulative skills, and cognitive integration of the communicative roles of infant and adult.

Part of our research program has been concerned with disambiguating the two major classes of theory concerning the development of pointing: namely whether it derives from prehension or whether it serves a species-typical communicative function from the outset. In one series of studies where we gave babies the opportunity to reach for or point to objects at different distances, we showed that babies at the outset of their pointing careers do not confuse pointing with reaching (Franco & Butterworth, 1991). Furthermore, cognitive asymmetry between the participants was not necessary because once pointing begins, a baby will point at an object for another baby, which shows that pointing by the baby does not depend upon contingent behavior from an adult, as Vygotsky might have supposed (Franco, Perrucchini, & Butterworth, 1992). Thus, pointing from its inception occurs when a social recipient for the communicative gesture is available. Checking with the social partner and vocalization are also closely associated with the pointing gesture and constitute further evidence for the sociocommunicative purpose of the act (Franco & Butterworth, 1991).

The most plausible interpretation of our data, when taken in this wider context, is that pointing is neither socially transmitted nor is it derived from prehension. Our findings support the view that pointing is a species specific form of reference, basic to human nonverbal communication.

Focal and Ambient Attention Processes and Pointing

In another program of studies we considered the relationship between attention processes and pointing. It would seem intuitively that when we point, we intend to bring an object into the focus of another person's attention. We carried out a pilot study using a radio-controlled toy truck, which was very successful in eliciting pointing in babies as young as 8 months and 3 weeks, who were seated in the laboratory with their mother (Butterworth & Adamson-Macedo, 1987). Preliminary data analyses showed that although the incidence of index finger pointing increased with age from 8 months to 21 months, the rate of pointing was similar in all age groups. Babies would point to the truck, vocalize and check with their mother that their interest in the truck was being reciprocated by the adult. The babies in this study generally pointed with the ipsilateral hand; that is, when the toy truck was on the baby's right they pointed with the right hand, and when the toy truck was on their left they pointed with the left hand. Pointing was generally suppressed when the truck was in motion and tended to occur during stationary periods, when the truck was quite near the baby. It seemed possible that the index finger might have privileged access to the mechanisms controlling attention and so we set out to investigate this hypothesis more systematically.

A series of experiments was carried out to investigate the relationship between focal and ambient attention processes and handedness of pointing in babies. A "family" of 6 remotely controlled doll figures was placed in a semicircle at a constant distance from the infant and extending between 50° to the left and right of the baby so that targets were available both focally and peripherally. The dolls were activated singly or in pairs so that their arms and legs moved up and down in a repeated cycle. This arrangement proved to be very effective in eliciting pointing both during the doll movement and in the intertrial interval when the dolls were stationary. We found that there was no effect for focal or peripheral target positions on the probability that any target position would elicit pointing. However, we found a highly significant sex difference in handedness of pointing between boys and girls aged 16.5 months. Boys pointed with the ipsilateral hand to the periphery (50°, whether to left or right) and were equally likely to use either hand at all positions in between. Girls were right-handed from the right periphery, across the midline to 15° on the left, where they became equally likely to use left or right hands for the more peripheral positions (Graupner, Butterworth, & Franco, 1993). Two interpretations seem possible. The simpler is that girls develop faster than boys and the differences in hand-edness of pointing reflect the earlier subordination of the pointing gesture to the dominant hemisphere controlling language. The second is that boys and girls may acquire language differently and this is reflected in the differential handedness of the pointing gesture. These intriguing possibilities await further investigation.

CONCLUSION

Our program of research demonstrates that even very young babies may enter into a communication network with others through comprehension of an adult's direction of gaze: Communication is not solely dependent upon the greater cognitive sophistication of the adult. The direction of an adult's gaze has a signal function from early in infancy. At 6 months, the signal value of the mother's head and eye movement will indicate the general direction (left or right) in which to look. Communication occurs because the easily distractible baby will attend to the same attention-compelling features of the objects in the environment as the mother. Such an agreement on the objects of shared experience might be reasonably considered as a proto-communicative behavior. When seen in a social context, the earliest ecological mechanism allows communication in relation to publicly shared objects through their common effects on the intrinsic attention mechanisms of mother and baby. This basic intermental process depends on the fact that attentional mechanisms in infant and adult operate in much the same way.

During the first year, joint visual attention remains limited to locations within the infant's own visual space. The infant behaves as if its own field of vision is shared with the adult and this gives us an insight into the nature of infant intersubjectivity. The infant in the first year is limited by the boundaries of the immediate visual field but this nevertheless allows communication. Although the cognitive development of the participants in the interaction is at very different levels, the process of immediate perception provides a basis for agreement on the objects experienced. Superimposed on this basic mechanism with cognitive development comes more precise geometric localization of the referent of the mother's gaze. This seems to be one of the cognitive changes necessary for the comprehension of manual pointing. A geometric mechanism lessens the ambiguity of reference, because now, targets that are identical in all respects except position can be singled out by the infant. Once this geometric mechanism is available, communication does not require that differential, intrinsic properties of the object be singled out; the infant will choose the correct object in relation to the angular displacement of the mother's head and arm. This change enables the comprehension of manual pointing, itself an important, species typical, social means for redirecting attention and for entry into language.

The production of manual pointing operates in an interpersonal context from its inception. It comprises a specialized posture of the index finger, vocalization, social referencing, and attentional processes involved in object identification. It does not develop out of prehension but makes use of the specialized evolutionary adaptations of the hand for referential communication.

Finally, our research shows the importance of constituent attentional and motor subsystems for understanding the earliest origins of language. We are currently investigating the role of focal and peripheral vision in the production of pointing (Graupner, Butterworth, & Franco, 1993). We can already say that although pointing generally terminates in focal attention, it is not elicited solely by targets in focal or peripheral vision. Infants point because they are attracted by interesting events, whether they first occur focally or peripherally, and wish to share them with others. We are beginning to find links with cerebral lateralization and with sex differences in handedness of pointing which promise important connections with the early aspects of speech. This line of research promises to reunite the characteristics of objects in the ecology (the ecological mechanism which makes objects attention worthy) with processes of referential communication (which draws the attention of others to attention-worthy objects) in a comprehensive theory of the origins, development, and functions of joint attention in infancy.

ACKNOWLEDGMENT

The research summarized here was supported by a series of grants from the Economic and Social Research Council of Great Britain.

REFERENCES

Bruner, J. S. (1983). Child's talk. Oxford, England: Oxford University Press.

Butterworth, G. E. (1987). Some benefits of egocentrism. In J. S. Bruner & H. Haste (Eds.), Making sense: The child's construction of the world (pp. 62–80). London: Methuen.

Butterworth, G. E. (1991a). The ontogeny and phylogeny of joint visual attention. In A. Whiten (Ed.), Natural theories of mind (pp. 223–232). Oxford, England: Blackwell.

Butterworth, G. E. (1991b). Evidence for the geometric comprehension of manual pointing. Paper presented at the meeting of the Society for Research in Child Development, Seattle.

Butterworth, G. E., & Adamson-Macedo, E. (1987). The origins of pointing: A pilot study. Paper presented at the Annual Conference of the Developmental Psychology Section, British Psychological Society, York, England.

Butterworth, G. E., & Cochran, E. (1980). Towards a mechanism of joint visual attention in human infancy. International Journal of Behavioural Development, 3, 253–272.

Butterworth, G. E., & Grover, L. (1988). The origins of referential communication in human infancy. In L. Weiskrantz (Ed.), Thought without language (pp. 5–25). Oxford, England: Oxford University Press.

Butterworth, G. E., & Jarrett, N. L. M. (1991). What minds have in common is space: Spatial mechanisms serving joint visual attention in infancy. British Journal of Developmental Psychology, 9, 55–72.

Franco, F., & Butterworth, G. E. (1991). Infant pointing, prelinguistic reference and co-reference. Paper presented at the meeting of the Society for Research in Child Development, Seattle.

Franco, F., Perrucchini, P., & Butterworth, G. E. (1992). Referential communication between babies. Paper presented at the Fifth European Conference on Developmental Psychology, Seville, Spain.

Fogel, A., & Hannan, T. E. (1985). Manual actions of nine to fifteen week old human infants during face to face interactions with their mothers. Child Development, 56, 1271–1279.

Graupner, L., Butterworth, G. E., & Franco, F. (1993). Dynamic aspects of visual event perception and the origins of pointing in human infants. Paper presented at the Sixth European Conference on Developmental Psychology, Bonn, Germany.

Grover, L. (1988). Comprehension of the manual pointing gesture in human infants. Unpublished doctoral dissertation, University of Southampton, England.

Guillaume, P. (1971). Imitation in children. Chicago: University of Chicago Press.

Hilton, C. E. (1986). *Hands across the old world: The changing hand morphology of the hominids.* Unpublished manuscript, University of New Mexico.

Landau, B., & Spelke, E. (1988). Geometric complexity and object search in infancy. *Developmental Psychology, 4,* 512–521.

Leung, E. H. L., & Rheingold, H. (1981). Development of pointing as a social gesture. *Developmental Psychology, 172,* 215–220.

Piaget, J. (1952). *The origins of intelligence in the child.* New York: Basic Books. (Original work published 1945)

Preyer, W. (1896). *The senses and the will.* New York: Appleton-Century-Crofts.

Scaife, M., & Bruner, J. S. (1975). The capacity for joint visual attention in the infant. *Nature, 253,* 265–266.

Schaffer, R. (1984). *The child's entry into a social world.* New York and London: Academic Press.

Vygotsky, L. (1962). *Thought and language.* Cambridge, MA: MIT Press. (Original work published 1926)

Chapter 3

The Eye Direction Detector (EDD) and the Shared Attention Mechanism (SAM): Two Cases for Evolutionary Psychology

Simon Baron-Cohen
University of Cambridge

To be a viable hypothesis about human psychological architecture, the design proposed must be able to meet both solvability and evolvability criteria [emphasis added]: It must be able to solve the problems that we observe modern humans routinely solving and it must solve all the problems that were necessary for humans to survive and reproduce in ancestral environments.
—Tooby & Cosmides, 1992, p. 110

Imagine that you are walking onto a crowded train. You see a remaining empty seat, so you go across and sit down. You get out your book, and settle into it. During the journey, you become aware of a feeling that someone is looking at you. You glance along the carriage and, sure enough, someone *is* looking at you. As soon as you make eye contact with this stranger, he looks away. To my mind, this phenomenon is rather striking in that it is not immediately obvious how you would have known that someone was looking at you if you were already engaged in another activity. One possibility is that as the train was going along you were occasionally rapidly scanning the other passengers' faces. Given that there was quite a crowd, perhaps your perceptual system only superficially processed those faces whose eyes were directed away from you, because to have processed each and every face in any deeper way would have led to information overload, and would be of little adaptive value. But among that sea of faces there was one whose *eyes were directed at you*, which your perceptual system processed in more detail. In this chapter, I discuss the evidence that "eyes looking at me" are especially salient.

In doing this, I pursue the idea that evolution has produced a neurocognitive system for the rapid detection of the eyes of another organism, because of the considerable adaptive significance of such a mechanism. This system is called the *Eye Direction Detector*, or *EDD*. Its ontogenesis in humans is described more fully elsewhere (Baron-Cohen, 1994, 1995), as is its neurobiology (Baron-Cohen & Ring, 1994). In this chapter, the focus is on its evolution, and on its relationship to a second mechanism, the *Shared Attention Mechanism*, or *SAM*. This second mechanism functions to verify if you and another organism are attending to the same thing.[1] I argue that SAM is not only essential for joint attention, but also for the development of a "theory of mind" in the human child.

Back to EDD. To get more of a flavor of the evolution of EDD, consider its use in a second example. This time the scenario involves an encounter between Alex, who has just entered a new social group, and Thalia, with whom Alex is keen to become acquainted:

> Alex stared at Thalia until she turned and almost caught him looking at her. He glanced away immediately, and then she stared at him until his head began to turn toward her. She [quickly looked toward the ground], but as soon as Alex looked away, her gaze returned to him. They went on like this for more than 15 minutes, always with split-second timing. Finally, Alex managed to catch Thalia looking at him. He made the friendly eyes . . . [and then] approached [her]. (Leakey & Lewin, 1992, pp. 287–288)

You could be forgiven for assuming that this couple was human; in fact, Alex and Thalia are members of a troop of baboons that live near Eburru Cliffs, 100 miles northwest of Nairobi, on the floor of the Great Rift Valley. The aforementioned observation was made by Barbara Smuts, a primatologist at the University of Michigan, who studied the social life of this troop over several years. Discussing this particular social interaction, Smuts comments, "It was like watching two novices in a singles bar" (Leakey & Lewin, 1992, p. 288).

In this example we see the split-second timing of eye direction detection, as one animal checks to see if the other is looking at him or her, and as each animal tries to avoid the other animal's being aware that they are checking this. Like the baboon, humans are very accurate at identifying when someone is looking at them. Given that there may be only a small difference in geometric angle between *you* being looked at and *something next to you* being looked at, the psychophysics of EDD are likely to be impressive. (This remains to be studied in detail in different species). The example with Alex and Thalia also shows how in some species there is a risk that eye contact from a stranger can be

---

[1]This owes a lot to those who have drawn attention to the primitive nature of joint attention (e.g., Bruner, 1983; Butterworth, 1991; Hobson, 1993; Tantam, 1992; Tomasello, Kruger, & Ratner, 1994). As will become apparent, my proposal is somewhat different from these in suggesting the modularity of this mechanism, and in discussing the unique class of representations it processes.

misinterpreted as threatening, and how, if one's intentions are prosocial as Alex's were, eye contact must be offered in small doses at the start of such an encounter, if this risk is to be avoided.

EVOLUTIONARY PSYCHOLOGY

In my opening two examples, I jumped from humans to baboons. This was a deliberate strategy to help introduce the approach being adopted here, that of evolutionary psychology. This is defined as "psychology informed by the fact that the inherited architecture of the human mind is the product of the evolutionary process" (Cosmides, Tooby, & Barkow, 1992, p. 7). This phrase should of course strike a chord with the more well-known phrase "evolutionary biology," which has transformed the science of biology. As Cosmides et al. suggest, the time is ripe to integrate psychology with biology via evolutionary theory.

In this spirit, the adaptive problem I initially discuss is the rapid prediction of another organism's next action. By adaptive problem I mean a "problem whose solution can affect reproduction, however distally" (Cosmides et al., 1992, p. 8). It is evident, I think, that if another organism's immediate goal is that you should be its lunch, it would pay to know about it quickly! This is one key function of EDD because "eyes directed at me" is something it was evolved specifically to detect, and because eye direction tends to specify the object upon which an agent's next action is targeted. Of course, just because another organism is looking at you, it does not mean the goal of its next action is necessarily predatory or aggressive. It may be interested in you for some other reason (e.g., to signal that it wants to communicate with you, or that it is sexually attracted to you, etc.).[2] However, recognizing any of these motives in another organism is also likely to affect reproduction, however distally.

The Environment of Evolutionary Adaptedness (EEA): An Intensely Social Environment

I return to the specific evolution of EDD shortly. First, I want to say something about evolutionary psychology more broadly. Cosmides et al. (1992) remind us that modern human history is only about 10,000 years old (if one dates this from the advent of agriculture, for example), and that nothing about our biology is likely to be an adaptation to changes during this period. In contrast, the period relevant to human evolution can be seen as spanning two phases: the Pleistocene epoch (roughly the last 2 million years, when we lived as hunter–gatherers), and then several hundred million years before that (when we lived as one kind of

---

[2]I thank Alison Gopnik for suggesting that I invoke the old joke here: that EDD allows one to predict that another animal is interested in you for one of the three F's: fight, food, or sex.

forager or another). They point out that these time spans are important to keep in mind, because "they establish which set of environments and conditions defined the adaptive problems the mind was shaped to cope with: Pleistocene conditions, rather than modern conditions " (Cosmides et al., 1992, p. 5). That there was massive neurocognitive evolution during the Pleistocene epoch is beyond any doubt. Figure 3.1, for example, shows that a threefold increase in brain size occurred in the 3 million years since *Australopithecus afarensis* evolved, going from around 400 cubic cm to its current size of about 1,350 cubic cm.

The causes of the brain size increase are likely to reflect many factors, but one major factor upon which many theorists agree was the need for greater "social intelligence" (Brothers, 1990; Dunbar, 1993; Humphrey, 1984). This is because the vast majority of primate species are social animals, living in groups that range from as few as two individuals to as many as 200. If one looks at different kinds of social organization in existing primates, one is struck by the variety: from lifelong monogamy (e.g., the gibbon), to unimale polygyny (e.g., the gorilla, where a single male has control over a group of females and their offspring), to multimale polygyny (e.g., the chimpanzee, where several males cooperate to defend a group of widely distributed females and their offspring), to "exploded" unimale polygyny (e.g., the orangutan, where a single male defends

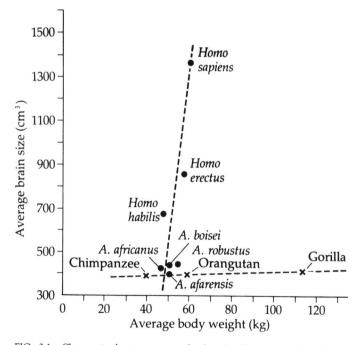

FIG. 3.1. Changes in brain size over the last 3 million years. From *Human Evolution*, p. 127, by R. Lewin (1989), Oxford, England, Blackwell Scientific Publications. Reprinted with permission.

a group of females and their offspring, but where the females do not live as a group but instead are distributed over a wide area).[3] These different models hint at how primate social environments are enormously more complex than those of other social groups, even those that live in comparably sized groups, such as the antelope. The difference in complexity lies in the nature of the social interactions. "The group is . . . the center of intense social interaction that has little apparent direct bearing on the practicalities of life: In the human sphere we would call it socializing, the making and breaking of friendship and alliances" (Lewin, 1992, p. 46). The challenge for the primate was (and remains) to predict and manipulate the behavior of others in the group, what Humphrey (1984), and Byrne and Whiten (1988) depict as the Machiavellian nature of social interaction. It is this social intelligence that determines who wins higher status. Consider Lewin again on this point:

> When you observe other mammal species and see instances of conflict between two individuals, it is usually easy to predict which one will triumph: the larger one, or the one with the bigger canines or bigger antlers, or whatever is the appropriate weapon for combat. Not so in monkeys and apes. Individuals spend a lot of time establishing networks of "friendships", and observing the alliances of others. As a result, a physically inferior individual can triumph over a stronger individual, provided the challenge is timed so that friends are at hand to help the challenger and whilst the victim's allies are absent. (Lewin, 1992, p. 129)

Leakey and Lewin (1992) reached a similar conclusion: "In higher primates, the greatest reproductive success (in both males and females) is shaped much more by social skills than by physical displays, either of strength or appearance" (p. 293). So, the evolution of primates can be characterized by an increase in the complexity of social interaction, requiring on the cognitive level an increase in rapid and adaptive social intelligence, and on the biological level an increase in different brain mechanisms, to support this. I argue that EDD and SAM are two such brain mechanisms.[4]

In evolutionary psychology, then, a claim about an evolved neurocognitive system needs to be considered in the light of its adaptedness. Again, in standard biological terminology, a system with proposed adaptedness should have design features that would "exploit the enduring properties of the environment in which it evolved (termed its environment of evolutionary adaptedness, or EEA) and . . . solve the recurring problems posed by that environment" (Tooby & Cosmides, 1992, p. 69). Here, the recurring problem that the organism would need

---

[3] This survey comes from Lewin (1989).

[4] Another such brain mechanism that is postulated to have evolved for social intelligence is the *Theory of Mind Mechanism* (or *ToMM*; Leslie, 1991). This is touched upon at the end of this chapter, though because this book concentrates on joint attention, it is not discussed in depth here. For further details, see also Leslie (1994), Baron-Cohen (1994, 1995), and Baron-Cohen and Ring (1994).

to solve is predicting another organism's next move, and the enduring property of the environment that natural selection is postulated to have exploited to solve this problem is that an animal's eye direction reliably correlates with its next action. Animals, human beings included, tend to look at what they are about to act upon.[5]

EDD

From Reptiles to Humans. EDD can be likened to other visual mechanisms. For example, the retina of the rabbit has a "hawk detector" (Marr, 1982) and the retina of the frog has a "bug detector" (Barlow, 1972, cited in Tooby & Cosmides, 1992). I propose that EDD fires in response to eye-like stimuli, and fires most strongly if the direction of these eye-like stimuli are "looking at me." In this section I give a sketch of the range of species that show fine sensitivity to eyes and eye direction.

Ristau (1990, 1991) carried out some elegant experiments with plovers, to test whether these birds were sensitive to eye direction, and whether they reacted to eyes directed at them as a threat. The birds were observed in the dunes on the beaches of Long Island, New York, where they nest. Ristau used two human intruders, one of whom looked towards the dunes, the other of whom looked towards the ocean. Each intruder walked up and down the same path along the coastline, about 15–25 meters from the dunes. Trials began when an incubating parent plover was on her nest. Ristau found that the birds moved off and stayed off their nests for longer periods when the intruder was gazing toward the dunes than when the intruder was gazing toward the ocean. Moving away from the nest was interpreted as a sign of the parent bird attempting to lead the intruder away from the nest. Ristau interpreted this as evidence that these birds were capable of detecting whether an intruder was looking at them on their nest, and that the birds reacted to gaze so directed as a threat. (One should note that in this study the birds had both eye direction and head direction available as cues.)

Snakes have also been reported to be sensitive specifically to eye direction as a cue to a potential threat (Burghardt, 1990). For example, if an intruder is about 1 m from a hog-nosed snake, and looks directly at the snake, the snake will feign death for longer than if the intruder averts its eyes. The same is true of chickens, who also engage in tonic immobility for longer in the presence of a human who is staring at them than one who is not looking at them (Gallup, Cummings, & Nash, 1972). The phenomenon of *tonic immobility* has been documented in a range of other species, such as the lizard (Hennig, 1977), the blue

---

[5]If you need a more concrete image of this generalization, picture where your cat looks before she pounces on the ball of wool you teasingly dangle in front of her.

crab (O'Brien & Dunlap, 1975), and ducks (Sargent & Eberhardt, 1975). (See Arduino & Gould, 1984, for a review.)

Many animals do not react to the eyes with tonic immobility, but nevertheless react with avoidance and fear. For example, macaque monkeys look less at photographic slides of faces with eye contact than with no eye contact (Keating & Keating, 1982), and infant macaque monkeys show more emotional disturbance when confronted by a picture of a full face with eye contact than by a picture of a face turned away to profile with gaze averted (Mendelson, Haith, & Goldman-Rakic, 1982). Perrett and Mistlin (1990) further demonstrated that appeasement behaviors (lip smacking and teeth chattering) by macaque monkeys are controlled by gaze angle and head posture, in that they occur more often to a human face looking directly at the animal (from a distance of 1.5 m, whether full face or half-profile), than to a human face tilted backward.

Mutual gaze, particularly in the form of a stare, is a well-documented component of threatening displays in many nonhuman primates, for example, adult male baboons (Hall & Devore, 1965), gorillas (Schaller, 1964), macaques (Altmann, 1967), and a number of other old world monkeys and apes (van Hooff, 1962). Chance (1967) described how struggles for dominance are often only ended with one animal averting its gaze, what he calls a "visual cutoff," possibly as a mechanism for reducing the physiological arousal produced by direct gaze (Nichols & Champness, 1971; Wada, 1961). This array of studies showing a fear response to eye direction is one source of evidence in support of the notion that there is an eye direction detector, one function of which is to detect threat. Note that recognizing that another animal's eyes are directed at you need not only be a form of threat detection. It may also signal to you that the other animal has you as its target for prosocial reasons. For example, eye contact occurs as part of grooming, greeting, and play facial expressions in old world monkeys and apes (van Hooff, 1962). However, Argyle and Cook (1976), in their important review of the literature, conclude that it is only in primates that gaze functions as an affiliative as well as an aggressive cue.

The Neurophysiology of EDD. Specific cells in the Superior Temporal Sulcus (STS) of the monkey brain appear to respond to the perspective view of the head (Perrett et al., 1985). Perrett's group found that different cell types in the STS of the macaque monkey brain respond selectively to the different views of the head, some to the left profile, others to the back of the head, and so forth. The STS is shown in Figure 3.2. Other studies have found that specific STS cells respond selectively to direction of gaze (Perrett et al., 1985; Perrett et al., 1990). For example, Perrett et al. (1985) found that 64% of the cells responsive to the face or profile views of the head were also selective for the direction of gaze. Other evidence for the neurophysiological basis of eye direction detection comes from neuropsychology. Lesions in the STS produce an impairment in the ability to discriminate gaze direction by monkeys (Campbell, Hey-

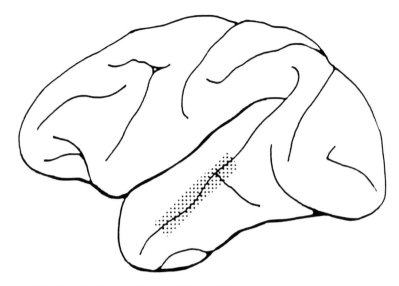

FIG. 3.2. The Superior Temporal Sulcus (STS: lateral view), in the macaque brain. From "The social brain: A project for integrating primate behaviour and neurophysiology in a new domain," by L. Brothers (1990), *Concepts in Neuroscience, 1*, 27–51. Reprinted with permission.

wood, Cowey, Regard, & Landis, 1990). Some patients with prosopagnosia are also impaired in this ability (Campbell et al., 1990; Heywood & Cowey, 1992). Perrett and his colleagues, in their most recent publications (e.g., Perrett, Hietanan, Oram, & Benson, 1992) refer to the cells in the STS that respond to gaze direction as cells responsive to the direction of attention of the other individual, and that have the primary function of detecting where another individual is looking. These studies suggest that EDD may be localized either regionally within the brain, or within specific neural circuits.

EDD's Representations: Dyadic. In the human case, I suggest that whenever EDD detects eyes, it gradually builds representations of eye behavior. These I call *dyadic representations*.[6] They are constructed by at least 4 months of age in humans, if not sooner (Johnson & Vicera, 1993). Dyadic representations specify the presence of two entities (Agent and Self; or Agent and Object; or Self and Object) standing in a relation to each other. Dyadic representations thus have one of four forms:

1. *[Agent–Relation–Self]*. Here, the relation term is bidirectional, because both elements are agents and thus capable of an active relation with something. Examples of this form are:

---

[6] This term is derived from Bakeman and Adamson (1984).

[Mummy-sees-me], or
[I-see-Mummy].

2. [Agent–Relation–Proposition]. Here, the relation term is unidirectional, because one of the elements is not an agent. An example of this form is:
[Mummy-sees-the bus].

3. [Agent₁–Relation–Agent₂]. Here, again, the relation term is bidirectional,
because both elements are agents. Examples of this are:
[Mummy-sees-Daddy], or
[Daddy-sees-Mummy].

4. [Self–Relation–Proposition]. Here, the relation term is unidirectional. So an
example of this form is:
[I-see-the house].

The form of these dyadic representations presumes that the organism has a
concept of *seeing*, a concept of *self*, and even a concept of *itself seeing*. All of
these concepts could be fairly simple. For example, seeing at the simplest level
could be an awareness of the distinction between "eyes open" (light) and "eyes
closed" (dark), which presumably even young infants have. Self could be quite
low level too, namely, an awareness of the distinction between dual stimulation
(when you touch yourself) and single stimulation (when you touch anything
else; Gallup, 1970).

In summary, the first adaptive problem to which EDD is a solution is identifying whether another organism is looking at you, because of the obvious
benefits of detecting this. There is, however, a second adaptive problem that
would be worth solving: if the other animal is not looking at you, then what *is*
he or she looking at? Might he or she have spotted something that would be
worth knowing about? A food source, a rival, a mate, or a predator, for example?
I have assumed that EDD can perform some geometric analysis to compute the
direction that another animal is looking in, because this also only requires dyadic
representation. Chimpanzees, for example, have been observed to use another
animal's eye direction to search for a hidden object in a location being looked
at (Menzel & Halperin, 1975). However, this is just about the limit of EDD's
power. To see how EDD is used in more complex ways, I need to introduce the
second mechanism, SAM.

SAM

Triadic Representations. The Shared Attention Mechanism (or SAM)
functions to identify if you and another organism are both attending to the same
thing. This is a further adaptive problem that it would be important to be able to
solve, but EDD just cannot solve it. This is because EDD is limited to building
dyadic representations, and according to my analysis, what is needed in order to
verify if you and someone else are both attending to the same thing is what I call

a *triadic* representation.[7] These are the special representations that SAM alone can build. Triadic representations differ in structure from dyadic representations in that they include an embedded element which specifies that Agent and Self are both attending to the same object. To capture this, they have one of two forms:

1. *[Self–Relation–(Agent–Relation–Proposition)]*. Here, the first relation term is bidirectional, so examples of this form are:
   [I-see-(Mummy-sees-the bus)], and
   [Mummy-sees-(I-see-the bus)].
   Because this representation specifies that both I and Mummy are seeing the same bus at the same time, this fulfills the function of the triadic representation, namely, to identify shared attention.
2. *[Self–Relation–(Agent₁–Relation–Agent₂)]*. Here, both relation terms are bidirectional. So examples of this form are:
   [I-see-(Mummy-sees-Daddy)], or
   [I-see-(Daddy-sees-mummy)], or
   [Mummy-sees-(I-see-Daddy)], or
   [Mummy-sees-(Daddy-sees-me)], etc.

These formal descriptions are my attempt at specifying what triadic representations represent. However, it is questionable whether one can fully capture the complexity of the relations with such formal descriptions. The alternative spatial description, depicted in Figure 3.3, may be both more comprehensive, and simpler to "read." In the text, however, I use the aforementioned formal descriptions, because these are adequate for present purposes.

As is clear, the embedded term in triadic representations is the main advance over dyadic representations. It is this term that enables the animal to specify within the triadic representation that they are looking at the same object that the other animal is looking at. My theory proposes that the capacity to construct triadic representations is necessary for joint attention, and suggests that in the first instance, SAM builds these representations using dyadic representations it obtains from EDD's output. This is because triadic representations can be built more easily in the visual modality than can be done in other modalities. However, in children born blind, but in whom SAM is otherwise intact, shared attention can be achieved by building triadic representations via touch or audition, thus establishing joint tactile or joint auditory attention. This is not easy, but in principle possible.

The clearest pieces of evidence for SAM's functioning are in gaze monitoring, and in the "protodeclarative" pointing gesture (Bates, Benigni, Bretherton,

---

[7]This term is also derived from Bakeman and Adamson (1984), and Trevarthen (1979). Hobson (1993) also refers to triadic relations. Note, however, that in my account, these are a class of *representations*.

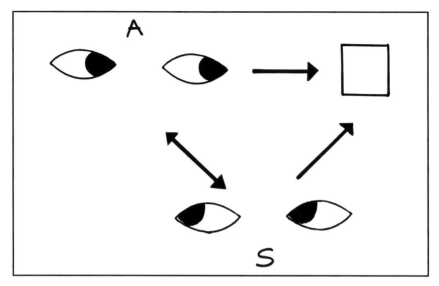

FIG. 3.3. A spatial description of the triadic representation [Agent–Relation–(Self–Relation–Proposition)]. Reproduced from "How to build a baby that can read minds: Cognitive mechanisms in mindreading," by S. Baron-Cohen (1994), *Cahiers de Psychologie Cognitive/Current Psychology of Cognition, 13*(5), 513–552. Reprinted with permission.

Camaioni, & Volterra, 1979), that is, the joint visual attention behaviors. There is some anecdotal evidence that chimpanzees and baboons may look in the same direction as another animal is looking, but this remains to be experimentally investigated (Cheyney & Seyfarth, 1990). Certainly, spontaneous gaze monitoring emerges clearly in human infants by the end of the first year, and is universally established between 9 and 14 months of age (Butterworth, 1991, this volume; Corkum & Moore, this volume; Desrochers, Morissette, & Ricard, this volume; Scaife & Bruner, 1975). Similarly, protodeclarative pointing emerges during the same period in normal development (Bates et al., 1979; Butterworth, 1991). Gaze monitoring continues to be present in human children (Leekam, Baron-Cohen, Perrett, Milders, & Brown, 1993). The communicative function of gaze in human adults has also been amply documented (Argyle & Cook, 1976).

SAM's Role in the Development of a Theory of Mind. My suggestion is that in the human case, SAM has two other key functions. First, it imports volitional terms like "want" or "goal" into the relation slot of its triadic representations. These are some of the earliest mental state concepts that the human child possesses (Wellman, 1990). SAM can do this because volitional terms are themselves relation terms. It is adaptive to do this because it gives the child a way of inferring a person's desires and goals from the direction of their gaze. Secondly, SAM plays a necessary though not sufficient role in triggering a later mechanism, ToMM (or the *Theory of Mind Mechanism*; see Leslie, 1991).

Regarding evidence for SAM's function of inferring a person's goal from eye direction, Phillips, Baron-Cohen, and Rutter (1992) investigated this with normal infants ranging from 9 to 18 months. The child was presented either with an ambiguous or an unambiguous action. One ambiguous action comprised blocking the child's hands during manual activity by the adult cupping her hands over the child's. A second ambiguous action comprised offering an object to the child, but then at the last minute teasingly withdrawing it, just as the child began to reach for it. The unambiguous action simply comprised giving or presenting an object to the child. This study found that, on at least half of the trials, 100% of the infants responded to the ambiguous actions by instantly looking at the adult's eyes (within the first 5 seconds after the tease or the block), whereas only 39% of them did so following the unambiguous action. This suggests that under conditions in which the goal of an action is uncertain, the first place young children (and indeed adults) look for information to disambiguate the goal is the eyes.

In a further study, we demonstrated that it is indeed eye direction that children use to infer a person's goal (Baron-Cohen, Campbell, Karmiloff-Smith, Grant, & Walker, in press). Thus, when 3–4-year-olds were asked "Which sweet will Charlie take?" after being shown a display of four sweets and with Charlie's face looking at one of these confections, they tended to pick the one he was looking at as the goal of his next action (see Fig. 3.4).

Regarding SAM's function of inferring a person's desire from eye direction, Baron-Cohen et al.'s (in press) study presented normal 3–4-year-olds with the display of the four sweets, and placed the cartoon face of Charlie in the center of the display. Again, Charlie's eyes were depicted as pointing toward one of the four sweets, randomly selected (see Fig. 3.4). The subject was asked "Which one does Charlie want?". In another condition, the subject was asked "Which one does Charlie say is the (x)?", in order to see if they used eye direction to infer a person's intended referent. Children of this age had no difficulty at all in inferring Charlie's desire (or his intended referent) from his eye direction. Note that Baldwin (1991, this volume) has also reported 18-month-olds' ability to use eye direction to infer a person's intended referent.

In summary, there is growing evidence that is consistent with the idea that in the human case SAM identifies when shared attention has been achieved, and infers a person's goal, desire, and intention to refer, from eye direction. Regarding SAM's function as a necessary (but not sufficient) precursor to a theory of mind, the evidence comes from autism.[8]

---

[8]In this chapter I simply mention one precursor to a theory of mind: joint attention. However, our earlier work (Baron-Cohen, Allen, & Gillberg, 1992) has shown that the combination of joint attention deficits and pretend deficits at 18 months predicts cases of autism. It is therefore likely that this same combination of deficits predicts impairments in theory of mind. If this is confirmed, then it suggests that both joint attention and pretend play may be precursors to theory of mind. Quite why these two behaviors should lie in this intimate relationship is not yet clear.

FIG. 3.4. The Four Sweets Display. From "Are children with autism blind to the mentalistic significance of the eyes?", by S. Baron-Cohen, R. Campbell, A. Karmiloff-Smith, J. Grant, & J. Walker (in press), *British Journal of Developmental Psychology*.

EDD, SAM, and Autism

EDD appears to be intact in children with autism, while SAM is in almost all cases impaired. Thus, children with autism are able to detect whether eyes are looking at them (Baron-Cohen et al., in press), but they show little if any joint-attention behaviors (Baron-Cohen, 1989a; Leekam et al., 1993; Phillips et al., 1992; Sigman, Mundy, Ungerer, & Sherman, 1986). This dissociation is consistent with the idea that children with autism can use EDD to build dyadic representations, but are impaired in using SAM to build triadic representations. If this is the case, then they should also fail to go on to import volitional mental state terms (*goal*, *desire*, and *intention-to-refer*) into triadic representations. There is some evidence consistent with these assumptions.

Phillips et al. (1992) tested very young children with autism for their ability to use SAM to detect a person's goals from their eye direction, using the ambiguous and unambiguous actions described earlier. However, these children did not seem to use eye contact to disambiguate the ambiguous actions, looking as little in both conditions (less than 11% looking, in each). Baron-Cohen et al. (in press) also tested children with autism on the Four Sweets Task and found significant impairments in the use of eye direction in inferring want, goal, and refer. For the case of refer, this has also been replicated using Baldwin's (1991) paradigm by Baron-Cohen, Baldwin, and Crowson (1995).

If children with autism are not capable of processing triadic representations, how are they able to pass visual perspective-taking tasks, which a number of experiments show that they do (Baron-Cohen, 1989a, 1991b; Hobson, 1984; Tan & Harris, 1991)? One possibility is that they do this by employing dyadic representations of the form [Agent–Relation–Proposition]. As mentioned earlier, what is missing from these is the embedded term that is a necessary feature of triadic representations, and the possibility of employing other mental state terms in the relation slot. This would explain why they do not show spontaneous gaze monitoring, or attempt to direct another person's attention to an object, as an end in itself.

It follows from my earlier claim about the precursor relation between SAM and theory of mind that I see the joint-attention deficits in autism as developmentally related to their later theory of mind deficits.[9] The theory of mind deficits in autism is not reviewed here, but some references to this literature are Baron-Cohen, Leslie, and Frith (1985); Perner, Frith, Leslie, and Leekam (1989); Baron-Cohen (1989c, 1989d, 1990, 1993); Leslie and Roth (1993); and Frith (1989). Suffice it to say that children with autism appear severely and selectively impaired in many tasks that require judging another person's mental state. If this account is correct, it implies that the origins of theory of mind may lie in the apparently simple acts of joint attention in infancy, the origin of which may itself lie deep in the evolutionary history of the brain.

SUMMARY

In this chapter I described two neurocognitive mechanisms that have each evolved to solve a different, key adaptive problem. One is concerned with identifying if you are the target of another organism's attention, and the other is concerned with establishing a shared focus of attention with another organism. The first of these is achieved by building dyadic representations specifying whether the eyes of another organism are directed toward you or not. This can function both as an "early warning system" that a predator has you (literally) within its sights, or that it has other (more prosocial) designs on you. EDD has evolved to build such dyadic representations, and to build them rapidly. The second problem, establishing a shared focus of attention with another organism, requires the construction of triadic representations, which SAM has evolved specifically to build. Although these representations could in principle be built in a number of different modalities, it is far easier in the visual modality, hence SAM exploits EDD to perform this function.

However, EDD and SAM have evolved over vastly different time scales.[10] EDD is very old (indeed, work reviewed in this chapter identifies it in reptiles and birds, as well as primates, for example), whereas SAM appears only com-

---

[9]See Baron-Cohen (1989a, 1991a), Tantam (1992), and Sigman et al. (1986), for similar arguments.

[10]I am grateful to the editors of this volume for helping me clarify this.

paratively recently in evolution. It is best documented in humans, though it remains possible that it is present in some of the higher primates. These two mechanisms probably evolved in different EEA's: EDD is likely to have evolved in environments in which sighted organisms are preyed upon by other sighted organisms. Clearly this encompasses a large set of species, independent of how social such species are. SAM, on the other hand, is likely to have evolved only in highly social species because the benefits of SAM would be more obvious in such cases. Finally, in the human case, SAM appears to play a crucial role in the ontogenesis of a theory of mind.

ACKNOWLEDGMENTS

During the preparation of this work I was a member of the Departments of Child Psychiatry and Psychology, The Institute of Psychiatry, University of London. I am grateful for the support from the Mental Health Foundation and the Medical Research Council. Parts of this paper first appeared in Baron-Cohen (1994), and were presented at the Society for Research in Child Development Conference, New Orleans, March, 1993, the British Psychological Society, Welsh Branch, "Faces" Conference, University of Wales College of Cardiff, September, 1993, and the British Society for the Philosophy of Science "Roots of joint reference" Conference, University of Bristol, November, 1993. Chris Moore, Phil Dunham, and Alison Gopnik all gave me valuable feedback on the first draft of this chapter. I am also grateful to Digby Tantam, Leslie Brothers, Dave Perrett, Annette Karmiloff-Smith, Pierre Jacob, and Ruth Campbell for discussions of these ideas.

REFERENCES

Altmann, S. (Ed.). (1967). *Social communication among primates.* Chicago: University of Chicago Press.

Arduino, P., & Gould, J. (1984). Is tonic immobility adaptive? *Animal Behaviour, 32,* 921–922.

Argyle, M., & Cook, M. (1976). *Gaze and mutual gaze.* Cambridge, England: Cambridge University Press.

Bakeman, R., & Adamson, L. (1984). Coordinating attention to people and objects in mother-infant and peer-infant interaction. *Child Development, 55,* 1278–1289.

Baldwin, D. (1991). Infants' contribution to the achievement of joint reference. *Child Development, 62,* 875–890.

Baron-Cohen, S. (1989a). Perceptual role-taking and protodeclarative pointing in autism. *British Journal of Developmental Psychology, 7,* 113–127.

Baron-Cohen, S. (1989b). Joint attention deficits in autism: Towards a cognitive analysis. *Development and Psychopathology, 1,* 185–189.

Baron-Cohen, S. (1989c). The autistic child's theory of mind: A case of specific developmental delay. *Journal of Child Psychology and Psychiatry, 30,* 285–298.

Baron-Cohen, S. (1989d). Are autistic children behaviourists? An examination of their mental-physical and appearance-reality distinctions. *Journal of Autism and Developmental Disorders, 19,* 579–600.

Baron-Cohen, S. (1990). Autism: A specific cognitive disorder of "mind-blindness." *International Review of Psychiatry, 2,* 79–88.

Baron-Cohen, S. (1991a). Precursors to a theory of mind: Understanding attention in others. In A. Whiten (Ed.), *Natural theories of mind* (pp. 233–252). Oxford, England: Basil Blackwell.

Baron-Cohen, S. (1991b). The development of a theory of mind in autism: Deviance and delay? *Psychiatric Clinics of North America, 14,* 33–51.

Baron-Cohen, S. (1993). From attention-goal psychology to belief-desire psychology: The development of a theory of mind, and its dysfunction. In S. Baron-Cohen, H. Tager-Flusberg, & D. Cohen (Eds.), *Understanding other minds: Perspectives from autism* (pp. 59–82). Oxford, England: Oxford University Press.

Baron-Cohen, S. (1994). How to build a baby that can read minds: Cognitive mechanisms in mindreading. *Cahiers de Psychologie Cognitive, 13*(5), 513–552.

Baron-Cohen, S. (1995). *Mindblindness.* Cambridge, MA: MIT Press/Bradford Books.

Baron-Cohen, S., Allen, J., & Gillberg, C. (1992). Can autism be detected at 18 months? The needle, the haystack, and the CHAT. *British Journal of Psychiatry, 161,* 839–843.

Baron-Cohen, S., Baldwin, D., & Crowson, M. (1995). *Do children with autism use eye-direction to infer linguistic reference?* Unpublished manuscript, University of Cambridge, Department of Experimental Psychology.

Baron-Cohen, S., Campbell, R., Karmiloff-Smith, A., Grant, J., & Walker, J. (in press). Are children with autism blind to the mentalistic significance of the eyes? *British Journal of Developmental Psychology.*

Baron-Cohen, S., & Cross, P. (1992). Reading the eyes: Evidence for the role of perception in the development of a theory of mind. *Mind and Language, 6,* 173–186.

Baron-Cohen, S., Leslie, A. M., & Frith, U. (1985). Does the autistic child have a "theory of mind"? *Cognition, 21,* 37–46.

Baron-Cohen, S., & Ring, H. (1994). A model of the Mindreading System: Neuropsychological and neurobiological perspectives. In P. Mitchell & C. Lewis (Eds.), *Origins of an understanding of mind* (pp. 183–210). Hillsdale, NJ: Lawrence Erlbaum Associates.

Bates, E., Benigni, L., Bretherton, I., Camaioni, L., & Volterra, V. (1979). Cognition and communication from 9 to 13 months: Correlational findings. In E. Bates (Ed.), *The emergence of symbols: Cognition and communication in infancy.* New York: Academic Press.

Bayliss, G., Rolls, E., & Leonard, C. (1985). Selectivity between faces in the responses of a population of neurons in the cortex in the superior temporal sulcus of the monkey. *Brain Research, 342,* 91–102.

Brothers, L. (1990). The social brain: A project for integrating primate behaviour and neurophysiology in a new domain. *Concepts in Neuroscience, 1,* 27–51.

Bruce, C., Desimone, R., & Gross, C. (1981). Visual properties of neurones in a polysensory area in superior temporal sulcus of the macaque. *Journal of Neurophysiology, 46,* 369–384.

Bruner, J. (1983). *Child's talk.* Oxford, England: Oxford University Press.

Burghardt, G. (1990). Cognitive ethology and critical anthropomorphism: A snake with two heads and hog-nosed snakes that play dead. In C. Ristau (Ed.), *Cognitive ethology: The minds of other animals.* Hillsdale, NJ: Lawrence Erlbaum Associates.

Butterworth, G. (1991). The ontogeny and phylogeny of joint visual attention. In A. Whiten (Ed.), *Natural theories of mind* (pp. 223–231). Oxford, England: Basil Blackwell.

Byrne, R., & Whiten, A. (1988). *Machiavellian intelligence: Social expertise and the evolution of intellect in monkeys, apes, and humans.* Oxford, England: Oxford University Press.

Byrne, R., & Whiten, A. (1991). Computation and mindreading in primate tactical deception. In A. Whiten (Ed.), *Natural theories of mind* (pp. 127–142). Oxford, England: Basil Blackwell.

Campbell, R., Heywood, C., Cowey, A., Regard, M., & Landis, T. (1990). Sensitivity to eye gaze in prosopagnosic patients and monkeys with superior temporal sulcus ablation. *Neuropsychologia, 28,* 1123–1142.

Chance, M. (1956). Social structure of a colony of *Macaca mulatta. British Journal of Animal Behaviour, 4,* 1–13.

Chance, M. (1967). The interpretation of some agonistic postures: The role of "cut-off" acts and postures. *Symposium of the Zoological Society of London, 8,* 71–89.

Cheyney, D., & Seyfarth, R. (1990). *How monkeys see the world.* Chicago: University of Chicago Press.

Cosmides, L., Tooby, J., & Barkow, J. (1992). Introduction: Evolutionary psychology and conceptual integration. In J. Barkow, L. Cosmides, & J. Tooby (Eds.), *The adapted mind* (pp. 3–18). New York: Oxford University Press.

Desimone, R., Albright, T., Gross, C., & Bruce, C. (1984). Stimulus selective properties of inferior temporal neurons in the macaque. *Journal of Neuroscience, 8,* 2051–2062.

Dunbar, R. (1993). Coevolution of neurocortical size, group size and language in humans. *Brain and Behavioral Sciences, 16,* 681–735.

Frith, U. (1989). *Autism: Explaining the enigma.* Oxford, England: Basil Blackwell.

Gallup, G. (1970). Chimpanzees: Self recognition. *Science, 167,* 341–343.

Gallup, G., Cummings, W., & Nash, R. (1972). The experimenter as an independent variable in studies of animal hypnosis in chickens (*Gallus gallus*). *Animal Behaviour, 20,* 166–169.

Gomez, J. C. (1991). Visual behaviour as a window for reading the minds of others in primates. In A. Whiten (Ed.), *Natural theories of mind* (pp. 195–208). Oxford: Basil Blackwell.

Hall, K., & Devore, I. (1965). Baboon social behavior. In I. Devore (Ed.), *Primate behavior.* New York: Holt, Rinehart & Winston.

Hennig, C. (1977). Effects of simulated predation on tonic immobility in *Anolis carolinensis*: The role of eye contact. *Bulletin of the Psychonomic Society, 9,* 239–242.

Heywood, C., & Cowey, A. (1992). The role of the "face cell" area in the discrimination and recognition of faces in monkeys. In V. Bruce, A. Cowey, A. Ellis, & D. Perrett (Eds.), *Processing the facial image: Philosophical Transactions of the Royal Society of London, B 335* (pp. 1–128). Oxford, England: Oxford University Press.

Hobson, R. P. (1984). Early childhood autism and the question of egocentrism. *Journal of Autism and Developmental Disorders, 14,* 85–104.

Hobson, R. P. (1993). *Autism and the development of mind.* East Sussex: Lawrence Erlbaum Associates.

Humphrey, N. (1984). *Consciousness regained.* Oxford, England: Oxford University Press.

Johnson, M., & Vicera, S. (1993). Cortical parcellation and the development of face processing. In B. de Boysson-Bardies, S. de Schonen, P. Jusczyk, P. McNeilage, & J. Morton (Eds.), *Developmental neurocognition: Speech and face processing in the first year of life.* Dordrecht, Netherlands: Kluwer.

Keating, C., & Keating, E. (1982). Visual scan patterns of rhesus monkeys viewing faces. *Perception, 11,* 211–219.

Kendrick, K., & Baldwin, B. (1987). Cells in the temporal cortex of conscious sheep can respond preferably to the sight of faces. *Science, 236,* 448–450.

Leakey, R., & Lewin, R. (1992). *Origins reconsidered.* London: Little, Brown, & Company.

Leekam, S., Baron-Cohen, S., Perrett, D., Milders, M., & Brown, S. (1993). *Eye-Direction Detection: A dissociation between geometric and joint-attention skills in autism.* Unpublished manuscript, University of Kent, Canterbury, UK.

Leslie, A. (1991). The theory of mind impairment in autism: Evidence for a modular mechanism of development? In A. Whiten (Ed.), *Natural theories of mind* (pp. 63–78). Oxford, England: Blackwell.

Leslie, A. (1994). ToMM, ToBY, and Agency: Core architecture and domain specificity. In L. Hirschfeld & S. Gelman (Eds.), *Mapping the mind: Domain specificity in cognition and culture.* Cambridge, England: Cambridge University Press.

Leslie, A., & Roth, D. (1993). What autism teaches us about metarepresentation. In S. Baron-Cohen, H. Tager-Flusberg, & D. Cohen (Eds.), *Understanding other minds: Perspectives from autism* (pp. 83–111). Oxford, England: Oxford Medical Publications.

Lewin, R. (1989). *Human evolution.* Oxford, England: Blackwell Scientific Publications.

Marr, D. (1982). *Vision.* San Francisco: Freeman.

Mendelson, M., Haith, M., & Goldman-Rakic, P. (1982). Face scanning and responsiveness to social cues in infant monkeys. *Developmental Psychology, 18,* 222–228.

Menzel, E., & Halperin, S. (1975). Purposive behavior as a basis for objective communication between chimpanzees. *Science, 189,* 652–654.

Nichols, K., & Champness, B. (1971). Eye gaze and the GSR. *Journal of Experimental Social Psychology, 7,* 623–626.

O'Brien, T., & Dunlap, W. (1975). Tonic immobility in the blue crab (*Callinectes sapidus,* Rathbun): Its relation to threat of predation. *Journal of Comparative and Physiological Psychology, 89,* 86–94.

Perner, J., Frith, U., Leslie, A. M., & Leekam, S. (1989). Exploration of the autistic child's theory of mind: Knowledge, belief, and communication. *Child Development, 60,* 689–700.

Perrett, D., Harries, M., Mistlin, A., Hietanen, J., Benson, P., Bevan, R., Thomas, S., Oram, M., Ortega, J., & Brierley, K. (1990). Social signals analyzed at the single cell level: Someone is looking at me, something touched me, something moved! *International Journal of Comparative Psychology, 4,* 25–55.

Perrett, D., Hietanen, M., Oram, W., & Benson, P. (1992). Organization and function of cells responsive to faces in the temporal cortex. In V. Bruce, A. Cowey, A. Ellis, & D. Perrett (Eds.), *Processing the facial image: Philosophical Transactions of the Royal Society of London, B 335* (pp. 1–128). Oxford, England: Oxford University Press.

Perrett, D., & Mistlin, A. (1990). Perception of facial characteristics by monkeys. In W. Stebbins & M. Berkley (Eds.), *Comparative perception: Vol II. Complex signals.* New York: Wiley.

Perrett, D., Oram, M., Harries, M., Bevan, R., Hietanen, J., Benson, P., & Thomas, S. (1991). Viewer-centered and object-centered codings of heads in the macaque temporal cortex. *Experimental Brain Research, 86,* 159–173.

Perrett, D., Rolls, E., & Cann, W. (1982.) Visual neurones responsive to faces in the monkey temporal cortex. *Experimental Brain Research, 47,* 329–342.

Perrett, D., Smith, P., Potter, D., Mistlin, A., Head, A., Milner, A., & Jeeves, M. (1984). Neurones responsive to faces in the temporal cortex: Studies of functional organization, sensitivity to identity, and relation to perception. *Human Neurobiology, 3,* 197–208.

Perrett, D., Smith, P., Potter, D., Mistlin, A., Head, A., Milner, A., & Jeeves, M. (1985). Visual cells in the temporal cortex sensitive to face view and gaze direction. *Proceedings of the Royal Society of London, B223,* 293–317.

Phillips, W., Baron-Cohen, S., & Rutter, M. (1992). The role of eye-contact in the detection of goals: Evidence from normal toddlers, and children with autism or mental handicap. *Development and Psychopathology, 4,* 375–383.

Ristau, C. (Ed.). (1990). *Cognitive ethology: The minds of other animals.* Hillsdale, NJ: Lawrence Erlbaum Associates.

Ristau, C. (1991). Attention, purposes, and deception in birds. In A. Whiten (Ed.), *Natural theories of mind* (pp. 209–223). Oxford, England: Basil Blackwell.

Sargent, A., & Eberhardt, L. (1975). Death feigning by ducks in response to predation by red foxes (*Vulpes fulva*). *American Midland Naturalist, 94,* 108–119.

Scaife, M., & Bruner, J. (1975). The capacity for joint visual attention in the infant. *Nature, 253,* 265–266.

Schaller, G. (1964). *The mountain gorilla.* Chicago: Chicago University Press.

Sigman, M., Mundy, P., Ungerer, J., & Sherman, T. (1986). Social interactions of autistic, mentally retarded, and normal children and their caregivers. *Journal of Child Psychology and Psychiatry, 27,* 647–656.

Tan, J., & Harris, P. (1991). Autistic children understand seeing and wanting. *Development and Psychopathology, 3,* 163–174.

Tantam, D. (1992). Characterizing the fundamental social handicap in autism. *Acta Paedopsychiatrica, 55,* 88–91.

Tomasello, M., Kruger, A., & Ratner, H. (1994). Cultural learning. *Behaviour and Brain Sciences.*

Tooby, J., & Cosmides, L. (1992). The psychological foundations of culture. In J. Barkow, L. Cosmides, & J. Tooby (Eds.), *The adapted mind* (pp. 19–136). New York: Oxford University Press.

Trevarthen, C. (1979). Communication and cooperation in early infancy: A description of primary intersubjectivity. In M. Bullowa (Ed.), *Before speech*. Cambridge, England: Cambridge University Press.

van Hooff, J. (1962). Facial expressions in higher primates. *Symposium of the Zoological Society of London, 8,* 97–125.

Wada, J. (1961). Modification of cortically induced responses in brainstem by shift of attention in monkeys. *Science, 133,* 40–42.

Wellman, H. (1990). *The child's theory of mind.* Cambridge, MA: MIT Press.

Yamane, S., Kaji, S., & Kawano, K. (1988). What facial features activate face neurons in the inferior temporal cortex? *Experimental Brain Research, 73,* 209–214.

Chapter 4

Development of Joint Visual Attention in Infants

Valerie Corkum
Chris Moore
Dalhousie University

The understanding of attention (in particular, the emergence of joint or shared attention) has been identified as playing a number of important roles in the social and cognitive development of the infant (see Adamson & Bakeman, 1991, for a review). Butterworth (1991) believes that attention serves an important communicative function during the prelinguistic period in that it permits basic information about objects of interest or desire to be conveyed. For example, joint attention plays an integral part in both the protodeclarative and protoimperative gestures first identified by Bates and her colleagues (e.g., Bates, Camaioni, & Volterra, 1979). Further, joint attention is also implicated in the phenomenon of social referencing whereby emotional information about an ambiguous object or event is conveyed from adult to infant (e.g., Feinman, 1982; Hornik, Risenhoover, & Gunnar, 1987; Sorce, Emde, Campos, & Klinnert, 1985). Bruner (1983) believes that joint attention provides the basis of shared experience necessary for the acquisition of language. In support of this notion, both the production of conventionalized acts (including referential and regulative words and gestures) toward the end of the first year (Bakeman & Adamson, 1986) as well as novel word learning in 17-month-olds (Tomasello & Farrar, 1986), 18-month-olds (Dunham, Dunham, & Curwin, 1993), and 16–19-month-olds (Baldwin, 1991), have been found to be greatly facilitated by involvement with an adult in joint attention toward an object. Finally, other authors (e.g., Baron-Cohen, 1991, this volume; Mundy, Sigman, Ungerer, & Sherman, 1986) have proposed that understanding attention in others may be a necessary precursor to the development of a "theory of mind," and that it is this understanding that is initially disrupted in autism.

Joint visual attention (JVA) is a type of shared attention that refers to the ability to follow another's direction of gaze or quite simply, "looking where someone else is looking" (Butterworth, 1991, p. 223). The current body of work on joint visual attention focuses on a number of developmental changes in this important behavior including age of onset (Scaife & Bruner, 1975), accuracy of target localization (Butterworth & Cochran, 1980; Butterworth & Grover, 1990; Butterworth & Jarrett, 1991), and the cues or behaviors important for establishing joint visual attention which include pointing (e.g., Butterworth, 1991; Churcher & Scaife, 1982; Lempers, 1979; Leung & Rheingold, 1981; Morissette, Ricard, & Gouin-Decarie, 1992; Murphy, 1978; Murphy & Messer, 1977), and the relative importance of head and eye orientation (Butterworth & Jarrett, 1991; Lempers, 1979).

The earliest investigators to explore the emergence of joint visual attention in infants were Scaife and Bruner (1975), who established the "prototypical" joint attention paradigm. In this paradigm, an experimenter engages in a face-to-face interaction with each infant. After establishing eye contact with the infant, the experimenter delivers a cue for change in the direction of his or her attention and the infant's response is noted. Subsequent trials are conducted in the same manner with the experimenter first reestablishing eye contact with the infant and then delivering a cue for change in the direction of his or her attention. Cases in which the infant changes his or her direction of gaze to align with the experimenter's are recorded as episodes of joint visual attention. In the Scaife and Bruner study, each experimental session consisted of just two trials of change in the experimenter's gaze direction—one to each side. On each trial, the experimenter turned head and eyes together 90° to fixate a target that was not visible to the infant. Scaife and Bruner judged infants as having established joint visual attention if they turned to look in the same direction as the experimenter on one out of the two trials. The results of this study indicated that 30% of the infants as young as 2 months turned their heads to follow a model's line of regard. The percentage of infants turning to follow the model's gaze increased steadily with age so that by 11–14 months of age, 100% of the infants tested demonstrated head turning in the appropriate direction on at least one of the two experimental trials.

Butterworth and colleagues (Butterworth & Cochran, 1980; Butterworth & Grover, 1990; Butterworth & Jarrett, 1991; see also Butterworth, this volume) employed the joint attention paradigm (with each infant's mother assuming the role of the experimenter), to examine the accuracy with which infants of different ages could localize the targets of another's attention. Butterworth and colleagues documented three age-specific mechanisms for joint visual attention between 6 and 18 months. At 6 months of age, infants reliably turn their heads to the correct side of the room for targets within their own visual field but only correctly locate the first target within their path of scanning (ecological mechanism). At 12 months of age, infants correctly pinpoint both the direction and location of targets regardless of positioning along the path of scanning (geometric mechanism); however, they fail to search for targets located behind them. Finally, at 18 months of age, infants not only correctly pinpoint both the direction and location of targets regardless of positioning along the path of scanning, but they now search for targets that are located behind them; however, they only do so when their own visual field is empty of targets (spatial-representational mechanism).

Work on the cues or behaviors important for the establishment of joint visual attention has been focused primarily in two areas: pointing and the relative importance of head and eye orientation. Over the years, pointing has been studied not only as a signal for the direction of another's attention (i.e., following another's points) but also as a tool for directing the attention of others (i.e., producing points oneself). In general, the research on pointing indicates that infants tend to follow another's points to nearby objects from approximately 9 months (Murphy & Messer, 1977) or 10 months of age (Butterworth, 1991; Leung & Rheingold, 1981) while points to more distant objects are followed by infants at about 14 months (Murphy & Messer, 1977) or 15 months of age (Morissette et al., 1992). In contrast, it is not until the end of the first year or beyond that a majority of infants are found to be reliably producing points of their own (Lempers, 1979; Leung & Rheingold, 1981). (See Butterworth, and Desrochers, Morissette, & Ricard, this volume, for a more thorough review of the work on pointing and the implications for joint attention.)

Like pointing, head and eye orientation are two perceptual cues that play an important role in the establishment of joint visual attention. The majority of research on joint visual attention to date has made use of a single signal (i.e., congruent head and eye orientation) for indicating change in direction of another's attention. Functionally, head and eye orientation are often equally good predictors of direction of attention because they are frequently congruent (i.e., we usually turn our head and eyes together). However, there are cases when the two cues are in conflict (e.g., the more subtle movement of turning our eyes but not our head) and in these cases, eye orientation alone provides the most accurate information regarding direction of attention. The issue of the relative effectiveness of changes in head plus eye orientation versus changes in eye orientation alone as cues for joint visual attention has thus far been investigated in two studies: Lempers (1979), and Butterworth and Jarrett (1991, Experiment 2). Butterworth and Jarrett studied head turning to localize targets in 18-month-olds in response to changes in a model's eye orientation only as well as congruent changes in head and eye orientation. The work by Lempers examined the same basic issue as Butterworth and Jarrett but in a variety of ages (9-, 12-, and 14-month-olds) with an additional condition in which only the "new" head plus eye orientation was viewed by the infant while the physical movement of the model to this new orientation was not. In general, the results of both studies indicate that a combined change in head and eye orientation is a somewhat more effective cue for joint attention than a change in eye orientation alone. In addition, Lempers found that the addition of movement enhanced the saliency of the head-plus-eyes cue. Finally, although Lempers found that no 9-month-olds engaged in joint attention based on the eyes alone cue, about 50% of the 12- and 14-month-olds did so. Likewise, Butterworth and Jarrett found that 18-month-olds successfully reoriented their own gaze on 42% of the trials when the cue was a change in the experimenter's eye orientation.

Our work on joint visual attention has primarily grown out of an interest in learning more about the nature of emerging social understanding in infants. The recent burgeoning literature on young children's social understanding has rather neglected the developmental connections between the social–cognitive changes seen in the preschool period and earlier signs of social sensitivity in infancy (Moore & Frye, 1991). One of the most significant milestones to occur in the first year of life is the onset of the period of what has been termed *secondary intersubjectivity* (Trevarthan & Hubley, 1978). Some examples of secondary intersubjectivity include such behaviors as social referencing (e.g., Feinman, 1982; Hornik et al., 1987; Sorce et al., 1985), protoimperative and protodeclarative gestures (e.g., Bates, 1979; Bates et al., 1979), and joint attention. Despite differences in form (and some would argue intent) among these exemplars of secondary intersubjectivity, the common theme that unites them lies in the fact that they all involve a coordination of the infant's attention toward both a social partner and an object of mutual interest. It is this important change in the young infant's behavior that signals the beginnings of a different type of social awareness and further, lays the foundation for full-fledged social understanding later on.

The present work represents the first stage in a program of research designed to investigate the nature of infant's social understanding over the first two years of life (portions of it were described in Corkum & Moore, 1992, 1993), and has three main purposes. First, while the appearance of social referencing (e.g., Feinman, 1982; Hornik et al., 1987; Sorce et al., 1985) and protoimperatives and protodeclaratives (e.g., Bates, 1979; Bates et al., 1979) has not been documented until the end of the first year of life, there is substantial evidence (e.g., Butterworth & Cochran, 1980; Butterworth & Grover, 1990; Butterworth & Jarrett, 1991; Scaife & Bruner, 1975) to suggest that joint visual attention, unlike these other types of secondary intersubjectivity, emerges much earlier around the 6 month mark. Given this curious developmental discrepancy, in the present work we were interested in identifying more clearly the age of onset of joint visual attention. Second, in keeping with our interest in joint attention as a line of insight into the nature of the infant's social understanding, we wished to explore what it is that infants know about other people that allows them to engage in joint visual attention. Of particular interest to us were the perceptual features that infants employ for determining another's direction of gaze and aligning with it. Therefore, in the present work we examined, systematically, developmental changes in the social cues that infants rely on for establishing joint visual attention. Finally, given the importance of joint attention in relation to later social understanding, we wished to turn to an issue that was unaddressed in the joint attention literature; that is, the origins of the joint attention response. In particular, we were curious about learning as a possible route of acquisition for joint attention. In keeping with this notion, we examined to what extent it was possible, with the provision of contingent reinforcement, to condition infants to make a "joint attention-like" head turn.

In order to address these issues, our work has employed two related but different paradigms: the joint attention paradigm described earlier (with some modifications) and a conditioned head turn paradigm (used quite frequently in work on infant perception but never before in the area of joint attention). In this chapter, we describe two studies using these paradigms.

SOCIAL CUES IN THE DEVELOPMENT
OF JOINT ATTENTION

In the first study described, we employed the joint attention paradigm to examine the age of onset of joint visual attention and the perceptual cues that infants of different ages use for determining the direction of another's gaze and aligning with it. However, in order to even address these issues we first needed to be able to accurately identify the occurrence of joint visual attention. To meet this end, our study incorporated two important features. First, we excluded targets from the experimental setup in the interest of reducing the occurrence of false positive responses (i.e., infant head turns that match the model's direction of gaze but that are a function of visual search of the experimental cubicle rather than responses to cues from the model). Although the absence of targets for infants to fixate is not consistent with all of the joint attention literature (e.g., work by Butterworth & colleagues) it certainly is not without precedent (e.g., Scaife & Bruner, 1975) and we believed it would assist us in the accurate identification of episodes of joint visual attention.

The second feature designed to permit the accurate identification of episodes of joint visual attention in the first study was the adoption of a more stringent operational definition of joint visual attention. In order to conclude that infants are reliably engaging in joint visual attention, we believe that it must be clear that they are shifting their own attention to match a model's direction of gaze significantly more frequently than they shift it to the opposite direction or "mismatch" with the model. The majority of research to date on joint attention in infants reports simply the frequency or percentage of correct responses or matches with a model's direction of gaze, but excludes the corresponding frequency of mismatches. Therefore, based on this technique for reporting findings, we believe that any conclusions that may be drawn are necessarily limited to age-related changes in the simple frequency of correct responses, and indeed these researchers all report developmental increases in frequency of matching with a model's direction of gaze. However, in the absence of information regarding the corresponding proportion of mismatches to matches, we believe that it is not possible to draw meaningful conclusions with respect to whether or not infants are actually engaging in joint visual attention at any particular age. Therefore, our studies employed a more stringent operational definition of joint visual attention in which matches with adult direction of gaze were compared with mismatches. (Morissette et al., 1992, adopted a similar definition.) According to this new operational definition, we created a difference score in which the number of infant head turns that mismatched the experimenter's direction of gaze were subtracted from the number of infant head turns that matched it, and we required infants to match the experimenter's direction of gaze significantly more frequently than they mismatched it (i.e., show a difference score significantly > 0) in order for joint visual attention to be reliably demonstrated. In this way, we were able to more accurately identify the occurrence, and thus the age of onset, of joint visual attention.

Finally, this study extended the previous research on the perceptual cues employed for joint visual attention by systematically varying both head and eye orientation in isolation (i.e., head only and eyes only) as well as in combination (i.e., head and eyes move in the same direction; head and eyes move in opposite directions) in order to determine their relative importance as cues for establishing joint visual attention. In addition, we included infants ranging in age from 6 to 19 months in order to gain a more complete picture of the developmental changes in sensitivity to these different cues.

In summary, our first study employed the joint attention paradigm (with some added features) in order to identify the age of onset of joint visual attention, and the perceptual cues that infants of different ages employ for establishing joint visual attention.

STUDY 1

Sixty infants, equally divided into five age groups—6–7, 9–10, 12–13, 15–16, and 18–19 months—participated in the first study. The experimental sessions were conducted in a 3.19 m × 1.75 m cubicle enclosed with curtains to minimize distractions. The parent sat on a chair facing the experimenter (.75 m away) with the infant seated on the parent's lap while the experimenter sat on a small stool so that her eyes were at approximately the same level as the infant's. The parent wore glasses with the lenses covered in black paper in order to obscure his or her view of the experimenter.

The experimental session was comprised of 16 trials of change in either the experimenter's head orientation, eye orientation, or both. Each trial commenced with the experimenter's eyes and head oriented frontward, directly facing the infant. The trial began once the infant's head and eyes were, likewise, frontward, facing the experimenter. The experimenter established eye contact with the infant by vocal means and then changed the orientation of either her head or her eyes to suit one of the following four types of trials: H (head orientation changed but eyes remained fixated on the infant); E (head maintained a frontward orientation facing the infant but eyes changed their direction of orientation); H + E (both head and eyes changed orientation in the same direction); or H − E (both head and eyes changed orientation but in opposite directions). Because no targets were present, small fixation points were marked with tape on the curtain behind the mother and infant to ensure a uniform deviation on each cue presentation. For the H, E, and H + E trials, the deviation of gaze was 61° from the midline, whereas for the H − E trials, the eye and head orientations deviated 31° each to opposite sides of the midline. Each change in orientation was maintained for approximately 7 sec. After 7 sec had elapsed, the experimenter turned back to face the infant and reestablished eye contact in order to begin the next trial.

Two trials of each of the four types were conducted to the right and left sides for a total of 16 trials. Within each session, the trials were presented in two randomized blocks so that each cue was presented once to each side in each half of the session. Each block was further subdivided into two segments comprised of one trial of each of the four trial types. Six randomized presentation orders were recorded on audiotape and played back via earphone during the session to cue the experimenter. Equal numbers of infants in each age group were tested using each of the six presentation orders.

The entire session was recorded on videotape via two video cameras; one positioned behind the experimenter facing the infant and the other positioned behind the mother facing the experimenter. A full-face view of the experimenter and a full-body view of the infant were combined into a split screen display. A coder naive to the hypotheses of the study scored the videotapes for the direction of the first infant head turn in the horizontal plane to occur during each trial. Each infant head turn was then designated as either a match or a mismatch with the criteria for this judgement differing depending upon trial type. In the case of the H, E, and H + E trials, a match was defined as an infant head turn in the same direction as the trial executed by the experimenter while a mismatch was defined as an infant head turn that was opposite in direction to the trial executed by the experimenter. However, in the case of the H − E trials, because head and eyes are oriented in opposite directions, a match was defined as an infant head turn that followed the direction of the experimenter's head orientation while a mismatch was defined as an infant head turn that followed the direction of the experimenter's eye orientation. In this way, the H − E difference score reflected the extent to which infants tended to follow the experimenter's head orientation in preference over her eye orientation. A sample of 25% of the videotapes, 3 subjects from each age group, was randomly selected for reliability coding by a second coder. Coefficient kappas calculated for each age group were as follows: 6–7 months, $k = .91$; 9–10 months, $k = .97$; 12–13 months, $k = .96$; 15–16 months, $k = .97$; and 18–19 months, $k = .91$.

A three-way analysis of variance (ANOVA) was conducted with Age (five levels: 6–7, 9–10, 12–13, 15–16, and 18–19 months) as a between-subjects variable and Block (two levels: one and two) and Trial type (four levels: H, E, H + E, & H − E) as within-subjects variables. The match minus mismatch difference score described earlier was the dependent variable in all analyses.

No significant effects involving the Block variable were found. In order to analyze further for possible performance differences early and late in the experimental session the data were collapsed across Trial type and an Age by Segment ANOVA was performed. The results of this two-way ANOVA yielded no significant effects involving the Segment variable. Because the results of this second analysis confirmed an absence of overall performance differences across the experimental session, the data were collapsed across both Segment and Block, and a two-way ANOVA was conducted with Age as a between-subjects variable and Trial type as a within-subjects variable. Table 4.1 provides an overall summary of the mean number of trials in which infants of each age turned to match or mismatch each trial type. Figure 4.1 illustrates the mean difference score obtained for each trial type as a function of age.

Results of the Age by Trial type ANOVA indicated a significant Trial type effect, $F(3, 165) = 5.86$, $p = .001$, indicating that infants showed higher match − mismatch difference scores for the H + E trials than for any of the others; H,

TABLE 4.1
Mean Frequency of Experimental Trials in Which Infants of Each
Age Turned to Match or Mismatch Each Trial Type in Study #1

Age (months)	Trial Type							
	H		E		H + E		H − E	
				Matches				
6–7	.917	(.793)	.917	(.669)	.833	(.718)	1.000	(.953)
9–10	1.167	(.835)	1.167	(.718)	1.500	(.905)	1.333	(.492)
12–13	.833	(.835)	.583	(.900)	1.250	(.866)	1.167	(1.267)
15–16	.917	(.900)	.833	(.835)	1.667	(1.231)	.750	(.754)
18–19	.417	(.515)	.583	(.900)	2.000	(1.279)	.500	(.674)
				Mismatches				
6–7	.917	(.793)	1.333	(.888)	1.083	(.996)	.750	(.965)
9–10	1.000	(.853)	.917	(.793)	.917	(.793)	1.000	(.603)
12–13	.500	(.674)	.417	(.515)	.417	(.669)	.583	(.996)
15–16	.417	(.515)	.750	(.965)	.500	(.674)	.750	(.866)
18–19	.750	(.866)	.333	(.492)	.083	(.289)	.417	(.669)

Note. Four trials of each type were presented in the session. Values in parentheses are SD.

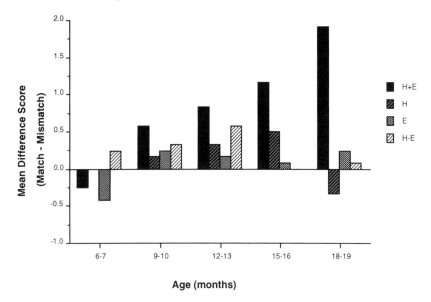

FIG. 4.1. Mean match – mismatch difference score calculated for each trial type as a function of age in Study #1.

$t(1, 165) = 3.43$, $p < .001$; E, $t(1, 165) = 3.75$, $p < .001$; H – E, $t(1, 165) = 2.87$, $p < .01$; with no significant differences in the difference scores for the remaining three trial types (H, E, & H – E).

In addition, a significant Trial type by Age effect was found, $F(3, 165) = 1.88$, $p = .04$. Post hoc testing indicated that at 6–7, 9–10 and 12–13 months of age there were no significant differences among the difference scores for the four trial types nor were the difference scores for any of the trial types found to be significantly different from 0. For the purposes of further post hoc testing, the difference scores were pooled across H, H + E, and H – E trial types at each age in order to construct an overall difference score that would reflect the extent to which infants at each age tended to align (rather than misalign) with the experimenter's head orientation. The pooled difference scores at 6–7, 9–10, and 12–13 months were found to be 0, 0.361, and 0.583, respectively. While the pooled difference score at 12–13 months was found to be significantly larger than 0, $t(1, 165) = 2.49$, $p < .025$, those at 6–7 and 9–10 months were not.

Further post hoc testing of the Trial type by Age effect revealed that infants at 18–19 months showed higher difference scores for the H + E trials than any other trial type: H, $t(1, 165) = 4.82$, $p < .001$; E, $t(1, 165) = 3.57$, $p < .001$; H – E, $t(1, 165) = 3.93$, $p < .01$; with no significant differences in the difference scores for the remaining three trial types (H, E, & H – E). In addition, the difference score for the H + E trial type at 18–19 months of age was found to be significantly greater than 0, $t(1, 165) = 4.10$, $p < .001$. Finally, the 15–16-month-olds, like the 18–19 month group, showed higher difference scores for H

+ E than the E, $t(1, 165) = 2.32$, $p < .025$ and H − E, $t(1, 165) = 2.49$, $p < .025$ trial types. In addition, the 15–16-month-olds also had a difference score for the H + E trial type that was significantly greater than 0, $t(1, 165) = 2.50$, $p < .025$ and they showed no significant differences among the difference scores for the remaining three trial types (H, E, & H − E). However, unlike the 18–19 month group, the 15–16-month-olds showed no significant difference in their difference scores for the H + E and H trial types.

When Does Joint Visual Attention Start?

The results of this study provide a somewhat different picture of the age of onset of joint visual attention from the previous literature on the topic. While both Scaife and Bruner (1975) and Butterworth and colleagues (Butterworth & Cochran, 1980; Butterworth & Grover, 1990; and Butterworth & Jarrett, 1991) have reported that a significant proportion of infants engage in joint visual attention from 6 months of age, our work suggests that it is not until somewhat later that joint visual attention is reliably demonstrated. In the strictest sense, it was not until 15 months of age that the infants in our study demonstrated a joint attention response that was characterized by significantly more matches than mismatches with the experimenter's direction of gaze (i.e., a difference score which was significantly different from 0). However, evaluation of the difference scores pooled across trial type indicated a developmental difference such that 12–13- but not 6–7- and 9–10-month-olds have pooled difference scores that were significantly greater than 0. This suggests that the rudiments of a reliable joint attention response may be evidenced by 12 months. While this age of onset for joint visual attention is somewhat later than previous investigators have reported, we believe that the modifications in scoring and procedure that we adopted may well account for the discrepancy.

One notable modification in our study was the exclusion of targets for the infants to fixate should they align with the experimenter's direction of gaze. While the bulk of studies on joint attention have included targets, the majority of them have been carried out by the same group of researchers (Butterworth and colleagues) for the purpose of examining the issue of target localization. Consequently, the inclusion of targets was a necessary part of their design. Although we realized that the exclusion of targets from the setup would compromise somewhat the ecological validity of our paradigm, we did so in the interest of reducing the occurrence of false positive responses resulting from a visual search of the experimental cubicle. As we saw it, the main risk of not having targets for the infants to fixate was an order effect that would have been manifested as extinction of infant looking (or some other change in response pattern) over the course of the experimental session. Because the data analyses showed no performance differences over the course of the experimental session, even when the session was broken down into four 4-trial segments, this potential problem was not realized. Despite the fact that there were no targets for them to look at, infants maintained their age-specific patterns of response throughout the lengthy experimental session. In contrast with our view, Butterworth and colleagues would argue, based on their ecological mechanism for joint visual attention in 6-month-olds, that we did not see joint attention in this age group in this study precisely because targets are an integral part of the context necessary for eliciting joint visual attention at this age, and by excluding the targets we effectively removed the possibility for joint visual attention. We would argue first, that the absence of targets in studies of joint attention is not without precedent (e.g., Scaife & Bruner, 1975), and second, that not all of the studies to include targets find an age of emergence for joint visual attention that is as early as that purported by Butterworth and colleagues. In fact, the weight of the empirical evidence suggests that age of onset of joint visual attention hinges more solidly on the criteria employed for scoring it than on the presence or absence of targets in the experimental setup. Whereas Butterworth and colleagues did employ targets in their paradigm, Scaife and Bruner did not; yet both groups reported very early ages of onset for joint visual attention (i.e., from about 6 months). The critical similarity in the work of these two groups lies in the fact that both adopted scoring criteria that included matches or alignments with adult direction of gaze but excluded misalignments or mismatches. In contrast with this work, Morissette et al. (1992) did include targets in their experimental setup but they also adopted a more stringent operational definition of joint attention that compared matches, mismatches, and no responses. Instead of the early age of onset reported by Scaife and Bruner, and Butterworth and colleagues, Morissette et al., in keeping with our findings, found that it was not until about 12 months of age that infants reliably engaged in joint visual attention. In a similar vein, Lempers (1979) tested 9-, 12-, and 14-month-olds in a paradigm that included targets but required infants to fixate the same target as a model on both experimental trials (one to each side) in order for them to be judged as correctly aligning with the model's gaze (i.e., if infants failed to look or misaligned on even one trial, their performance was judged to be incorrect). In keeping with the findings of both our study and that of Morissette et al., it was not until 12 months of age that Lempers found a majority of infants (83%) engaging in joint visual attention according to this more stringent definition. In light of this concordance between our findings and those of Lempers and Morissette et al., we conclude that joint visual attention does not emerge until somewhat later than previously reported, and that the most likely explanation for the discrepancy between our findings and those of previous studies which report a 6 month age of onset is the more stringent operational definition of joint attention.

What Social Cues Do Infants Use?

The pattern of performance exhibited by 6–7- and 9–10-month-olds suggests that these infants are not reliably engaging in joint attention based on information from any of the cues. Their difference scores were not found to be significantly greater than 0, indicating that they turned in the opposite direction or mismatched the direction of the experimenter's gaze as frequently as they matched it. Therefore, this age group will not be considered with respect to the issue of cues employed for joint visual attention.

In contrast to the two youngest age groups, the findings for 15-month-olds indicate that these infants do reliably engage in joint visual attention, and they appear to do so based primarily on information about head position. This was evidenced by a difference score for the H + E trials (but no other trial type) that was significantly greater than 0, indicating that they turned their heads to match the direction of the H + E trials significantly more frequently than they mismatched them; by a significantly higher difference score for H + E than for E trials; and by a lack of significant differences in the difference scores for the H and H + E trial types. However, because the 15–16-month-olds did have a significantly higher difference score for the H + E than the H – E trial types, it appears that at least some awareness of eye orientation as a signal for direction of attention is present at this age.

In keeping with the findings for 15–16-month-olds, analysis of the pooled difference scores constructed for the 12–13 month age group indicated that these infants, like the 15–16-month-olds, seem to be making a joint attention response based primarily on information about the experimenter's head orientation, as the pooled difference scores that reflect tendency to follow head position were significantly different from 0.

In contrast with the 12–16 month infants, the 18–19-month-olds seem to rely on congruent head and eye orientation for determining direction of gaze and joining attention because: (a) their difference score for the H + E trials only was significantly greater than 0, indicating that they turned their heads to match the H + E trials significantly more frequently than they mismatched them; (b) they matched the H + E trials significantly more frequently than they matched any of the other trial types; and (c) there were no significant differences among the difference scores for the remaining three trial types.

Finally, at no age did infants align with the direction of the model's gaze based on information about eye orientation alone, whether presented in the context of the E or H – E cues. This finding is inconsistent with Lempers (1979) and Butterworth and Jarrett (1991), who found that a significant proportion of 14- and 18-month-olds, respectively, were able to employ changes in a model's eye orientation alone as a cue for establishing joint attention. Lempers found that 50% of 14-month-olds engaged in joint visual attention on the basis of change in a model's eye orientation alone while 90% of them did so when the cue was congruent change in head and eye orientation. Similarly, Butterworth and Jarrett reported that 18-month-olds turned their heads in the same direction to a change in eye orientation alone on 42% of occasions compared to 50% of occasions when the cue was congruent head and eye orientation. In these two studies, therefore, it appears that both 14-month-olds and 18-month-olds were reasonably good at establishing joint attention on the basis of eye orientation alone. Because research on infant vision (Mayer & Dobson, 1982) indicates visual acuity levels from birth sufficient for resolution of the changes in eye orientation presented at the proximate distance employed in our study, the differing findings are clearly not the result of a problem in detecting the cues presented. Instead, a difference in procedure between our work and that of Lempers, and Butterworth and Jarrett may well account for the apparent discrepancy. Both Lempers, and Butterworth and Jarrett presented E and H + E trials separately. Butterworth and Jarrett presented them in separate blocks, while Lempers presented them as completely separate tasks. This procedural difference may have acted to enhance the saliency of the E trials in these two studies. By comparison, in our study, there were more types of trials and the different trial types were presented in random order, which may have made discrimination of the E trials more difficult.

Notwithstanding this difference, all the relevant studies have found that H + E was a more salient cue to 18-month-olds for joint attention than E alone. By way of explanation, Butterworth and Jarrett have proposed that congruent eye and head movements may simply be a clearer signal for change in attention than eye movements alone. We would add that it is also possible that congruent head and eye movements signal something about the target that is not signalled by eye movements alone (e.g., that it is more interesting or more enduring, and thus more worthy of a turn).

In summary, the results of this study indicate that infants do not reliably engage in joint visual attention until about 12 months of age. Prior to this age not only do infants fail to distinguish between the four trial types but they mismatch (or turn in the opposite direction) as frequently as they match any of them. From about 12–16 months of age, infants seem to establish joint visual attention based primarily on head position alone while at 18 months, head and eye congruence seems to be important. At no age did the infants in this study establish joint visual attention based on information about eye orientation alone.

LEARNING AND THE ORIGINS OF JOINT ATTENTION

In a second study we addressed two issues: the age of onset of joint visual attention, and the origins of the joint attention response, an issue that had not yet been addressed in the literature. In order to examine these issues we adopted a somewhat unconventional methodology for joint attention research: the conditioned head turn paradigm.

The conditioned head turn paradigm was particularly appropriate for our purposes for a number of reasons. First, notwithstanding the earlier arguments against the absence of targets in the first study as a methodological problem, an empirical test of this notion remained to be completed. Because the conditioned head turn paradigm necessitates the addition of targets to act as reinforcers, it permitted us the opportunity to empirically examine the possibility that our earlier finding—later emergence of joint visual attention—was an artifact of the absence of targets for the infants to fixate. Second, we wished to learn something about the origins of the joint attention response. In particular we were curious about learning as a possible route of acquisition for joint attention (Moore & Corkum, in press). In light of the findings of the first study indicating that infants under 12 months were not spontaneously engaging in joint visual attention, we wondered if it would be possible to condition infants in this age range to make a "joint visual attention-like" head turn response. Because developmental psychologists have successfully employed the conditioned head turn paradigm for decades to delimit the parameters of infant perception, we knew that conditioning of a simple head turn response to visual or auditory stimuli was possible (e.g., Bower, 1966; Werker & Tees, 1984). However, what was not clear was whether infants in this age group could learn to make differential head turn responses to more complex social stimuli that differed in only one crucial aspect: orientation of gaze. By attempting to condition infants to make a gaze following head turn in this study we believed that we would be able to learn something about not only the age of acquisition of joint visual attention but, perhaps more importantly, about the possible origins of the joint attention response.

STUDY 2

Sixty-three infants, equally subdivided into three age groups (6–7-, 8–9-, and 10–11-month-olds) completed the study. Sessions took place inside the same cubicle as used in the first study. The only targets present inside the cubicle were the two toys, one on each side, used as reinforcers. These toys were located behind a plexiglass window and could be illuminated and made to move by remote control. An observer located in an adjacent room watched the proceedings of the session on a video monitor and was responsible for remote control of the toys. Both toys were visible to the infant at all times but activation was contingent upon the behavior of both the experimenter and the infant as well as the particular phase of the session.

During the session the experimenter participated in a face-to-face interaction with the infant who was seated on the parent's lap. Each session consisted of a maximum of 28 trials or changes in the experimenter's direction of gaze either to the right or left. The duration of each trial was 7 sec, and prior to initiating a trial the experimenter established eye contact with the infant. The trials were divided into three phases. Table 4.2 outlines the events that took place during each experimental phase. During Phase I (Baseline) there were four trials of a change in the experimenter's direction of gaze (two trials to each side) throughout which the targets remained inactive. This phase permitted assessment of a spon-

TABLE 4.2
Outline of Events in Study #2

Phase	# Trials	Event
Baseline	4	Both targets visible but inactive
Noncontingent	4	Target of experimenter's gaze activated after 2 sec delay
Contingent		Target of experimenter's gaze activated contingent
	20	upon concurrent fixation by infant

taneous joint attention response in the presence of targets. During Phase II
(Noncontingent Toy) there were also four trials (two to each side) but this time,
regardless of the infant's behavior, the target to which the experimenter turned
was activated approximately 2 sec after the change in the experimenter's direction
of gaze. This phase assisted in shaping the gaze following head turn response.
Finally, during Phase III (Contingent Toy) there was a maximum of 20 trials
(10 to each side) during which a toy was activated only if the infant made a
head turn that matched the direction of the experimenter's gaze. This phase
allowed for further shaping and a test of learning. Although a maximum of 20
Contingent trials was possible, the exact length of the Contingent phase varied
as a function of individual performance. A criterion measure was employed by
the observer online in each session such that the Contingent phase was termi-
nated at the end of the four-trial block in which infants demonstrated a reliable
joint attention response. In order to demonstrate a reliable joint attention response the infant was required to make five consecutive alignments with the experimenter's direction of gaze. If no such response was demonstrated, the Contingent phase continued to a maximum of 20 trials. A full-face view of the
experimenter and a full-body view of the infant were recorded with separate
videocameras and the two images were combined on a split screen.

As in the first study, a coder naive to the hypotheses of the study scored the
videotapes for the direction of the first infant head turn in the horizontal plane
to occur during each trial. Each infant head turn was then designated as either
a match or a mismatch, respectively, depending upon whether the turn was
aligned with (match) or in the direction opposite (mismatch) the orientation
of the experimenter's gaze. A difference score was then calculated by subtracting
the frequency of mismatches from the frequency of matches demonstrated in
each four-trial block of the session. A sample of 30% of the videotapes (7 subjects
from each age group) was randomly selected for reliability coding by a second
coder. Coefficient kappas calculated for each age group were as follows: 6–7
months, $k = .95$; 8–9 months, $k = .95$; 10–11 months, $k = .97$.

Based on the pilot work conducted for this study, it became clear that the
question we were posing in this conditioning study was not so simple as whether
infants in this age range could or could not learn to make a reliable head turn
response that aligned with a model's direction of gaze. Even within the relatively

narrow 6–11 month age range tested, infants generated qualitatively different patterns of response that could not be adequately captured by simply comparing the overall frequency of matches and mismatches as we had done in the first study. While we were still committed to the notion (as outlined in the operational definition of joint visual attention employed in the first study) that infants must demonstrate more matches than mismatches in order to be judged as reliably engaging in joint visual attention, it was necessary to add some additional criteria in this study in order to describe the full range of response patterns obtained. Our results suggested three primary patterns of response: Spontaneous Joint Visual Attention, Learning, and Perseveration. Table 4.3 outlines the criteria for these response patterns.

In keeping with the operational definition of joint visual attention adopted in the first study, infants who demonstrated a pattern of Spontaneous Joint Visual Attention engaged in more matches than mismatches during the Baseline phase; that is, there was a match minus mismatch difference score of two or greater in the four-trial Baseline phase. In addition to satisfying this Baseline requirement, Spontaneous joint visual attenders went on to reach a criterion of five consecutive matches with the experimenter's direction of gaze during the Contingent phase (with a conservative estimate of the probability of infants engaging in five consecutive matches at $p < .05$). In contrast, infants who demonstrated a pattern of Learning did not meet the Baseline criterion for Spontaneous Joint Visual Attention but did go on to meet the Contingent phase criterion of five consecutive matches with the experimenter's direction of gaze. Finally, infants who demonstrated a pattern of Perseveration failed to reach both the Baseline and Contingent phase criteria outlined earlier. However, Perseverators did meet an alternative criterion during the Contingent phase whereby they engaged in either a majority of head turns in one direction (70% or greater) or several sequences of turns in the same direction (three or more sequences of

TABLE 4.3
Criteria for Each of Three Response Patterns Identified in Study #2

Response Type	Phase Criteria	
	Baseline	Contingent
Spontaneous JVA	Match – mismatch difference score of 2 or greater	5 or more consecutive matches
Learning	Failure to meet Baseline criterion for Spontaneous JVA	5 or more consecutive matches
Perseveration	Failure to meet Baseline criterion for Spontaneous JVA	70% or more head turns to one side OR 3 or more sequences of 3 or more turns to one side

three or more consecutive turns in the same direction). Since these three response categories were not exclusive (i.e., it was possible for an infant to meet the criteria for more than one category) decisions regarding categorization were made in a conservative fashion. For example, infants who met criteria for both Perseveration and Learning were assigned to the Perseveration category. In addition, it should be noted that the response categories were not exhaustive (i.e., 3 out of the 63 infants tested did not meet criteria for any of the patterns). However, all of the infants demonstrating an "other" response pattern fell into the youngest (6–7 month) age group.

A chi-square test, performed on the data indicated clear developmental differences in the three primary response patterns, $\chi^2(4, N = 60) = 26.66, p < .001$. Figure 4.2 illustrates the number of infants in each age group exhibiting each response pattern. In the 6–7 month age group the majority of infants (17 out of 21) engaged in a pattern of Perseveration. Only one infant in the 6–7 month group showed a pattern of Learning while no infants demonstrated Spontaneous Joint Visual Attention. In contrast, in the 8–9 month age group there were far fewer Perseverators (10 out of 21) and far more Learners (8 out of 21) than at 6–7 months. In addition, there were a few infants (3 out of 21) demonstrating Spontaneous Joint Visual Attention in the 8–9 month group. Finally, in the 10–11 month age group there were even fewer Perseverators (only 3 out of 21) than in the 8–9 month group, but roughly the same number of Learners (7 out of 21). However, the pattern demonstrated by the greatest number of infants in

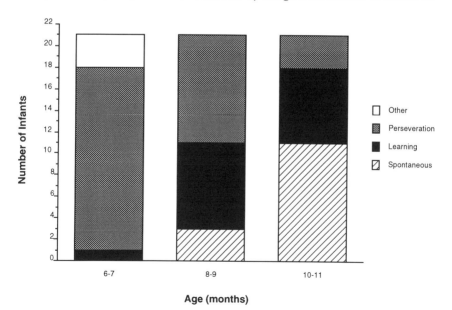

FIG. 4.2. Number of infants demonstrating each response pattern as a function of age in Study #2.

the 10–11 month group (11 out of 21) was one of Spontaneous Joint Visual Attention.

In line with the findings of the first study, the pattern of results obtained in this study clearly indicates that joint visual attention does not emerge until somewhat later than thought by previous investigators (Butterworth & Cochran, 1980; Butterworth & Jarrett, 1991; Scaife & Bruner, 1975). Even with the addition of targets, there were no 6–7-month-olds who spontaneously engaged in joint attention and only a very small proportion (less than 5%) of them were able to learn to align with the direction of another's gaze even with the assistance of contingent reinforcement. In addition, very few 8–9-month-olds but a large number of 10–11-month-olds engaged in spontaneous joint attention. We therefore conclude that it is not until sometime around 10 months of age that joint visual attention becomes a reliable part of the infant's behavioral repertoire. However, given the high proportion of 8–9-month-olds who were able to learn to align with the direction of another's gaze this age appears to be the critical one for the acquisition of this response.

In summary, the findings of this study indicate that even when targets are present, joint visual attention is not spontaneously demonstrated by infants until about 10 months of age. However, given the appropriate feedback infants are able to acquire a gaze-following response from about 8 months on. This pattern of findings suggests that learning is a possible mode of acquisition for joint visual attention.

CONCLUSION

Given the results of these two studies, let us consider again the three issues raised in the introduction to this chapter.

Age of Emergence of Joint Visual Attention

Although the findings of our first study indicate that infants do not reliably engage in joint visual attention until about 12 months of age, the results of the second study demonstrate that a significant proportion of infants are able to align with another's direction of gaze from as early as 10–11 months. Based on the findings of these two studies we conclude that it is not until sometime around the end of the first year, between 10 and 12 months of age, that joint visual attention is reliably demonstrated.

This 10–12 month age of onset for joint visual attention is considerably later than that reported by Scaife and Bruner (1975) and by Butterworth and colleagues (Butterworth & Cochran, 1980; Butterworth & Grover, 1990; Butterworth & Jarrett, 1991) who suggest that even 6-month-olds engage in joint visual attention. This discrepancy in age of onset may be accounted for by the fact that our research employed a more stringent operational definition of joint attention, one which compares both matches and mismatches, and by the fact that other researchers such as Lempers (1979) and Morissette et al. (1992), who used similar, more stringent coding procedures, also found a later age of onset.

In addition, given that our second study represents the first attempt to employ a new paradigm for the study of joint attention, the qualitatively different response patterns documented in the narrow age range tested in our second study suggest that the joint attention conditioning paradigm may, in fact, be more sensitive to subtle developmental differences in the emergence of the joint visual attention response. In this way, this study may provide a more "finely tuned" estimate of infants' abilities with respect to joint visual attention.

In terms of the broader context of infant social development, the 10–12 month age of onset for joint attention documented in the present work is certainly much more in keeping with the emergence of other types of secondary intersubjectivity such as social referencing (e.g., Feinman, 1982; Hornik et al., 1987; Sorce et al., 1985) and protoimperative and protodeclarative gestures (e.g., Bates, 1979; Bates et al., 1979) at around the end of the first year. Consequently, the present findings provide for a greater degree of consistency in the nature of the infant's social understanding in the first year of life than has the previous work on joint attention.

Social Cues Employed for Joint Visual Attention

The findings of our first study suggest that 6–7- and 9–10-month-olds do not engage in joint visual attention based on information from any of the cues as they mismatch as frequently as they match any of them. In contrast, from 12 months of age infants appear to be engaging in joint attention based primarily on information about head orientation based on the finding that these infants show more matches than mismatches to the head and head plus eyes cues. Despite the fact that from birth, infants are not only able to detect changes in eye orientation (Mayer & Dobson, 1982) but also spend more time scanning the eye region of the face than any other area (Hainline, 1978; Haith, Bergman, & Moore, 1977), it appears that in the early stages of joint visual attention infants do not yet understand the significance of eye orientation as an indicator of direction of visual attention because they do not take the model's eye orientation into consideration in aligning their gaze.

In contrast to the younger infants, the results of our work indicate that by 18 months, infants do seem to appreciate the importance of eye orientation to joint attention even though they do not follow another's direction of gaze on the basis of eye orientation alone. For the 18–19-month-olds in Study #1, head and eye congruence seemed to be the most important factor as these infants aligned significantly more frequently than they misaligned with the head plus eyes cue but also aligned with the head plus eyes cue significantly more frequently than they aligned with either the head alone or eyes alone cues. Despite the fact that these infants did seem to take the experimenter's eye orientation into consideration in establishing joint visual attention, they did not reliably align with the experimenter's changes in eye orientation alone. Although this finding is inconsistent with the work of Butterworth and Jarrett (1991) and Lempers (1979) who found that a significant proportion of infants in this age range aligned with changes in eye orientation, it is possible that the salience of the eyes-alone cue in our work was significantly diminished due to a randomized rather than blocked presentation of the various cue types. Despite this discrepancy in findings, both our work and that of Butterworth and Jarrett and Lempers found changes in head and eye orientation to be a much more salient cue for joint visual attention in 18-month-olds than changes in eye orientation alone.

This pattern of findings suggests definite developmental differences in the perceptual cues employed by infants for establishing joint visual attention and in the associated understanding that infants have of joint attention. In the early stages of joint attention infants seem to rely on information about another's head orientation alone. This finding raises important questions about the nature of the infant's understanding of joint attention. If infants do not appreciate the role of eyes in joint attention, then it is questionable whether they can be said to understand that the other person is attending to an object at all. Rather, our results are consistent with the idea that joint attention has its origins in infancy in a response that makes use of another's head orientation as a stimulus to make a head turn in the same direction (Moore & Corkum, in press). Such an orienting response would work well in many instances because eye and head orientation are frequently congruent, and thus, in normal circumstances, one would expect the proportion of hits to misses yielded by such a response to be high. As development progresses, infants come to employ information about both head and eye orientation in establishing joint visual attention and to understand better the importance of eye orientation as the best indicator of where another is looking. Our results do not allow us to draw conclusions about when infants understand the nature of joint attention in the sense of understanding that attention to an object can be shared. However, we would suggest that the use of eye orientation is a likely index of this understanding. Finally, the oldest infants are quite responsive to subtle changes in eye orientation alone and reliably engage in joint visual attention based on the eyes-alone cue. In support of this last stage, the work of both Lempers (1979), and Butterworth and Jarrett (1991) reported that a substantial proportion of infants (14- and 18-month-olds, and 18-month-olds, respectively) establish joint visual attention based on changes in another's eye orientation alone. In addition, some further work of our own conducted with the joint attention conditioning paradigm (Corkum & Moore, 1994) indicates that while a substantial proportion of infants are able to acquire a joint attention-like head turn response to changes in a model's head and eye orientation from about 8–9 months of age, it is not until well after 10 months that we have been able to condition even a small proportion of infants to make the same response to the more subtle cue of changes in eye orientation alone.

Role of Learning in the Development
of the Joint Visual Attention Response

Our second study indicates clear age-related differences in infants' abilities to spontaneously engage in joint attention or to even acquire a gaze-following head turn response. While the most frequent response generated by 10–11-month-olds was Spontaneous Joint Visual Attention, no 6–7-month-olds and only a very small number of 8–9-month-olds showed this pattern. In contrast, a considerable number of 8–11-month-olds but only a couple of 6–7-month-olds were able to learn to make head turns that reliably aligned with the experimenter's direction of gaze. Although these findings do not constitute evidence that joint visual attention is acquired via a process of learning, they certainly indicate that it is possible to acquire, through learning, a gaze-following response to a model's head turn. Consequently, our findings are consistent with the notion that learning is a possible route of acquisition for the joint attention response.

Having said that, however, we do not wish to endorse a simple conditioning account of the acquisition of joint visual attention (see Moore & Corkum, in press). In line with general sensorimotor development, joint visual attention may be tied to the infant's emerging ability to respond flexibly to two separate spatial locations on the basis of different cues. At the initial stage of this development, infants show a basic awareness of the changes in behavior that accompany the reorientation of a model's gaze and of the appearance of the targets. However, at this stage they seem unable to effectively integrate these two domains of information in order to produce differential responding, even with the assistance of contingent feedback. Later, infants are able to respond differentially to the model's cues for change in gaze orientation. However, at this stage contingent feedback is necessary in scaffolding the integration of model and target information. Finally, infants spontaneously generate differential responses to the experimenter's cues for change in gaze orientation without the need for specific feedback.

This account is consistent with a view of the developmental progression in the infant's understanding of joint attention that reverses the order of events often assumed to be the case. Perhaps the more common view (e.g., Baron-Cohen, this volume; Tomasello, this volume) is that the infant must first understand something about the model's attention to a potential object in order to engage in joint attention. Instead, we propose (see also Barresi & Moore, 1993; Moore & Corkum, in press) that other mechanisms such as learning can get the infant involved in joint attention without the infant's understanding the nature of attention in the model. However, once the infant is reliably engaging in joint attention, the experiences offered by this new triadic interactive form of behavior will afford progress in the infant's conceptualization of attention and set the child on the road to the discovery of all forms of social life that rest on sharing attention with others.

REFERENCES

Adamson, L. B., & Bakeman, R. (1991). The development of shared attention during infancy. *Annals of Child Development, 8*, 1–41.

Baldwin, D. (1991). Infants' contribution to the achievement of joint reference. *Child Development, 62*, 875–890.

Bakeman, R., & Adamson, L. B. (1986). Infants' conventionalized acts: Gestures and words with mothers and peers. *Infant Behavior & Development, 9*, 215–230.

Baron-Cohen, S. (1991). Precursors to a theory of mind: Understanding attention in others. In A. Whiten (Ed.), *Natural theories of mind: Evolution, development, and simulation of everyday mindreading* (pp. 234–251). Oxford, England: Blackwell.

Barresi, J., & Moore, C. (1993). Sharing a perspective precedes the understanding of that perspective. *Behavioral and Brain Sciences, 16*, 513–514.

Bates, E. (1979). Intention, conventions, and symbols. In E. Bates, L. Benigni, I. Bretherton, L. Camaioni, & V. Volterra (Eds.), *The emergence of symbols* (pp. 33–42). New York: Academic Press.

Bates, E., Camaioni, L., & Volterra, V. (1979). The acquisition of performatives prior to speech. In E. Ochs & B. Schieffelin (Eds.), *Developmental pragmatics* (pp. 111–129). New York: Academic Press.

Bower, T. G. R. (1966). The visual world of infants. *Scientific American, 215*, 80–92.

Bruner, J. (1983). *Child's talk: Learning to use language*. New York: Norton.

Butterworth, G. (1991). The ontogeny and phylogeny of joint visual attention. In A. Whiten (Ed.), *Natural theories of mind: Evolution, development, and simulation of everyday mindreading* (pp. 223–232). Oxford, England: Blackwell.

Butterworth, G., & Cochran, E. (1980). Towards a mechanism of joint visual attention in human infancy. *International Journal of Behavioral Development, 3*, 253–272.

Butterworth, G., & Grover, L. (1990). Joint visual attention, manual pointing, and preverbal communication in human infancy. In M. Jeannerod (Ed.), *Attention and performance XIII* (pp. 605–624). Hillsdale, NJ: Lawrence Erlbaum Associates.

Butterworth, G., & Jarrett, N. (1991). What minds have in common is space: Spatial mechanisms serving joint visual attention in infancy. *British Journal of Developmental Psychology, 9*, 55–72.

Churcher, J., & Scaife, M. (1982). How infants see the point. In G. Butterworth & P. Light (Eds.), *Social cognition: Studies of the development of understanding* (pp. 110–136). Chicago: University of Chicago Press.

Corkum, V. L., & Moore, C. (1992, May). *Cues for joint visual attention in infants*. Poster presented at the International Conference on Infant Studies, Miami.

Corkum, V. L., & Moore, C. (1993, March). *Origins of joint visual attention*. Paper presented at the meeting of the Society for Research in Child Development, New Orleans.

Corkum, V. L., & Moore, C. (1994, June). *Conditioning of a joint attention response to two different cues*. Poster presented at the International Conference on Infant Studies, Paris, France.

Dunham, P. J., Dunham, F., & Curwin, A. (1993). Joint-attentional states and lexical acquisition at 18 months. *Developmental Psychology, 29*(5), 827–831.

Feinman, S. (1982). Social referencing in infancy. *Merrill-Palmer Quarterly, 28*, 445–470.

Hainline, L. (1978). Developmental changes in visual scanning of face and nonface patterns by infants. *Journal of Experimental Child Psychology, 25*, 90–115.

Haith, M. M., Bergman, T., & Moore, M. J. (1977). Eye contact and face scanning in early infancy. *Science, 198*, 853–855.

Hornik, R., Risenhoover, N., & Gunnar, M. (1987). The effects of maternal positive, neutral, and negative affective communications on infant responses to new toys. *Child Development, 58*, 937–944.

Lempers, J. D. (1979). Young children's production and comprehension of nonverbal deictic behaviors. *The Journal of Genetic Psychology, 135*, 93–102.

Leung, E. H. L., & Rheingold, H. L. (1981). Development of pointing as a social gesture. *Developmental Psychology, 17*(2), 215–220.

Mayer, D. L., & Dobson, V. (1982). Visual acuity development in infants and young children, as assessed by operant preferential looking. *Vision Research, 22*, 1141–1151.

Moore, C., & Corkum, V. L. (in press). Social understanding at the end of the first year of life. *Developmental Review*.

Moore, C., & Frye, D. (1991). The acquisition and utility of theories of mind. In D. Frye & C. Moore (Eds.), *Children's theories of mind: Mental states and social understanding* (pp. 1–14). Hillsdale, NJ: Lawrence Erlbaum Associates.

Morissette, P., Ricard, M., & Gouin-Decarie, T. (1992, May). *Comprehension of pointing and joint visual attention: A longitudinal study*. Poster presented at the 8th biennial International Conference on Infant Studies, Miami.

Mundy, P., Sigman, M., Ungerer, J. A., & Sherman, T. (1986). Defining the social deficits in autism: The contributions of nonverbal communication measures. *Journal of Child Psychology & Psychiatry, 27*, 657–669.

Murphy, C. M. (1978). Pointing in the context of shared activity. *Child Development, 49*, 371–380.

Murphy, C. M., & Messer, D. J. (1977). Mothers, infants, and pointing: A study of gesture. In H. R. Schaffer (Ed.), *Studies in mother-infant interaction* (pp. 325–354). London: Academic Press.

Scaife, M., & Bruner, J. S. (1975). The capacity for joint visual attention in the infant. *Nature, 253*, 265–266.

Sorce, J. F., Emde, R. N., Campos, J. J., & Klinnert, M. D. (1985). Maternal emotional signaling: Its effects on the visual cliff behavior of 1-year-olds. *Developmental Psychology, 21*, 195–200.

Tomasello, M., & Farrar, M. J. (1986). Joint attention and early language. *Child Development, 57*, 1454–1463.

Trevarthan, C., & Hubley, P. (1978). Secondary intersubjectivity: Confidence, confiding, and acts of meaning in the first year. In A. Lock (Ed.), *Action, gesture, and symbol* (pp. 183–229). London: Academic Press.

Werker, J. F., & Tees, R. C. (1984). Cross-language speech perception: Evidence for perceptual reorganization during the first year of life. *Infant Behavior and Development, 7*, 49–63.

Chapter 5

Two Perspectives on Pointing in Infancy

Stéphan Desrochers
Paul Morissette
Marcelle Ricard
University of Montreal

In the mid-1970s, infant psychologists began to verify empirically the existence of a relationship between early pointing gestures and the acquisition of language. Elizabeth Bates (Bates, Camaioni, & Volterra, 1975) was a pioneer in interpreting the different pointing gestures produced during infancy in terms of Austin's concept of speech acts. Since then, many researchers have worked within this perspective in order to support or to restrict its validity. In the first part of this chapter, results regarding the relationship between early production of pointing and later language development are presented. In addition, the possibility of a link between the comprehension of pointing and language is investigated.

Recently, other researchers have also become interested in the production of pointing inasmuch as it may represent the beginning of a theory of mind in infancy. Wellman (1990, 1993) and Moore and colleagues (Barresi & Moore, 1994; Moore, 1992; Moore & Corkum, in press) tried to define the moment at which an infant produces a pointing gesture for the purpose of orienting another person toward an object of interest. This capacity is believed to be important because it involves an implicit notion of "intentionality," a fundamental characteristic of mental states according to Searle (1983) and Fodor (1985). In the second part of this chapter, we explore this new perspective on the production of pointing and present some results regarding the infant's increasing ability to relate the mother to an external object or event from 12 to 18 months.

COMPREHENSION AND PRODUCTION
OF POINTING IN RELATION TO LANGUAGE

The idea that the infant's production of pointing may be a precursor of language has been present in developmental psychology for a good while. Werner and Kaplan (1963) were among the first to underscore the analogy between the production of pointing and naming. In their view, because pointing was a referential act produced in a social context, it could be considered as a first step toward true symbolisation.

This hypothesis was appealing to other researchers, many of whom found that infants' production of pointing correlated positively with emerging verbal behaviors (Bates, Benigni, Bretherton, Camaioni, & Volterra, 1979; Camaioni, Castelli, Longobardi, & Volterra, 1991). For these researchers, the link between pointing and language was strong enough for the gesture to be included in recent language tests, such as the Bzoch and League (1980) Receptive–Expressive Emergent Language Scale or the Fenson and Dale (1990) MacArthur Communicative Development Inventory: Infants. These facts and others led Bates, O'Connell, and Shore (1987) to state that "pointing—an act that is carried out in the visual-gestural modality—may be one innate component of the human language acquisition device" (p. 163).

This point of view is far from being accepted by everyone. Although the experimental results are not contested, their interpretation is. Petitto (1988), for one, agreed that the learning of language is facilitated by some pragmatic and social behaviors, among them, pointing gestures and symbolic gestures, but nevertheless considered that a distinction between language and these behaviors should be preserved. This argument was based on the observations made on deaf infants. These infants used spontaneous pointing in the same way and at the same age as hearing infants. But this ability did not help them when they later had to learn personal pronouns in American Sign Language, which are expressed by pointing gestures. In other words, spontaneous pointing is not easily transferred into a linguistic system. According to Petitto the correlations found in various studies between pointing and language could be due to the fact that the gesture provokes some social and verbal exchanges between infants and adults, thus facilitating the acquisition of language.

This position could gain some support from the work of other researchers who observed that pointing by the child is usually accompanied by denomination by the adult. Bruner (1978), for example, reported how pointing and naming are associated within book reading games. Hannan (1992) found that between 20 and 50 months, children observed in natural settings point mainly to name things, and that the response of adults is usually to name what is pointed. Dobrich and Scarborough (1984) also came to the conclusion that pointing and language are not part of the same system. Pointing is not replaced when language appears but keeps on accompanying it, even in 2-year-olds who have high mean length of utterances (MLU) for their age. Moreover, these authors did not observe any relation between formal measures of pointing (e.g., configuration of the hand) and language. They nevertheless found some relation between what they called "functional aspects" of these two systems, particularly between the frequencies of pointing and of vocalization. They concluded that pointing and language are linked by social rather than cognitive factors.

Despite the numerous writings examining whether or not production of pointing and language are part of the same system, nobody, as far as we know, has ever tried to systematically investigate the links between comprehension of pointing and language.

In the existing literature, comprehension of pointing has been examined either in itself or in relation to the production of pointing. In the first case, researchers have mainly strived to assess the effect of the target position on the infant's comprehension of another person's pointing gesture. For example, does the infant need to see simultaneously both the pointing hand and the target to connect them? (For those spatial aspects, see Butterworth & Grover, 1988; Butterworth & Jarrett, 1991; Lempers, 1979; Lempers, Flavell, & Flavell, 1977; Morissette, Ricard, & Gouin Décarie, 1992a; Murphy & Messer, 1977). All of these studies, except the one by Morissette et al., were performed cross-sectionally. As to the relationship between comprehension and production of pointing, the studies are scarce, none are longitudinal, and they have yielded somewhat inconclusive results (Lempers, 1979; Lempers et al., 1977; Leung & Rheingold, 1981; Renard, 1964).

Because production of pointing seems to relate differently to receptive and expressive aspects of language (see Bates, Thal, Whitesell, Fenson, & Oakes, 1989), one purpose of our study was to examine more carefully how the comprehension of pointing relates to these same aspects. Another purpose was to determine whether the relationship between production and comprehension of pointing is analogous to the one observed between comprehensive and expressive aspects of language.

Method

Twenty-five subjects (13 girls and 12 boys) took part in the study. They came from upper-middle class families living in the neighbourhood of the University of Montreal. They were seen at the laboratory every 3 months from the age of 6 to 18 months and once again at 24 months. One baby did not complete the study, his parents having moved out of town. For all experimental sessions, comprehension of pointing was evaluated first, followed by production of pointing. As this experiment was part of a larger project, the subjects were also evaluated on a number of other gestural communication tasks. Thus, the tasks on comprehension and production of pointing were separated by about 45 min.

In the comprehension tasks, the infant was seated in a small seat, facing the mother. Halfway between them were four pegs, each one with an identical little colorful plastic truck on its top. The four pegs formed a straight line from left to right and were equally distant from the mother and the child. The two pegs at the extremities of the line, one on the left and one on the right, were at 2.11 m each from the mother and the infant, forming an angle of 70° with the imaginary line of sight going between the mother and the infant. The two other pegs were near the center of the straight line (see Fig. 5.1). The mother was asked to make visual contact with the infant and then to point (arm extended) and to look at a specific truck for a period of 5 sec. She then resumed visual contact with her infant and pointed the same way at the three other trucks. Only the results concerning the two 70° targets were analyzed. The infant was attributed a correct response when he or she looked directly at the target for at least 1 second. (For more details about the procedure or the results of these tasks, see Morissette, Ricard, & Gouin Décarie, in press.) The subjects were not evaluated at 24 months on this dimension as their performances were almost perfect at 18 months, and as the tasks had lost their capacity to interest them.

To assess the production of pointing, a procedure inspired by Leung and Rheingold (1981) was adopted. Three different events were presented at approximately 2 m in front of the infant: slides appearing on a screen, a jumping jack clown, and a mobile made of frogs and flowers. These events were activated twice, from outside the room, while the infant was seated in a baby chair beside the mother. Two categories of responses were noted according to the noncommunicative or communicative function of the gestures. Noncommunicative pointing consisted of pointing at the event without looking at the mother's face, whereas communicative pointing consisted of pointing at the event and looking at the mother's face within 1 sec regardless of whether the look occurred before, during, or after the gesture.

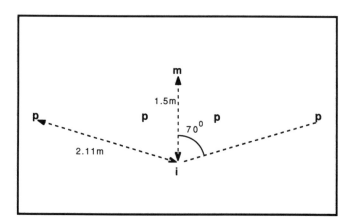

FIG. 5.1. Experimental setting for the comprehension tasks.

Finally, the Reynell (1977) Developmental Language Scales test was administered at 24 months. This test provided information about the infant's mastery of both the expressive and comprehensive aspects of language.

Results

In the comprehension tasks, as can be seen in Table 5.1, it is only at 15 months that the infants looked at the pointed target more often than elsewhere. Previously, at most ages, the main mistake was to look at the pointing hand. Whatever the age, other mistakes were relatively infrequent and consisted of looking at a wrong target, looking where there was no target, or looking at the mother's face.

For analytic purposes, the age at which half of the subjects or more could understand the pointing gesture was determined. To demonstrate this capacity, a subject had to look at the two targets pointed to by the mother within a given session. The criterion of two targets was chosen because it reduced the likeliness that the infant would reach it by chance, as could be the case if he or she had to look at only one correct target. The cumulative proportion of subjects meeting this criterion at each age was as follows: No subjects at 6 and 9 months, 27% of the subjects at 12 months, 64% at 15 months, and 86% at 18 months. Thus, more than half of the subjects understood the pointing gesture at 15 months.

As for the production of pointing, the age at which more than 50% of the infants were able to produce noncommunicative pointing (pointing without looking at the mother) was 12 months. At this age, 67% either produced the response at least once or had produced it in a previous session. Because the production of pointing cannot be done by chance, contrary to its comprehension, it was not necessary for the subjects to produce the gesture twice. Using the same criterion, it was at 15 months that more than half of the infants (54%) were able to produce communicative pointing (pointing and looking at the mother). The gradual increase in the number of subjects who were capable of producing each category of pointing appears in Table 5.2. As can be seen, at 6 and 9 months no subjects were able to produce either response.

TABLE 5.1
Comprehension of Pointing: Number of Responses
of Each Category at Each Age

Age (in months)	Looking at the Pointed Target	Looking at the Pointing Hand	Other Responses
6	4	20	24
9	9	28	11
12	21	17	10
15	36	10	2
18	37	4	5

Note. Two responses are lacking at 18 months due to mistrials.

TABLE 5.2
Production of Pointing: Cumulative Proportion of Subjects Able
to Produce Each Category of Pointing at Each Age

Age (in months)	Noncommunicative Pointing	Communicative Pointing
6	0.00	0.00
9	0.00	0.00
12	0.67	0.13
15	0.89	0.54
18	1.00	0.79
24	1.00	1.00

In order to examine the relationships between production or comprehension of pointing and language development, the subjects were classified as "precocious" or "late" with regard to their comprehension or production of pointing. To be considered precocious, a subject had to demonstrate a given capacity at or before the age of acquisition for the majority of the subjects, as established previously. If not, the subject was said to be late. Thus, the age of 15 months was the breaking point for the comprehension of pointing. As for the production of pointing, the criterion of 12 months was adopted to determine whether a subject was precocious or late in noncommunicative pointing, and 15 months for communicative pointing.

The scores of these subgroups (precocious vs. late) on the language test at 24 months were compared. The subjects who were precocious in their production of communicative pointing obtained higher total scores than their late peers on both the expressive (mean scores of 37.25 vs. 28.73, $t(21) = 2.16$, $p < .05$) and the comprehensive (mean scores of 36.17 vs. 28.90, ($t(21) = 2.13$, $p < .05$) components of the language test. There was no significant relation between the production of noncommunicative pointing and language.

Data analyses yielded only one significant result regarding the relationship between the comprehension of pointing and language: The subjects who were precocious in their comprehension of pointing obtained higher scores than the late subjects in the "vocabulary expression" subpart of the language test (mean scores of 13.07 vs. 8.75 $t(21) = 2.39$, $p < .05$). There were no differences in their total scores on either the expressive or comprehensive components of the language test.

Finally, a Spearman rank correlation tested the relationship between the onset of both comprehension and production of pointing. This analysis showed no link between the comprehension of pointing and the production of either noncommunicative ($r = .05$, n.s.) or communicative ($r = .206$, n.s.) pointing. Thus, to understand pointing early did not mean that a subject would also produce it early, with or without looking at the mother. In contrast, the Pearson correlation between the comprehensive and the expressive parts of the language test was relatively high ($r = .85$, $p < .001$).

Discussion

First, our results showed longitudinally that there seems to be no relationship between the comprehension and the production of pointing. Lempers (1979) also came to this conclusion from his cross-sectional study. The learning achieved in one domain does not transfer to the other domain. On this issue, pointing seems to differ from language, where the understanding and uttering of words appear to be closely related to each other. As a matter of fact, in our experiment, the correlation between production and comprehension of language was high. In everyday life, comprehension of pointing by the infant happens in a situation where the adult is trying to include an object in the interaction already going on between him or her and the infant, using, to do so, the kind of expertise adults possess in attention directing, as described by Zukow (1990). This is quite different from production of pointing by the infant: In that case the infant tries to include the adult in the relation that he or she is having with an object. This difference in the tasks could explain the lack of relation between comprehension and production of pointing observed in our study.

Our results concerning the production of communicative pointing are also similar to those found in other studies. They confirm, with a larger and older group of infants, that communicative pointing is related to both the comprehension (Bates et al., 1979) and the production (Camaioni et al., 1991) of language.

As seen earlier, most researchers admit the existence of a link between the production of pointing and language development, but there is a controversy about the nature of this link. By resorting to the moment of appearance of the behavior instead of its frequencies, as is generally the case in existing research, our study may bring some weight to the idea that pointing and language do belong to the same system.

At least it casts doubt on the hypothesis proposed by some authors (Dobrich & Scarborough, 1984; Petitto, 1988) that the link between pointing gestures and language is "socially mediated"; that is, the more an infant points, the more his or her caretaker is likely to name the things that are pointed at, thus providing the infant with occasions to learn language. In other words, if the moment of appearance of the pointing gesture can predict, at least partly, an infant's linguistic performance, without the frequencies of the gesture being taken into account, then the existence of a systemic link between production of pointing and language cannot be discarded.

More surprisingly, our data do not show any significant relation between the production of noncommunicative pointing and language. Although contrary to the findings of Bates et al. (1979) relative to various aspects of language, this negative result makes some sense: Even if noncommunicative pointing shares a referential aspect with language—in the sense of making reference for oneself, an idea proposed by Werner and Kaplan (1963)—it nevertheless lacks the usual communicative aspect of language, thus decreasing the probability of a significant relationship. Here again, because we did not assess the frequencies of the behavior, there was no possibility to observe a relation due to the tendency of the adult to name what is pointed at, even if from the infant's perspective the gesture had no communicative intent.

Our results concerning the relationship between comprehension of pointing and language seem harder to explain because they cannot be compared to previous work and yielded only a limited and surprising relation. Surprising, indeed, because a link between comprehension of pointing and comprehension of language was expected more than a link with a part of expressive language. Comprehension of pointing (an arbitrary gesture used by the adult to refer to something) shares at least formal resemblance with the comprehension of language (an arbitrary group of signs used to refer to things). But, as understanding pointing at distant objects implies a capacity to orient properly one's gaze in space, our task may have measured the ability to use the spatial information conveyed by the gesture in addition to its referential meaning. This hypothesis which was put forward by Butterworth and Grover (1988) and by Morissette et al. (1992b), would also possibly explain the lack of relation between comprehension and production of pointing.

This explanation still leaves us with no answer to the question of why comprehension of pointing was found to be related to the "vocabulary expression" subpart of the language test (keeping in mind that it is a limited result and that it should be replicated before considering it definitive). Procedural factors could account for this observation. When administered that subpart of the language test, subjects were facing a situation formally similar to the one used in our task on the comprehension of pointing: For some items of the test, the adult directed the attention of the infant toward an object and asked "What's that?" As in the task on comprehension of pointing, it supposed that the infant would be able to focus on the same thing as the adult before he or she could name what was indicated. Thus, the relation found between the comprehension of pointing and the "vocabulary expression" subpart of the language test may reflect the isomorphism of the tasks instead of a common cognitive process.

PRODUCTION OF POINTING AND THE BEGINNING OF A THEORY OF MIND IN INFANCY

Since the beginning of the 1990s, researchers have become interested in the place of early production of pointing within the genesis of the child's theory of mind. This theoretical perspective was the background of our next experiment to which we now turn.

Most of the studies that have been carried out to study the development of a theory of mind in childhood required that the subjects understand language (see Astington, Harris, & Olson, 1988; Frye & Moore, 1991; Wellman, 1990; Whiten, 1991). This constraint led to a serious neglect of nonverbal behaviors that may demonstrate the beginning of a theory of mind in infancy.

However, Bretherton, McNew, and Beeghly-Smith (1981) have already suggested that the onset of intentional communication might show that infants have an implicit theory of mind. When infants point, they "attribute an internal state of *knowing* and *comprehending* to the mother . . ." (p.339). Besides, some authors tried to identify the origins in infancy of the understanding of a specific mental state, that is, intention. Thus, Poulin-Dubois and Shultz (1988), Premack (1990, 1991), and Shultz (1991) claimed that the notion of intention in preschool children may arise out of a comprehension of agency in infancy.

More recently, Barresi and Moore (1994), Moore and Corkum (in press), and Wellman (1993) proposed a general characteristic of the mind to which the infants might be sensitive. This characteristic, often mentioned in philosophical works such as Dennett (1987), Fodor (1985), or Searle (1983), is the *intentionality* or "aboutness" of mental states. According to these philosophers, mental states cannot exist on their own, but are always related to something: I believe in something, I desire something, or I have the intention to do something. Those states do not appear in isolation; their existence always depends on the object to which they are related.

Before understanding this intentionality of mental states during the preschool years, infants, according to Wellman (1993) and Barresi and Moore (1994), show an earlier capacity that allows them to conceive of people and objects as connected together. In other words, the beginning of a theory of mind in infancy might happen when the baby has the capacity to relate a person to an event or object in the world. This form of understanding represents a kind of implicit notion of intentionality.

Thus, Wellman (1993) suggested that social behaviors such as social referencing, giving an object when the mother is requesting it by palm-up gestures, or the production of pointing gestures, demonstrate that 12-month-old infants already begin to appreciate that the mother is related to a given object. Even though Wellman (1993) admitted that the data were far from decisive, he also stipulated that these behaviors demonstrate an understanding that the mother has a psychological relation to the object, that she is having an inner *experience* of it.

For example, according to Wellman (1993), social referencing reveals a sensitivity to the mother's emotion toward an object, while giving the object could be interpreted as a sensitivity to the mother's desire. Similarly, the production of pointing gestures at 12 months represents an early understanding of perception or attention, the infant's wanting the mother to attend to an object, for her to have a perceptive experience of it.

But Barresi and Moore (1994) and Moore and Corkum (in press; see also Corkum & Moore, this volume) do not believe that behaviors such as social referencing, production of pointing, and especially joint visual attention (JVA), reveal an implicit notion of intentionality at 12 months. Based on their general theory of intentionality, Barresi and Moore (1994) stipulated that 1-year-olds do not appreciate that another person has a psychological relation to a given object when they show these social behaviors. Rather, these authors propose that the infant's as well as the mother's relations are trapped in an undifferentiated "we," whereby the infant is unable to appreciate that the mother has an independent relation to an external object. Only at 18 months, as pretend play emerges, will the infant show such an appreciation in a clear manner.

In this same line of thought, regarding the production of pointing, Moore and Corkum (in press) suggest that "the initial use of protodeclaratives towards the end of the first year appears more likely to be the use of an object to elicit a particular form of adult behavior to the infant rather than to the object" (p.18), such as laughters, smiles, and eye contacts.

Nevertheless, both Wellman (1993) and Barresi and Moore (1994) admit the existence of an evolution in the production of pointing gestures during the second year. Wellman (1993) states that in the second year the infant points at an object but also in increasingly sophisticated ways, while Barresi and Moore (1994) note that pointing gestures may be used in a self–other distinction manner only at 18 months, such as to pick out individual others or the self.

Therefore, they all agree that the infant's capacity to appreciate that the mother is related to a given object when he or she points at it increases during the second year. It is then plausible that some developmental transformations of this behavior during this period can be observed. The claim that infants point at an object in different ways during the second year has often been made in the literature (Bates et al., 1979; Butterworth, 1991; Cox, 1986; Lempers et al., 1977; Masur, 1983).

In fact, Butterworth (1991) and Cox (1986) reported an identical developmental transformation in the production of pointing during the second year. This transformation, related to the different types of looks that accompany the pointing gesture, has never been tested experimentally. Based on these suggestions, our second longitudinal study investigated the development of three different levels of the pointing gesture produced in infancy. The three levels were: (1) pointing without looking at the mother's face; (2) pointing first and then looking at the mother's face within 1 sec; (3) looking at the mother's face within 1 sec before pointing, or pointing and looking at the mother's face simultaneously.

We believe that these levels represent an operationalization of the infant's increasing capacity to relate the mother with a given object (Barresi & Moore, 1994; Wellman, 1993), because they demonstrate a developing ability that allows the infant to ensure that the mother will be related to the object of interest when he or she points at it. This growing ability, from Level 1 to Level 3, is associated in our study with the moment at which the infant takes the mother's face into account by looking at it.

In fact, it is plausible to think that pointing accompanied by a look to the mother is a more efficient strategy than pointing alone, the infant's goal being to orient the mother toward the object. Moreover, looking even before pointing is clearly the most sophisticated way to ensure that the production of a pointing gesture will not be inefficient in fulfilling its goal.

Method

Thirty subjects (13 girls and 17 boys) aged 6 months at the beginning of the study were observed during a twelve month period at 6, 9, 12, 15, and 18 months. Babies were selected randomly from the birth records of the City of Montreal. Most infants came from middle-class families. Five babies did not complete the study: Four refused to cooperate in one or another session and another moved out of town. Those babies are not included in the present report. At each age level, the pointing gestures were elicited by the same procedure as the one described in the first study.

Results

First, pointing gestures appeared to be produced significantly at 12 months, that is, when more than 50% of the subjects pointed at least once. Moreover, all three levels of pointing were observed at this same age. But it was only at 15 months that more than 50% of the subjects produced a pointing gesture accompanied by a look.

Second, ANOVAs revealed a significant age effect for each level of pointing: Level 1, $F(4, 96) = 6.29$, $p < .001$; Level 2, $F(4, 96) = 6.72$, $p < .001$; Level 3, $F(4, 96) = 7.29$, $p < .001$. Fisher PLSD multiple comparisons showed that all three levels of pointing were significantly higher at 12 months compared to the previous ages ($p < .05$). After 12 months, pointing gestures characteristic of Levels 1 and 2 remained stable while Level 3 pointing increased. In other words, only the proportion of pointing gestures devoted to Level 3 was greater at 18 months (26.22%) compared to 12 months (12.37%): the critical PLSD difference being 12.03, $p < .05$.

Discussion

Even if all three levels of pointing had been observed as soon as pointing seemed established, a certain evolution is evident. In fact, only the use of the most sophisticated strategy (Level 3) increased at 18 months compared to 12 months. Therefore, the pattern of pointing gestures was found to change during the second year and this change seemed to be related to the infant's increasing ability to ensure that the mother will be related to the given object when he/she points at it.

As mentioned previously (Wellman, 1993), one might simply conclude that the infants increasingly appreciated from 12 to 18 months that the mother has a psychological relation to a given object. On the other hand, this evolution may also be linked to the fact that the infants, in their intentional relations, developed a gradual self–other distinction during the second year (Barresi & Moore, 1994). If this is the case, the 12-month-old infants would not have recognized that the mother has a relation to an object, and would have come later to appreciate that their perceptive experience may differ from the mother's. Thus, pointing at 12 months may not be intended to elicit adult attention to an object but simply to elicit adult attention toward the infant (Moore & Corkum, in press).

The present study can only tell that an evolution does take place from 12 to 18 months, but it cannot resolve the opposition between these two possible interpretations. However, a few points are worth mentioning regarding the infant's capacity to conceive of people as related to an object.

It is well known that infants understand causal relations between two objects or between an object and a person at around 12 months or even before (Desrochers, Ricard, & Gouin Décarie, in press; Goulet, 1974/1972; Harding & Golinkoff, 1979; Oakes & Cohen, 1990; Piaget, 1954/1937). Moreover, infants of that age can distinguish between psychological causality (agency) and physical causality (Poulin-Dubois & Shultz, 1990), which means that they also have very specific expectations about relations involving a person and an object.

Therefore, one should be cautious in denying 12-month-olds the capacity to relate a person to an object. Even if they might not appreciate that another person has a psychological relation to an external object (Moore & Corkum, in press), infants of that age may well be able to, at least, relate a person (not necessarily this person's subjective experience) to an object. Thus, the first and simplest form of intentionality or aboutness the infant has to discover in order to later develop an efficient theory of mind, will probably be achieved when the infant acquires the capacity to relate a person (not necessarily this person's mental states) to an object or event in the world.

One of our previous studies (Desrochers, Ricard, Gouin Décarie, & Allard, 1994) demonstrated that when infants become able to understand that one object or person may be related causally to another object or person (stage V–VI of Piagetian sensorimotor causality), they also become able to seek out information from the mother in order to cope with an ambiguous situation (social referencing). In other words, there seems to exist a developmental synchrony between social referencing and the development of Piagetian causality at 12 months.

Thus, social behaviors involving an object at 12 months (social referencing, pointing, giving, etc.) may well demonstrate at least the infant's capacity to relate a person to an object in the physical world but not necessarily in a psychological way like Wellman (1993) has suggested. Only later on, around 18 months, when the infant possesses the representational ability, would these behaviors demonstrate a sensitivity to the other's subjective psychological experience.

Hence, we would suggest that by the act of pointing, the 12-month-old infant is trying to relate the mother to the object of interest, but not necessarily in a psychological relation such as attention or perception. It might be a more "behavioral way," such as orienting the mother's face or eyes toward the given object, an alternative suggested by Wellman himself (1993). With the representational ability, at around 18 months, this behavior probably demonstrates that the infant has now become sensitive to the mother's subjective experience of attention or perception. This interpretation would be highly compatible with the results of the present study. The increase of the most sophisticated Level 3 strategy between 12 and 18 months can be linked with the emergence of the representational ability at 18 months that allows the infant to appreciate, over the simple physical or behavioral relation, the subjective experience of the mother when trying to relate the mother to the object of interest.

Thus, there might be a sensitivity to the person as an object existing in the world before a sensitivity to the person's subjective experience. Moreover, before discovering the ontological and causal aspects of specific mental states (desire, intention, belief) in early childhood, the sensorimotor infant would first have to discover the independency and causal characteristics of the objects in the world, which includes the human being.

Conclusion

Our report offers some conclusive results regarding the production of pointing. On the whole, a sample of 49 subjects aged 6 months at the beginning of the studies, was observed during a 12 month period using the same experimental design. From these observations, we can conclude that the pointing gesture is reliably produced by the infant at 12 months, where more than 50% of our subjects showed this behavior. But it is only at 15 months that more than 50% of these same subjects produced a pointing gesture accompanied by a look at the mother.

There is agreement in the literature about the existence, early in life, of a hand configuration, not directed at any object, but similar in its formal aspect to the pointing gesture discussed in the present chapter. Fogel and Hannan (1985) observed it in 9- to 15-week-old subjects and Degril (1984) in 4- to 6-month-olds. There is also agreement about the appearance of a pointing gesture directed at objects, but not performed for somebody else (a pointing–for–self), around 9 months of age. According to Werner and Kaplan (1963), this pointing gesture is a way for the infant to differentiate himself or herself from the object, while for Degril (1984) it also serves to explore close objects. Lempert and Kinsbourne (1985) hypothesized that it could be an orienting response released by the presence of some interesting stimulus. This leads to the dilemma faced by both perspectives presented in this chapter: When does the infant stop producing a pointing gesture for himself or herself and, instead, produce it in order to show an object or event to the mother?

From the first perspective, the production of pointing gestures is considered to be a precursor of language. The question then becomes: Which pointing gesture represents a real communicative behavior? An often used criterion is the presence of a look addressed to an adult while pointing occurs. But Cox (1986) noted that in some situations (e.g., book reading games), this criterion is not needed as the infant is aware that the adult is already looking at the target, so that not all researchers have demanded it. Also, Lempert and Kinsbourne (1985) mentioned that pointing–for–self keeps on being produced after the onset of pointing–for–others. Therefore, the only way to make sure that a pointing gesture is addressed to someone else is to require the presence of a look directed at the adult, but by doing so there is a risk of classifying as pointings-for-self some pointings-for-others. In order to validate that criterion, one can turn to external evidence, such as relation to language. In the first study presented in this chapter, only this type of pointing was linked to later language development. From there, it is difficult not to conclude that only when the production of pointing is accompanied by a look at the mother should this behavior be considered as a communicative act. This condition was not met by our subjects before the age of 15 months.

From the second perspective, where the production of pointing gestures might convey an implicit notion of intentionality or aboutness, the question becomes: When does the infant actually try to relate the mother to a given object? In the second part of this chapter, we used facts from the infant's understanding of causal relations to argue that the 1-year-old infant possesses everything needed to relate the mother with a given object when pointing at it. It is plausible to think that the pointing gestures produced by our 12-month-old subjects already had this very function.

Because of this apparent contradiction, we believe that further investigations or theoretical proposals are necessary. One should stop using external criteria (language or causality) to decide whether the infant points for himself or herself or in order to show an event or object to the mother. Instead, efforts should be made to find appropriate methodologies for a thorough evaluation of whether the infant can or cannot appreciate that the mother is "object oriented" in a particular experimental design. In this sense, Moore and colleagues' general theory of intentionality (Barresi & Moore, 1994; Moore, 1992; Moore & Corkum, in press) could serve as a useful framework.

Finally, the fact that comprehension and production of pointing seem to develop independently, as shown in our first study, is still intriguing. It may indicate that one should be prudent in designing a single theoretical account for all the different behaviors involving an object during infancy, be it social referencing, production and comprehension of pointing, or joint visual attention.

ACKNOWLEDGMENT

The first study reported in this chapter was part of Paul Morissette's doctoral dissertation, and the second one, part of Stéphan Desrochers'. They both worked under the supervision of Marcelle Ricard. This research was supported by grants to Thérèse Gouin Décarie and Marcelle Ricard from the Fonds pour la Formation de chercheurs et l'Aide à la Recherche (FCAR) of the Province of Quebec (No. EQ-2331) and from the Social Sciences and Humanities Research Council of Canada (No. 410-87-1360), and by postgraduate fellowships to Stéphan Desrochers and Paul Morissette from the Natural Sciences and Engineering Research Council of Canada and the Social Sciences and Humanities Research Council of Canada.

REFERENCES

Astington, J. W., Harris, P. L., & Olson, D. R. (Eds.). (1988). *Developing theories of mind*. New York: Cambridge University Press.

Barresi, J., & Moore, C. (1994). *Intentionality and social understanding*. Manuscript submitted for publication.

Bates, E., Benigni, L., Bretherton, I., Camaioni, L., & Volterra, V. (1979). *The emergence of symbols: Cognition and communication in infancy*. New York: Academic Press.

Bates, E., Camaioni, L., & Volterra, V. (1975). The acquisition of performatives prior to speech. *Merrill-Palmer Quarterly, 21*, 205–226.

Bates, E., O'Connell, B., & Shore, C. (1987). Language and communication in infancy. In J. D. Osofsky (Ed.), *Handbook of infant development* (2nd ed.) (pp. 149–203). New York: Wiley.

Bates, E., Thal, D., Whitesell, K., Fenson, L., & Oakes, L. (1989). Integrating language and gesture in infancy. *Developmental Psychology, 25*, 1004–1009.

Bretherton, I., McNew, S., & Beeghly-Smith, M. (1981). Early person knowledge as expressed in gestural and verbal communication: When do infants acquire a 'theory of mind'? In M. E. Lamb & L. R. Sherrod (Eds.), *Infant social cognition* (pp. 333–373). Hillsdale, NJ: Lawrence Erlbaum Associates.

Bruner, J. S. (1978). Acquiring the uses of language. *Canadian Journal of Psychology, 32*, 204–218.

Butterworth, G. E. (1991). The ontogeny and phylogeny of joint visual attention. In A. Whiten (Ed.), *Natural theories of mind: Evolution, development and simulation of everyday mindreading* (pp. 223–232). Oxford, England: Basil Blackwell.

Butterworth, G. E., & Grover, L. (1988). The origins of referential communication in human infancy. In L. Weiskrantz (Ed.), *Thought without language* (pp. 5–21). Oxford, England: Oxford University Press.

Butterworth, G. E., & Jarrett, N. (1991). What minds have in common in space: Spatial mechanisms serving joint visual attention in infancy. *British Journal of Developmental Psychology, 9*, 55–72.

Bzoch, K. R., & League, R. (1980). *Assessing language skills in infancy.* Baltimore: University Park Press.

Camaioni, L., Castelli, M. C., Longobardi, E., & Volterra, V. (1991). A parent report instrument for early language assessment. *First Language, 11,* 345–359.

Cox, M. V. (1986). *The child's point of view.* New York: St. Martin's Press.

Degril, C. (1984). *La conventionnalisation de l'indication à travers le geste de pointage chez le bébé* [Conventionalization of indication through the pointing gesture in the baby]. Unpublished doctoral dissertation, Université de Provence, France.

Dennett, D. C. (1987). *The intentional stance.* Cambridge, MA: Bradford Books, MIT Press.

Desrochers, S., Ricard, M., & Gouin Décarie, T. (in press). Understanding causality in infancy: A reassessment of Piaget's theory. *Current Psychology of Cognition.*

Desrochers, S., Ricard, M., Gouin Décarie, T., & Allard, L. (1994). Developmental synchrony between social referencing and Piagetian sensorimotor causality. *Infant Behavior and Development, 17,* 301–307.

Dobrich, W., & Scarborough, H. S. (1984). Form and function in early communication: Language and pointing gestures. *Journal of Experimental Child Psychology, 38,* 475–490.

Fenson, L., & Dale, P. S. (1990). *Technical manual for the MacArthur Communicative Development Inventories.* San Diego: San Diego State University.

Fodor, J. A. (1985). Fodor's guide to mental representations: The intelligent auntie's vade-mecum. *Mind, 94,* 76–100.

Fogel, A., & Hannan, T. E. (1985). Manual actions of 9- to 15-week-old human infants during face-to-face interaction with their mothers. *Child Development, 55,* 1271–1279.

Frye, D., & Moore, C. (Eds.). (1991). *Children's theories of mind: Mental states and social understanding.* Hillsdale, NJ: Lawrence Erlbaum Associates.

Goulet, J. (1974). The infant's conception of causality and his reactions to strangers. In T. Gouin Décarie (Ed.), *The infant's reactions to strangers* (J. Diamanti, Trans.) (pp. 59–96). New York: International Universities Press. (Original work published 1972)

Hannan, T. E. (1992). An examination of spontaneous pointing in 20 to 50-month-old children. *Perceptual and Motor Skill, 74,* 651–658.

Harding, C. G., & Golinkoff, R. M. (1979). The origins of intentional vocalizations in prelinguistic infants. *Child Development, 50,* 33–40.

Lempers, J. D. (1979). Young children's production and comprehension of nonverbal deictic behaviors. *Journal of Genetic Psychology, 135,* 93–102.

Lempers, J. D., Flavell, E. R., & Flavell, J. H. (1977). The development in very young children of tacit knowledge concerning visual perception. *Genetic Psychology Monographs, 95,* 3–53.

Lempert, H., & Kinsbourne, M. (1985). Possible origin of speech in selective orienting. *Psychological Bulletin, 1,* 62–73.

Leung, H. L., & Rheingold, H. L. (1981). Development of pointing as a social gesture. *Developmental Psychology, 17,* 215–220.

Masur, F. E. (1983). Gestural development, dual-directional signaling, and the transition to words. *Journal of Psycholinguistic Research, 12,* 93–109.

Moore, C. (1992, May). *Theory of mind and the self-other distinction.* Paper presented at the Twenty-Second Annual Symposium of The Jean Piaget Society, Montreal.

Moore, C., & Corkum, V. (in press). Social understanding at the end of the first year of life. *Developmental Review.*

Morissette, P., Ricard, M., & Gouin Décarie, T. (1992a, May). *Comprehension of pointing and joint visual attention: A longitudinal study.* Poster presented at the Eighth International Conference on Infant Studies, Miami.

Morissette, P., Ricard, M., & Gouin Décarie, T. (in press). Joint visual attention and pointing in infancy: A longitudinal study of comprehension. *British Journal of Developmental Psychology.*

Murphy, C. M., & Messer, D. J. (1977). Mothers, infants, and pointing: A study of gesture. In H. R. Schaffers (Ed.), *Studies in mother-infant interaction* (pp. 325–354). London: Academic Press.

Oakes, L. M., & Cohen, L. B. (1990). Infant perception of a causal event. *Cognitive Development*, *5*, 193–207.
Petitto, L. (1988). "Language" in the prelinguistic child. In F. Kessel (Ed.), *Development of language and language researchers* (pp. 187–222). Hillsdale, NJ: Lawrence Erlbaum Associates.
Piaget, J. (1954). *The construction of reality in the child*. (M. Cook, Trans.). New York: Basic Books. (Original work published 1937)
Poulin-Dubois, D., & Shultz, T. R. (1988). The development of the understanding of human behavior: From agency to intentionality. In J. W. Astington, P. L. Harris, & D. R. Olson (Eds.), *Developing theories of mind* (pp. 109–125). New York: Cambridge University Press.
Poulin-Dubois, D., & Shultz, T. R. (1990). The infant's concept of agency: The distinction between social and nonsocial objects. *Journal of Genetic Psychology*, *15*, 77–90.
Premack, D. (1990). The infant's theory of self-propelled objects. *Cognition*, *36*, 1–16.
Premack, D. (1991). The infant's theory of self-propelled objects. In D. Frye & C. Moore (Eds.), *Children's theories of mind: Mental states and social understanding* (pp. 39–48). Hillsdale, NJ: Lawrence Erlbaum Associates.
Renard, R. M. (1964). *Premiers développements du geste de désignation* [First developments of the indicative gesture]. Unpublished master's thesis, Université Catholique de Louvain, Belgium.
Reynell, J. (1977). *Reynell developmental language scales* (rev. ed.). Windsor, England: NFER-Nelson Publishing Co. Ltd.
Searle, J. R. (1983). *Intentionality: An essay in the philosophy of mind*. Cambridge, England: Cambridge University Press.
Shultz, T. R. (1991). From agency to intention: A rule-based, computational approach. In A. Whiten (Ed.), *Natural theories of mind: Evolution, development and simulation of everyday mindreading* (pp. 79–98). Oxford, England: Basil Blackwell.
Wellman, H. M. (1990). *The child's theory of mind*. Cambridge, MA: MIT Press.
Wellman, H. M. (1993). Early understanding of mind: The normal case. In S. Baron-Cohen, H. Tager-Flusberg, & D. Cohen (Eds.), *Understanding other minds: Perspectives from autism* (pp. 10–39). Oxford, England: Oxford University Press.
Werner, H., & Kaplan, B. (1963). *Symbol formation*. New York: Wiley.
Whiten, A. (Ed.). (1991). *Natural theories of mind: Evolution, development and simulation of everyday mindreading*. Oxford, England: Basil Blackwell.
Zukow, P. G. (1990). Socio-perceptual bases for emergence of language: An alternative to innatist approaches. *Developmental Psychobiology*, *23*, 705–726.

Chapter 6

Joint Attention as Social Cognition

Michael Tomasello
Emory University, Georgia

We have been thinking about joint attention—what it is, where it comes from, and its role in human development—for almost 2 decades now. Most of the research has focused on two sets of phenomena. Ontogenetically first is the tendency of human infants, in the months immediately preceding their first birthday, to follow or to direct the visual attention of adults to outside entities (e.g., Bates, 1976; Butterworth & Cochran, 1980; Corkum & Moore, this volume; Scaife & Bruner, 1975). Ontogenetically second is the tendency of somewhat older children, in their second year of life, to participate with adults in more extended bouts of joint visual attention as they begin to acquire their first linguistic conventions (e.g., Bakeman & Adamson, 1984; Baldwin, this volume; Dunham & Dunham, this volume; Ninio & Bruner, 1978; Tomasello & Todd, 1983). More recently, however, researchers with a more strictly cognitive bent have begun to look at children's joint attentional skills as "precursors" to their representational theories of mind (e.g., Baron-Cohen, 1991, 1993; Meltzoff & Gopnik, 1993; Wellman, 1993). This new perspective has opened up a whole new set of questions about the cognitive and social-cognitive bases of joint attention.

In the context of this new perspective, Tomasello, Kruger, and Ratner (1993) have argued and presented evidence that what underlies infants' early skills of joint attention is their emerging understanding of other persons as intentional agents; that is, their understanding of human activity in terms of the outcomes it is designed to achieve. When infants begin to view others as intentional they begin to comprehend that: Other persons may attend selectively (intentionally) to some things in the environment and ignore others; Other persons may intend for them

103

to selectively attend to some things in the environment and ignore others; With certain behaviors they may induce other persons to intentionally attend to new things in the environment. Implicit in this proposal is the theoretical proposition, following Gibson and Rader's (1979) trenchant analysis, that attention should be considered as intentional perception: A sightseer and a mountain climber attend to very different aspects of a mountain (e.g., to its coloration or its slopes) in light of their very different goals. The implication for infant social cognition is that in order to understand what an adult is attending to when he or she looks at, reacts to, or behaves toward an entity in the environment, and thus to enter into a joint attentional interaction with him or her, infants must understand something of the adult's intentions in the situation.

From the point of view of theory of mind research, the Tomasello et al. (1993) proposal is that infants undergo a revolution in their understanding of persons at around their first birthday that is just as coherent and dramatic as the one they undergo at around their fourth birthday. Just as 4-year-olds come to understand others as mental agents in terms of their thoughts and beliefs about reality, 1-year-olds come to understand others as intentional agents in terms of their concrete goals and the sensorimotor and attentional activities designed to achieve them. Instead of viewing children's understanding of intentions as a precursor to their theories of mind, the proposal is that these two phenomena represent related but distinct steps in the understanding of other persons. And indeed, Tomasello et al. (1993) argue that it is the understanding of intentions, not beliefs, that is foundational: Children's theories of mind develop out of their ontogenetically prior understanding that other persons are intentional agents whose attention and behavior to outside entities may be actively followed, directed, or shared. This way of looking at 1- to 2-year-old children makes for a much more coherent and continuous view of social-cognitive development than the view that there is only one interesting developmental milestone worth studying—theory of mind—and that all other manifestations of children's understanding of other persons are either precursors or sequelae (see, e.g., Leslie, 1987).

In this chapter I explore further the Tomasello et al. (1993) proposal about the social cognition of 1- to 2-year-olds. I do this by means of a more or less systematic analogy to children's development of a theory of mind that emerges at around 3 to 4 years of age. I take the central features of the development of a theory of mind to be the following:

1. Children understand other persons in terms of their thoughts and beliefs;
2. Children understand that others have thoughts and beliefs that may differ from their own;
3. Children understand that others have thoughts and beliefs that may not match with the current state of affairs (false beliefs).

The attempt is to show that children in their second year of life develop an analogous understanding of other persons, but in terms of concrete intentions rather than thoughts and beliefs. Thus, the proposal is that by the end of their second year of life:

1. Children understand other persons in terms of their intentions.
2. Children understand that others have intentions that may differ from their own.
3. Children understand that others have intentions that may not match with the current state of affairs (accidents and unfulfilled intentions).

In all cases, the term "intention" is meant to refer to the concrete goals or purposes by which human beings guide their behavior, not to the philosophical sense of intentionality including all mental activity showing "aboutness" (Powers, 1973). Following Piaget (1952), the operational definition I employ relies on the clear differentiation of means and ends in instrumental acts.

I attempt to support this account of human social cognition in the second year of life by examining the different types of joint attentional interactions that occur during three developmental periods; the first 9 months of life when skills of joint attention have yet to fully emerge, the period from 9 to 18 months when infants begin to follow and direct the attention and behavior of other persons, and the period from 18 to 24 months when joint attention begins to manifest itself in many complex ways in children's learning and use of language. The different nature of the joint attentional interactions at these three periods, I argue, is a direct result of children's emerging understanding of other persons as intentional agents. The precise developmental mechanisms underlying this ontogeny are not known, though there is no shortage of speculations to which I will add my own.

SIMULTANEOUS LOOKING IN THE FIRST 9 MONTHS

Attention is not the same thing as visual orientation. A person may visually orient to a location in space but on different occasions attend to different aspects of what is at that location, for example, to an object, its color, its shape, its activity, and so forth ad infinitum. If we take seriously the notion of joint attention, we must stipulate the existence of two persons attending to the same aspect of their common environment. It is presumably the case that 6-month-old infants quite often orient to the same spatial location as adults, but focus on a different aspect of what is at that location. In such cases we may talk of simul-taneous looking or simultaneous orienting to a location, but not of joint atten-tion. Joint attention is not just a geometric phenomenon concerning two lines of visual orientation.

Given that we can establish that indeed two persons are simultaneously fo-cused on the same aspect of the environment at the same time, we still do not have joint attention the way it has been conceptualized or even operationalized by most researchers—the attentional focus of the two persons must be truly joint in the sense that both participants are monitoring the other's attention to the outside entity. There are at least two very common kinds of adult–child interactions that lack this criterion of jointness. First, both an infant and adult may look to an object and focus on the same aspect of the object but do this independently; the adult may simply watch the child engaging with an object (what Bakeman & Adamson, 1984, call "onlooking"); the child may simply watch the adult engaging with an object (also onlooking); or both child and adult may have their attention drawn to the same thing fortuitously, as when barking leads each of them to look to a dog out separate windows of the house. In none of these cases is the attention joint in the sense that each participant knows of the other's attentional focus. Second, the infant may look to where the adult is looking, focusing on the same aspect of the environment perhaps, but does so only as a case of cued looking in which he or she has learned that looking in the direction another individual is looking often results in interesting sights (see Corkum & Moore, this volume). The use of the head orientation of others as a cue is very common in the animal kingdom (Baron-Cohen, this volume), and demonstrations of the ease with which neonates may be conditioned to turn their heads in one direction or another (e.g., Haith, Hazen, & Goodman, 1988) make it a plausible explanation of some infant gaze following. Again in this case, the reason cued looking is not joint attention is because the attention is not joint; the infant does not know the adult is attending. Thus, just as joint attention is not simply a geometric phenomenon concerning two lines of visual orientation, it is also not simply a psychological phenomenon concerning two foci of visual attention.

Joint attention is primarily a social, or social-cognitive, phenomenon: Two individuals know that they are attending to something in common. For most researchers this mutual knowledge is judged to be present if both participants are simultaneously looking at the same entity in the environment and, because the adult's knowledge of the child's attentional focus is typically assumed, the child looks to the face of the adult during their joint focus or gaze alternation, thus demonstrating his or her knowledge of the adult's attention. But even here we must be careful, as gaze alternation is not an infallible indicator of joint attention. For example, an infant may look to an object the adult is looking at, and then, perhaps because the adult moves or talks, have his or her attention drawn to the adult, and then, perhaps because the object moves or makes noise, back to the object. This alternating of attention between an object and a person is not joint attention because the child is not concerned with the adult's attention to the object; this is what happens quite often in what Bakeman and Adamson, 1984, call "passive" or "supported" joint attentional interactions. Nor is it joint attention when the child looks up spontaneously to see if the adult is preparing to reward or punish him or her for reaching for a forbidden object, for example, because, once again, the child's gaze alternation is not serving to monitor the adult's attentional focus to the object.

The overall point is that joint attention does not just mean two people looking at the same thing at the same time. Nor is it just one person looking on while another engages with an object, nor is it the child alternating her attention between two phenomena (person and object) of equal interest. In joint attention the child coordinates her attention to the object and the adult at the same time that the adult coordinates her attention to the same object and the child. And in both cases this coordination is of a very special nature. The coordination that takes place in joint attentional interactions is accomplished by means of an understanding that the other participant has a focus of attention to the same entity as the self. This implies an understanding of the other participant *not* as an object or capturer of attention or potential punisher, but as a *person* who intentionally perceives a certain aspect of the environment that is *the same* as one's own, or could be made to be *the same*. There is thus a notion that the participants are sharing an intentional relation to the world (Hobson, 1989).[1]

It is very unlikely that infants below 9 months of age engage in joint attention of this type. It is unclear in most cases whether they are focused on the same aspect of the environment as adults, but, more importantly, it is especially unclear whether they know that they are. Thus, prior to 9 months of age, there is some simultaneous looking that results from both adult and infant having their attention attracted to the same thing. There is also some gaze following (Butterworth & Jarrett, 1991; Scaife & Bruner, 1975). Corkum and Moore (this volume) report, however, that before 10 to 11 months of age their infant subjects were just as likely to respond to adult head turns by looking in the opposite direction as they were by looking in the same direction. They also found that 6- and 7-month-olds could not be conditioned to consistently follow the gaze of an adult to an interesting sight, that 8- and 9-month-olds could be so conditioned, and that 10- and 11-month-olds did not need to be conditioned as they followed adult gaze spontaneously. It is thus very likely that instances of gaze following prior to 9 months of age are either random coincidences or conditioned responses in which the infant has learned to look in the direction of adult head turns in order to see interesting things. It is also important that before 9 months of age there is very little spontaneous gaze alternation between adult and object; when infants do follow adult gaze or engage with an adult and an object, they seldom look back spontaneously to check on the adult's attentional focus.

The most plausible interpretation of these observations in young infants, therefore, is that prior to 9 months of age adult–infant simultaneous looking is

---

[1]It is easy to get into an infinite loop here: The child attends to the adult attending to his or her attention, with the adult attending to that, and so on. Newman (1986) presented a very useful discussion of why such mental gymnastics are not necessary; we may simply assume that at some point human children understand that they are in a situation of "mutual knowledge" or, in Hobson's terms, of "sharing experience."

either fortuitous, a case of onlooking, a case of alternating attention, or results from infant gaze following as a learned response in which an adult head turn is used as a discriminative cue that an interesting sight is to be found in a particular direction. There is no joint attention or any other indication that infants at this age understand others as intentional agents.

UNDERSTANDING PERSONS AT 9 TO 18 MONTHS

In the period from 9 to 18 months of age infants engage in a variety of behaviors that evidence a new understanding of other persons and how they work. Most important for current purposes, recent research has shown a qualitative shift in infants' skills of joint visual attention at some time around their first birthdays. In addition, however, it is important that this shift occurs synchronously with the emergence of, or qualitative changes in, a host of other related social behaviors such as social referencing, imitative learning, and intentional communication. The developmental synchrony of all these changes is strong evidence of an underlying commonality, and my candidate for that commonality is that they all rely on the infant's emergent understanding of other persons as intentional agents who have a specific relation to the world that may differ from their own.

At around 12 months of age the earliest attempts at systematic gaze alternation occur in a variety of contexts including following into the adult's attention and attempting to direct it. As argued previously, gaze alternation is not by itself a sufficient criterion of joint attention, but it becomes a much more convincing criterion when it occurs spontaneously (not elicited by adult behavior) and when it is integrated with the ongoing social interaction in appropriate ways. Thus, at around the time of their first birthday, infants will follow the gaze of an adult to an object and then immediately look back, seeming to check on the adult's continued attentional focus, unprecipitated by adult behaviors (Butterworth, 1991). Similarly, at this same age, when infants point to or show adults objects, they often alternate their attention between the object and the adult spontaneously, again without any discernable adult provocation (Bates, 1976). And perhaps most importantly, it is at around this same age that infants and mothers first engage in extended periods of coordinated joint attention, where coordinated joint attention refers to relatively lengthy interactions in which the child actively coordinates her attention to adult and object, almost always involving a spontaneous, unprecipitated look to the adult during their joint play (Bakeman & Adamson, 1984).

The conditioned learning explanation may be applicable to all of these cases as well, especially if, following Moore and Corkum (in press), we posit that just making eye contact with an adult, or seeing him or her smile, is rewarding to young infants. But the conditioning interpretation is much less plausible in the case of these new joint attentional behaviors than in the case of those occurring prior to 9 months of age. Most importantly, the quality of the looks, especially their timing, the affect they express, and their coordination with the ongoing interaction, is not consistent with the view that children learn to look to interesting objects and to people under separate sets of contingencies (Adamson & Bakeman, 1985). The child does not look to the adult or attempt to secure their attention at random moments, but rather looks to the adult or points to an object when surprised by something, pleased with something, afraid of something, or in other socially meaningful situations. The child does not look to the object and adult in the same way either; he or she expresses affect when looking to the adult and even when looking on as the adult looks to the object (Adamson & Bakeman, 1985). This kind of coordinated interaction, I would argue, is an unlikely candidate for the conditioning explanation. In any case, while conditioning explanations can never be ruled out completely, children's spontaneous gaze alternations, and the way they are coordinated with their ongoing social interactions at around 12 months of age, makes less plausible the conditioning explanation and more plausible the view that the child understands that the adult is a separate person who has intentions and attention that may differ from its own.

This more cognitive view of 1-year-olds' interactions with adults gains in plausibility even further when other infant behaviors at this same age are considered. In addition to following into adults' attention to objects, infants at this age also follow into other adult behaviors. Social referencing is a case in point (see Uzgiris, 1989). In its classic formulation, the young child follows into the adult's attention to an outside entity, and monitors the emotional reaction to it, typically then adopting that same emotional attitude. There are other simpler interpretations of course; for example, the child may be either mimicking the adult's behaviors to the object or else experiencing something like emotional contagion in which he or she is "infected" with the adult's emotion (something like contagious crying in neonates). The best test of these interpretations is a study by Walden and Ogan (1988) in which young infants were presented with objects as their mother reacted either positively or negatively as determined experimentally. After a brief delay, the child was given the opportunity to play with the objects alone. It was not until they were around 12 months old that children showed in their solitary play a significant effect of the mother's expressed emotional attitude toward the objects. In terms of interpretation, it did not seem that infants were blindly mimicking the behaviors of their mothers as they often showed different specific behaviors; for example, they simply avoided what their mothers expressed fear toward. An interpretation in terms of emotional contagion cannot account for the child's behavior in the later solitary play period, but it could happen that the child is infected with the adult's emotion while looking at the object and so the object becomes associated, through conditioning, with the emotion (Moore & Corkum, in press). Once again, however, it is also plausible that infants in this situation understand their mothers as intentional agents who either like or dislike the object they are looking at, an attitude that differs from their own as yet unformed attitude.

Another way that infants may follow into the behavior of others is in their imitative learning of new behaviors. Imitative learning has not been typically considered a relevant phenomenon when researchers talk of joint attention, but, obviously, it involves a following into adult behavior and attention in some sense. This is very clear in the case of imitation of actions on objects. The earliest evidence that children might imitatively learn novel adult actions on objects comes at around 9 months of age. Meltzoff (1988a) showed infants simple actions on novel objects, and they then produced many of those same actions themselves. The problem is that precisely what was learned from the model is not totally clear. Although there were some control conditions, it is possible that what the child learned in this study was nothing other than the affordances of the objects involved: that the toy egg made a noise, that the hinge folded, and so forth. In cases in which there is only one plausible action leading to a given result on a given object, given the structure of the human body, the behavior of the observer and demonstrator will match. This is one version of what I have previously called emulation learning, in which the observer repro- duces the demonstrator's end result but does so in its own idiosyncratic way or in a way that matches another's behavior accidentally (Tomasello, 1990). What is needed to show that the child understands the intention of the demonstrator is a behavior that has different possible means to the same end. The earliest demonstration of this type is provided by Meltzoff (1988b) who had 14-month- old infants watch an adult demonstrator bend at the waist to touch his forehead to a panel which activated a light. Children reproduced this action, even though they might more plausibly have used their hand on the panel to produce the same end result. Children in the control group did not reproduce the bending- at-the-waist behavior. The success of these 14-month-olds suggests strongly that they did not just tune into a change in the state of the object, but also understood something about the adult's strategy in producing that change of state in the object. Again it is hard to understand why or how a child might do such a thing if he or she does not appreciate the fact that the adult is an individual person who has intentions in the situation that may be different from its own.

In addition to following into the attention and behavior of adults, infants at this same age also do a number of things to actively manipulate adult behavior and attention. In the technical parlance, prelinguistic children use protoimpera- tives to solicit adult help in obtaining a desired object or activity, and protode- claratives to direct adult attention to an object or activity of interest (Bates, 1976). Both of these behaviors could conceivably be conditioned responses. In the case of imperatives, it could easily be the case that the child does something like reach for an object, the adult responds in a rewarding fashion by getting the object, and the child learns to use the reaching in an intentionally communicative way, perhaps stylized into pointing. This explanation is less applicable to the protoimperative pointing of the 12–14-month period because it is very often accompanied by the kind of spontaneous gaze alternation that seems to indicate that the child expects from the adult a self-initiated, intentional response rather than a mechanical one. It is also important that the child looks to the eyes of the adult rather than to the hand or any other body part that will directly effect the desired change (Butterworth, 1991; Gomez, 1991). My interpretation of protoimperative pointing in the 12- to 14-month period, therefore, is that the child is attempting not just to obtain the object but to change the adult's intentions so that they become aligned with its own.

Declaratives present an even more compelling story. In this case the child simply shows or shares something with an adult, which would not seem amenable to a conditioning explanation as there are no apparent rewards involved. But if human beings are rewarded by smiles and other signs of acknowledgement from adults, then they might be conditioned in their use of protodeclaratives as well (Moore & Corkum, in press). In addition to the fact that this stretches the conditioning explanation somewhat out of shape, it is also important to note that, as in the case of imperatives, the 12- to 14-month period signals the onset of spontaneous gaze alternation between object and adult as the child points or shows objects (Butterworth, 1991). It is also telling in this connection that autistic children do not spontaneously produce protodeclaratives (Baron-Cohen, 1991), nor do chimpanzees in their natural habitats, and they are very rare in chimpanzees taught humanlike means of communication (Carpenter, Tomasello, & Savage-Rumbaugh, 1993; Gomez, Sarria, & Tamarit, 1993). In the interpretation of many researchers, including myself, declaratives have the purely social motive of sharing attention to something, which would seem by itself to be indicative of children's understanding that others have perspectives on things that may differ from their own (see also Baron-Cohen, 1993; Gomez et al., 1993).

Over and above all of these phenomena, I would argue that the single most compelling piece of evidence that 12–14-month-old infants understand other persons as intentional agents is their learning and use of linguistic symbols. In addition to their use in communication as imperatives and declaratives accompanied by gaze alternation, symbols have another quality of special importance for the current discussion: Each linguistic symbol implies its own particular point of view on a situation. Thus, while adult and child are simultaneously looking at a ball, the adult may say that it is "Round" or "Blue" or "Rubber" or "Rolling," which are much more specific ways of manipulating attention than simple pointing or showing. For children to determine which aspect of the object is being singled out by the adult in such cases, they must determine something of the adult's attentional focus, for which gaze following is manifestly insufficient (Wittgenstein, 1953). Children show that they have understood the adult's attentional orientation in using a novel symbol when they respond to it appropriately. Better still, they show such understanding when they themselves reproduce the symbol in appropriate but novel circumstances by exhorting someone else to adopt a particular attentional orientation. The understanding implicit in comprehending and producing symbols in these ways is not present in the child's initial behaviors that appear on the surface to be linguistic comprehension and production: in the 9 to 12-month period infants often respond to verbal requests by relying on nonlinguistic cues, and they often produce sounds that resemble adult language but do not carry its referential meaning (e.g., Nelson & Lucariello, 1985). The full comprehension and use of communicative symbols (i.e., in multiple novel but appropriate circumstances) does not appear before around 13 months of age, at which time children use productively both conventional linguistic symbols (Bates, 1979) and idiosyncratic symbolic gestures as well (Acredolo & Goodwin, in press). I deal with language acquisition and use more fully in the section that follows, but for now the important point is simply that by learning and using linguistic symbols in a productive manner, 13-month-old children are demonstrating their understanding that other persons have points of view on a situation that may differ from their own.

Applying "lean interpretations" to behavior is always possible as evidenced by the continued existence of behaviorism. There is no decisive evidence in any single behavior just adduced that 1-year-old children understand other persons as intentional agents whose perspectives may differ from their own. I would argue, however, that viewing these behaviors as a whole provides several strong and converging lines of evidence of the first glimmerings of such an understanding at 12 to 14 months of age. Although in each case there are initial expressions at around 9 to 12 months for which it is unclear whether the child has taken an intentional stance toward the adult whose behavior or attention is being adopted, in each case there is also a subsequent period at around 12 to 14 months in which the child adopts adult behaviors or behavioral strategies in a flexible and appropriate manner requiring an understanding of the adult's intentions and attention in the situation and how these might differ from his or her own. And viewing these behaviors as a group makes theoretical sense because, whereas we call them each by a different name, they can each be seen as a different manifestation of the same basic process: The child adopts the visual attention of the other, the emotion of the other, or the instrumental or symbolic behavior of the other—or else attempts to get the adult to adopt an intention or attentional focus in line with his or her own. All of these behaviors can thus be seen to rely on the understanding of others as intentional agents, each of whom has their own intentional and attentional agenda. The view that each of these behaviors is conditioned one at a time, each under its own set of reinforcement contingencies, is implausible, I would argue, given the coordinated way in which each is integrated into the child's social interactions and affective exchanges with others, and given the general developmental synchrony with which they all emerge. A summary of the evidence for this developmental synchrony is presented in Table 6.1.

TABLE 6.1
Ontogeny of Early Social Cognition in Several Important Behavioral Domains

	9 Months	12 Months
Following Attention		
Gaze Following	[conditioned gaze follow]	Spontaneous gaze follow
Joint Engagement	[passive joint engagement]	Coordinated joint engagement
Following Behavior		
Social Referencing	[conditioned emotions]	Social referencing
Imitative Learning	[emulation]	Imitative learning of symbols, actions on objects
Directing Attention		
Declaratives		Declarative pointing (w/ gaze alternation)
		Symbol use
Directing Behavior		
Imperatives		Imperative pointing (w/ gaze alternation)

113

To be fair I should report, at least very briefly, on the most consistent and coherent skepticism about the social cognition of 12- to 14-month-olds. Barresi and Moore (1993; see also Moore & Corkum, in press) argue that the important transformation in infants' understanding of others does not take place until 18–24 months of age. They base their view on the relatively late emergence of two key behaviors. First, they argue that it is not until after 18 months of age that children show a clear differentiation of their own perspective from that of others by, for example, following an adult's gaze or pointing gesture to the space behind them (Butterworth, 1991). In this view, it is not until children follow adult directions to locations out of their own sight that infants can be said to truly understand that adults have perspectives different from their own. It is not clear to me, however, why the important advance in this behavior is not simply a new understanding of space, also manifest in infants' performance on Stage 6 object permanence tasks (in which they search for objects after invisible displacements) at this same age. The important phenomenon would seem to be the fact that infants look to some new place because an adult is looking; precisely where that new place is seems much less crucial. Second, Barresi and Moore also invoke the relatively late emergence of mirror self-recognition in infants, which also is not clearly present until around 18 to 24 months of age. But the implications of mirror self-recognition are currently a matter of some heated debate. Neisser (1991) and Rochat (1993) both argue and present evidence that infants clearly recognize their own bodies and differentiate them from the rest of the world from a very early age, by at least 3 months. The recognition of what is in reality just another body part—the face—is then not so special, and its late emergence depends mostly on the child's ability to deal with mirrors. I continue to believe, therefore, that the behaviors I have outlined are much more to the point about how infants are understanding the behavior of other persons than the two possibilities put forth by Barresi and Moore.

My conclusion is that it is at around 12 to 14 months of age that human infants begin to understand other persons as intentional agents whose intentions and attention may differ from their own. This new understanding makes itself felt in any behavior or behavioral domain that depends on or is affected by the child's understanding of other persons, with decalages in particular domains depending on any number of performance factors. These domains include both the child's attempts to follow into the attention or behavior of others (e.g., gaze following, social referencing, and the imitative learning of instrumental actions and symbols), as well as attempts to direct the attention and behavior of others for imperative and declarative purposes using either gestures or conventional symbols. In the analogy to 4-year-olds' theories of mind, however, one component is still missing. The component for which we still do not have evidence at 12–14 months is the child's understanding that the intentions of persons may on occasion not match with the current state of affairs (analogous to 4-year-olds' understanding of false beliefs). Although children of this age deal every day with the fact that they cannot always fulfill their intentions or achieve their goals, and they provide ample evidence of their displeasure when this occurs, we do not have any evidence that they understand this fact conceptually, either about themselves or about other persons. Evidence for such understanding comes during the 18- to 24-month period.

LANGUAGE ACQUISITION AND USE AT 18 TO 24 MONTHS

I take it as axiomatic that when humans use language to communicate referentially they are attempting to manipulate the attention of another person or persons (see Talmy, 1993). Moreover, if we take the Gibsonian view that attention is intentionally directed perception, we can view referential uses of language as attempts to get others to intentionally perceive certain aspects of the discourse context (including perceptual context), for example, such things as the shape, size, ownership, history, or activities of an object, all without changing direction of gaze, it might be added. In this view, then, linguistic reference may be seen as something of the form: "I *intend* for you to *attend* to X," that is to say, "I *intend* for you to *intend* to *perceive* X in such and such a way." When children hear new language addressed to them, therefore, they must determine not the adult's intention to an object, as many theories of reference assume, but rather the adult's intentions with respect to their attention. Reference is not directed to an object but to a person (see Tomasello, 1992). To play this attention manipulation game productively from the other direction, when it is the child who is encouraging another person to attend to something in their shared environment, the child must understand that all persons, including him or herself, have at least some intentional control over the attention switching process. The understanding of others as intentional agents thus comes out clearly both in children's attempts to learn new pieces of language by tuning into the attentional focus of others (comprehension) and in their attempts to use language in order to get others to tune into their attentional focus (production). I discuss each in turn.

As mentioned previously, most human infants begin to use conventional linguistic symbols at around 13 months of age. In these early months young children acquire the vast majority of their first words in joint attentional interactions with adults and objects (see Bruner, 1983; Tomasello & Todd, 1983). This is because such formats provide a referential frame within which the adult's attention to the outside world when using a piece of language is discernable to the child nonlinguistically. It has been found that object label acquisition is easiest for young children when adults follow into their already established attentional focus in these formats (Akhtar, Dunham, & Dunham, 1991; Dunham, Dunham, & Curwin, 1993; Tomasello & Farrar, 1986; Tomasello, Mannle, &

Kruger, 1986). But recent research has shown that even before their second birthdays, children are able to determine the adult focus of attention on objects in more active ways. Thus, when an adult and child are visually focused on two different objects and the adult utters a novel word, 18-month-old children learn the label not for the object on which they are focused but for the object on which the adult is focused (Baldwin, 1991, 1993a, 1993b). This indicates very clearly and directly that children of this age understand that other persons sometimes have intentions and attention toward the world that are different from their own.

Two experimental studies demonstrate the power of this understanding, and, in addition, show something of young children's ability to discriminate intentional and unintentional actions. In the first study, Tomasello and Barton (in press) taught children near their second birthdays a novel object label in a finding game. While facing a row of five identical buckets an adult said to the child "Let's find the *toma*. Where's the *toma*?" In the experimental condition, the adult first picked up one object and then replaced it in its bucket with a scowling face; she then repeated this performance with a second object; she then finally, on her third attempt, picked up an object gleefully and handed it over to the child. In this condition children had no trouble skipping over the two rejected objects to attach the adult's novel label to the target object, and in fact they learned to comprehend and produce the new word just as well in this condition as in a control condition where the target object was found straight-away, and they almost never learned the word for one of the rejected objects (see also Baldwin, 1993a, 1993b). The reason this word learning situation was so natural for 24-month-old children is that they understood the adult's intention to find the toma, and so they actively monitored the adult's facial and other nonverbal cues in her subsequent search activities to determine at what point that intention had been fulfilled. Children's pattern of learning showed that they clearly discriminated cases in which the adult's intention was fulfilled from those in which it was not, and that they knew the new language was being used only for intended entities.

In a second study Tomasello and Barton (in press) taught children near their second birthdays two novel verbs, one in each of two experimental conditions (see also Tomasello & Kruger, 1992). Two specially built apparatuses were used, each having two possible actions that could be performed on it. In the Target Last experimental condition an adult picked up a doll and said "Let's dax Mickey Mouse," while moving toward an apparatus. Upon arriving at the apparatus she then accidentally subjected the doll to one action (saying "Woops!") and then proceeded to perform the target action on the doll (saying "There!"). Each child then heard the other novel verb in association with the other apparatus and in the Target First experimental condition. In this condition, the experimenter, after announcing her intentions in the same way, first performed the target action intentionally and then performed the other action accidentally. Results showed that in the Target Last condition children had no trouble skipping over the intervening accidental action to attach the new verb to the second action the adult performed: The two experimental conditions produced equivalent learning and almost no children learned the word for the accidental action. Once again, the only way the children could have done this was through an understanding of the adult's intentions in using the new word: They had to clearly discriminate actions the adult performed intentionally from those she performed unintentionally and attach the new language only to the intentional actions.

The point is this: To acquire a new word—to learn to comprehend and produce it in conventionally appropriate contexts (one instance of what Tomasello et al., 1993, call cultural learning)—the child must enter into a state of joint attentional focus with an adult. On many occasions, this requires shifting his or her own attention so that it aligns with that of the adult, thus demonstrating an appreciation of their differing points of view. Children's tendency to ignore unintended objects and activities in this process demonstrates that they understand, not only that others have intentions that may differ from their own, but also that on some occasions those intentions do not accord with the actual situation; for example, people find objects they were not looking for or perform actions accidentally.

In terms of language use, children must now play the attention manipulation game from the opposite side. It is useful to consider this game from the point of view of a basic theoretical dichotomy in the study of the pragmatics of conversation: topic–comment. In this view each turn of a mature linguistic dialogue must make reference to the topic the speaker wishes the participants to focus on (perhaps previously established) and the comment (or predication) the speaker wishes to make about that topic. Briefly, the ontogeny of children's ability to control topic–comment structure is as follows (see Table 6.2; see Tomasello, 1988). Children's earliest forays in communication are the face-to-face "protoconversations" characteristic of primary intersubjectivity during early

TABLE 6.2
Correlation of Processes of Communication
and Predication in Human Development

Age	Process of Communication	Topic	Comment
0–6 Months	Primary Intersubjectivity	—	—
6–12 Months	Secondary Intersubjectivity	Nonlinguistic	—
12–18 Months	First Words	Linguistic	—
18–24 Months	First Predication	Nonlinguistic	Linguistic
24+ Months	Conversation	Linguistic	Linguistic

infancy. These direct emotional exchanges have no topic-comment structure. At around 9–12 months of age children begin to engage in communicative interactions aimed at drawing an adult's attention to some topic (declaratives), either with a nonlinguistic gesture or with a piece of language proper. These earliest forays into secondary intersubjectivity have topic but not comment structure. At around 18 months of age children begin establishing topic nonlinguistically, for example by holding up an object for the adult to see, and then adding a comment linguistically (e.g., "Wet"). Finally, sometime before their second birthdays children gain purely linguistic control of topic-comment structure, using conventional linguistic forms not only to direct a communicative partner to a topic but also to comment on that topic (e.g., "Shirt wet" or "It's wet").

The important point for current purposes is that children's use of predication demonstrates a very sophisticated level of social cognition in the 18- to 24-month period. When the child holds up a ball and says "Wet" or "Blue" or "Mine" or "Roll," she or he is assuming a shared focus of attention on the ball and then going further to ask the listener to attend to some specific aspect out of other possible aspects of that ball. Predication thus requires some notion that other persons can intentionally modulate their attention in response to linguistic and nonlinguistic means of communication, often while not changing their visual orientation at all. Children's use of language in pragmatically appropriate conversational turns demonstrates very dramatically their understanding that adults have intentional control over their attentional focus and that this attentional focus sometimes differs from their own. It also demonstrates their understanding that focus of attention is underdetermined by the actual perceptual situation, and thus that in one and the same shared perceptual situation they and an adult may have different foci of attention.

It is also relevant in this context to recall that 24-month-old children, when in conversation with adults, actively adjust their language depending on their understanding of what others know. For example, Tomasello, Farrar, and Dines (1983) found that 24-month-old children repair conversational breakdowns differently depending on whether the interlocutor is a familiar adult (their mother) or an unfamiliar adult experimenter: They repeat themselves for their mothers, assuming her ability to comprehend their linguistic signal, whereas they more often reformulate their misunderstood utterance for a stranger, because there is a greater possibility that the stranger does not know the idiosyncratic means of expression they sometimes use. Anselmi, Tomasello, and Acunzo (1986) also found differential adjustments depending on which part of the utterance the adult misunderstood (see also Akhtar, 1994). In these situations what young children are showing is a clear awareness that other persons may comprehend a communicative message in a way that they did not intend (Golinkoff, 1993). Perhaps the most powerful demonstration of this awareness is the fact that, in anticipation of such misunderstandings, children at this age even begin to make self-corrections of their own "speech accidents" (Clark, 1982). These kinds of modifications of linguistic expressions to take account of misunderstandings and anticipated misunderstandings would seem to be very powerful further evidence for the hypothesis that, during the last half of their second year of life, children know that the intentional and attentional states of others may conflict with the actual situation, in this case as represented by the message the child actually intends to send.

I would thus argue that language learning and use at 18 to 24 months of age demonstrate very clearly that children in this developmental period are operating with an understanding of other persons as intentional agents, and, moreover, that their understanding of intentionality has deepened to include the possibility of mismatches between intentions and actual situations. Their basic understanding of persons as intentional is demonstrated by their active shifting of attention to match that of adults' in learning new words, as well as by their use of language, especially in predication, to direct the attention of adults to aspects of the environment for which gaze direction is an insufficient cue. Their further understanding of intentionality is demonstrated by the way they actively monitor the intentions of adults in learning new words in nonostensive contexts, even ignoring as irrelevant objects or actions the adult marks as unintentional, as well as by the adjustments and self-corrections they make in their language use to accommodate to the misunderstandings, or anticipated misunderstandings, of listeners. Therefore, on analogy with the 4-year-old's understanding of others as mental agents with beliefs that differ from their own and sometimes from the current state of affairs, I believe it is plausible to posit that 18- to 24-month-old children understand other persons as intentional agents with intentions and attention that may differ from their own and sometimes from the current state of affairs.

POSSIBLE DEVELOPMENTAL MECHANISMS

The ontogenetic picture that emerges from the foregoing account is as follows. In the period prior to 9 months of age, although they are doing many interesting things, infants are not engaging with adults in joint attention of any kind. In the 9- to 18-month period, joint attentional interactions emerge in two phases. In the 9- to 12-month period infants begin following into and directing the attention and behavior of other persons, although it is not perfectly clear to what extent these behaviors rely on an understanding of others as intentional agents. In the 12- to 18-month period infants demonstrate an understanding of intentional agents through qualitative changes in the nature of their joint attentional interactions, the emergence of social referencing and of the imitative learning of instrumental and symbolic behaviors, and the use of gestures and language in symbolic communication. While these activities show the child's understanding that other persons have intentions and attention that may differ from his or her own, there is no evidence that children this young comprehend that the intentions of persons may not always match the current situation or what was intended to be expressed in an intentional communication. Children aged 18- to 24-months-old show a clear understanding of other persons as agents with intentional relations to a situation that may differ from their own and sometimes from the current state of affairs.

It may be too early in our knowledge of these things to make definitive theoretical pronouncements about possible developmental mechanisms that may underlie this ontogenetic sequence, but I would nevertheless like to make a few tentative comments in the context of some current theoretical debates. To orient the discussion, it is important, I believe, to begin by distinguishing two related but distinct aspects of children's early social-cognitive development that have been implicit in the foregoing account: infants' early identification with, but differentiation from, other persons, and the precise nature of how infants and young children understand the notion of person, both other persons and themselves. I will address each very briefly in turn.

With respect to infants' early identification with other persons, the two most interesting proposals are those of Meltzoff and Gopnik (1993; see also Gopnik & Meltzoff, 1993) and Moore and Corkum (in press; see also Barresi & Moore, 1993). Meltzoff and Gopnik argue for a kind of "starting state nativism" in which infants from the very beginning identify with and imitate others, and know when others are imitating them, so that their growing understanding of others is applied to themselves, and, conversely, their knowledge of themselves is applied to others. Citing Anisfeld's (1991) skeptical review of neonatal imitation research, Moore and Corkum believe that a certain type of social experience is necessary for children to learn the kind of self–other correspondences that Meltzoff and Gopnik posit as innate. Key in their account are situations in which adult and infant take similar intentional stances toward an outside entity and the infant attends to this convergence; for example, they both look to the same place or fear the same object. In such interactions, and only in such interactions, children have available both first-person information about their own intentional states and third-person information about the intentional states of the other (e.g., through their facial expressions and behavior). From these kinds of convergence experiences infants come to both identify and differentiate first- and third-person perspectives—the intentional states of themselves and others—in much the same way they come to differentiate and coordinate their sensorimotor schemes in general.

Clearly imitation and converging adult-child behaviors of all sorts are key to infants' identifying with other persons and understanding their similarity to them. However, both Meltzoff and Gopnik, and Moore and Corkum ignore situations in which infants interact with others reciprocally, for example, in protoconversations where their social and emotional behaviors and those of others do not match but rather complement one another: the adult tickles and the child smiles or the child coos and the adult laughs (Trevarthen, 1979). It seems clear that these types of reciprocal interactions are also of crucial importance because it is reciprocal interactions, not matching interactions, that provide infants with occasions for determining that, although they are "like" other persons, they have an individual identity that is separate and distinct. And this would seem to be bolstered by their own sense of self-identity as constructed through reciprocal interactions with the inanimate world (Rochat, 1993). One could argue in fact, following Trevarthen (1979), that it is the reciprocal, dialogic interactions that are primary, and that matching interactions which are relatively rare occurrences are but one type of dialogic interaction infants have with adults. In either case, for present concerns the important point is that from very early in life infants engage with others reciprocally, as well as in imitative and converging interactions, and it is very likely that these types of interactions are crucial to infants' emerging understanding that they are similar to, but not identical with, others.

With regard to the second major aspect of infants' early social-cognitive development, theories of how children come to understand the notion of person range from totally nativistic theories to almost totally cultural theories. Thus, Trevarthen (1979, 1993) believes that from birth infants understand other persons as intentional, mental, and reflective agents, and they coordinate this understanding with their own self-conscious sense of self from the beginning. There are no particular experiences, social or otherwise, that are necessary for the development of children's social cognition. Kaye (1982), on the other hand, believes that infants must learn about intentional agents and themselves through particular kinds of interactions with other persons. In this view, human infants are born into a cultural world in which virtually all of their experiences are socially framed and mediated. Infants' understanding of the personal agency of themselves and other persons is created by this mediation, most especially by the fact that adults treat children as intentional agents even before they are such agents. In this formulation, "parents create persons" by treating them intentionally. Although Meltzoff and Gopnik are not explicit on this point, in their account infants come to understand persons as intentional agents possessing specific intentional states by means of "highly powerful theory formation abilities" that are employed to explain their behavior. Moore and Corkum do not specifically address the development of the understanding of intentionality or intentional states other than to assume the child's ability to discern them in both their first-person and third-person forms.

None of these theories account adequately, in my opinion, for infants' understanding of the behavior of persons as intentional. The key to this understanding, I believe, is that late in their first year of life infants for the first time differentiate in their *own* behavior between the ends and means of instrumental acts; that is, they begin to behave intentionally. Piaget (1952) finds intentionality of this sort in the infant's removal of obstacles at around 9 months of age. In more carefully controlled experimental contexts, however, Frye (1991) found that infants do not clearly behave intentionally in the sense of differentiated ends and means until around 12 months of age. It is interesting—and not accidental, I would argue, that 9 months is the age at which many joint attentional behaviors emerge in their nascent forms, and that 12 months is the age at which joint attentional behaviors become more clearly intentional across a number of domains. My proposal, which is somewhat at variance with a previous proposal of mine that concentrated on infants' understanding of the behavior of other persons (Tomasello, 1993), is that it is in their own intentional behavior that infants first understand intentionality. Once their own behavior shows a clear separation between ends and means, infants' matching and reciprocal interactions with other persons, and perhaps their observation of the instrumental behaviors of other persons, provides the raw material for their understanding that others also act intentionally. In this version of what is essentially a simulation view of early social cognition it is children's knowledge of their own behavior—from the inside as it were—that is the impetus for new levels in their understanding of others.

Let me immediately make clear two things that this proposal does not imply and hopefully clarify it in the process. First, this proposal does not imply that infants conceptually understand the intentionality of their own behavior before they conceptually understand that of others. Infants can use experience of their own intentional activities such as having goals and pursuing them with varied means, to simulate the experience and behavior of other persons. To do this, they do not need to treat their own way of functioning as an object of conceptual thinking in which the various components are distinct and conceptually manipulable. The hypothesis here is that when children begin operating in their sensorimotor behavior with a clear differentiation of ends and means, they automatically begin seeing the behavior of others with whom they have previously identified, as specified by either Meltzoff and Gopnik or Moore and Corkum, in these same terms (see Gopnik, 1993; and especially Gordon, 1986, 1992, for a fuller discussion of this issue). As a corollary of this proposal, I should also stress that the primacy of self-understanding at the major ontogenetic transitions in how children understand persons does not mean that within a given level of understanding, for example, the understanding of others as intentional agents, the child cannot also develop various understandings about the specific behavior of other persons that could then be applied to itself. The only claim is that the major transitions in early social cognition—understanding persons in terms of intentions, beliefs, and reflective beliefs—are grounded in children's understanding of their own transactions with the environment.

Second, this view does not imply that children's understanding of persons simply unfolds with little help from the social environment as they robotically differentiate ends and means in their interactions with the inanimate world. It is very likely that interactions with other persons are necessary for the emergence of children's ability to attribute their newly emerging behavioral organization to the behavior of others, although experimental demonstrations of this necessity are, for obvious reasons, not available. What is available is a very convincing demonstration of the power of a structured cultural environment in the developing social-cognitive skills of chimpanzees. A number of recent studies have demonstrated important differences in the social cognition of normally reared chimpanzees and chimpanzees who have been raised in humanlike cultural environments with exposure to human artifacts, language, attention direction, and teaching. As opposed to their conspecifics in species-typical environments, chimpanzees raised in such environments show, in addition to their more well-known symbolic skills (Savage-Rumbaugh, McDonald, Sevcik, Hopkins, & Rupert, 1986), a number of humanlike joint attentional and imitative learning skills (Carpenter et al., in press; Tomasello, Savage-Rumbaugh, & Kruger, 1993). Although we do not know what all of the effective factors are in such cross-fostering experiments, one possibility is that what is of special importance are interactions in which infants are treated as intentional themselves, for example, when an adult tries to get an infant (of whatever species) to do something or understand something. In such interactions—which are not present routinely in the lives of chimpanzees in species-typical environments—the adult intends that the infant intend to do X. When the infant begins to behave intentionally itself, and so begins to understand the behavior of others in that way as well, there begins a recursive process of the child understanding the adult's intentions toward his or her intentions. This might be the basis for the infant's earliest self-concept—as they see themselves from the outside, as it were (Tomasello, 1993). And it might even provide the basis for understanding one's own behavior conceptually, as simulating the perspective of others toward the self may provide the basis for reflection on one's own activities (Tomasello et al., 1993), the importance of which has recently been demonstrated by Karmiloff-Smith (1992).

My specific account of the developmental mechanisms that underlie early social cognition is thus as follows. In the first 9 months of life, children are interacting with other persons regularly. In these interactions, they both match and reciprocate the interactive behaviors of others and they notice when others match and reciprocate their own interactive behaviors. This leads to identification with but differentiation from other persons: I am like them, but I am a separate individual. At around 9 months of age, infants begin to produce instrumental behaviors in which means and ends are clearly separated: They have goals "in mind" ahead of time and employ various means for achieving them, modifying those means as necessary in light of the goals. Because of their already existing ability to identify with others, infants begin to use their own new way of interacting with the world intentionally as the basis for their understanding of the intentional activities of other persons. At around 12 to 14 months of age, this understanding consolidates (see Adamson & McArthur, this volume, for the argument that joint attentional skills "consolidate" at this age) as does their own intentional behavior (Frye, 1991). From this point on, they simply see the behavior of others intentionally: When they watch mother trying to open a jar, for example, they see not her specific hand movements, but they see her intentionally trying to accomplish a goal in the same way in which they understand their own goal-directed behaviors. We do not really know the basis of this consolidation, but one possibility is that from individual acts of interacting with others as intentional during the previous 3–5 months, infants construct a generalized concept of persons as intentional agents. With such a generalized concept as a part of their conceptual apparatus, it is quite natural that 14-month-old infants begin to imitatively learn instrumental and symbolic behaviors from adults, to direct their attention with gestures and symbols, to social reference, and, in general, to tune into their intentional states.

With several months of experience operating in this way, and also responding to adults intentionally trying to influence their intentions, children refine their understanding of intentionality. In the months leading up to the 18–24-month age period, infants come to understand more deeply the nature of intentions as "mental" phenomena in the sense that they can be quite discrepant from the current state of affairs, can be frustrated and not fulfilled, and, in general, can be very different from the perceptual world around them. They then go on in the years that follow to construct the notion of belief and to understand the behavior of others in terms of beliefs. We know little of the developmental mechanisms underlying this development, but a straightforward application of the current approach would stress that young children construct such a concept as they differentiate in their own experience what they expect to occur from what actually does occur, perhaps especially in language-based discourse. They then use this notion of belief to explain both their own behavior and that of others.

CONCLUSION

It may seem that we have strayed very far away from joint attention. But I believe that we cannot understand joint attention except in the context of the child's developing social cognition as a whole. I would thus like to conclude by stressing both the cognitive aspect of the process, which joint attention theorists have mostly ignored, and the social aspect of the process, which theory of mind theorists have mostly ignored.

In theories of joint attention, the emphasis has always been on gaze following and gaze manipulation by young infants with very little discussion of the cognitive and social-cognitive bases of these behaviors. But, as I have argued, it is important to recognize that attention goes beyond visual orientation and so joint attention goes beyond simultaneous looking: Attention is inherently intentional and so joint attention is also. Children's understanding of other persons as intentional thus determines the developmental course of their joint attentional skills during the second year of life, as well as the developmental course of their other so-cial-cognitive skills during this same period. A number of theorists have recognized the underlying commonality among some of these skills by grouping together with joint attention such things as social referencing and gestural communication (e.g., Moore & Corkum, in press; see also Sigman & Kasari, this volume). I would like to add to the list the imitative learning of instrumental behaviors with objects and the acquisition and use of language as an instrument of attention manipulation, as both of these skills involve important social-cognitive interactions with other persons. My candidate for the commonality underlying all of these behaviors, for reasons I have hopefully made clear in the preceding, is their common reliance on the understanding of other persons as intentional agents.

In theories of children's theories of mind, it is the social aspect that has most often been neglected. This is clearest in views that emphasize issues of representation and metarepresentation in which children's emerging abilities to understand other persons are reduced to issues of cognitive computation (e.g., Leslie, 1987). But it is also true of a number of recent accounts in which some early social-cognitive competencies, including most prominently joint attention and protodeclarative communication, have been posited as precursors to a full-fledged, computational theory of mind. Wellman (1993) and Gomez et al. (1993), for example, both have accounts of early social cognition focusing on such things as children's understanding of the desires of others and the attention of others as evidenced by their protodeclarative behaviors. But by focusing only on behaviors that seem to be precursors to a theory of mind and metarepresentation they have neglected other social behaviors such as imitation and language, and so have missed the social-cognitive basis for the commonality among these behaviors. Similarly, Baron-Cohen (1993; this volume) posits an "attention-goal" psychology that bears some resemblance to the current account, but because of his emphasis on theory of mind as an endpoint and metarepresentation as a process, he also misses some key relations, especially that between attention and intention. He thus posits that children use the gaze direction of others to infer their goals, but he does not recognize that children must use their understanding of the goal of other persons to go beyond simple gaze following and on to an appreciation of their attentional focus. Overall, by choosing to focus purely on the cognitive (metarepresentational) side of the process, theory of mind theorists miss both the commonality among different social skills during infancy and the developmental continuities and discontinuities of infancy and early childhood. A focus on children's understanding of persons and its developmental trajectory from the understanding of intentional agents to mental agents overcomes both of these theoretical limitations.

There are still many things we do not know about children's early social cognition. We are especially ignorant of young children in the 9- to 18-month age period. In the analogy to children's theories of mind, about which there is currently much debate, this age is analogous to the 3- to 4-year age period; for example there are questions about 3-year-olds' skills of deception, which rely on an understanding that others' beliefs differ from one's own, but may or may not rely on an understanding that the beliefs of others may differ from reality (e.g., Sodian, Taylor, Harris, & Perner, 1991). Similarly in the current case, whether or not 9- to 18-month-old children are credited with the understanding of others as intentional agents depends on one's theoretical predilections and the choice of criteria this entails. It is reasonable to claim that 14-months-olds understand intentions because they clearly differentiate their own from those of others, but it is also reasonable to claim that until they understand accidents and unfulfilled intentions at 18 to 24 months they do not really understand intentions. In either case, there are many things we need to know about 9- to 18-month-old children. For example, it would be very useful to know more precisely how children of this age coordinate their gaze, emotional expression, actions with objects, and social behaviors as they interact with adults in naturalistic settings. It would also be useful to know more about the relation between joint attention and various types of social learning at this early period (see Carpenter et al., in press, for some general relations), and, more generally, about the ontogenetic relations among the various behaviors that have been hypothesized to be related. To my knowledge there has never been a longitudinal study of children of this age that documents, for example, the ages at which these various skills emerge. It would also be very useful to attempt to identify any possible behaviors, either naturally or experimentally, in which children of this age demonstrate a knowledge that intentions may not match the current state of affairs. In general, we simply need to know much more about all of the social and social-cognitive skills that emerge during this important transition period.

I close with two recommendations. First, if cognitively oriented researchers are going to embrace joint attention as a precursor to children's theories of mind, they should be as clear as they can about the underlying continuity that makes for this close relationship. Specifying the nature of this continuity will have to involve, in my opinion, attention to children's social cognition in terms of their understanding of other persons as intentional or mental agents (Tomasello et al., 1993). Second, I think cognitively oriented researchers should drop the precursor terminology. Those of us who have been studying joint attention might just as well refer to theory of mind as a postcursor to joint attentional skills. Indeed, a good case could be made that the first step in the ontogeny of social cognition—the understanding of other persons as intentional agents—is in an important sense foundational for all the rest. This in the sense that the other levels of social cognition including children's theories of mind depend on it, but also in the sense that it is at this level that we find what is already uniquely human. Although other primate species display impressive social intelligence in many ways in their daily lives, it is only humans who enter into joint attentional states with conspecifics, use symbols without special training, imitatively learn novel behaviors from conspecifics, intentionally teach their offspring, and, in general, interact with other persons as intentional beings. It is thus at the level of the social cognition of 1- to 2-year-old children—not 3- to 4-year-old children—that we see the basis of the uniquely human forms of social cognition that underlie the evolution of many uniquely human competencies, including language and other cultural skills.

ACKNOWLEDGMENTS

Thanks to Carolyn Mervis, Ann Kruger, Philippe Rochat, Ulric Neisser, Chris Moore, Nameera Akhtar, and Malinda Carpenter for comments on an earlier version of this manuscript.

REFERENCES

Acredolo, L., & Goodwin, S. (in press). Symbolic gestures versus words: Is there a modality advantage for the onset of symbol use? *Child Development.*

Adamson, L., & Bakeman, R. (1985). Affect and attention: Infants observed with mothers and peers. *Child Development, 56,* 582–593.

Akhtar, N. (1994). *Early strategies in responding to yes/no questions.* Manuscript submitted for publication.

Akhtar, N., Dunham, F., & Dunham, P. (1991). Directive interactions and early vocabulary development: The role of joint attentional focus. *Journal of Child Language, 18,* 41–50.

Anisfeld, M. (1991). Neonatal imitation. *Developmental Review, 11,* 60–97.

Anselmi, D., Tomasello, M., & Acunzo, M. (1986). Young children's responses to neutral and specific contingent queries. *Journal of Child Language, 13,* 135–144.

Bakeman, R., & Adamson, L. (1984). Coordinating attention to people and objects in mother-infant and peer-infant interactions. *Child Development, 55,* 1278–1289.

Baldwin, D. (1991). Infants' contributions to the achievement of joint reference. *Child Development, 62,* 875–890.

Baldwin, D. (1993a). Infants' ability to consult the speaker for clues to word reference. *Journal of Child Language, 20,* 395–418.

Baldwin, D. (1993b). Early referential understanding: Infants' ability to recognize referential acts for what they are. *Developmental Psychology, 29,* 832–843.

Barresi, J., & Moore, C. (1993). Sharing a perspective precedes the understanding of that perspective. *Behavioral and Brain Sciences, 16,* 513–514.

Baron-Cohen, S. (1991). Precursors to a theory of mind: Understanding attention in others. In A. Whiten (Ed.), *Natural theories of mind: Evolution, development, and simulation of everyday mindreading* (pp. 233–251). Oxford, England: Basil Blackwell.

Baron-Cohen, S. (1993). From attention-goal psychology to belief-desire psychology. In S. Baron-Cohen, H. Tager-Flusberg, & D. Cohen (Eds.), *Understanding other minds: Perspectives from autism* (pp. 59–82). Oxford, England: Oxford University Press.

Bates, E. (1976). *Language and context: The acquisition of pragmatics.* New York: Academic Press.

Bates, E. (1979). *The emergence of symbols: Cognition and communication in infancy.* New York: Academic Press.

Bruner, J. (1983). *Child's talk.* New York: Norton.

Butterworth, G. (1991). The ontogeny and phylogeny of joint visual attention. In A. Whiten (Ed.), *Natural theories of mind: Evolution, development, and simulation of everyday mindreading* (pp. 223–232). Oxford, England: Basil Blackwell.

Butterworth, G., & Cochran, E. (1980). Towards a mechanism of joint visual attention in human infancy. *International Journal of Behavioral Development, 19*, 253–272.

Butterworth, G., & Jarrett, N. (1991). What minds have in common is space: Spatial mechanisms serving joint visual attention in infancy. *British Journal of Developmental Psychology, 9*, 55–72.

Carpenter, M., Tomasello, M., & Savage-Rumbaugh, S. (in press). Joint attention and imitative learning in children, chimpanzees, and enculturated chimpanzees. *Social Development.*

Clark, E. (1982). Language change during language acquisition. In M. Lamb & A. Brown (Eds.), *Advances in developmental psychology* (pp. 171–195). Hillsdale, NJ: Lawrence Erlbaum Associates.

Dunham, P., Dunham, F., & Curwin, A. (1993). Joint attentional states and lexical acquisition at 18 months. *Developmental Psychology, 29*, 827–831.

Frye, D. (1991). The origins of intention in infancy. In D. Frye & C. Moore (Eds.), *Children's theories of mind* (pp. 15–38). Hillsdale, NJ: Lawrence Erlbaum Associates.

Gibson, E., & Rader, N. (1979). Attention: The perceiver as performer. In G. Hale & M. Lewis (Eds.), *Attention and cognitive development* (pp. 6–36). New York: Plenum Press.

Golinkoff, R. (1993). When is communication a meeting of the minds? *Journal of Child Language, 20*, 199–208.

Gomez, J. C. (1991). Visual behavior as a window for reading the mind of others in primates. In A. Whiten (Ed.), *Natural theories of mind: Evolution, development, and simulation of everyday mindreading* (pp. 195–207). Oxford, England: Basil Blackwell.

Gomez, J. C., Sarria, E., & Tamarit, J. (1993). The comparative study of early communication and theories of mind. In S. Baron-Cohen, H. Tager-Flusberg, & D. Cohen (Eds.), *Understanding other minds* (pp. 397–426). Oxford, England: Oxford University Press.

Gopnik, A. (1993). How we know our minds: The illusion of first-person knowledge of intentionality. *Behavioral and Brain Sciences, 16*, 1–15.

Gopnik, A., & Meltzoff, A. (1993). Imitation, cultural learning, and the origins of "theory of mind". *Behavioral and Brain Sciences, 16*, 521–523.

Gordon, R. (1986). Folk psychology as simulation. *Mind and Language, 1*, 158–171.

Gordon, R. (1992). The simulation theory: Objections and misconceptions. *Mind and Language, 7*, 87–103.

Haith, M., Hazen, C., & Goodman, G. (1988). Expectation and anticipation of dynamic visual events by 3.5-month-old babies. *Child Development, 59*, 467–479.

Hobson, P. (1989). On sharing experiences. *Development and Psychopathology, 1*, 197–203.

Karmiloff-Smith, A. (1992). *Beyond modularity.* Cambridge, MA: MIT Press.

Kaye, K. (1982). *The mental and social life of babies.* Chicago: University of Chicago Press.

Leslie, A. (1987). Pretense and representation: The origins of "theory of mind." *Psychological Review, 94*, 412–426.

Meltzoff, A. (1988a). Infant imitation and memory: 9-month-olds in immediate and deferred tests. *Child Development, 59*, 217–225.

Meltzoff, A. (1988b). Infant imitation after a one week delay: Long-term memory for novel acts and multiple stimuli. *Developmental Psychology, 24*, 470–476.

Meltzoff, A., & Gopnik, A. (1993). The role of imitation in understanding persons and developing a theory of mind. In S. Baron-Cohen, H. Tager-Flusberg, & D. Cohen (Eds.), *Understanding other minds* (pp. 335–366). Oxford, England: Oxford University Press.

Moore, C., & Corkum, V. (in press). Social understanding at the end of the first year of life. *Developmental Review.*

Nelson, K., & Lucariello, J. (1985). The development of meaning in first words. In M. Barrett (Ed.), *Children's single-word speech* (pp. 59–86). New York: Wiley.

Neisser, U. (1991). Two perceptually given aspects of the self and its development. *Developmental Review, 11*, 197–209.

Newman, D. (1986). The role of mutual knowledge in the development of perspective-taking. *Developmental Review*, 6, 122–145.

Ninio, A., & Bruner, J. (1978). The antecedents of labelling. *Journal of Child Language*, 5, 1–16.

Piaget, J. (1952). *The origins of intelligence in children*. New York: Norton.

Powers, W. (1973). *Behavior: The control of perception*. Chicago: Aldine-Atherton.

Rochat, P. (1993). Connaissance de soi chez le bébé. *Psychologie Française*, 38, 41–51.

Savage-Rumbaugh, S., McDonald, K., Sevcik, R., Hopkins, W., & Rupert, E. (1986). Spontaneous symbol acquisition and communicative use by pygmy chimpanzee (*Pan paniscus*). *Journal of Experimental Psychology: General*, 115, 211–235.

Scaife, M., & Bruner, J. (1975). The capacity for joint visual attention in the infant. *Nature*, 253, 265–266.

Sodian, B., Taylor, C., Harris, P., & Perner, J. (1991). Early deception and the child's theory of mind: False trails and genuine markers. *Child Development*, 62, 468–483.

Talmy, L. (1993). *The windowing of attention in language*. Unpublished manuscript.

Tomasello, M. (1988). The role of joint attention in early language development. *Language Sciences*, 11, 69–88.

Tomasello, M. (1990). Cultural transmission in the tool use and communicatory signaling of chimpanzees? In S. Parker & K. Gibson (Eds.), *Language and intelligence in monkeys and apes: Comparative developmental perspectives* (pp. 274–311). Cambridge, England: Cambridge University Press.

Tomasello, M. (1992). The social bases of language acquisition. *Social Development*, 1, 67–87.

Tomasello, M. (1993). The interpersonal origins of self-concept. In U. Neisser (Ed.), *Ecological and interpersonal aspects of self-knowledge*. Cambridge, England: Cambridge University Press.

Tomasello, M., & Barton, M. (1994). Learning words in nonostensive contexts. *Developmental Psychology*, 30, 639–650.

Tomasello, M., & Farrar, J. (1986). Joint attention and early language. *Child Development*, 57, 1454–1463.

Tomasello, M., Farrar, J., & Dines, J. (1983). Young children's speech revisions for a familiar and an unfamiliar adult. *Journal of Speech and Hearing Research*, 27, 359–363.

Tomasello, M., & Kruger, A. (1992). Joint attention on actions: Acquiring verbs in ostensive and nonostensive contexts. *Journal of Child Language*, 19, 311–333.

Tomasello, M., Kruger, A. C., & Ratner, H. H. (1993). Cultural learning. *Behavioral and Brain Sciences*, 16, 495–552.

Tomasello, M., Mannle, S., & Kruger, A. C. (1986). Linguistic environment of 1- to 2-year-old twins. *Developmental Psychology*, 22, 169–176.

Tomasello, M., Savage-Rumbaugh, S., & Kruger, A. C. (1993). Imitative learning of actions on objects by children, chimpanzees, and enculturated chimpanzees. *Child Development*, 64, 1688–1705.

Tomasello, M., & Todd, J. (1983). Joint attention and early lexical acquisition style. *First Language*, 4, 197–212.

Trevarthen, C. (1979). Instincts for human understanding and for cultural cooperation: Development in infancy. In M. von Cranach, K. Foppa, W. Lepenies, & D. Ploog (Eds.), *Human ethology: Claims and limits of a new discipline* (pp. 530–571). Cambridge, England: Cambridge University Press.

Trevarthen, C. (1993). Predispositions to cultural learning in young infants. *Behavioral and Brain Sciences*, 16, 534–535.

Uzgiris, I. (1989). The links between imitation and social referencing. In S. Feinman (Ed.), *Social referencing and the social construction of reality* (pp. 143–167). New York: Plenum.

Walden, T., & Ogan, T. (1988). The development of social referencing. *Child Development*, 59, 1230–1240.

Wellman, H. (1993). Early understanding of mind: The normal case. In S. Baron-Cohen, H. Tager-Flusberg, & D. Cohen (Eds.), *Understanding other minds* (pp. 10–39). Oxford, England: Oxford University Press.

Wittgenstein, L. (1953). *Philosophical investigations.* New York: Macmillan.

Chapter 7

Understanding the Link Between Joint Attention and Language

Dare A. Baldwin
University of Oregon

Some time ago, Bruner and his colleagues (1978, 1983; Scaife & Bruner, 1975) pointed out that joint attention plays a crucial role in children's acquisition of language. They argued that one of the primary tasks in language learning is for the child to link words and sentences with the correct objects, events, or properties in the world, and that mechanisms promoting joint attention between parent and child must certainly facilitate this mapping process. Clear empirical support can be found for this view. Parents readily provide attentional cues such as line-of-regard and gestures while speaking (e.g., Messer, 1983), and infants are able to make use of such cues from a relatively early age: They follow line-of-regard and pointing gestures to nearby objects by roughly 9–12 months (Butterworth, 1991; Butterworth & Jarrett, 1991; Corkum & Moore, 1992, this volume; Murphy & Messer, 1977; Scaife & Bruner, 1975). Further, when parents are more cooperative with respect to joint attention—they follow in on infants' own focus of attention when providing language—infants' vocabulary acquisition proceeds at a faster pace (e.g., Akhtar, Dunham, & Dunham, 1991; Dunham, Dunham, & Curwin, in press; Harris, Jones, Brookes, & Grant, 1986; Tomasello & Farrar, 1986). There is then every reason to agree with the essentials of this analysis: Mechanisms that serve joint attention enable parents and infants to achieve the social coordination necessary for language learning. But I would argue that something important is missing, or at least underemphasized, in this view. While it is clear that joint attention is critical to language learning, even more critical is what infants understand about the joint attention enterprise and especially, what they understand about its relevance to language. In other words, being aware that attention on some external thing is shared and understanding the significance of such intersubjectivity for communication would make all the difference for expediting language acquisition, and for that matter, any other kind of learning that is social in kind. What follows is an elaboration of this point, the result of which is twofold: a new understanding of some of the facts concerning early language learning, and a new approach to investigating the ontogeny of intersubjective understanding.

JOINT ATTENTION VERSUS INTERSUBJECTIVE UNDERSTANDING

Technically speaking, joint attention simply means the simultaneous engagement of two or more individuals in mental focus on one and the same external thing. Put this way, joint attention is likely a ubiquitous occurrence for all organisms that boast a complex central nervous system. For instance, two bushbabies, alerted by a predator's call, are caught in an instant of joint attention prior to pursuing their separate avenues of escape. Or to take a human case, perhaps you and I once unwittingly happened to watch "Dr. Strangelove" on the same night in the same time zone, thereby satisfying the criteria for joint attention. Clearly, this notion of simultaneous engagement fails to capture something central to our experience—the aspect of intersubjective awareness that accompanies joint attention, the recognition that mental focus on some external thing is shared. And of course, it is just this aspect of the joint attention experience—intersubjective awareness—that makes simultaneous engagement with some third party of such social value to us. It is because we are aware of simultaneous engagement that we can use it as a springboard for communicative exchange.

If all parties to a given interaction are unable to appreciate when attentional focus is shared, the only value that joint attention holds would be purely incidental. Sometimes organisms can be advantaged simply because similar responses are engendered in several individuals at once, as when a stampede results from several buffalo responding in like manner to the presence of a wolf, with the resultant ruckus in and of itself defeating the wolf's gustatory intentions. However, additional benefits of joint attention accrue even if only one participant possesses a sophisticated ability to assess when mental focus is shared. This would seem an accurate description, for example, of many interactions between adult humans and most other species. While we are reluctant to attribute an appreciation of intersubjective awareness to horses, for example, it is nevertheless clear that people can purposefully influence horses' thoughts, feelings, and behavior. Influence of this kind is part of what is implied by the term "training." Some aspects of training seem to be accomplished by virtue of our ability to appreciate, at least tacitly, what horses attend to, and how to influence a horse's mental focus. But the asymmetry in understanding that seems to hold between ourselves and horses places serious limits on the range of possibilities for social and communicative exchange. The party who lacks understanding plays no role in helping to coordinate shared attention, and hence opportunities for communicative exchange are more difficult to achieve and are noticeably one-sided. Further, the ignorant party cannot be regarded as either receptive to or even interested in communicative exchange, per se. Without an ability to appreciate that attentional focus is shared, there can be no recognition that communicative exchange is occurring.

Many theorists have suggested that, at some early point in development, human infants lack intersubjective awareness just as we suspect that horses and many other species do (e.g., Barresi & Moore, in press; Butterworth, 1991; Perner, 1991; Tomasello, this volume; Tomasello, Kruger, & Ratner, 1993). If so, the emergence of such awareness should have profound implications for the quality of their social interaction in general (Tomasello et al., 1993), and especially for their acquisition of language. Below I briefly review evidence that speaks to this question, and then turn to a description of my own recent attempts to fill in some of the remaining gaps in our understanding of the ontogeny of intersubjective awareness.

EXISTING EVIDENCE REGARDING EARLY INTERSUBJECTIVE UNDERSTANDING

Infants' Comprehension of Attentional Cues

As I mentioned earlier, we have known for some time that infants show some sensitivity to the attentional focus of others by their second year; they follow another's line of regard if they happen to notice that the other is looking elsewhere and they will follow pointing gestures to nearby objects. Yet these facts alone do not clarify whether infants possess an intersubjective appreciation of shared attention. An alternative possibility, endorsed by several others (e.g., Butterworth, 1991; Moore & Corkum, in press; Perner, 1991), is that infants follow line of regard and pointing gestures only because they have learned the predictive value of roving eyes and jabbing fingers. That is, such actions on others' part tend to be good predictors of interesting visual experiences and they also tend to predict the direction and target of others' subsequent actions. An understanding of predictiveness is not the same thing as intersubjective awareness. Appreciating such predictability could in principle lead infants to follow others' attentional cues without any awareness that following such cues results in shared attentional focus.

Infants' Production of Intentional Signals

There has been some inclination to interpret infants' communicative productions, via word or gesture, as evidence for intersubjective awareness (e.g., Baron-Cohen, 1991; Bretherton, 1991; Bretherton, McNew, & Beeghly-Smith, 1981).

Recognizable words (e.g., *Daddy, banana, ball*) and gestures (e.g., points, reaches, arms raised to request a lift up) start to be produced by many infants between 12 and 14 months (e.g., Bates, Benigni, Bretherton, Camaioni, & Volterra, 1977; Benedict, 1979; Bloom, 1973; Leung & Rheingold, 1981). But the mere fact that infants comprehend and produce gestures and words is not sufficient to clarify whether they appreciate that shared mental focus underlies their own or others' comprehension (e.g., Shatz, 1983). Along these lines, Lempert and Kinsbourne (1985) argued that infants' pointing gestures merely index their own shifting focus of attention, and are not actually communicative in nature. A similar argument could be constructed regarding infants' linguistic productions. They may produce object names, for example, as a result of having noticed the relevant object themselves rather than because they are trying to direct another's attention to that object. Even in cases where infants' language seems more clearly communicative, a lower level understanding may be operating. For instance, an infant who produces an utterance such as "Cheerio!" may not think beyond the fact that this vocalization fairly reliably elicits Cheerios from adults. To be fair, however, infants show some signs that they are doing more than just offering up their words and gestures without regard to the way these signals are received by others (e.g., Bretherton, 1991; Wellman, 1993). For example, there are an- ecdotal reports that infants of 14 months and older often glance back toward a parent immediately after producing a point (e.g., Bates et al., 1977). This kind of checking suggests some understanding that points can be regarded as successful only if the addressee ultimately orients attention toward the desired object. If we could be confident that this is indeed the source of infants' looks, such checking would clearly indicate an awareness of the significance of joint attention for communicative exchange. There are low level alternatives, however. Infants may check only because they expect a reaction from a parent following their point—a kind of anticipatory looking that infants are known to show in other sequence-learning contexts (e.g., Clohessy, Posner, & Rothbart, 1992; Haith, Hazan, & Goodman, 1988) that need not involve an underlying awareness of attentional focus. Or along the lines suggested earlier regarding gaze following more generally, infants may simply have learned that a person's line-of-regard predicts the target of his or her subsequent action.

Coordination in Parent-Infant Interaction

Another thread of evidence concerning the possibility of early intersubjective understanding stems from microanalytic observation of parent-infant interaction. Trevarthen and his colleagues (1977, 1980; Trevarthen & Hubley, 1978) have argued that even from birth infants are capable of "primary intersubjectivity," by which they mean an appreciation for the mutual engagement that occurs during highly regulated, harmonious interactions with caregivers. Infants' differ- ential emotional and behavioral response to people versus inanimate objects and their obvious distress at abrupt changes in parental behavior were taken as evidence for primary intersubjectivity. However, in their view it is not until infants reach about 9–12 months of age that they begin to show "secondary intersubjectivity"—the ability to recognize the mutuality inherent in joint attention on objects external to the participants in the interaction. It is this more advanced level of intersubjective understanding in Trevarthen's scheme with which I am concerned here; the ability to appreciate that mental focus on some external thing is shared with another. Signs of secondary intersubjectivity were inferred from the fact that infants of this age spontaneously initiate highly cooperative behavior, and show predictable emotional responses to others' object-directed actions. Examples include cases of accepting an object from a parent, smiling up at a parent after handling an object, showing or offering an object to the parent accompanied by a smile, or watching a parent's action on a toy with pleased anticipation, and then repeating the same maneuver when the toy is offered.

While Trevarthen's analysis is intuitively persuasive, there is reason to question whether infants' emotional responses in dynamic interaction supply definitive evidence for this kind of intersubjective awareness (Hobson, 1993). First, it is possible that the emotional responses that infants show have more to do with their enjoyment in controlling or predicting the parent's behavior than with an appreciation for the mutuality of focus per se. And infants' tendency to initiate and take pleasure in coordinated play with a parent (e.g., Bakeman & Adamson, 1984) may reflect their growing ability to coordinate their own actions with those of others via an understanding of means–ends relations, without any real accompanying understanding of the joint mental focus that underlies such complementary activity.

Social Referencing

Social referencing—the ability to use another's emotional display to guide one's own response to something novel—has been interpreted as another source of evidence concerning early intersubjectivity. The social referencing phenomenon is this: When infants as young as 8 to 12 months of age encounter a new person, object, or event, they will sometimes look toward a parent and subsequently respond to the novel circumstance in accord with the affective expression that the parent displays (e.g., Klinnert, 1984; Sorce, Emde, Campos, & Klinnert, 1985). For example, upon being approached by a remote control spider, an infant whose parent appears fearful will hesitate to approach the toy, whereas he or she will approach more readily and play more freely if the parent looks happy (Zarbatany & Lamb, 1985). Bretherton (e.g., Bretherton, 1984, 1991) in particular has argued that social referencing implies that infants as young as 12 months appreciate the existence of mental life in others and have skills for "interfacing" with other minds. The idea is that infants' tendency to consult others for emotional information regarding some external thing indicates that they recognize that emotions concerning third parties can be communicated or shared between people. If so, this would imply intersubjective understanding.

At present, however, the evidence regarding social referencing has not been detailed enough to provide definitive support for this analysis. One difficulty is that observations of social referencing have not made clear whether infants are purposefully seeking emotional information from another. The existing evidence on this point is problematic in two major respects. First, careful examination of the available data reveals that, contrary to widespread belief, infants frequently fail to look toward a parent before approaching the novel object or person (e.g., Walden & Ogan, 1988), and, when such spontaneous looks do occur, they are often either just a brief glance that does not include a look to the parent's face, or they seem to reflect a desire to share affect with the parent, rather than a desire to seek affective information to resolve uncertainty (e.g., Hornik & Gunnar, 1988). Second, spontaneous looks to the parent that might appear to indicate information-seeking, an endeavor hinging on intersubjective understanding, may well represent something considerably simpler and nonintersubjective. A low level alternative is that infants simply look to a parent to reassure themselves when feeling hesitant or threatened. This would carry no necessary implication of intersubjective understanding. Infants could simply look toward the parent due to a wish to gain comfort or to reassure themselves as to the parent's presence without appreciating that the parent might supply information regarding the object that is engendering uncertainty. (See Baldwin & Moses, 1994, for a review elaborating these, and related, considerations.)

In fact, several findings in the social referencing literature are consistent with this comfort-seeking interpretation. For instance, Dickstein, Thompson, Estes, Malkin, and Lamb (1984) found that infants' rate of referencing was negatively related to their proximity to the mother: The further infants were from the mother, the more frequently they looked in her direction. The authors themselves suggest comfort or reassurance seeking as a better way of interpreting infants' referencing looks "because proximity-seeking and referencing are alternative strategies for checking back with mothers in uncertain situations: Infants may use either a distal mode (i.e., referencing) or a proximal mode (i.e., approach) for reassurance" (p. 514). Further, in some studies infants have shown a higher frequency of looks to the parent when the parent displayed fear relative to when the parent displayed pleasure (e.g., Zarbatany & Lamb, 1985). Reassurance seeking makes sense of this pattern: Perhaps a display of fear leads infants to feel more threatened, leaving them more in need of reassurance and hence increasing their level of looks to the parent. Finally, social referencing studies differ considerably in the frequency of referencing that has been observed. In some cases, 100% of infants apparently spontaneously looked toward the parent following a look to the toy at some point during the session (Walden & Ogan, 1988); other studies using stricter criteria for crediting looks as referencing looks found that only a very small proportion of infants showed a prototypical referencing pattern (e.g., only 7% did so in Hornik & Gunnar, 1988). Studies reporting high rates of referencing have at least one thing in common: The object infants encountered was especially threatening—a visual cliff with a sizable drop off (Sorce, Emde, Campos, & Klinnert, 1985), or a remote control toy such as a robot or a spider that approached infants from across the room (e.g., Camras & Sachs, 1991; Klinnert, 1984; Walden & Ogan, 1988; Zarbatany & Lamb, 1985). Although the standard interpretation is that these stimuli elicit referencing because they are highly ambiguous and hence provoke infants to seek information to resolve uncertainty, it is also possible that these stimuli are perceived not as ambiguous but as threatening, and this leads infants to look to the parent for comfort rather than for information about the object. Until it is certain that this comfort-seeking alternative does not fully account for infants' social referencing, it will not be clear that true information seeking is occurring, and hence intersubjective understanding remains in question.

Another problem in taking social referencing as evidence for intersubjective understanding arises as well. It is unclear whether social referencing is indeed occurring, in the full sense of the term. It is possible that infants are receptive to a parent's emotion and influenced by it without actually understanding the referential quality of that emotion. That is, infants may not realize that the emotion refers to the specific object at hand. There are actually two issues to be dealt with in resolving this issue of referential understanding. Specificity is one. Do infants link the adult's emotional signal with a specific object or person, or does the affective display also affect infants' behavior toward objects other than that to which the adult intended to refer? If the latter, then a simple mood-modification mechanism could account for infants' responsiveness to adults' emotional displays. Two studies suggest that infants indeed show some degree of specificity in their use of adults' affective signals. In a study by Hornik, Risenhoover, and Gunnar (1987), infants of 12 and 18 months were shown a novel object toward which a parent displayed positive, negative, or neutral affect. Infants were later given the opportunity to play with the toy in a room littered with other toys. Contrary to the mood contagion hypothesis, Hornik et al. found that, although infants' behavior toward the target toy was influenced by parental affect, their behavior toward the other toys was unaffected. Moreover, this selective effect on infants' toy play persisted over time, even though parents displayed only neutral affect at the time of later assessment. Similarly, in a study by Walden and Ogan (1988), 6- to 22-month-old infants' responses to two toys were examined after positive parental affect had been directed at one and negative affect at the other. Walden and Ogan found that the time infants spent contacting each toy during a subsequent free-play period, when both toys were simultaneously available, was differentially related to the affect that had been directed earlier at each toy. And this was so despite the fact that no affective signaling was concurrently provided by parents at the time infants' responses were measured. Infants' differential responding in this subsequent play situation indicates that they registered a link between the parent's emotional display and a specific object, and maintained that link as a guide to their subsequent interactions with that object.

Evidence for such specificity cannot by itself resolve the issue of interest here, however. For social referencing to qualify as evidence for intersubjective understanding, it is critical to show that infants appreciate the referential intention underlying the adult's display of affect. That is, if infants truly comprehend the referential import of emotional signals, then they should realize that the individual displaying affect is the one who specifies the target of that affect, and that the individual's focus of attention is relevant for determining the specific referent of the affect. Although the findings of Hornik et al. (1987) and Walden and Ogan (1988) show that infants use parental affect in a specific way, they do not clarify whether a true appreciation of referential intent is present because, in those studies, infants were almost certainly already attending to the target object when parents provided the affective information. Hence infants could simply apply parental affect to the target object without considering the parent's focus of attention at all. Consequently, these studies do not tell us whether infants appreciate that parental affect might refer to something other than whatever happens to be at the center of their own attention. For example, an infant might respond warily to a stranger in accord with his mother's expression of worry not because he appreciates that the mother's attentional focus suggests that her expression relates to that person, but only because he himself happened to be preoccupied with that person when the mother's affect was glimpsed. The question is: Are infants sensitive to whether the person displaying emotion is concerned with or focused upon the same thing with which infants themselves are engaged? Until there is reason to believe that infants indeed appreciate that the other's attentional focus is relevant to interpreting the emotion displayed, there is no surety that the so-called social referencing phenomenon trades on intersubjective understanding.

Imitation

Infants' precocious imitation abilities have provided another source of speculation concerning early intersubjective awareness. Newborns imitate facial expressions (e.g., Meltzoff & Moore, 1989) and by at least 9 months infants will imitate another's actions on a novel object even after substantial delays such as a day or a week (e.g., Meltzoff, 1988a, 1988b). Meltzoff and Gopnik (1993; Gopnik & Meltzoff, 1994) suggest that such imitation abilities imply that infants perceive others as similar to self, and in this sense are aware of what is interpersonal or shared in an imitative interaction (see also Hay, Stimson, & Castle, 1991). However, this in itself does not clarify whether infants recognize what is mutual or shared when they and another are jointly focused on some external thing, which is the aspect of intersubjectivity at issue here. Nor does the deferred imitation of actions on objects illuminate this specific question. Infants might watch another's object-oriented actions and later reproduce them, without any awareness that the earlier shared focus on that object enabled them to acquire this new skill.

Summary

This review of existing evidence yields a suggestive but inconclusive picture: There are numerous hints that infants of 9–12 months and older have some awareness of others' mental focus and recognize when focus is shared, but the case for this has been far from compelling. Moreover, little information of any kind has been available to clarify whether infants take an active part in coordinating shared focus specifically for the purpose of facilitating communication. And of course it is this ability that is particularly relevant for language learning. This observation points to a different strategy of investigation: Given that intersubjectivity would profoundly influence the form that language learning could take, early language should show telltale traces of this understanding. Perhaps in this way language learning can serve as a tightly focused lens through which to view infants' level of intersubjective understanding.

LANGUAGE LEARNING AS A WINDOW ON EARLY INTERSUBJECTIVE UNDERSTANDING

Consider what would occur if infants lacked an understanding of attention and of the significance of shared attention. This limitation would not entirely stymie language learning, provided that infants were fortunate enough to interact with others who possess a sophisticated appreciation for joint attention. In other words, adults could orchestrate joint attentional experiences in such a way as to make links between language and the world transparent for infants, thereby enabling language learning to begin even were infants themselves to lack an appreciation for this process. But this state of affairs would leave infants highly dependent on adults in their acquisition of language. Establishing correct linkages between words and things in the world would hinge on whether the word being presented happened to match what infants were concurrently focused upon, and this would occur with regularity only if adults were painstakingly adapting the timing of their speech to infants' focus. In other words, a new word would be acquired because temporal contiguity between that word and the infant's focus on something in the external world engendered an associative link. At bottom, then, infants would learn language via a simple process of detecting co-occurrences between words and things out in the world. Adults' assistance in coordinating utterances with infants' focus, and infants' ability to follow adults' cues, would merely facilitate the covariation detection process. The question, then, is whether this is an accurate description of infants' abilities (or lack thereof) and of the process of early language learning.

As it turns out, there is good reason, on both logical and empirical grounds, to doubt this model of infants as nothing more than covariation detectors where language learning is concerned. To see this, one must consider the full implications of the covariation detection model of infants' approach to language. A covariation detector simply attempts to sort out which experiences in the world co-occur with which other experiences. And of course words co-occur with many things other than the specific external things to which they refer in the adult language. For instance, words co-occur with gestures, sounds of various kinds, even the presence of walls and ceilings. Likewise, other things than language covary with objects—sounds (e.g., barking sounds covary with dogs), gestures, and, again, walls and ceilings, among others. It is not clear how a pure covariation detector could ever sort out which co-occurrences are worth attending to and carry meaning, and which do not. This is a point made eloquently by Macnamara (1982), leading him to conclude that "it would be hopeless if the child took speech as nothing more than noisy behavior" (p. 171).

There is now some evidence suggesting that infants have abilities that help them to circumvent this logical problem plaguing simple covariation detection. In particular, even in the early phases of language learning infants apparently accord language, or at least language-like sounds, some special status as covariates. For example, Markman and I (Baldwin & Markman, 1989) found that 10- to 14-month-old infants attend longer to novel objects if a nearby adult talks about those objects as opposed to standing by silently. Infants might have shown increased attention to the speaker as a result of orienting to the source of the sound. Yet instead, they showed increases in attention to the novel object, not to the speaker, as if they expected the language to bear some relation to that object. Another study showed further that language facilitated infants' attention to a novel object over and above what pointing alone could accomplish, despite the fact that pointing is known to be a powerful technique for directing infants' attention. Finally, an additional finding was that language enhanced infants' attention only to the object pointed out; their attention to other nearby candidates was not increased. This suggests that infants interpreted the language as concerned with the specific object that was indicated at the time the utterance was produced, and for this reason showed sustained attention toward the object remarked upon.

It seems that infants are primed to treat language as relevant to things out in the world, and consequently show increased engagement with a novel object when language is provided. Thus, infants depart from the profile of a simple covariation detector in two respects. First, language-like sounds have some special status as covariates for infants (see Roberts, 1993, for a comparison of language sounds to other complex auditory stimuli). Second, infants seem to have some starting expectations about which things in the immediate surround are likely to be the relevant covariates for language. Objects that are salient or indicated by the speaker receive increased attention, while the speaker or other things in the setting do not.

These two additions to simple covariation detection ought to prime infants to register and establish correct word–world linkages. They need not incessantly make the error of noting the covariation between word and speaker with each new word, for example. Instead, infants would be predisposed to connect words with the things out in the world that seem relevant. Of course, these abilities might not be grounded in any particular knowledge about joint attention or intersubjectivity. Infants may simply have basic propensities to relate language-like sounds with things in the world, without appreciating that the attentional focus they share with the speaker is what warrants establishing a relation between word and object. In other words, infants might simply be "suped up" covariation detectors. If so, however, then they will remain susceptible to certain predictable difficulties in language learning. This is because covariation information in adults' speech to children remains fairly noisy even when infants realize that words should be related to external objects (see Gleitman, 1990, and Bloom, in press, for a similar point). Adults do not make a practice of talking about everything in sight on every occasion, so things are often within infants' view without mention of their corresponding labels. When adults do comment on the things that are in the immediate context, such comments may or may not include a label for the particular object or objects involved. Moreover, labels are not infrequently uttered when the objects they correspond to are absent, even in speech to children. And even if a label is provided for an object that is present, children often are focused on an entirely different object at the time of labeling. Finally, things tend to have more than one label.

It is easy to see that these properties of adult language would all undermine a simple process of covariation detection and, at the very least, make covariation detection a lengthy, error-ridden process involving the filtering out of a considerable level of noise over an extended period. Thus, to the extent that children's learning appears robust in the face of such noise in the input, a covariation detection model of infants' abilities, even one augmented by a tendency to accord language special status as a covariate, loses plausibility. In some cases, as will become apparent later, the ability to deal with noisy input on infants' part would seem to implicate some degree of intersubjective understanding. I now turn to an overview of work that has recently examined just this set of issues.

Infants' Ability to Deal With Labeling Decoupled From Joint Attention

Take the case, mentioned previously, where infants hear a word just when they happen to be focused on an incorrect object: This could occur anytime they happen to be playing with toys while a television or radio blares nearby, or when an adult is engaged in a telephone conversation. Figure 7.1 provides a graphic example.

FIG. 7.1. A scenario in which labeling is decoupled from joint attention.

From the perspective of covariation detection, a word (e.g., *mastodon*) uttered by an adult engaged in a phone conversation might covary with the infant's focus on an incorrect novel object (e.g., a bear) and the resultant link would carry the same status as any other word–object pairing. Hence an error would have entered the infant's system, to be eradicated over time only if the infant were later exposed to other occurrences of that word and that object with their appropriate partners. Adult learners would not be prone to this error, of course, and this is because adults appreciate that the speaker's focus of attention provides a critical source of information regarding the reference of the utterance. We are nonegocentric enough to realize that the utterances of television commentators and telephone conversationalists are unlikely to be relevant to the object of our own focus if we happen to be focused elsewhere. So if infants share any part of this adult-level understanding about the significance of the speaker's focus of attention, they too could avoid the errors predicted by the simple covariation detection approach.

To test this possibility, my colleagues and I (Baldwin et al., 1994) presented 16 infants of 18–20 months with a novel label in just this kind of situation. Infants were focused on a novel toy (e.g., a hand-held plastic telescope) when they heard the new label (e.g., "A *modi!*"), but the label was uttered by someone whose focus was elsewhere; in this case, the speaker was seated out of infants' view, behind a sound-conducting rice-paper screen. In this situation, called the decoupled condition, labeling was decoupled from joint attention, but the new label nevertheless covaried with infants' focus on a novel toy, which, on a covariation detection model, should promote a link between word and object. But if infants appreciate the importance of the speaker's focus of attention, they might regard the new label as irrelevant to the toy they were focused on at the time of labeling. As a basis for comparison, each infant also heard a different novel label (e.g., "A *dawnoo!*") uttered by a speaker who was sitting in view and engaged in joint focus with infants on a different novel object (e.g., a pair of miniature folding plastic binoculars). In this situation (the coupled condition), where labeling was coupled with joint attention, infants should regard the label as relevant to the novel object and hence register the mapping between word and object. In each condition infants heard the new label just three times in the format described and then they were asked comprehension questions about the new label.

The pattern of infants' answers to the comprehension questions across the two conditions should be telling regarding infants' level of understanding about the significance of joint attention to language. If infants are operating as simple covariation detectors, their comprehension responses should show that they have established a new word–object mapping in both the coupled and decoupled conditions given that in both cases they were focused on the novel object at the time the label was heard. In contrast, if infants understand about the speaker's focus of attention they should be more likely to establish a mapping in the coupled condition than in the decoupled condition. As can be seen in Figure 7.2, the findings fit the latter prediction: Infants selected the correct toy at above chance levels on comprehension questions in the coupled condition, but responded randomly to comprehension questions in the decoupled condition. Although covariation detection alone would have led infants to be equally likely to register word–object links in both conditions, infants seemed to regard labeling that was decoupled from joint attention as less noteworthy than labeling occurring within a joint attention context. This suggests that infants are indeed sensitized to the presence or absence of joint attention, and use it as a guide to establishing new word–object mappings. The implication here is that infants have some minimal awareness of joint attention, at least by 18–20 months, and that they recognize that joint attention is relevant to language. At least some glimmer of intersubjective understanding, an appreciation for the jointness of joint attention, has been gained.

Dealing With Discrepant Labeling

Perhaps, though, infants' intersubjective understanding at this early age is still quite superficial and limited. While capable of noting the occurrence of joint attention, infants may simply have a propensity to become more aroused, and

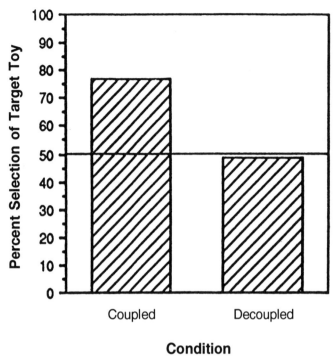

Condition

FIG. 7.2. Infants' mean percent selection of the target toy in response to comprehension questions.

hence to attend more, when they are engaged with another in joint focus, an infantile form of the infamous Hawthorne effect. The enhanced attention resulting from shared focus might be responsible for their greater ability to register word–object links in the coupled condition relative to the decoupled condition. It is possible, then, that infants of 18–20 months do not yet have any real understanding about the significance of shared attentional focus as a conduit for communicative exchange. If so, is this problematic for them in any way? Would anything be gained from a more advanced understanding? For one, a more sophisticated appreciation for the significance of shared focus would lead infants to spontaneously monitor others' attentional focus when communicative exchanges occur, and to seek shared focus in an active way when exchanges begin in the absence of shared focus. Such an ability would be especially helpful to infants in avoiding errors that would otherwise occur in cases of discrepant labeling; when a parent happens to provide a novel label at a time when the infant is focused on something other than a correct referent. In Figure 7.3, for example, a baby's attention is momentarily diverted to a gecko that is out of the parent's view, while the parent is labeling the rooster on which the baby's attention had been focused only a moment before.

FIG. 7.3. A scenario in which labeling occurs during discrepant focus.

The danger here, then, is that the baby will mistakenly link the term rooster with the gecko. The fact is that infants' attention is very mercurial, so such discrepancies cannot help but frequently occur (Collis, 1977; Harris, Jones, & Grant, 1983). The question is whether infants have any ability to deal with these discrepancies. If they realize that the speaker's focus of attention supplies information about the target of his or her utterance, then they would respond to discrepant labeling by looking toward the speaker, following his or her focus, and linking the utterance with the correct object. By actively gathering information about the others' attentional focus, and using that information to guide the interpretation of the new word they can avoid a mapping error, despite the fact that they were focused on an incorrect object at the time the new word was actually heard.

Based on some recent evidence, this too seems to be within 18-month-olds' abilities. Across two different studies (Baldwin, 1991, 1993a), I found that when infants of this age were faced with discrepant labeling—a new label was uttered just at the time infants were looking at an incorrect object—they spontaneously checked the speaker's focus, followed her line-of-regard, and linked the new label with the object of the speaker's focus. Figure 7.4 displays the results for the comprehension test that came immediately after infants had heard a new label in a discrepant labeling situation. The results are combined across the two studies, as the procedures were essentially the same. What is reported here is the percent of infants who met a criterion of consistently picking the same toy in response to comprehension questions. The criterion was either three or four selections of that toy in response to a total of four questions. Of interest is how often infants steadily selected the correct toy, the toy the speaker was focused on during labeling, as opposed to the incorrect toy, the toy the infant was actually looking at when the label was heard.

Without an understanding of the relevance of the speaker's attentional focus, we would expect to see many mapping errors. Instead, mapping errors scarcely occurred at all. Rather, the majority of infants established a firm mapping between the new word and the correct toy, the toy of the speaker's focus. This finding—that 18-month-olds do not make mapping errors when labeling occurs in the context of attentional discrepancies—has recently been corroborated in a study by other researchers (Dunham & Dunham, 1992).

So it seems that by 18 months infants have some appreciation for the necessity of shared attentional focus when interpreting another's utterance. When discrepancies of focus occur, infants themselves take trouble to coordinate attentional focus in the service of discovering the speaker's reference. They are not

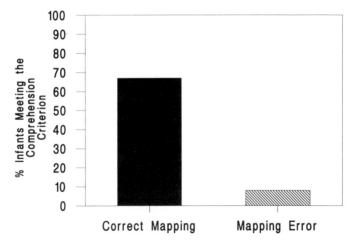

FIG. 7.4. Percent of infants meeting the comprehension test criterion for a correct mapping versus for a mapping error after discrepant labeling.

only sensitized to the occurrence of joint focus, but appreciate its import for language and communicative exchange. This level of understanding has important implications for language learning: Mapping errors that would otherwise occur can be avoided and infants have many additional opportunities for word learning given that by observing others they can search out the speaker's intended referent to establish new mappings.

What of the development of this ability to actively coordinate joint focus in the service of communication? Infants of 14–15 and 16–17 months also participated in the studies just described. Interestingly, at all ages infants spontaneously glanced at the speaker in response to hearing the novel label, and when a discrepancy of focus occurred, they followed the speaker's gaze to the object of her focus. This suggests that even the youngest infants were sensitive to discrepancies in focus and made use of the speaker's attentional cues to coordinate joint focus. However, both of these younger age groups showed random responding to subsequent comprehension questions after discrepant labeling, indicating that, unlike 18- to 19-month-olds, they had not succeeded in establishing a stable link between the new label and the object of the speaker's focus. On the one hand, such unsystematic responding is potentially interesting because it indicates that mapping errors did not occur, errors that would be expected on a simple model of covariation detection. On the other hand, it is difficult to draw strong conclusions based on such random performance. This is especially true for the youngest age group—the 14- to 15-month-olds. These infants showed random responding to comprehension questions not only after discrepant labeling, but even when a label was presented in the context of joint focus. Little can therefore be made of such generally unsystematic behavior. The 16- to 17-month-olds' performance was somewhat more interpretable: Their comprehension performance showed that they established a firm link between label and object when the label was presented in circumstances of joint focus (as did 18- to 19-month-olds), and hence this middle group's unsystematic performance following discrepant labeling seems noteworthy. However, this pattern yields a number of possible interpretations. A generous reading is that 16- to 17-month-olds realize the significance of the speaker's attentional focus for interpreting her utterance, and her attempt to use it, but that processing capacity limitations make it difficult for them to register and integrate all the information required to achieve a stable link between word and object (e.g., Tomasello & Farrar, 1986). Also possible, however, is that infants of 16–17 months were simply confused or distracted by discrepancies of focus, and for this reason were unable to make sense of new labels uttered during discrepant labeling. If so, this would suggest a less impressive level of understanding.

Distinguishing Referential From Nonreferential Acts

Although the findings do not yield a definitive developmental story, they demonstrate unambiguously that infants of 18 months and older understand the significance that joint attention has for communicative exchange. At this age infants already actively gather information about another's attentional focus in the service of interpreting his or her utterance. Other important questions arise, however. How skilled are infants at judging others' attentional focus? And are they truly concerned with attentional focus, per se, or are they simply responding to actions produced by others that happen to correlate with attentional focus? For example, in the studies just described we found that infants linked a new label with the toy toward which the speaker was looking at the time of labeling. Perhaps, though, infants checked the speaker's face simply as an orienting response to the sound of her utterance, and then her gaze direction (coupled with correlated cues such as body posture and voice direction) merely acted to enhance the salience of one toy over the other for infants, thus prompting them to link the label with the toy of her focus. In other words, infants may not have been consulting the speaker's line-of-regard specifically to ascertain her attentional focus with the purpose of using this information to guide the interpretation of her utterance. Rather, simpler mechanisms of salience may have been the source of their success in the discrepant labeling situation. If so, this falls short of what we mean by intersubjective understanding; infants would be nothing more than "super suped-up" covariation detectors, having a propensity to link language with whatever is salient in the immediate surround, with the speaker's actions and attentional cues being among the factors influencing salience.

As before, we should ask whether the higher level of understanding would have any implications for infants. Indeed it would. In the jungle of everyday interaction, language is overlaid on a complex flow of action, with events occurring rapidly, hands waving, fingers wiggling, eyes darting about, often at an incredible pace. It is not at all unusual for people to be acting on one thing while talking about something completely different. A concrete example, shown graphically in Figure 7.5, is helpful to register this point. Imagine that a father and infant are cleaning up prior to heading for bed. In the midst of picking up toys, the father happens to say "Time for bed!" just as he reaches to grasp a dinosaur. Now of course this utterance does not refer directly to the dinosaur toward which the father's action is directed, and it would be a mistake for the child to map the term bed to the dinosaur.

So, again, the general point is that people's actions quite often coincide with labels only through happenstance. In such cases actions are not intended by the speaker to clarify anything about the reference of an utterance, and should not be taken by an addressee as evidence concerning the speaker's mental focus or referential intent. On the other hand, there are times when people purposely engage in actions that follow from their mental focus and that are intended to clarify the immediate reference of their utterances. Infants would be at a marked advantage if they were able to sort out these two fundamentally different types of scenarios, which I will call referential versus nonreferential acts.

One way to test whether infants can make such a distinction is to present them with a nonreferential situation where a speaker happens to produce sali-

FIG. 7.5. A scenario in which a label is uttered in the context of a nonreferential act: The father's action of grasping the dinosaur coincides with a label only through happenstance.

ence-enhancing actions at the time of labeling, but the speaker's attentional focus does not correspond to the object targeted by these actions. If we find that infants disregard the salience-enhancing actions and persist in using the speaker's attentional focus to interpret utterances, intersubjective understanding would be strongly implicated.

To pursue this possibility, we should ask first how infants might distinguish nonreferential acts, where salience-enhancing action fails to coincide with attentional focus, from referential acts, where action is supplied as a cue to mental focus. Are there any extralinguistic cues that might help to clarify when a speaker intends an utterance to be interpreted as directly referring to the objects acted upon? Unfortunately, little in the way of hard data is available to answer this question. My sense is that there is quite a large variety of cues, and that we are sensitive to concatenations of these cues in our decisions about other people's mental focus and referential intent. Intuition, corroborated by recent evidence from evolutionary psychology (e.g., Baron-Cohen, this volume) suggests that line-of-regard is likely somewhat privileged. If language is produced at the same time that the speaker is manipulating an object, we might be inclined to infer that the utterance refers to that object if the speaker is also looking at it, whereas the action of manipulating may be viewed as nonreferential if it is unaccompanied by gaze toward the object involved. The question, then, is whether infants would have similar intuitions.

I should briefly explain the overall strategy I have used to investigate this question (Baldwin, 1993b). In a first study, 16 infants between 19 and 20 months heard a new label that was accompanied by referential action toward a novel toy, the speaker looked at the toy while manipulating the container it was in, and they were tested to determine whether they used the action to guide their interpretation of the new word. Demonstrating this unequivocally required that infants' performance be observed across two experimental conditions: the conflict and coincide conditions that will be explained. Then in a second study a different group of 19- to 20-month-olds heard the novel label, but its presentation was accompanied by *nonreferential action*—manipulating that was unaccompanied by looking. At issue, then, was whether infants would link the new label with the relevant object in the context of referential action, but inhibit such a link when nonreferential action was involved.

Turning to the first of this pair of studies, the goal was to show that infants indeed used the speaker's referential action to guide a new word–object mapping. The alternative—that infants are merely setting up a simple association between a toy they are interested in and a label that happens to be heard—must be ruled out. This in mind, the conflict condition was designed in which a speaker's referential action would conflict with associative information, that is, temporal contiguity.

A group of 19- to 20-month-old infants were given two novel toys to play with for about 60 seconds, then the toys were hidden in opaque containers (infants did not know which object was in which container). The experimenter proceeded to raise the lid of one container, peer in, and provide the novel label (e.g., "It's a *modi*! A *modi*. There's a *modi* in here!"). In other words, referential action was provided at the time of labeling to indicate which toy was being labeled. Then the experimenter turned to the other container, extracted the toy that had not been labeled, and handed it to infants. Finally, after at least 10 seconds had passed, the experimenter extracted the toy that had been labeled from its container and offered it to infants. Thus immediately after hearing the label infants viewed an incorrect object (the first toy), and only after an interval of 10 or more seconds saw the correct object (the second toy), the toy that had earlier been specified via referential action.

To summarize, the point of the conflict condition was to have the speaker's referential action suggest one object as the referent for the novel label (the second toy), while temporal contiguity suggested a different referent (the first toy). The question of interest was whether infants would make use of the speaker's referential action to guide any mapping that they established, in which case they should select the second toy in response to subsequent comprehension questions, or whether temporal contiguity would determine the mapping, in which case they should select the first toy.

For comparison purposes, another group of infants between 19–20 months participated in the coincide condition where temporal contiguity and referential action coincided to specify the same toy as the referent of the speaker's utterance. In this condition, the experimenter peered into one container while uttering the novel label, and then immediately handed infants the toy from that container. Ten or more seconds later, infants were given the toy from the other container. So the only difference between the conflict and coincide conditions was in which toy infants were given first after hearing the novel label. In the coincide condition, the first toy was the correct toy from the point of view of referential action, and it was also the toy that had temporal contiguity operating in its favor. When infants were later asked comprehension questions in the coincide condition, there was every reason to expect them to choose the first toy. The question is how this would compare with the conflict condition: Would infants be any less likely to select the first toy in the conflict condition relative to the coincide condition? They should be, if referential action is what matters to them.

As it turned out, infants linked the label with the toy dictated by referential action across both conditions. In response to comprehension questions following the coincide condition they tended to select the first toy, whereas they tended to select the second toy, not the first toy, in response to comprehension questions following the conflict condition. This pattern indicates that they relied on the speaker's referential action to guide their interpretation of her utterance.

In a second study, a different group of infants had the same scenario in either the conflict or coincide condition with just one difference: The labeling utterance was accompanied by nonreferential action. That is, the experimenter manipulated the lid of one of the buckets while labeling (saying "I'll show you a *modi*! Want to see a *modi*? A *modi*!"), but refrained from looking at the bucket, instead looking in infants' direction. So, from the adult point of view, the experimenter's action on the container just happened to coincide with her utterance, but was nonreferential. At issue, then, was whether infants would establish a link between the label and the object hidden inside the container that was manipulated nonreferentially as they had in the previous study when referential action occurred. It is important to note that infants found the nonreferential action quite salient. When this action was performed, they reliably looked toward the container that was being acted on. This means that infants were looking at the container that nonreferential action was directed toward at the time they heard the new label.

Infants' comprehension performance showed quite a different pattern than what was observed in the previous study, despite the subtle differences in procedure. When labeling accompanied a nonreferential action, infants subsequently showed random selection patterns in response to comprehension questions in both coincide and conflict conditions. As can be seen in Figure 7.6, this stood out in clear contrast to their highly systematic selections in the prior study in which the speaker provided referential action at the time of labeling. The findings

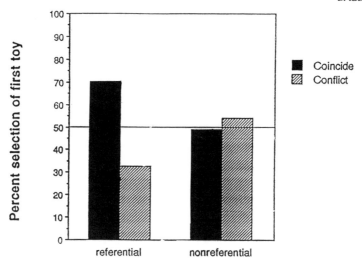

Condition

FIG. 7.6. Infants' mean percent selection of the first toy in response to comprehension questions.

from this research show that, for infants as young as 19 months, some actions are interpreted as indicating focus on and reference to an immediate object, and others are not. A similar demonstration has recently been made with slightly older children in a series of studies by Tomasello and Barton (in press). Infants will link a new label with a novel object only if the speaker shows clearcut signs of referring to that object. What is noteworthy here is that infants are not merely linking new words with the objects made salient by speakers' actions. Instead, they seem to be making inferences concerning another's attentional focus and referential intent based on close observation of how language is overlaid on subtle aspects of behavior. Already infants are treating language as linked with mental life. This is intersubjective understanding in clear relief, and it is being skillfully recruited in the service of language learning.

CONCLUSION

I began by arguing that adult humans have an experience of joint attention that goes beyond the mere fact of simultaneous attentional engagement with another on some external thing. It includes an awareness that focus is shared and an appreciation for what this shared focus makes possible in the form of communicative exchange. This level of intersubjective awareness does not seem to be necessary for learning to occur through social channels, provided a more sophisticated interactive partner is available, but having it greatly expedites the learning process. A brief review of existing evidence failed to clarify definitively whether intersubjective understanding of the kind at issue here is within infants' repertoire. A different empirical strategy—using language learning as a window on intersubjective understanding—has yielded a new body of information. Were infants to lack intersubjective awareness altogether, then from the point of view of language learning they would be covariation detectors, nothing more. Yet a simple covariation detection model of language learning fails on a number of counts, at least for infants of 18–19 months and up. And in each case, only an appreciation for the import of joint attention could supply the advantage needed to account for infants' success. One study showed that infants of 18–20 months do not simply link a label with an object if they happen to hear that label while looking·at the object involved. Instead, they seem to regard shared focus as crucial in justifying the establishment of a new word–object mapping. Another study demonstrated that in cases where 18- to 19-month-olds hear a new label at a time of discrepant focus, they actively gather information to help coordinate attentional focus with the speaker and use this information to help in interpreting the new word. A final series of studies showed that 19- to 20-month-olds do not link labels with objects simply because those objects are made salient by a speaker via action at the time of labeling. On the contrary, infants appear to make relatively subtle judgments concerning the speaker's focus and referential intent and establish new mappings only if attention and referential intent toward the relevant object is perceived. Together, these findings provide a convincing case that older infants are aware of others' attentional focus and appreciate that shared attentional focus is crucial for communicative success.

It is surely not coincidental that such intersubjective understanding is in place at the time in late infancy when linguistic skill blossoms rapidly. At about 18–20 months vocabulary begins to be acquired at an extraordinarily fast pace; new words are learned each and every day and children's productive vocabularies have been known to double within a month's time (e.g., Bloom, Lifter, & Broughton, 1985; Dromi, 1986; Goldfield & Reznick, 1990; Nelson, 1973). At this time children also begin producing multiword utterances (e.g., Nelson, 1973), spontaneously initiating conversations about absent objects (e.g., Sachs, 1983), and they are for the first time relying on language, without accompanying gestures, for communication (e.g., Zinober & Martlew, 1985). It seems improbable that simple covariation detection is responsible for such rapid acquisition, given the pitfalls that I and others have shown to be dotting the path of a learner so ill-equipped to cope with the jungle of human linguistic interaction. It is also difficult to imagine how such sophisticated use of language could occur (e.g., extended conversation concerning absent objects) were infants to lack a basic understanding of the intersubjective nature of language and communicative exchange.

One question to be considered is whether intersubjective understanding arises initially as a specialized ability within the language domain, and only later is extended to guide infants' understanding of other kinds of human interaction, for example, interactions involving the communication of emotions. The literature on language acquisition is replete with discussion concerning the possibility that language may be a developmentally privileged domain, operating under a unique set of learning mechanisms (e.g., Chomsky, 1988), and it is of course possible that intersubjective understanding is among those abilities special to language, at least early on. An alternative possibility is that intersubjective understanding emerges as a general piece of social understanding that infants can recruit to guide knowledge acquisition in the language domain as well as in other domains.

Some evidence that I and my colleagues have recently obtained concerning early social referencing abilities (Baldwin & Moses, in press; Baldwin, Moses, & Tidball, in preparation) favors the latter proposal. Although I argued earlier that existing evidence regarding social referencing fails to speak to intersubjective awareness, it is nevertheless possible to obtain such evidence within the social referencing context. The question is whether infants incorporate information about another's focus of attention in their interpretation of the affect provided. An answer to this question requires observing whether infants can use information about focus of attention to disambiguate the referent of another's emotional message in circumstances where at least two potential referents are available. If infants possess this richer ability then they should be able to figure out the referent even when their own focus of attention differs from that of the other. We found that infants both 12 and 18 months were able to do just that. Specifically, even in cases of discrepant attentional focus they noticed which object was the target of an adult's vocal affect (pleasure or disgust), and behaved toward that object in accord with the quality of the emotion displayed. Interestingly, like others (e.g., Mumme, 1993; Walden & Ogan, 1988), we also found signs of "generalization" of affect. That is, while the adult's emotional message had the greatest influence on infants' behavior toward the toy the adult referred to, it nevertheless also had a clearly detectable impact on their response to the toy that had been ignored by the adult. On the one hand, these generalization findings suggest that mechanisms such as mood modification are partly responsible for infants' responsiveness to adult emotional displays. On the other hand, these findings also indicate that infants of both 12 and 18 months actively coordinate attentional focus to help in interpreting another's emotion if that emotion is produced in the context of discrepant focus. Infants actively consulted cues to the adult's focus of attention, and used them to determine the target of referential intent. Thus even infants as young as 12 months are showing an intersubjective ability in the emotions domain that parallels the abilities we have seen at older ages in the language domain. Clearly, early intersubjective understanding is not confined to the language domain; rather, it seems that language learning is advantaged because infants can capitalize on a general appreciation for the communicative significance of shared focus.

The basic insight provided by the research reported here is that the purest diagnostic for intersubjective understanding is the skill, or lack thereof, shown in acquiring information that is fundamentally social in kind. Language, perhaps the most dazzling of human social skills, has served this diagnostic purpose admirably with infants of 18 months and older. Emotions promise to serve as a more sensitive window on intersubjective abilities at a younger age. Perhaps even more exciting is the possibility that using these techniques in the emotions domain could provide a new source of information regarding the question of intersubjective understanding in other species, a question that is currently undergoing a renaissance of interest and research activity (e.g., Byrne & Whiten, 1986; Cheney & Seyfarth, 1990; Parker & Gibson, 1990; Parker, Mitchell, & Boccia, 1994; Whiten, 1991). Pursuing this question may help us to understand in what ways our own learning abilities diverge from those of even our closest phylogenetic relatives.

REFERENCES

Akhtar, N., Dunham, F., & Dunham, P. J. (1991). Directive interactions and early vocabulary development: The role of joint attentional focus. *Journal of Child Language*, 18, 41–49.

Bakeman, H., & Adamson, L. B. (1984). Coordinating attention to people and objects in mother-infant and peer-infant interaction. *Child Development*, 55, 1278–1289.

Baldwin, D. A. (1991). Infants' contribution to the achievement of joint reference. *Child Development*, 63, 875–890.

Baldwin, D. A. (1993a). Infants' ability to consult the speaker for clues to word reference. *Journal of Child Language*, 20, 395–418.

Baldwin, D. A. (1993b). Early referential understanding: Infants' ability to recognize referential acts for what they are. *Developmental Psychology*, 29, 832–843.

Baldwin, D. A., & Markman, E. M. (1989). Establishing word-object relations: A first step. *Child Development*, 60, 381–398.

Baldwin, D. A., Markman, E. M., Bill, B., Desjardins, R. N., Irwin, J., & Tidball, G. (1994). *Infants' reliance on a social criterion for establishing word-object relations.* Unpublished manuscript, University of Oregon.

Baldwin, D. A., & Moses, L. J. (1993). *The ontogeny of social information-seeking.* Unpublished manuscript, University of Oregon.

Baldwin, D. A., & Moses, L. J. (1994). Early understanding of referential intent and attentional focus: Evidence from language and emotion. In C. Lewis & P. Mitchell (Eds.), *Origins of an understanding of mind* (pp. 133–156). Hillsdale, NJ: Lawrence Erlbaum Associates.

Baldwin, D.A., Moses, L. J., & Tidball, G. (in preparation). *Social referencing versus social receptiveness: Infants' use of others' attentional cues to clarify the reference of emotional displays.*

Baron-Cohen, S. (1991). Precursors to a theory of mind: Understanding attention in others. In A. Whiten (Ed.), *Natural theories of mind: Evolution, development, and simulation of everyday mindreading* (pp. 233–251). Oxford, England: Basil Blackwell.

Barresi, J., & Moore, C. (in press). Intentional relations and social understanding. *Behavioral and Brain Sciences*.

Bates, E., Benigni, L., Bretherton, I., Camaioni, L., & Volterra, V. (1977). From gesture to the first word: On cognitive and social prerequisites. In M. Lewis & L. Rosenblum (Eds.), *Interaction, conversation, and the development of language*. New York: Wiley.

Benedict, H. (1979). Early lexical development: Comprehension and production. *Journal of Child Language*, 6, 183–200.

Bloom, L. (1973). *One word at a time: The use of single-word utterances before syntax*. The Hague, Netherlands: Mouton.

Bloom, L., Lifter, K. L., & Broughton, J. (1985). The convergence of early cognition and language in the second year of life: Problems in conceptualization and measurement. In M. Barret (Ed.), *Children's single-word speech* (pp. 149–180). New York: Wiley.

Bloom, P. (in press). Theories of word learning: Rationalist alternatives to associationism. In T. K. Bhatia & W. C. Ritchie (Eds.), *Handbook of language acquisition*. New York: Academic Press.

Bretherton, I. (1984). Social referencing and the interfacing of minds: A commentary on the views of Feinman and Campos. *Merrill-Palmer Quarterly*, 30, 419–427.

Bretherton, I. (1991). Intentional communication and the development of an understanding of mind. In D. Frye & C. Moore (Eds.), *Children's theories of mind: Mental states and social understanding*. Hillsdale, NJ: Lawrence Erlbaum Associates.

Bretherton, I., McNew, S., & Beeghly-Smith, M. (1981). Early person knowledge as expressed in gestural and verbal communications: When do infants acquire a "theory of mind"? In M. E. Lamb & L. R. Sherrod (Eds.), *Infant social cognition*. Hillsdale, NJ: Lawrence Erlbaum Associates.

Bruner, J. (1978). From communication to language: A psychological perspective. In I. Markova (Ed.), *The social context of language* (pp. 255–287). New York: Wiley.

Bruner, J. (1983). *Child's talk*. New York: Norton.

Butterworth, G. (1991). The ontogeny and phylogeny of joint visual attention. In A. Whiten (Ed.), *Natural theories of mind: Evolution, development, and simulation of everyday mindreading* (pp. 223–232). Oxford, England: Basil Blackwell.

Butterworth, G., & Jarrett, N. (1991). What minds have in common is space: Spatial mechanisms serving joint visual attention in infancy. *British Journal of Developmental Psychology*, 9, 55–72.

Byrne, R. W., & Whiten, A. (1986). *Machiavellian intelligence: Social expertise and the evolution of intellect in monkeys, apes and humans*. Oxford, England: Oxford University Press.

Camras, L. A., & Sachs, V. B. (1991). Social referencing and caretaker expressive behaviour in a day-care setting. *Infant Behaviour and Development*, 14, 27–36.

Cheney, D. L., & Seyfarth, R. M. (1990). *How monkeys see the world*. Chicago: University of Chicago Press.

Chomsky, N. (1988). *Language and problems of knowledge*. Cambridge, MA: MIT Press.

Clohessy, A., Posner, M. I., & Rothbart, M. K. (1992, June). *Stability in anticipatory eye movement learning from 4 months to adulthood*. Paper presented at the International Conference on Infant Studies, Miami.

Collis, G. M. (1977). Visual co-orientation and maternal speech. In H. R. Schaffer (Ed.), *Studies in mother-infant interaction* (pp. 355–375). London: Academic Press.

Corkum, V., & Moore, C. (1992). *Cues for joint visual attention in infants*. Paper presented at the 8th International Conference on Infant Studies, Miami, FL.

Dickstein, S., Thompson, R. A., Estes, D., Malkin, C., & Lamb, M. E. (1984). Social referencing and the security of attachment. *Infant Behaviour and Development*, 7, 507–516.

Dromi, E. (1986). The one-word period as a stage in language development: Quantitative and qualitative accounts. In I. Levin (Ed.), *Stage and stucture: Reopening the debate: Vol. 1. Human development* (pp. 220–245). Norwood, NJ: Ablex.

Dunham, P., & Dunham, F. (1992). Lexical development during middle infancy: A mutually driven infant-caregiver process. *Developmental Psychology*, 28, 414–420.

Dunham, P. J., Dunham, F., & Curwin, A. (in press). Joint-attentional states and lexical acquisition at 18 months. *Developmental Psychology*.

Gleitman, L. R. (1990). The structural sources of word meaning. *Language Acquisition*, 1, 3–55.

Goldfield, B. A., & Reznick, J. S. (1990). Early lexical acquisition: Rate, content, and the vocabulary spurt. *Journal of Child Language*, 17, 171–184.

Gopnik, A., & Meltzoff, A. N. (in press). Minds, bodies and persons: Young children's understanding of the self and others as reflected in imitation and "theory of mind" research. In S. Parker & R. Mitchell (Eds.), Self-awareness in animals and humans. New York: Cambridge University Press.

Haith, M. M., Hazan, C., & Goodman, G. S. (1988). Expectation and anticipation of dynamic visual events by 3.5-month-old infants. Child Development, 59, 467–479.

Harris, M., Jones, D., Brookes, S., & Grant, J. (1986). Relations between non-verbal context of maternal speech and rate of language development. British Journal of Developmental Psychology, 4, 261–268.

Harris, M., Jones, D., & Grant, J. (1983). The nonverbal context of mothers' speech to infants. First Language, 4, 21–30.

Hay, D. F., Stimson, C. A., & Castle, J. (1991). A meeting of minds in infancy: Imitation and desire. In D. Frye & C. Moore (Eds.), Children's theories of mind: Mental states and social understanding. Hillsdale, NJ: Lawrence Erlbaum Associates.

Hobson, P. (1993). Understanding persons: The role of affect. In S. Baron-Cohen, H. Tager-Flusberg, & D. J. Cohen (Eds.), Understanding other minds: Perspectives from autism (pp. 204–227). Oxford, England: Oxford University Press.

Hornik, R., & Gunnar, M. R. (1988). A descriptive analysis of infant social referencing. Child Development, 59, 626–634.

Hornik, R., Risenhoover, N., & Gunnar, M. (1987). The effects of maternal positive, neutral, and negative affective communications on infant responses to new toys. Child Development, 58, 937–944.

Klinnert, M. (1984). The regulation of infant behaviour by maternal facial expressions. Infant Behaviour and Development, 7, 447–465.

Lempert, H., & Kinsbourne, M. (1985). Possible origin of speech in selective orienting. Psychological Bulletin, 97, 215–220.

Leung, E. H., & Rheingold, H. L. (1981). Development of pointing as a social gesture. Developmental Psychology, 17, 215–220.

Macnamara, J. (1982). Names for things: A study of human learning. Cambridge, MA: MIT Press.

Meltzoff, A. N. (1988a). Infant imitation and memory: Nine-month-olds in immediate and deferred tests. Child Development, 56, 62–72.

Meltzoff, A. N. (1988b). Infant imitation after a 1-week delay: Long-term memory for novel acts and multiple stimuli. Developmental Psychology, 24, 470–476.

Meltzoff, A. N., & Gopnik, A. (1993). The role of imitation in understanding persons and developing a theory of mind. In S. Baron-Cohen, H. Tager-Flusberg, & D. Cohen (Eds.), Understanding other minds: Perspectives from autism (pp. 335–366). Oxford, England: Oxford University Press.

Meltzoff, A. N., & Moore, M. K. (1989). Imitation in newborn infants: Exploring the range of gestures imitated and the underlying mechanisms. Developmental Psychology, 25, 954–962.

Messer, D. J. (1983). The redundancy between adult speech and nonverbal interaction: A contribution to acquisition? In R. M. Golinkoff (Ed.), The transition from prelinguistic to linguistic communication (pp. 147–159). Hillsdale, NJ: Lawrence Erlbaum Associates.

Moore, C., & Corkum, V. (in press). Social understanding at the end of the first year of life. Developmental Review.

Mumme, D. L. (1993). Rethinking social referencing: The influence of facial and vocal affect on infant behavior. Unpublished doctoral dissertation, Stanford University, Stanford, CA.

Murphy, C. M., & Messer, D. J. (1977). Mothers, infants, and pointing: A study of gesture. In H. R. Schaffer (Ed.), Studies in mother-infant interaction (pp. 325–354). London: Academic Press.

Nelson, K. (1973). Structure and strategy in learning to talk. Monographs of the Society for Research in Child Development, 38(1–2, Serial No. 149).

Parker, S. T., & Gibson, K. R. (1990). "Language" and intelligence in monkeys and apes: Comparative developmental perspectives. Cambridge, England: Cambridge University Press.

Parker, S., Mitchell, R., & Boccia, M. L. (1994). Self-awareness in animals and humans. New York: Cambridge University Press.

Perner, J. (1991). *Understanding the representational mind.* Cambridge, MA: MIT Press.

Roberts, K. (1993, March). *Covariation between speech input and attentional focus facilitates 15-month-olds' categorization in the absence of noun-labels.* Paper presented at the biennial meeting of the Society for Research in Child Development, New Orleans, LA.

Sachs, J. (1983). Talking about there and then: The emergence of displaced reference in parent-child discourse. In K.E. Nelson (Ed.), *Children's language* (Vol. 4, pp. 1–28). Hillsdale, NJ: Lawrence Erlbaum Associates.

Scaife, M., & Bruner, J. (1975). The capacity for joint visual attention in the infant. *Nature, 253,* 265–266.

Shatz, M. (1983). Communication. In J. Flavell & E. Markman (Eds.), P. Mussen (Gen. Ed.), *Cognitive development. Handbook of child psychology* (4th ed., pp. 841–890). New York: Wiley.

Sorce, J., Emde, R. N., Campos, J. J., & Klinnert, M. (1985). Maternal emotional signalling: Its effect on the visual cliff behavior of 1-year-olds. *Developmental Psychology, 21,* 195–200.

Tomasello, M., & Barton, M. (in press). Learning words in nonostensive contexts. *Developmental Psychology.*

Tomasello, M., & Farrar, M. J. (1986). Joint attention and early language. *Child Development, 57,* 1454–1463.

Tomasello, M., Kruger, A. C., & Ratner, H. H. (1993). Cultural learning. *Behavioral and Brain Sciences, 16,* 495–552.

Trevarthen, C. (1977). Descriptive analyses of infant communicative behavior. In H. R. Schaffer (Ed.), *Studies in mother-infant interaction* (pp. 227–270). New York: Academic Press.

Trevarthen, C. (1980). The foundations of intersubjectivity: Development of interpersonal and cooperative understanding in infancy. In D. Olson (Ed.), *The social foundations of language and thought: Essays in honor of J. S. Bruner.* New York: Norton.

Trevarthen, C., & Hubley, P. (1978). Secondary intersubjectivity: Confidence, confiders, and acts of meaning in the first year of life. In A. Lock (Ed.), *Action, gesture, and symbol.* New York: Academic Press.

Walden, T. A., & Ogan, T. A. (1988). The development of social referencing. *Child Development, 59,* 1230–1240.

Wellman, H. M. (1993). Early understanding of mind: The normal case. In S. Baron-Cohen, H. Tager-Flusberg, D. Cohen, & F. Volkmar (Eds.), *Understanding other minds: Perspectives from autism* (pp. 10–39). Oxford, England: Oxford University Press.

Whiten, A. (1991). *Natural theories of mind: Evolution, development, and simulation of everyday mindreading.* Oxford, England: Basil Blackwell.

Zarbatany, L., & Lamb, M.E. (1985). Social referencing as a function of information source: Mothers versus strangers. *Infant Behaviour and Development, 8,* 25–33.

Zinober, B., & Martlew, M. (1985). The development of communicative gestures. In M. D. Barrett (Ed.), *Children's single-word speech* (pp. 183–215). New York: Wiley.

Chapter 8

Optimal Social Structures and Adaptive Infant Development

Philip J. Dunham
Frances Dunham
Dalhousie University

Given the negative developmental consequences observed in classic research on the effects of early social deprivation (Bowlby, 1951, 1969; Spitz, 1950, 1965), most developmental psychologists readily accept the view that humans, like other altricial species, require the social input of adult caregivers for adaptive development. Over the past several decades, research concerned with early social stimulation has gradually shifted from a focus on the effects of social deprivation per se, to questions concerned with the influence of qualitative differences in our early social experiences. Indeed, much of the contemporary literature shares a pervasive assumption that various qualitative properties of social stimulation are optimal for adaptive development above and beyond the quantity of stimulation experienced.

The purpose of this chapter is to present an overview of our recent research concerned with the developmental consequences of various social structures described as optimal during infancy. The first section of the chapter is devoted to the early infancy period and a theoretical approach to those issues we have previously described as the *social contingency hypothesis* (e.g., Dunham & Dunham, 1990). Then, moving forward in developmental time, the second section of the chapter considers the middle and late infancy periods of development and a theoretical assumption frequently described as the *shared attention hypothesis* (e.g., Adamson & Bakeman, 1991). As will be evident later in the discussion, we believe that these two hypotheses typically associated with different periods of infant development can be conceptualized as variations on the same basic theme at the level of defining operations.

OPTIMAL SOCIAL STRUCTURES: EARLY INFANCY

Reciprocity (Brazelton, Tronick, Adamson, Als, & Wise, 1975), *contingency* (Seligman, 1975; Watson, 1985), *interpersonal accommodation* (Jasnow & Feldstein, 1986), *protocommunication* (Fafouti-Milenkovic & Uzgiris, 1979), *matching monadic phases* (Tronick, Als, & Brazelton, 1980), *attunement* (Stern, 1986), and *primary intersubjectivity* (Trevarthen, 1979) are just a few of the many terms that have been used to describe optimal infant-caregiver social structures. Although each of these concepts is to some extent distinct, we have argued in other contexts that most share a fundamental assumption that episodes of contingent, reciprocating social responses between infant and caregiver are optimal for various dimensions of early human development. We call this generic assumption the *social contingency hypothesis* (Dunham & Dunham, 1990), and before we examine some of the research associated with this hypothesis, it is perhaps important to clarify some of the relevant terminology.

The social contingency hypothesis essentially identifies a measurable social behavior emitted by an infant (e.g., a vocalization that occurs while gazing at the adult) and a social behavior emitted by the adult partner (e.g., a vocalization that occurs while gazing at the child). If each of these behaviors is viewed as an individual element in a potential interactional structure, a number of different relations can exist between these elements as they occur across time. In the social contingency hypothesis, the terms *contingent* and *reciprocating* are the critical concepts describing the generic social relationships that various contemporary researchers have identified as optimal across different versions of the hypothesis.

The term contingent describes an interaction in which a sequentially dependent, close temporal relationship exists between the infant's social behavior and the adult's reply. A substantial number of variations on this sequential structure are possible. For example, in a perfect contingency structure, the designated adult response would occur after each instance of the designated infant behavior, but at no other time during the interaction. A number of contingency structures also deviate from this perfect case. For example, if each designated adult element occurs with a probability of less than one following the designated infant element, but at no other time during the interaction, the relationship continues to be contingent, but less than perfect. Indeed, as most readers will realize, the many ways in which an adult element can be sequentially related to the infant element parallels a wide variety of scheduling operations that researchers have devised to manipulate instrumental contingencies in the context of operant conditioning research (see Watson, 1985, for a relevant discussion).

Alternatively, the term *noncontingent* is generally used to describe the various conditions in which a contingency structure between the infant and adult elements has been disrupted. Perhaps the purest operation for eliminating a contingency structure in a simulated social interaction would be to schedule the occurrence of each element with an independent, random probability generator. Under these conditions, the two social elements occur randomly in time at some predetermined density. By definition, no predictable sequential dependency exists between the elements. Again, the conditioning literature provides a long list of operations for disrupting contingency structures.

The point to appreciate is that many theoretical accounts of optimal social stimulation appear on the surface to be very different; however, at the level of defining operations most share the assumption that a sequentially dependent, contingent relationship between the infant and adult element is an optimal form of social stimulation for various aspects of early infant development. These versions have essentially operationalized the popular notion that infants thrive best in the presence of highly responsive caregivers; the more responsive the better. We should also note in passing, however, that there are theoretical variations on the contingency assumption that deviate in interesting ways from the intuitively appealing view that more is better. For example, Watson (1985) has suggested that moderately responsive caregivers may facilitate development more effectively than highly responsive caregivers in certain contexts. As we discuss in more detail later in the chapter, he argues that a "moderately responsive" caregiver may be an optimal condition for the process of differentiating self from other during the early infancy period.

Consider next the term reciprocating. Although this concept has a long and somewhat inconsistent semantic history in research concerned with early social interactions (see Ross, Cheyne, & Lollis, 1988, for a thorough review), in the context of the social contingency hypothesis we will use this term to describe the assumption that an adult's social response is optimal when, in addition to being contingent, it acknowledges (i.e., reciprocates) certain theoretically specified properties of the infant's preceding behavior. Essentially, the reciprocity assumption operationalizes the generally accepted notion that not all adult social responses are created equal. Some contingent behaviors are assumed to be more influential than others, and they are presumed to exert this influence above and beyond the effects of the contingency structure per se. Indeed, it is these diverse variations on the reciprocity concept that give this literature much of its theoretical richness.

Specific versions on the reciprocity assumption differ with respect to the particular dimension(s) of the infant element that must be reciprocated for optimal influence. Stern (1986), for example, uses the term *attunement* to describe a contingent adult element that reciprocates the infant element by matching the intensity and temporal patterning of the infant's social behavior during the interaction. He is not particularly concerned with the specific nature of the caregiver's action (touching, smiling, vocalizing, etc.), but argues instead that any contingent adult response that underestimates or overestimates the intensity of the infant's behavior will be less optimal than actions matching the intensity of the infant's actions.

Given these basic definitions, it should be clear that the designated adult social input can occur in either a contingent or noncontingent structure relative to the infant element, and when a contingent structure has been established, the contingent adult element can either reciprocate some property of the infant element, or fail to reciprocate. The label social contingency hypothesis is intended to capture both of these dimensions. An interactional structure is generally assumed to be optimal for adaptive development when it is both contingent and reciprocating as these terms have been elaborated across different theoretical positions. Note also that the term optimal is used in the sense of exerting a maximal influence on the particular developmental process under consideration. For example, some researchers discuss social structures that are maximally effective for changing the infant's motivational states (e.g., a sense of control or helplessness, e.g., Seligman, 1975; Skinner, 1985); others emphasize structures that are maximally effective for influencing basic cognitive processes such as contingency detection and differentiating self from others (e.g., Stern, 1985; Watson, 1985; Wellman, 1990).

Before we proceed, a few additional points need to be made about the term reciprocity as it is used in the context of this chapter. First, it is important to emphasize that our use of the term reciprocity should not be confused with other more theory-laden uses often encountered in the current literature. For example, some researchers use the term reciprocity to imply the existence of a theoretical dyadic state in which both infant and caregiver have a shared understanding of the other's intentions during the interaction (cf., Ross, Cheyne, & Lollis, 1988). We are not using the term to describe this inferred state of social understanding. We are using the term reciprocity in a more generic operational sense to describe various physical or structural characteristics of adult social stimulation that different researchers have identified as having special properties above and beyond the properties of the contingency structure per se. As the present chapter evolves, it will be evident that our bias on this particular issue is to assume that early contingent and reciprocating social structures can, in many situations, have wide-ranging effects on various dimensions of infant development in the absence of any understanding by the infant of the shared attentional states underlying these structures. At the present time, our working assumptions are that; experiences with early contingent and reciprocating social structures may be building important structural foundations during infancy that permit a social understanding of shared attentional states (and other mental states) to emerge near the end of the second year, and this phase shift in social cognition near the end of the second year may be triggered by an independently occurring change in the child's representational system at that time. Some of the data discussed near the end of this chapter addresses this working hypothesis in more detail.

It is also important to note that our use of the term reciprocity in this chapter is not limited to imitative or matching interactive social behaviors. We noted earlier that Stern's concept of attunement (1986) assumes that it is important for the adult partner's contingent social behavior to match the intensity of the infant's social behavior during an interaction. Stern's intensity matching condition should be viewed, however, as just one of many possible examples of our more broadly defined reciprocity concept. Stern's views can, for example, be contrasted with Tomasello's (this volume) suggestion that a young infant's social understanding of adults as intentional agents is facilitated "when others match and reciprocate their own interactive behaviors" (p. 123). Much like Stern, Tomasello uses the term *matching* to underline the potential importance of contingent adult imitation or matching during early social interactions. Tomasello also proceeds, however, to use the term reciprocity in a unique manner to describe contingent adult social behaviors that do not simply match or imitate, but complement in various ways the infant's preceding social overture. Indeed, he suggests that complementary adult social responses may be more influential than matching or imitative behaviors in facilitating certain aspects of early social understanding. Essentially, Stern and Tomasello each describe special properties of the adult's social behavior above and beyond the contingency structure, as optimal for certain dimensions of early social development. Stern uses the term *attunement* to describe one such property; Tomasello uses the terms matching and reciprocity to describe two different properties and emphasizes the importance of the latter. Although these two points of view raise some interesting theoretical and empirical questions, the important point is that within the social contingency hypothesis, the term reciprocity is used to subsume all such variations on the fundamental assumption that some special property of the adult's social behavior will have an impact on infant development above and beyond the contingency structure and the total amount of social stimulation per se.

Finally, with reference to these structural concepts, it is also important to realize that the terms contingency and reciprocity are defined in the present chapter as "unidirectional influences of the adult social input on the infant." We realize of course that the "social string pulls both ways," and that each of the definitions outlined in the preceding discussion can also be used to discuss the effects of the infant's social behavior on the adult. When, for example, infant interactional behaviors are defined as contingent and/or reciprocating, we assume that those social behaviors can be more or less optimal in their influence on the adult caregiver. Anyone who has observed a young infant contingently reciprocate a mother's smiles or sounds can document the substantial changes in the mother's behavior and social attributions accompanying these events. In the present chapter, however, we focus primarily on procedures designed to study the influence of adult social behaviors on the infant. Eventually, as our research program evolves, we plan to explore a parallel set of questions in which the social string is manipulated to pull in the opposite direction.

Contingency Structure: Early Infancy

Most versions of the social contingency hypothesis predict that a contingent, reciprocating social structure during early infancy holds an infant's attention effectively and tends to be associated with positive affect. In general, reviews of existing literature reveal a substantial amount of evidence supporting this gener-alization (see Adamson & Bakeman, 1991; Dunham, Dunham, Hurshman, & Alexander, 1989; Field & Fox, 1985; and Schaffer, 1977). However, when we first developed an interest in these issues, we noted at least two problems with the existing research. First, the relevant evidence consisted largely of correlations observed among various measures of contingency structure and measures of infant affect and attention during unconstrained adult-infant interactions. A more rigorous test of the contingency hypothesis requires behavioral comparisons when infants are randomly assigned to one of two different social treatment conditions: an interaction with an adult partner who responds contingently in a consistent, specified manner to a designated infant response; and an interaction with an adult partner who delivers an identical pattern and density of social responses to the infant in the absence of any contingency structure (i.e., a yoked, noncontingent adult partner). Differences in infant affect and attention observed across these two experimental conditions would provide more convincing evidence for the direct effects of the contingency structure on infants during the interaction.

The second recurring problem in this literature is that researchers have focused almost exclusively on changes in infant behavior observed during social inter-actions. If, however, differential experience with social contingency structures is to be taken seriously as a factor influencing development, it is particularly important to demonstrate that the different social experiences also modify un-derlying emotional-motivational and/or perceptual-cognitive processes in a man-ner that transfers across both time and context (Bronfenbrenner, 1979). Relevant theoretical perspectives include the suggestion that the different social experi-ences may affect an infant's ability to perceive a contingency structure in other subsequent social or nonsocial contexts (e.g., Watson, 1985), may affect the infant's sense of control and motivation to participate in subsequent contingency structures (e.g., Seligman, 1975), and/or may affect the development of a sense of control (Skinner, 1985) and a sense of self (e.g., Stern, 1986; Wellman, 1990).

Much of the research conducted in our own laboratory over the past few years has been explicitly designed to address these two weaknesses in the existing literature. To investigate these issues, we have developed a transfer paradigm that permits us to compare the effects of contingent and yoked, noncontingent social structures on various aspects of young infants' behavior both during an initial social interaction phase and during a subsequent nonsocial contingency task. This transfer procedure permits us to determine whether experience with the social contingency structure has effects on the infant that generalize across both time and context when the total density and pattern of social stimulation received during previous contingent and noncontingent social experiences are identical.

Our initial work with the transfer paradigm has provided additional experi-mental support for several of the assumptions implicit in the social contingency hypothesis. In our first series of experiments, 3-month-old infants participated in a brief social interaction with either a contingent or a yoked, noncontingent adult. Immediately following the interaction they were placed in an infant seat and tested in a nonsocial context. In this nonsocial contingency transfer test, each visual fixation on a target light activated a multimodal pattern of lights and tones for as long as the infant maintained a visual fixation. Across three different experiments involving minor variations on this procedure, we observed essentially the same pattern of results: (a) during the initial social interaction phase, the contingent adult structure tended to produce more of the required infant social behavior (vocalizations, leg kicks) and less gaze aversion than the equivalent density and pattern of stimulation delivered in a yoked, noncontingent structure; and (b) in the subsequent nonsocial, contingency transfer task, the infants tended to activate the nonsocial stimulus for longer periods of time, and to leave the stimulus off for shorter periods of time than infants who had previously experienced an equivalent amount of social stimulation from a noncontingent adult. In effect, the density of nonsocial stimulation produced during the subsequent transfer task was significantly higher in infants who had prior experience with a social contingency structure (see Dunham et al., 1989).

In a subsequent attempt to enhance the ecological validity of these laboratory manipulations, we also asked whether these same phenomena would be observed when individual differences in the contingency structure of more natural mother–infant interactions were measured and then correlated with the infant's performance on the same, subsequent nonsocial transfer task (see Dunham & Dunham, 1990). Using these procedures, we again observed that individual differences in the contingency structure of the mother–infant interactions correlated positively with infant affect during the interaction, and with the infants' subsequent performance on the nonsocial contingency task (i.e., infants in dyads with high contingency structure ratings also activated and maintained a higher density of nonsocial stimulation during the subsequent contingency transfer task). Considered together, these data corroborated existing correlational evidence for the direct effects of different social structures on infant affect and attention, and they also provided much-needed experimental evidence for those versions of the contingency hypothesis arguing for effects that generalize beyond the immediate social interaction.

These transfer phenomena suggest that brief social interactions can produce changes in infants that generalize in some form across short periods of time and to a different nonsocial context. What inferences can we make about the mechanisms that mediate this generalization process at a very early stage of development? We believe that two kinds of mechanisms might be operating, and one is considerably more interesting than the other. Neither, we should note, requires us to infer that the infant has an understanding of the caregiver's intentions or a sophisticated mental representation of the different social structures involved.

The more interesting of the two explanations can be described as a *contingency detection mechanism*. This perceptual–cognitive explanation assumes that experience with the contingent social structure increases the infants' sensitivity to other contingency relations in their physical and social environment. Or, conversely, experience with the random social partner inhibits subsequent contingency detection. As such, the differences in performance we observed during the contingent transfer task can be interpreted as differences in the ability of these two groups to detect the contingent property of the transfer task following the contingent and noncontingent social experiences.

A second, and less interesting explanation of these generalized effects is perhaps best described as a simple *stimulus tolerance mechanism*. If one assumes that a given amount of random social stimulation is functionally more intense than an equivalent amount of contingent social stimulation, then the noncontingent infants may simply have less tolerance for additional stimulation during the transfer task. The data we obtained during the transfer task are also compatible with this explanation given that the noncontingent group exposed themselves to a lower density of nonsocial stimulation during the task.

Which of these two explanations best explains the generalized effects of these prior social experiences? In order to explicitly test the stimulus tolerance explanation, we recently replicated the Dunham et al. (1989) experiment and added a potentially informative variation on the transfer test. As in previous studies, two groups of infants were randomly assigned to either contingent or noncontingent social partners. Following these interactions, half of the infants in each group replicated our previously used transfer contingency task (i.e., each visual fixation on a target activated nonsocial, multimodal stimulation). The other half participated in a transfer contingency task that reversed the consequences of fixating the visual target (i.e., the nonsocial stimulation was continuously present during the transfer contingency task, and the infant's visual fixations on the target deactivated the stimulation for the duration of each fixation). Note that the stimulus tolerance explanation makes very different predictions about the noncontingent infants' behavior across these two versions of the transfer task. Consider first those infants required to fixate the target during the transfer task in order to activate the nonsocial stimulation. The stimulus tolerance hypothesis predicts that infants with previous noncontingent social experiences, if they detect the contingency and are motivated to reduce the density of subsequent stimulation, should fixate on the target for shorter periods, and look away from the target for longer periods; this strategy will reduce the density of the nonsocial stimulation relative to their contingent counterparts. This specific result in these two groups replicates the earlier data reported by Dunham et al. (1989) using essentially the same stimulus activation transfer task.

However, during the second transfer task requiring the infants to fixate the target in order to deactivate the ongoing nonsocial stimulation, the stimulus tolerance explanation predicts that the noncontingent infants should fixate the target for longer periods and look away from the target for shorter periods than their contingent counterparts. This response strategy in the deactivation task would actively reduce the density of stimulation following their noncontingent social experience.

The results illustrated in Figure 8.1 were informative. First, in the two groups repeating the Dunham et al. (1989) procedure, the original transfer results were replicated. Following the noncontingent social experience, infants adopted a response strategy in the activation version of the transfer task that decreased stimulus density relative to their contingent counterparts. Of more interest, the two groups of infants who received the deactivation transfer task adopted the same response strategy following a noncontingent social experience. These infants also fixated the target in the transfer task for shorter periods of time and looked away for longer periods than their contingent counterparts, even though this response strategy increased stimulus density relative to their contingent counterparts. These results clearly argue against a simple stimulus tolerance explanation of the generalized effects.

Given these more recent data, our working hypothesis identifies a *contingency detection mechanism* as perhaps the most reasonable explanation for the data presented in Figure 8.1. Murray and Trevarthen (1985), Seligman (1975), Tronick

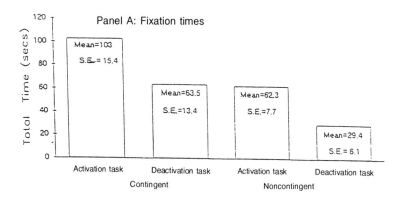

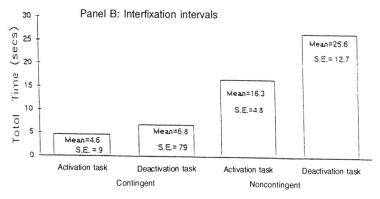

FIG. 8.1. Fixation times and interfixation intervals during activation and deactivation tasks following contingent and noncontingent social interactions.

(1989), and Watson (1985) have each discussed different versions of this mechanism, sharing in common the assumption that exposure to less than optimal social stimulation (e.g., a random social partner) disrupts infants' ability to detect subsequent contingent relationships and/or reduces their motivation to participate in subsequent contingency tasks; or stated positively, exposure to contingent social stimulation increases infants' sensitivity to contingent relationships and/or increases their motivation to participate in subsequent contingency tasks.

The infants' behavior in the transfer task was compatible with the contingency detection explanation. As indicated in Figure 8.1, the noncontingent infants essentially displayed the same patterns of behavior in both versions of the transfer task (activation and deactivation) regardless of the stimulus consequences. They were slow to orient toward the target that controlled the nonsocial stimulation, and when they fixated the target it did not hold their attention for long, relative to the contingent group. Indeed, when observing these infants, it seems that they gradually lose interest in external events during the noncontingent social interaction, and this lack of interest in their environment carries forward into the transfer task. This pattern of behavior has characteristics resembling those described by Seligman (1975) as *learned helplessness*.

Questions for Future Research: Early Infancy

We believe that Watson (1985) has raised some of the most interesting questions in the current literature concerned with the influence of various contingency experiences on infant development. He suggests, for example, that both perfect and truly random contingency structures are more easily detected by the infant (i.e., perceptible) than intermediate, less than perfect contingency structures. Intermediate levels of contingency, on the other hand, are suggested to maintain the infant's attention and an optimal level of arousal more effectively. Several interesting questions arise when Watson's analysis is considered in the context of our transfer paradigm. For example, will an experimental simulation of a moderately contingent social partner more effectively maintain attention and positive affect during the interaction than perfectly contingent and yoked, noncontingent partners? More importantly perhaps, which of these contingency structures (relative to yoked, noncontingent controls) will most effectively produce generalized differences in a subsequent nonsocial contingency transfer task? Although a more perceptible, perfect social contingency may, as Watson suggests, maintain less attention and positive affect during the interaction, we suspect that the more easily detected perfect social contingency will also more readily generalize across time and context to influence performance during the transfer task.

As noted earlier in the chapter, Watson (1985) also suggests that the infant's ability to perceive differences in contingency structures may be an important factor in the early differentiation of self from other. His reasoning can be paraphrased as follows. For every self-initiated action an infant directs toward herself (e.g., thumb sucking), she experiences a perfectly contingent consequence (e.g., the response of thumb sucking produces a perfectly predictable set of tactile sensations from the thumb and mouth). Alternatively, for every act directed toward a social other (e.g., a gaze at caregiver), the contingent consequences are typically less predictable. He argues that these different contingency structures associated with self-directed behaviors (perfect contingency) and other-directed behaviors (less than perfect contingency) may establish the first primitive representations of self and other, and further speculates that particular variations on the less than perfect contingency structures often associated with significant others may define some of the infant's early social categories (e.g., caregiver vs. stranger). Watson's arguments in this domain have much in common with similar positions outlined by Lewis and Brooks-Gunn (1979, pp. 223–224), Stern (1985, p. 80), and Wellman (1990, pp. 238–239).

Finally, before we leave this discussion of the early infancy period, we should note that most of the issues raised thus far involve tampering with the contingency structure and observing both the direct and generalized (i.e., transfer) consequences of this tampering. We also believe that additional research is needed to explore the effects of various reciprocating conditions infants encounter within a contingency structure. Research concerned with the role of reciprocity during early infancy essentially pits a contingent adult caregiver who reciprocates some theoretically specified property of the infant's behavior against a contingent adult caregiver who fails to reciprocate the specified property. This basic rationale permits one to determine if the reciprocating property accounts for any variance in the infant's behavior above and beyond the contingency structure per se. Consider again Stern's (1985, 1986) particular variation on the social contingency hypotheses called attunement. As discussed earlier, he assumes that a caregiver who contingently reciprocates an infant's social behaviors by matching intensity is optimal for generating positive affect and maintaining mutual social attention. While some descriptive data support this theoretical perspective (Stern, Hofer, Haft, & Dore, 1985), we think it is important to determine at various points in developmental time whether the contingency structure alone is sufficient to explain any direct or generalizable effects of the adult partner, or whether some of the changes in behavior can, as Stern implies, be attributed to the specified reciprocating properties of the adult behavior. Until rigorous experimental simulations of various reciprocating properties are employed, with contingent structure held constant, we cannot know whether a contingent adult who consistently replies, for example, to the 2-month-old infant by reciprocating some specified property (e.g., a contingent, intensity matching adult) will enjoy more success in the interaction than a contingent adult who does not reciprocate (e.g., a contingent, but nonmatching adult). It is conceivable that the contingency structure is far more important than the reciprocating structure during the earliest stages of infancy, and that the reciprocating properties specified in different versions of the social contingency structure begin to account uniquely for some variance in the infant's behavior only at later points in development (or vice versa).

Optimal Social Structures: Middle and Late Infancy

Most researchers acknowledge that a fundamental change in the structure of infant–caregiver social interactions begins to emerge in the second half of the infant's first year. Episodes of contingent turn-taking considered to be optimal during the first 4 or 5 months of development become increasingly difficult to maintain as the infant finds objects and events in the external environment more compelling and shows a reduced interest in the caregiver per se. While most would agree that it remains important for the adult to respond contingently and to reciprocate the infant's direct social overtures, the infant's changing social agenda at this age has been described as an attempt to integrate a new interest in external objects and events into the previously established interactional structure (e.g., Bakeman & Adamson, 1984; Bruner, 1977, 1983; Tomasello, 1992; Trevarthen, 1979; Werner & Kaplan, 1963). Bakeman and Adamson (1984) describe this important transition as ". . . the emergence of a 'triadic' (infant-object-other) interactive system" (p. 1288), and suggest that the process of learning to coordinate attention on objects and events with the social input of an adult caregiver continues to unfold across the remainder of the infancy period. Just as episodes of interpersonal turn-taking have been widely viewed as optimal during the first few months of life, researchers interested in the developmental phenomena during middle and late infancy have identified episodes of shared attention on objects or events as an optimal interactional structure during this period.

We suggest that the shared attention hypothesis is, at the level of defining operations, best conceptualized as an extension of the previously discussed generic social contingency hypothesis. Establishing a shared attentional state on an object essentially involves contingently responding to a designated infant response and reciprocating some specified property of the infant's behavior (e.g., when the infant reaches for a noisy rattle, the adult contingently reciprocates this behavior by helping the infant shake it). The joint attentional episode will not be established if the adult fails to respond contingently (i.e., does not act in response to the designated infant behavior) or if the adult fails to reciprocate (i.e., if the adult reaches for a different toy each time the infant reveals an interest in the rattle). In the same sense that establishing mutual infant–caregiver attention (i.e., exchanging gaze) can be described as a contingent, reciprocating structure during early infancy, establishing joint attention on an object or event can be operationally defined as a contingent, reciprocating structure emerging during later infancy. Again, we believe that questions about the extent to which this social structure has an influence on the infant can be posed without a priori assumptions about the infant's understanding of the social structure (e.g., attributions of shared perceptions or intentions). The consequent data may or may not justify inferences about the infant's social cognition (see chapters by Baldwin and Tomasello in this volume for additional discussion).

The notion that episodes of shared attention are optimal for adaptive development during middle and late infancy has been customized in many different ways to deal with various changes in behavior emerging at different points in the infant's second year. Boccia and Campos (1989), for example, in their research on social referencing, describe the importance of episodes of shared attention in early emotional development, arguing that they are influential in the emergence of emotional phenomena like stranger distress. Others have implicated episodes of shared attention as "hot spots" for various aspects of early language and communicative development, and for the emergence of early mental attributions (see Tomasello, 1988, 1992). Although researchers in each separate domain have tailored the specific characteristics of the joint attentional episode to fit the specific developmental phenomena under consideration, all versions are essentially variations on a generic theme assuming that stimulation experienced within this basic social structure is particularly influential.

In the remainder of this chapter we focus on two specific areas of research on this period of development where we have made some progress in the past couple of years. First, we consider the role of joint attentional episodes in lexical development during the middle infancy period; and then, we turn our attention to the late infancy period and the role of joint attentional episodes in communicative development and in children's emerging mental attributions.

Shared Attention and Lexical Development

Tomasello (1988, 1992) has, in our opinion, outlined the most comprehensive theoretical account of the role of shared-attentional episodes in early lexical development. Working in the rich tradition of Vygotsky (1986), Jakobson (1960), Werner and Kaplan (1963), Bruner (1977, 1983), and Kaye (1982), he suggests that a fine grain analysis of the adult–infant interactional structure during this period reveals that periods of joint attention on a particular object or event can be established in one of two ways, each with different implications for lexical development. During an interaction, the adult partner can respond to the infant's interest in a particular object by following the infant's existing focus of attention, or the partner can require the infant to switch his or her attention to an object on which the infant is not currently focused. Note that either strategy will potentially establish an episode of shared attention on an object, and that in both cases the adult's response has been contingent on a preceding infant behavior. We, therefore, view this conceptual framework as yet another variation on the operational distinction drawn earlier between reciprocating and nonreciprocating contingent adult responses customized in this context to deal with lexical development.

Specifically, lexical acquisition is assumed to be easier when the contingent adult is reciprocating the infant's gaze (i.e., attention-following), and more difficult when the contingent adult is not reciprocating the infant's gaze (i.e., attention-switching). Essentially, the reciprocating (i.e., attention-following) contingency is assumed to make lexical acquisition easier by solving the ubiquitous problem of reference for the infant during new word learning.

A substantial amount of evidence relevant to this general issue has accumulated over the past decade. First, a number of correlational studies have been generated by Bruner's (1977, 1983) initial, more general arguments, suggesting that infants with more extensive exposure to episodes of joint attention in their social history will display more advanced lexical development. Various studies searching for this global association have tended to find support for it (e.g., Dunham & Dunham, 1992; Harris, Jones, Brookes, & Grant, 1986; Rocissano & Yatchmink, 1983). Microanalytic approaches to infant–caregiver interactions have also directly explored Tomasello's *attentional mapping* version of this hypothesis. Again, most of the evidence relevant to the attentional mapping assumption has been positive. Correlational studies of individual differences in the relevant infant–caregiver interactional structures have observed that exposure to an attention-following strategy during social interactions tends, as predicted, to be positively correlated with more advanced infant lexical development, and to a lesser degree, that attention-switching styles tend to predict slower development (e.g., Akhtar, Dunham, & Dunham, 1991; Tomasello & Farrar, 1986; Tomasello & Todd, 1983).

Again, in parallel with the point made earlier in our discussion of the social contingency hypothesis, the major weakness in this literature is the almost exclusive dependence of these arguments on correlational data. In these descriptive studies other structural differences in the dyadic interaction are potentially co-varying with the presumed optimal conditions for lexical acquisition, and the discussion of causal influence can easily be reversed to argue that infants with advanced vocabulary skills are better able to support the optimal dyadic structure than infants with less advanced vocabularies. Indeed, to the best of our knowledge, there has been only one attempt to test Tomasello's specific version of the shared attention hypothesis using more rigorous experimental simulations of the social structures designated as optimal. In an initial study, Tomasello and Farrar (1986) trained 10 infants between 14 and 23 months of age on a lexical acquisition task in which two objects were repeatedly labeled by an adult experimenter using an attention-following strategy, and two others were labeled using an attention-switching strategy. A subsequent comprehension test revealed that the children were more likely to learn the labels in the attention-following condition. While these data provided tentative experimental support for Tomasello's predictions, several aspects of their procedure confounded other conditions with the attention-following and attention-switching strategies (see Dunham, Dunham, & Curwin, 1993).

In a recent attempt to provide a more rigorous test of the attentional mapping hypothesis we designed a different lexical acquisition task that eliminated some of the methodological problems encountered in previous research. Two groups of 18-month-old infants were observed during a relatively natural play session in a large room with an adult experimenter and several toys. The experimenter demonstrated that certain manipulations performed on each toy would send small plastic objects careening down a noisy chute into a tray below. The children were then free to play with any toy in the room during an 8-minute play session. Each time a child activated one particular toy, the specific plastic object associated with that toy was called a "dodo" by an experimenter using either an attention-following strategy (i.e., introducing the label when the infant was already focused on the dodo object) or an attention-switching strategy (i.e., introducing the label for the dodo object when the infant was focused on an alternative object). When a number of potentially confounded factors such as the frequency of exposure to the label, the infant's motivation, and infant compliance during a separate comprehension test were equated across the two groups of children, the children in the attention following group were more likely to learn the dodo label for the appropriate object. These data provided substantial support for the attentional mapping hypothesis.

Although these data corroborate the existing correlational studies, additional research is required to fully understand these results. Although Tomasello's explanation suggests that the attention-switching strategy places attentional demands on the infant that make word learning more difficult, before accepting this view, we think it is also important to examine the properties of the attention-switching and attention-following structures in more detail. Consider, for example, the child's experiences in a natural play session. When an object is labeled during an attention-following episode, the infant will typically be handling and manipulating the object as the label is delivered. Alternatively, when the object is labeled during an attention-switching episode, by definition the child will be engaged in another activity and the sensory experiences associated specifically with the object during labeling will typically be limited to the visual domain (i.e., he or she will look at it when the adult points to it). Does experiencing the object across several sensory modalities during the word learning process give the infant in the attention-following condition a memory encoding advantage not enjoyed by the attention-switching counterpart? Although the experiment remains to be conducted, data concerned with lexical acquisition suggests that children do more readily learn names for objects that support active manipulation and exploration (Ross, Nelson, Wetstone, & Tanouye, 1986).

Again, the point to appreciate is that demonstrating that a particular social structure influences early development is only the first step in the difficult task of elucidating the particular mechanisms that underlie this influence. With respect to the research on early lexical development, it is possible that the multimodal input associated with the attention-following strategy is facilitating the word learning and memory process. If so, we may need to reconsider interpretations based on assumed differences in attentional mapping demands in the two structures, and related interpretations that assume a child is more likely to infer a shared attentional state in the attention following structure (see Baldwin in present volume for relevant discussion).

Shared Attention, Verbal Discourse, and Mental Attributions

In the recent literature, true conversation during early childhood has been defined as maintaining a topic-comment structure across successive verbal turns on a shared focus of attention (Collis, 1985; Kaye, 1982; Tomasello, 1988). Children's use of this topic-maintaining, predicative discourse structure suggests that; the child understands that a particular object or event is a shared focus of attention (the topic), and the child realizes that their partner's attentional state can be directed to various properties of the object or event (the comment).

In several analyses of early adult-child verbal interactions (e.g., Bloom, Rocissano, & Hood, 1976; Kaye, 1982; Kaye & Charney, 1980; Tomasello, 1988, 1992), there is a general consensus that true conversation begins to emerge late in the infant's second year. Again, Tomasello (1988, 1992) has developed perhaps the most detailed theoretical account of this process. He conceptualizes this change in pragmatic communicative development as a cultural learning process in which certain structural characteristics of infant-caregiver social interactions play a major role. As children approach 2 years of age, he suggests that an adult partner can directly facilitate the child's transition into true conversation by consistently maintaining the child's topic and expanding on it briefly during episodes of shared attention. This emphasis on the importance of topic-maintaining expansions during episodes of shared attention also finds a theoretical heritage in similar ideas discussed by Vygotsky (1986), Bruner (1977, 1983) and Kaye (1982).

The adult's consistent use of topic-maintaining expansions at this transition point in communicative development is assumed to be optimal for two reasons. First, by expanding briefly on the child's preceding utterance, the adult both maintains a joint focus of attention with the child and "scaffolds" or illustrates the more advanced predicative structure by making a brief comment on some new aspect of the shared topic (see also Kaye's, 1982, *discourse framing hypothesis*). Second, the episodes of joint attention associated with the adult's use of topic-maintaining expansions are also assumed to facilitate the children's understanding of the adult partner as an intentional, mental agent. The emergence of these mental attributions is portrayed as a major step forward in the development of communicative competence, and in the child's emerging theory of mind. With reference to this second assumption, we should perhaps note that the nature of the 2-year-old's understanding of another person's mental life is a matter of considerable debate (see Astington, Harris, & Olson, 1988; Frye &

Moore, 1991; Wellman, 1990, for relevant discussions). Tomasello's (1992) theoretical account is, however, explicit on this point. Exposure to the topic-maintaining expansions during episodes of shared attentional discourse are assumed to facilitate children's understanding of their partner's ". . . global characteristics as intentional or mental agents" (Tomasello, 1992, p. 84).

As noted earlier, the evidence directly relevant to these theoretical assumptions about early discourse is sparse, and primarily descriptive in nature. For example, in one of the more frequently cited studies of adult-child discourse near the end of the child's second year, Kaye and Charney (1980) observed that adults were particularly effective in eliciting an adjacent verbal response from the child when the adult utterances consisted of *turnabouts* ". . . building on what the child had just done or said and attempting to elicit something more on the topic" (p. 222). While these descriptive data are compatible with Tomasello's topic-expansion version of the scaffolding hypothesis (see also, Barnes, Gutfreund, Satterly, & Wells, 1983; Bloom et al., 1976; Penner, 1987; Scherer & Olswang, 1984), they must be interpreted with caution. As most of these researchers acknowledge, one cannot conclude from these data that adult expansions are facilitating the child's discourse skills when many other dimensions of the adult's conversational structure are free to covary with variations in the use of topic-maintaining expansions. For example, as defined, the adult turnabouts are very likely confounded with the frequency of questions in the adult's speech. Similarly, the correlational data do not permit one to determine the direction of influence during the interaction; more competent children may simply facilitate the adult's tendency to use topic-maintaining expansions rather than vice versa.

Similar problems undermine claims that adult topic-maintaining expansions function to facilitate children's mental attributions at this age. Although a child's reply at any point in a conversation might suggest a predicative structure (i.e., imply that the child attributes a shared attentional state to the adult), an observed association between the adult's expansions and a child's predicative replies does not require inferences about the child's mental attributions or the existence of a causal relationship between adult topic-expansions and the children's presumed mental attributions. It is just as reasonable, perhaps even more compelling, to suggest that a competent adult partner has anticipated when the 2-year-old child is about to speak and manages to anticipate the next topic and comment the child is most likely to make in that specific context. If so, the child's apparently predicative structure (i.e., a reply that implies shared attentional understanding) can be interpreted alternatively as the adult successfully "reading the child's mind" rather than the child "reading the adult's mind."

In addition to these interpretive problems, we should note that there are other descriptive data in the literature hinting that the 2-year-old's understanding of these verbal conversational structures may not be as sophisticated as Tomasello's theoretical mechanism implies. For example, Bordeaux and Willbrand's

(1987) descriptive analysis of early telephone discourse confirms the typical household experience of most parents; it is almost impossible to maintain a 2-year-old's interest in a phone conversation beyond a few minutes (see also Ervin-Tripp, 1979). The child's verbal interactions on the telephone clearly lack the temporal, sequential topic structure of face-to-face verbal interactions Kaye and Charney (1980) reported at this age. This difference suggests that the verbal structure of the adult's replies (e.g., topic-expansions) may not have the illocutionary force assumed in existing theoretical accounts of verbal discourse at this age (e.g., Tomasello, 1988; Kaye, 1982). Although a competent adult's verbal input is not constrained during telephone discourse, the 2-year-old child's interest and/or ability to maintain adjacent, topic-maintaining conversation drops precipitously in this context. We note in passing that additional research varying the structure of adult verbal replies during telephone discourse may be a particularly informative approach to dissecting the contributions of various verbal and nonverbal structures to the maintenance of discourse.

Other descriptive data also suggest that children's mental attributions may not be a particularly important factor in their conversations at 2 years of age. For example, in an extensive analysis of 2-year-olds' attempts to initiate conversation during social interactions, Ervin-Tripp and Gordon (1986) reported that "... 89 percent of the times when 2-year-olds addressed somebody who was already busy with someone else, they made their requests without first attempting to gain attention" (p. 68). These observations suggest that 2-year-olds are oblivious to the adult partner's mental (attentional) state. By implication, theoretical accounts of early communicative development that ascribe a central role to the 2-year-old child's mental attributions should be accepted with some caution.

To summarize, several investigators have suggested that an adult's verbal replies provide optimal support for episodes of topic-maintaining discourse if those replies are contingent and have a topic-expanding (reciprocating) semantic relationship to the child's preceding utterance. However, given the fundamental problems with the data supporting these intuitively appealing arguments, it remains to be determined, in our opinion, whether a 2-year-old's attempts to engage in verbal discourse with an adult are influenced by variations in either the verbal contingency structure or the verbal topic-maintaining structure of the adult partner's speech. Furthermore, the extent to which these particular structures also facilitate the emergence of mental attributions about the adult partner remains, at this point, a matter of speculation.

In an effort to address some of these questions in a more rigorous experimental context, we recently developed a procedure in which children are introduced to a small, immobile robot dressed in a hat and sweater. A hidden experimenter observes the child and responds verbally to the child's speech through a speaker mounted in the robot's chest. If, for example, a child points to a toy pig and says "dat, piggy," the robot might reciprocate with the comment, "yes, the piggy is in the barn." Most of the children we observe in this context are willing to engage in conversations with the robot as they play. For example, in our initial research with this procedure, we instructed the robot to speak only in response to the child's speech during the play session and to use only topic-expansions when replying. Much to our surprise, the robot's verbal replies produced as much adjacent, topic-maintaining discourse as mothers had been able to produce during earlier, unconstrained play sessions with their child in this same playroom (Dunham, Dunham, Tran, & Akhtar, 1991). Apparently, the robot is an effective verbal playmate for the child, and, unlike a human partner, the robot permits us to control precisely both the verbal and nonverbal input a child receives during any given social interaction. Thus far, we have completed two experiments using the robot as a social partner. Both experiments were designed to test the assumption that contingent, topic-maintaining expansions facilitate discourse near the end of the second year

In the first experiment Dunham et al. (1991) explored the properties of the contingency structure by comparing 2-year-old children's tendency to engage in adjacent, topic-maintaining discourse under two conditions. In one group of children (the contingent condition), each time the child spoke, the robot would reply by repeating the topic and expanding briefly on it. The robot's vocalizations were also tape recorded in this group so that they could be used with a second group of children in a noncontingent condition. In the noncontingent condition, each child was yoked to a child in the contingent group. As such, each child in the noncontingent group heard a series of vocalizations identical to his or her contingent counterpart, but delivered by the robot in a noncontingent structure. These procedures permitted us to equate the verbal and nonverbal social stimulation across the two treatment groups except for the difference in contingency structure.

The results of this experiment clearly demonstrated that the 2-year-old child does differentiate between these two verbal discourse structures. Consistent with the above-described theoretical predictions, a verbal social partner using contingent, topic-expanding replies facilitated both the total amount of adjacent discourse, and the tendency for the children to maintain the topic of conversation during these verbal interactions. To the best of our knowledge, this is the first experimental evidence supporting the assumption that children's discourse at 2 years of age is influenced by the verbal contingency structure.

Several other aspects of the children's behavior during these play sessions with the robot were also of interest in this initial study. For example, the social behavior of some children implied that they perceived the robot as animate. Some children said "Robie play ball," and tossed the nerf balls to the robot; one child said "Watch me juggle," and proceeded to toss balls in the air. Some attempted to dance with Robie, others showed him various objects, and one child, after falling on the robot, showed some concern that Robie might be experiencing pain. While at first glance these observations are compatible with

Tomasello's (1988) suggestion that topic-expanding verbal replies facilitate children's mental attributions at this age, we did not consider these anecdotal observations conclusive. For example, Tomasello's arguments also imply that the noncontingent robot should not support mental attributions, yet some of the children in the noncontingent condition did engage in these same attributional social behaviors. There were also striking individual differences in the tendency for children in both groups to make these animate attributions. Many of the children never engaged in attributional acts other than their verbal conversation, an act obviously consistent with animate attributions.

Given these initial data establishing that children are sensitive to differences in the verbal contingency structure when the total amount and patterns of verbal input are held constant (i.e., the quality vs. quantity assumption), we have proceeded to expand this rationale in several directions permitting a more detailed analysis of these issues. Note first that the above-described experiment confounded two dimensions of the robot's verbal behavior across the contingent and noncontingent conditions. This confounding was necessary in order to contrast the difference in contingency structure while, at the same time, controlling for the absolute quantity of verbal stimulation the child experienced. Specifically, the children in the contingent condition experienced both a *contingency condition* (i.e., there was a programmed sequential dependency between the child's vocalizations and the robot's replies), and an *on-topic reciprocating condition* (i.e., the robot's verbal replies had a consistent semantic relationship to the child's preceding vocalization or reference). The noncontingent group experienced neither the contingency nor the topic maintenance condition. If we want to know whether the reciprocating, topic-maintaining property alone has any influence above and beyond the effects of the contingency structure, an additional experiment is required in which two different contingent robots are compared: a robot that contingently replies to the child's vocalizations with on-topic expansions and a robot that contingently replies to the child's vocalizations with off-topic responses. This comparison is particularly important in the context of Tomasello's analysis, given his emphasis on the importance of the topic-sharing property across conversational turns. The question of interest when comparing the on-topic and off-topic groups is whether 2-year-old children are sensitive to the differences in the topic-structure of the conversations when contingency structure is not confounded with topic maintenance. Again, to the best of our knowledge, this fundamental difference in discourse structure has never been examined in an experimental setting at this important transition stage of early communicative development. It is conceivable, for example, that any timely, contingent adult verbal reply will effectively maintain a 2-year-old's verbal discourse whether or not that reply is semantically related to the child's preceding utterance.

We would also argue that the inanimate robot as a social partner provides a particularly stringent test of Tomasello's assumption that joint episodes of topic-maintaining conversation will facilitate the child's mental state attributions.

According to this hypothesis, certain kinds of social behavior should be more probable during interactions with the topic-maintaining robot. For example, if children in this treatment condition are attributing a shared-attentional state to the robot, they should behave in various ways indicating that they are assessing and actively manipulating the robot's presumed attentional state (e.g., show and offer objects to the robot, point at objects, and ask the robot questions about objects in the playroom). This cluster of joint-attentional behaviors provides an index of the extent to which children in the different treatment conditions conceptualize this plastic playmate as an animate, sentient organism capable of sharing their attention and perceptual experiences (see also Baron-Cohen, 1991).

Finally, as noted earlier, in our initial research using the robot (Dunham et al., 1991) some children made animate attributions and others did not. These individual differences were perplexing, and led us to believe that there may be some important changes in the children's cognitive development during this period that moderate the impact of the different discourse structures. In thinking about these individual differences, Perner's (1991) description of fundamental changes in children's representational skills occurring near the end of the second year seem particularly relevant. He suggests that a child's mental representations during middle infancy are best described as a single, updating "reality model" of the immediate perceptual world. He describes this reality model as a primary representational system in which changing perceptual experiences are continuously being converted directly into mental representations. Near the end of the second year, a more sophisticated secondary representational system is assumed to develop in which children begin to compare multiple mental models of their external world. Among other things, Perner argues that this fundamental change in the representational system is necessary for the child to compare mental representations based on their direct perceptual experiences with representations based on the various kinds of symbolic input they are beginning to process at this age (e.g., pictures, physical models, and linguistic information).

Consider several implications of Perner's theoretical analysis in the context of our experiment comparing the properties of a contingent, on-topic social partner and a contingent, off-topic partner. It seems to us that a 2-year-old child's ability to differentiate between the on-topic and off-topic discourse structures during verbal interactions presupposes some degree of competence in dealing with multiple mental representations of the world. Panel A of Figure 8.2 illustrates the representational process described by Perner when a partner's discourse is contingent and on-topic; and Panel B illustrates the partner's discourse as contingent and off-topic. To detect these semantic differences (reciprocating and nonreciprocating semantic conditions) in the verbal contingency, Perner would argue that the child must be able to comprehend the linguistic input from the robot and compare two mental models of the world; one based on direct visual experience (seeing the piggy in the barn) and one based on the symbolic linguistic information provided by the robot (e.g., the nonreciprocating

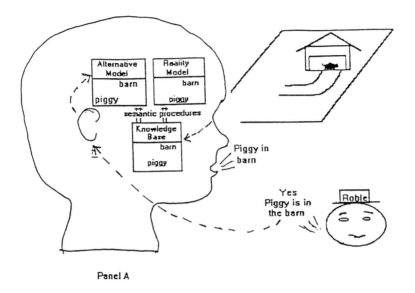

Panel A

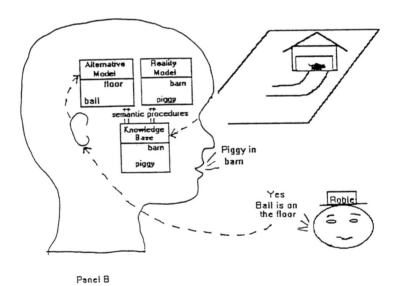

Panel B

FIG. 8.2. Perner's (1991) conceptualization of the 2-year-old's representational processes in the context of "on-topic" (Panel A) and "off-topic" (Panel B) conversational partners.

verbal statement, "yes, the ball is on the floor"). If Perner is correct, the child's secondary representational skills should be an important moderator variable in any procedure designed to assess the effects of these two different verbal discourse structures. Although there are several possible variations on the counterfactual robot portrayed in Panel B of Figure 8.2, according to Perner's analysis, the basic on-topic and off-topic difference illustrated in Panels A and B should have a minimal impact on children lacking these secondary representational skills, whereas children with more developed secondary representational skills should respond differentially to the discourse of the on-topic and off-topic robot.

The minimum requirement for testing these implications of Perner's analysis is a measure of children's secondary representational skills independent of the social interactional context in which the skills are suspected to be important. In discussing these individual differences, Perner (1991) describes several approaches to this measurement problem. He suggests, for example, that children's ability to differentiate mirror-image representations from direct representations of reality provides one index of their emerging secondary representational skills near the end of their second year. To illustrate his argument, consider a teddy bear dangled above and behind a 2-year-old child who is looking in a mirror. According to Perner's analysis, if the child turns around to look at the actual teddy bear, he or she reveals an ability to compare two different representations of the world and respond appropriately; the teddy bear in the mirror and the teddy bear in reality. Alternatively, a child with less developed secondary representational capacities should react to the teddy bear in the mirror as a single updating perceptual model of the world (primary representation), and respond accordingly by examining only the mirror image of the teddy bear. In the context of an on-topic and off-topic verbal contingency, the question of interest is whether children who pass the teddy bear test will more readily differentiate between an on-topic and off-topic structure than children with less advanced secondary representational skills.

Our most recent experiment with the robot was designed to explore each of these issues in more detail. In this experiment, a female experimenter once again replied contingently to the child's vocalizations through a speaker mounted in the robot's chest. In one group of 14 children, during an 8-minute play session, the robot replied to each vocalization by repeating the child's topic and expanding briefly on it (e.g., the child says "ball," the robot replies "Yes, that's a red ball"). In the other group of 14 children, the robot responded to each utterance with an off-topic reply (e.g., the child says "baby," the robot replies "Yes, that's a big truck"). The off-topic replies were selected from a list of topic-maintaining expansions the experimenter had delivered to a child in the on-topic group. Once again, this yoked control procedure permitted us to strictly control the lexical content, prosody, and other paralinguistic cues the child hears across the two discourse structures; only the reciprocating or nonreciprocating semantic nature of the contingent replies differed.

Naive observers coded several different measures from videotapes of the play sessions with the robot. First, with respect to verbal discourse, we asked whether the on-topic robot produced more adjacent vocalizations, and encouraged the child to maintain the topic when he or she replied adjacently. In scoring the tapes, we used the same definitions for adjacency and topic-maintenance employed in our initial research (see Dunham et al., 1991). In addition, we measured the total number of nonadjacent vocalizations during the session and vocalizations directed to the mother. As an index of the children's mental attributions, we measured the frequency of several joint-attentional behaviors directed toward the robot: (a) pointing at objects for the robot, (b) showing objects to the robot, and (c) giving the robot an object by placing it in front of him. In order for these behaviors to be counted as mental (i.e., joint-attentional) attributions, each of these acts had to be accompanied by a vocalization directed to the robot, and had to be enacted in a manner that acknowledged the robot's visual perspective. Finally, in addition to these joint-attentional behaviors, we also measured the frequency of "WH" questions addressed to the robot (e.g., "Where horsey?"; "Whazatt?") on the assumption that this verbal construction provides us with an index of the extent to which the child assumes that the robot has various forms of perceptual knowledge that can be shared.

In a second phase of the procedure, conducted immediately following the robot play session, a female experimenter invited the child to play with some new toys on the floor in front of a large mirror covered by a window blind. A few minutes into this play session, the experimenter raised the blind to reveal the mirror. Each child looked into the mirror during this brief pretest, but none turned around to look at any reflected feature of the room behind them. The blind was then lowered, and several minutes later it was raised for a second time and remained in the raised position for the duration of the play session. After the blind was raised for the second time, when the child looked into the mirror, an assistant, hidden behind a partition, lowered a bouncing teddy bear into position above and behind the child where it was visible in the mirror. The children's responses to the mirror image were judged as falling into one of three categories. Children who reacted within 10 seconds of seeing the teddy bear in the mirror by turning around to look at the actual toy were scored as passing the teddy bear test. Children who reacted to the teddy bear in the mirror by visually or tactually exploring only the mirror image were scored as failing the test. Finally, there was a small percentage of children who were judged as not reacting to the mirror image in any detectable way. In the final data analyses, we combined these latter children with the group who failed the teddy bear test (note that the same conclusions were permissible with or without the latter children included in the failure category).

In considering the results of this experiment, it is instructive to examine first the direct effects of the on-topic and off-topic social partner on the children's discourse and attributional behaviors ignoring, for the moment, the teddy bear

TABLE 8.1
Effects of On-Topic and Off-Topic Discourse Structure
on Adjacent Topic-Maintaining Discourse and
Children's Mental Attributions at 2 Years of Age

Discourse Measures	On-Topic Partner (N = 14)		Off-Topic Partner (N = 14)	
	M	SD	M	SD
Frequency adjacent replies*	31.71	25.60	15.43	10.70
Proportion topic maintaining*	0.51	0.14	0.36	0.15
Frequency speech to mother	12.43	11.10	13.79	12.30
Attributional Measures	M	SD	M	SD
Point, show, offer*	4.29	5.70	1.64	1.78
Frequency WH questions*	2.93	3.87	.71	1.14

*Difference significant at .05 level.

test as a potential moderator variable. The measures of discourse reported in Table 8.1 reveal that 2-year-old children are significantly more likely to make adjacent replies following the robot's utterance in the on-topic group; and that a greater proportion of their replies maintain the topic of the conversation. Given that the frequency of children's utterances directed toward the silent mother during the play session did not differ across the two different treatment conditions, these differential effects of the on-topic and off-topic robot are apparently specific to discourse with the robot. The various measures of attributional behavior reported in Table 8.1 also indicate that children are more likely to engage in joint-attentional behaviors with the on-topic robot, and to ask the on-topic robot WH questions. The children are more likely to direct the on-topic robot's attention to objects and events in the environment by showing and offering objects or pointing to objects and events in a manner that takes into account the robot's visual perspective.

Consider next, the data in Table 8.2, comparing the effects of the on-topic and off-topic robot across children who either passed or failed the teddy bear test. Paired-comparison tests following 2 × 2 ANOVAs on the three measures presented in Table 8.2 revealed substantial moderating effects of the teddy bear measure. First, with reference to the proportion of topic maintaining replies, the on-topic and off-topic treatment produced a significant difference in this measure of discourse only in those children who passed the teddy bear test. Similarly, with respect to the children's mental attributions, the on-topic and off-topic robot produced a significant difference in the frequency of joint-attentional behaviors only in the children who passed the teddy bear test. And finally, when we examined the proportion of WH questions in the children's utterances directed to the robot, the on-topic robot supported significantly more WH ques-

TABLE 8.2
Topic-Maintaining Replies and Mental Attributions With On-Topic
and Off-Topic Partner in Children Who Passed and Children
Who Failed the Teddy Bear Mirror Image Task

	Passed Teddy				Failed Teddy			
	On-Topic		Off-Topic		On-Topic		Off-Topic	
	M	SD	M	SD	M	SD	M	SD
Proportion topic-maintaining	.54	.11	.32	.16*	.48	.17	.41	.15
Frequency WH question	.12	.05	.03	.04*	.02	.02	.01	.03
Frequency joint-attentional (point, show, and offer)	6.71	7.06	1.00	1.15*	1.86	2.54	2.29	2.14

*Difference significant at .05 level.

tions only in the group of children who passed the teddy bear test. We note also that the differences in Table 8.2 that were associated with the teddy test cannot be attributed to confounded differences in language production skills. Vocabulary checklists completed by the mothers revealed no significant differences in language production between children who passed and children who failed the teddy test.

Considered together, this comparison of contingent on-topic and contingent off-topic verbal partners indicates that children's verbal discourse and their joint-attentional behaviors are facilitated by a robot that contingently replies to their vocalizations with topic-expansions, and that these facilitating effects are moderated by individual differences in the ability to differentiate between a mirror-image representation and reality in the teddy bear test. If, as Tomasello assumes, these differences in discourse and social behavior are an index of differences in children's mental attributions, the data provide much-needed experimental support for his suggestion that topic-expansions are optimal input for facilitating true conversation and an emerging theory of mind at this age. If, as Perner suggests, the teddy bear task is an index of the children's secondary representational skills, the data also suggest a corollary to accompany Tomasello's arguments. This corollary indicates that topic-expanding replies can facilitate these changes in early communicative development only after the child has, in Perner's terms, a well-developed secondary representational system.

Although this conceptual framework combining Tomasello's analysis of communicative development and Perner's developmental analysis of representational skills provides a tidy theoretical account of our research thus far on verbal discourse and mental attributions during late infancy, we remain cautious in promoting this interpretation. A more parsimonious interpretation would argue that hearing your speech repeated (with minor variations) each time you speak is simply a pleasant emotional experience for the child, and children are therefore reacting to the on-topic robot's replies by engaging in various verbal and behavioral routines that consistently produce this pleasant outcome. In this more conservative view, describing the children's behaviors with the on-topic robot in terms of predicative, topic-maintaining discourse and mental attributions would be inappropriate.

On the other hand, this more conservative explanation is also difficult to reconcile with the moderating influence of the teddy-bear task. If, as described above, the children in the on-topic condition are simply engaging in previously acquired verbal and gestural routines, it is not clear why their tendency to use these routines would be moderated in any way by their secondary representational skills (i.e., their ability to differentiate mirror-image representations from reality in the teddy-bear task).

CONCLUSIONS

At the beginning of the chapter we asked whether certain qualitative properties of the social stimulation experienced by infants could explain some of the variance in their development above and beyond the quantity of stimulation they receive. We argued that the various theoretical positions exploring this general question across the infancy period share in common the assumption that two structural properties of early social experiences are optimal for various aspects of the infant's development. Different versions of this generic social contingency hypothesis generally agree that (a) social stimulation is most influential when it occurs in a contingency structure, and that (b) within the contingency structure, social stimulation is most effective when the adult's contingent social behavior reciprocates some theoretically specified property of the infant's behavior. We described these theoretical positions as variations on a generic social contingency hypothesis during early infancy. Researchers have described similar attention-reciprocating structures as shared episodes of attention during the middle and late infancy period.

The data discussed in the current chapter provide considerable support for several different variations on the social contingency hypothesis. The general picture painted by these data is one in which a theoretically specified contingent, reciprocating social structure induces or facilitates specific changes in the infant's behavior at a particular point in developmental time. A lesser amount of data also suggest that these changes in behavior generalize across both time and context. The specific examples explored in the present chapter included socially induced changes in attention, positive affect, contingency detection, word learning, verbal discourse, and mental attributions.

Given this overview, we believe that the theory and research in this area needs to be expanded in several related directions. First, research demonstrating that specific developmental changes in behavior can be produced by certain structural properties of social stimulation is only the first step in the process of

understanding these early social influences on development. Once specific optimal social structures have been identified, it is then necessary to elucidate the
mechanisms mediating the influence of these structures. Consider, as an example,
the presumed optimal influence of attention-following structures (i.e., the contingent reciprocation of attention on objects) on early infant lexical development. We cited a considerable amount of correlational and experimental evidence in this chapter consistent with this assumption. However, we also indicated
that several different functional explanations for the optimal properties of the
attention-following structure must be explored in order to understand the processes underlying the demonstrated structural influence. This same point applies
in general to each of the developmental phenomena we discussed in this chapter.
Important progress has been made in terms of identifying the optimal social
structures for certain aspects of development during infancy, but we still know
very little about the emotional, motivational, and cognitive processes that presumably underlie the influence of these structures.

A second, related point concerns the nature of existing theories. With few
exceptions (see Tomasello, Kruger, & Ratner, 1993), the theoretical accounts
of phenomena discussed in this chapter are perhaps best described as a collection
of "miniature theories" each designed to deal with specific developmental phenomena at certain points in developmental time (e.g., Stern's, 1986, attunement
hypothesis; Tomasello's, 1988, attentional mapping hypothesis; Kaye's, 1982,
discourse framing hypothesis). As our understanding of the mechanisms underlying these specific phenomena increases, we believe it will be important to
replace these circumscribed approaches with a more integrated conceptual framework. We hope that our attempt to define and differentiate the fundamental
operations underlying many of the existing variations on the concept of an
optimal social structure will facilitate this process.

ACKNOWLEDGMENT

Research supported by a grant from the Social Sciences and Humanities Research
Council of Canada to Philip J. Dunham.

REFERENCES

Adamson, L., & Bakeman, R. (1991). The development of shared attention during infancy. In R.
    Vasta (Ed.), Annals of child development (Vol. 8, pp. 1–41). London: Kingsley.
Akhtar, N., Dunham, F., & Dunham, P. (1991). Directive interactions and early vocabulary
    development: The role of joint attentional focus. Journal of Child Language, 18, 41–49.
Astington, J., Harris, P., & Olson, D. (1988). Developing theories of mind. Cambridge, England:
    Cambridge University Press.

Bakeman, R., & Adamson, L. (1984). Coordinating attention to people and objects in mother-infant and peer-infant interaction. *Child Development, 55,* 1278–1289.

Baron-Cohen, S. (1991). Precursors to a theory of mind: Understanding attention in others. In A. Whiten (Ed.), *Natural theories of mind* (pp. 234–251). Oxford, England: Blackwell.

Barnes, S., Gutfreund, M., Satterly, D., & Wells, G. (1983). Characteristics of adult speech which predict children's language development. *Journal of Child Language, 10,* 65–84.

Bloom, L., Rocissano, L., & Hood, L. (1976). Adult-child discourse: Developmental interaction between information processing and linguistic knowledge. *Cognitive Psychology, 8,* 521–552.

Boccia, M., & Campos, J. (1989). Maternal emotional signals, social referencing, and infants' reactions to strangers. In N. Eisenberg (Ed.), *Empathy and related emotional responses* (pp. 25–49). San Francisco: Jossey-Bass.

Bordeaux, M., & Willbrand, M. (1987). Pragmatic development in children's telephone discourse. *Discourse Processes, 10,* 253–266.

Bowlby, J. (1951). *Maternal care and mental health.* Geneva: World Health Organization.

Bowlby, J. (1969). *Attachment and loss: Vol. 1. Attachment.* New York: Basic Books.

Brazelton, T. B., Tronick, E., Adamson, L., Als, H., & Wise, S. (1975). Early mother–infant reciprocity. In M. Lewis & L. Rosenblum (Eds.), *The effect of the infant on its caregiver* (pp. 49–76). Amsterdam: Association of Scientific Publishers.

Bronfenbrenner, U. (1979). *The ecology of human development: Experiments by nature and design.* Cambridge, MA: Harvard University Press.

Bruner, J. (1977). Early social interaction and language acquisition. In H. R. Schaffer (Ed.), *Studies in mother-infant interaction* (pp. 271–289). New York: Academic Press.

Bruner, J. (1983). *Child's talk: Learning to use langauge.* New York: Academic Press.

Collis, G. (1985). On the origins of turn-taking: Alternation and meaning. In M. Barret (Ed.), *Children's single word speech* (pp. 217–230). New York: Wiley.

Dunham, P., & Dunham, F. (1990). Effects of mother-infant social interactions on infants' subsequent contingency task performance. *Child Development, 61,* 785–793.

Dunham, P., & Dunham, F. (1992). Lexical development during the middle infancy period: A mutually driven infant-caregiver process. *Developmental Psychology, 28,* 414–420.

Dunham, P., Dunham, F., & Curwin, A. (1993). Joint-attentional states and lexical acquisition at 18 months. *Developmental Psychology, 29,* 827–831.

Dunham, P., Dunham, F., Hurshman, A., & Alexander, T. (1989). Social contingency effects on subsequent perceptual-cognitive tasks in young infants. *Child Development, 60,* 1486–1496.

Dunham, P., Dunham, F., Tran, S., & Akhtar, N. (1991). The nonreciprocating robot: Effects on verbal discourse, social play, and social referencing at 2 years of age. *Child Development, 62,* 1489–1502.

Ervin-Tripp, S. (1979). Children's verbal turn-taking. In E. Ochs & B. Schiefflen (Eds.), *Developmental pragmatics* (pp. 391–414). New York: Academic Press

Ervin-Tripp, S., & Gordon, D. (1986). The development of requests. In R. Schiefelbusch (Ed.), *Language competence: Assessment and intervention* (pp. 61–95). San Diego: College Hill.

Fafouti-Milenkovic, M., & Uzgiris, I. (1979). The mother-infant communication system. *New Directions for Child Development, 4,* 41–56.

Field, T., & Fox, N. (1985). *Social perception in infants.* Norwood, NJ: Ablex Press.

Frye, D., & Moore, C. (1991). *Children's theories of mind: Mental states and social understanding.* Hillsdale, NJ: Lawrence Erlbaum Associates.

Harris, M., Jones, D., Brookes, S., & Grant, J. (1986). Relations between the nonverbal context of maternal speech and rate of language development. *British Journal of Developmental Psychology, 4,* 261–268.

Jakobson, R. (1960). Linguistics and poetic. In T. Sebeok (Ed.), *Style in language* (pp. 350–357). New York: Wiley.

Jasnow, M., & Feldstein, S. (1986). Adult-like temporal characteristics of mother-infant vocal interactions. *Child Development, 57,* 754–761.

Kaye, K. (1982). The mental and social life of babies. Chicago: University of Chicago Press.

Kaye, K., & Charney, R. (1980). How mothers maintain "dialogue" with 2-year-olds. In D. R. Olson (Ed.), The social foundations of language and thought: Essays in honor of Jerome S. Bruner (pp. 211–230). New York: Norton.

Lewis, M., & Brooks-Gunn, J. (1979). Social cognition and the acquisition of self. New York: Plenum.

Murray, L., & Trevarthen, C. (1985). Emotional regulation of interactions between 2-month-olds and their mothers. In T. Field & N. Fox (Eds.), Social perception in infants (pp. 177–198). Norwood, NJ: Ablex

Penner, S. (1987). Parental responses to grammatical and ungrammatical utterances. Child Development, 58, 376–384.

Perner, J. (1991). Understanding the representational mind. Cambridge, MA: MIT Press.

Rocissano, L., & Yatchmink, Y. (1983). Language skill and interactive patterns in prematurely born toddlers. Child Development, 54, 1229–1241.

Ross, H., Cheyne, J., & Lollis, S. (1988). Defining and studying reciprocity in young children. In S. Duck (Ed.), Handbook of personal relationships (pp. 143–160). New York: Wiley.

Ross, G., Nelson, K., Wetstone, H., & Tanouye, E. (1986). Acquisition and generalization of novel object concepts by young language learners. Journal of Child Language, 13, 67–83.

Schaffer, H. R. (1977). Studies in mother-infant interaction. London: Academic Press.

Scherer, N., & Olswang, L. (1984). Role of mother's expansions in stimulating children's language production. Journal of Speech and Hearing Research, 27, 387–396.

Seligman, M. E. P. (1975). Helplessness: On depression, development, and death. San Francisco: Freeman.

Skinner, E. (1985). Action, control judgements, and the structure of control experience. Psychological Review, 92, 39–58.

Spitz, R. (1950). Possible infantile precursors of infantile psychopathology. American Journal of Orthopsychiatry, 20, 240–248.

Spitz, R. (1965). The first year of life. New York: International Universities Press.

Stern, D. (1985). The interpersonal world of the infant. New York: Basic Books.

Stern, D. (1986). Development of the infant's sense of self. New York: Basic Books.

Stern, D., Hofer, L., Haft, W., & Dore, J. (1985). Affect attunement: The sharing of feeling states between mother and infant by means of intermodal fluency. In T. Field & N. Fox (Eds.), Social perception in infants (pp. 249–268). Norwood, NJ: Ablex.

Tomasello, M. (1988). The role of joint attentional processes in early language development. Language Sciences, 10, 69–88.

Tomasello, M. (1992). The social bases of language acquisition. Social Development, 1, 68–87.

Tomasello, M., & Farrar, J. (1986). Joint attention and early language. Child Development, 57, 1454–1463.

Tomasello, M., Kruger, A., & Ratner, H. (in press). Cultural learning. Behavioral and Brain Sciences.

Tomasello, M., & Todd, J. (1983). Joint attention and early lexical acquisition style. First Language, 4, 197–212.

Trevarthen, C. (1979). Communication and cooperation in early infancy: A description of primary intersubjectivity. In M. Bullowa (Ed.), Before speech: The beginnings of interpersonal communication (pp. 321–346). Cambridge, England: Cambridge University Press.

Tronick, E. (1989). Emotions and emotional communication in infants. American Psychologist, 44, 112–119.

Tronick, E., Als, H., & Brazelton, T. B. (1980). Monadic phases: A structural descriptive analysis of infant-mother face-to-face interaction. Merrill-Palmer Quarterly, 26, 3–24.

Vygotsky, L. (1986). Thought and language. (A. Kozulin, Trans.) Cambridge, MA: MIT Press.

Watson, J. (1985). Contingency perception in early social development. In T. Field & N. Fox (Eds.), Social perception in infants (pp. 157–176). Hillsdale, NJ: Lawrence Erlbaum Associates.

Wellman, H. (1990). The child's theory of mind. Cambridge, MA: MIT Press.

Werner, J., & Kaplan, B. (1963). Symbol formation. New York: Wiley.

Chapter 9

Joint Attention Across Contexts in Normal and Autistic Children

Marian Sigman
Connie Kasari
University of California at Los Angeles

In the last few years, a great deal of research has focused on the use of joint attention by the infant and young child. For the most part, this research has examined normative patterns of development. Less attention has been paid to individual differences within typically developing groups or to differences due to developmental delay or psychopathology. Yet, children vary in their ability to regulate attention, their level of social understanding, and their interest in the reactions of other people. For this reason, it seems worthwhile to investigate the extent to which individuals differ and how these differences might be related to cognitive and language development.

Joint attention has been defined both narrowly and broadly in the research literature. In the narrower definition, the term joint attention refers to "looking where someone else is looking" (Butterworth, 1991, p. 223). This occurs when infants notice that another person has turned their eyes or head in a certain direction and the infants follow suit, or when infants move their head or eyes in the same direction as someone is pointing. Besides this kind of responsive joint attention, infants can also initiate joint attention by holding up something for another person to see or by pointing at something themselves. The broader definition of joint attention includes these responsive and initiating behaviors as well as the checking of another person's face that occurs while the infant is playing with something, when the infant has accomplished some task, after the infant has pointed to something, or in an ambiguous situation. We have used this broader definition in our previous work and continue to do so in this chapter. While some authors in this book use the narrower definition, our definition resembles what Adamson and McArthur (this volume) refer to as "opening or maintaining a communicative channel with the partner." Similarly, Landry (this volume) defines coordinated joint attention in infants as "moving their attention from a toy to mother and back to the toy" so that visual checking of the other's face is included in the definition.

The young child's motives, intentions, and understanding in attending to another person vary across contexts. Attention to the faces of others seems to be used for affective sharing in some situations and for obtaining information or reassurance in others. If the infant is looking to seek information, it is often not clear what kind of information is wanted or what is obtained. For example, infants may be looking to ask "What is this?" or "What do I do with this?" or "Why are you doing that?" or, perhaps less likely, "What do you think of this?" As a corollary, the extent to which joint attention reflects the beginning of social and emotional understanding is unknown. The infant may use the person's face as a kind of traffic light, to get a signal how to act, with little attribution of thought or feeling to the other person. Alternatively, joint attention may be a precursor of "theory of mind" in that the infant may be demonstrating a beginning sense of awareness that another person has feelings and thoughts that may be useful to consider.

In our view, joint attention must involve an integration of information processing and emotional responsiveness. If joint attention is seen as an instrumentally conditioned behavior reinforced by the experience of seeing the object of the mother's attention (Moore & Corkum, in press), one has to explain how and why the infant finds looking where the mother looks to be reinforcing. Such an explanation requires establishing why the mother is reinforcing and identifying some mechanism that makes what the mother plays with and looks at reinforcing to the child. Infants' emotional reactions and sensitivity to the emotions of others are likely to be important in explaining how the mother's views gain this kind of valence. Moreover, many episodes of infant initiated joint attention tend to be marked by vivid affect on the faces of infant and social partner. The role of this affect in these interchanges has to be considered.

Joint attention has been studied in several contexts with each line of inquiry fairly independent of the others. The most thoroughly researched lines of developmental inquiry are as follows: (a) joint gaze and shared verbal reference; (b) social referencing of adults, usually in ambiguous situations; and (c) responses to the distress of others. The first purpose of this chapter is to review the research on joint attention in different contexts. We have found parallel increases in the use of joint attention in these contexts, suggesting that the processes assessed have some shared base.

A second issue addressed by this chapter is the extent to which there are consistent individual differences across contexts. The identification of individual consistencies across contexts may aid in determining the extent to which all forms of joint attention share a common base and the nature of this base. Finally, we discuss the evidence for the notion that joint attention is a necessary precursor to language acquisition. We do this by examining the associations between joint attention and language skills in both normal children and children with autism. Children with autism do not use joint attention in the same way as typically developing children. Moreover, preliminary evidence suggests that those children with autism who do use joint attention to some extent are more likely to acquire language skills than autistic children who do not use joint attention.

NORMAL DEVELOPMENT OF JOINT ATTENTION IN DIFFERENT CONTEXTS

Shared Gaze and Verbal Reference

One line of inquiry has been concerned with the development of joint gaze between the infant and a social partner. After 6 months of age, infants begin to integrate their attention with that of others. At first, this appears in occasional glances back and forth between an object and a person. By 8–9 months of age, infants follow another person's line of regard, although this does not become standard until 12 months (Corkum & Moore, this volume; Scaife & Bruner, 1975). Infants follow pointing gestures to the side or ahead by 9 months of age but not across the body until 14 months (Murphy & Messer, 1977). By the end of the first year, the infant follows the mother's glance and looks back at her face if she looks off in space (Butterworth, 1991).

While infants are clearly able to follow gaze, they engage in little coordinated attention until the second year of life (Adamson & Bakeman, 1985; Bakeman & Adamson, 1984). Before this time, the caregiver provides a great deal of support for shared attention. In the earliest period, caregivers hold up objects for infants to see. Early joint engagement is also supported by caregivers in such shared activities as book reading (Ninio & Bruner, 1978) and hide and seek (Ratner & Bruner, 1978). Infants do not routinely check the caregiver's gaze until 14–18 months, and coordinated joint attention in which the infant attempts to maintain engagement with the caregiver does not take up sizeable amounts of play time until 18 months (Bakeman & Adamson, 1984).

The child's awareness of the caregiver's interest influences not only attention but also emotional responses. By 10 months of age, infants smile more at caregivers who are looking at them during toy play than at caregivers who are inattentive (Jones, Collins, & Hong, 1991). This effect is quite specific in that attentiveness of caregivers does not appear to affect the infant's interest or pleasure in the toy. By 12 months, the normal infant also shows a differentiated emotional expression depending on the message to be communicated. Like adults, infants smile when they are sharing an experience with another person but fail to smile when they are attempting to obtain an object or assistance (Mundy, Kasari, & Sigman, 1992).

Understanding the significance of another person's gaze can be documented by verbal understanding when infants are 18 months of age. If an adult labels an object that he or she is looking at when the infant is looking at a different object, when asked to which object the label applies, the infant will select the object of the adult's gaze (Baldwin, 1991). At earlier ages in these studies, infants did not show evidence of having word–object mappings so it was impossible to evaluate whether they actually understood the significance of shared reference (Baldwin, in press). However, by 19 to 20 months, it is clear that the infant can distinguish between referential and nonreferential acts (Baldwin, this volume).

This ability is critical for language learning as the infant has to be able to detect the object being labelled if she or he is going to learn verbal labels. Caregivers appear to try to make language learning easier by following the infant's line of regard or pointing gestures and labeling the object on which the infant's attention is focused (Collis, 1977; Leung & Rheingold, 1981; Masur, 1983; Murphy, 1978). Moreover, caregivers who do this more frequently have children with better verbal skills (Akhtar, Dunham, & Dunham, 1991; Tomasello, Mannle, & Kruger, 1986; Tomasello & Todd, 1983). On the other hand, caregivers do not carry all the responsibility for language learning as indicated by evidence that their labels correspond to infant attention about 50 to 70% of the time (Collis, 1977; Harris, Jones, & Grant, 1983). For this reason, the infant's ability to link the adult's gaze with the object labelled is an important component in learning language.

Social Referencing of Adults in Ambiguous Situations

At least part of the motive for sharing gaze appears to be an inherent interest in the other person and the object of that person's gaze. However, infants also seem to look at other people's faces for information or reassurance. For example, the infant will look at the mother or another adult when faced with a situation that is ambiguous or mildly threatening. This is true for the visual cliff (Sorce, Emde, Campos, & Klinnert, 1985), an unfamiliar adult (Feinman & Lewis, 1983), a moving robot (Gunnar & Stone, 1984), or a rabbit in a cage (Hornik & Gunnar, 1988). If the adult blocks the child's hand when the child is manipulating an object or offers an object and then pulls back, the infant will gaze at the adult's face (Phillips, Baron-Cohen, & Rutter, 1992). In all of these situations, it appears as if the infant is checking the adult's face to determine something about the situation or even, perhaps, the adult's intentions.

Although a child may be most likely to check the face of another person in an ambiguous situation, the child references in unambiguous situations as well. When infants were placed on the shallow side as opposed to the deep side of the visual cliff, they unhesitatingly crossed to their mothers without referencing their mothers' faces. On the other hand, infants will reference if the mother verbally expresses strong affect and will respond to verbal messages from caregivers even when these are unsolicited (Hornik & Gunnar, 1988).

The behavioral effects of visual referencing vary depending on the situation. The most dramatic effects have been shown in the visual cliff situation. When the infant is presented with an unfamiliar robot, the affect shown by the caregiver's face may influence distance from the caregiver rather than manipulation of the unfamiliar toy. On the other hand, some studies have documented clear behavioral effects on toy play in infants from 10 to 13 months of age (Hornik, Risenhoover, & Gunnar, 1987; Walden & Baxter, 1989; Walden & Ogan, 1988). In the one study investigating the responses of infants older than 13 months, the infants actually preferred the toy that the mother treated as fearful. Some of these infants seemed to be trying to convince their mothers that the toy was really not dangerous (Walden & Ogan, 1988).

Only a few studies have investigated developmental changes, most of these comparing 12- to 18-month-olds (Hornik & Gunnar, 1988; Klinnert, 1984; Walden & Baxter, 1989; Walden & Ogan, 1988). In several of these studies, older children visually referenced more quickly and more often. In addition, in two studies, older children were more likely to look at their mothers' faces before acting rather than after acting. Younger children were equally likely to act before looking as to look before acting. In spite of this, Hornik and Gunnar (1988) point out that only a few infants followed the classically defined pattern of attention to the novel object followed by social referencing and then physical approach.

Responses to the Distress of Others

Just as infants respond to emotions of fear and disgust in others, so they respond to distress in others. As early as 10 weeks, infants discriminate between facial and vocal expressions of joy, anger, and sadness displayed by their mothers and show increases in mouth movements to sadness (Haviland & Lelwica, 1987). They begin to show prosocial responses to the distress of others by 12 months and show a full range of prosocial behaviors by 20 to 24 months (Zahn-Waxler, Radke-Yarrow, Wagner, & Chapman, 1992).

There are clear developmental trends in prosocial behaviors and empathetic concern over the second year of life, particularly in response to witnessed episodes of naturally occuring distress in the home (Zahn-Waxler et al., 1992). In reactions to simulated episodes of distress, empathetic concern but not prosocial behaviors increased with age in a sample of twins (Zahn-Waxler, Robinson, & Emde, 1992). Girls showed more empathetic concern than boys for witnessed distress in one study, and more prosocial behaviors, empathetic concern, hypothesis testing, and self-distress in response to simulated episodes of distress in the second study. These results support other evidence that girls display more empathy than boys (Brody, 1985; Eisenberg & Lennon, 1983).

Few studies of infant responses to distress have focused specifically on gaze behaviors in this context either to the distressed adults or to other adults in the environment. We noted very high levels of attention to a distressed adult among our normal control sample in a study comparing the responses of autistic, mentally retarded, and normal children. One would expect that infants would reference other adults present in the room and not show any comforting behaviors if an unfamiliar adult showed a marked degree of distress. Even at nursery school age, children do not respond to a peer who is distressed if an adult is present (Caplan & Hay, 1989).

PARALLELS IN THE DEVELOPMENT
AND MANIFESTATION OF JOINT ATTENTION
ACROSS CONTEXTS

There are both differences and similarities in the use of joint attention across contexts. On the one hand, the infant's goals appear to vary somewhat across the situations. Thus, they display more effort to share attention and affect in some situations and more effort to use the emotions of others to make sense of puzzling encounters in other situations—a differentiation described by Hornik and Gunnar as "share looks" and "reference looks." Despite these differences, the infant responses observed in these situations all seem to index some early form of social awareness. In all cases, the infant seems to be interested in un-derstanding the attention and emotional expressions of other people. If these behaviors are tapping a similar core process, then similar developmental changes should appear in responses to the three types of situations. Furthermore, there may be individual differences in that infants who are attentive in one situation may also be attentive in the others.

Parallels in the Use of Gaze With Development

In order to investigate this question, we examined the gaze behavior of a group of 51 normal children ranging in age from 8 to 30 months (Sigman & Kasari, 1994). The children were studied in all three contexts. Each child was observed during a 30 minute semistructured play interaction with the experimenter (Seibert, Hogan, & Mundy, 1982) in order to examine shared attention. Coding of gaze behaviors was done from videotapes of these sessions. Gaze behaviors coded included eye contact to the experimenter while holding a toy, gaze alter-nation between the experimenter and the toy, pointing, and showing of toys. Responses to pointing by the experimenter to the side or behind the infant were also recorded. The results indicated that there were developmental changes in all these behaviors except for showing which was rarely observed in this situation. Eye contact while holding the toy declined with age, whereas gaze alternation, pointing, and responding to points increased as the children matured.

In a similar fashion, there were developmental changes in the frequency with which normal children looked at their parent in the social referencing situation and in a situation in which the experimenter showed distress. In the social referencing situation, the parent and an experimenter showed either fear or amusement upon entry of a small, moving robot and for 30 seconds afterwards. The behaviors of the child, parent, and experimenter were videotaped and the child's gaze behaviors to parent, experimenter, and robot were observed and recorded. Older children looked more frequently at the parent than younger children and shifted their gaze more frequently from adult to robot particularly in the fear situation. In order to investigate the infants' responses to someone else's distress, the experimenter pretended to hurt her finger with a hammer while showing the child how to play with a small pounding toy. The infants generally looked at the experimenter for nearly the whole 30 second period, after which the experimenter showed the infant that her finger was better. However, older infants both looked at the experimenter more frequently and turned to reference their parent sitting behind them more frequently than younger infants.

Thus, there appear to be parallel changes with development in the frequency with which infants shift gaze from an adult's face to a toy and look at the adult's face in ambiguous and possibly disturbing situations. These findings suggest that there is some core similarity in the kinds of social understanding and responsiveness measured in these situations.

Individual Difference in Gaze Across Contexts

Additional support for this hypothesis comes from evidence that there were consistencies in the responses of individuals across the situations. Infants who alternated gaze between toy and adult in the social play observation also looked more frequently and for longer durations at the experimenter in the social referencing situation and looked at the distressed adult longer. Infants who looked longer at the experimenter in the social referencing situation also looked longer at the distressed experimenter. These associations were independent of chronological age. Thus, infants appeared to vary in the extent to which they were likely to focus attention on the experimenter during pleasant, ambiguous and disturbing situations. This finding suggests that one component of joint attention is interest in the facial expressions of an unfamiliar adult. Some infants are more likely than others to look at an unfamiliar adult regardless of the function served by looking.

We suggested earlier in this chapter that joint attention might be important for language learning and there is some evidence for this hypothesis. Regardless of age, children who followed points behind themselves more frequently and turned to reference their parents more frequently and for longer periods when the experimenter was distressed also had higher scores on a measure of expressive language. Thus, responsive joint attention and referential looking were associated with sophistication of language use.

An unanticipated observation in this study was that female infants referenced the experimenter more than male infants during the robot situation. Girls also looked slightly longer at the distressed adult than did male infants. While girls have been reported to show more empathetic concern than boys at 14 months of age, as far as we know, this is the first time that gender differences have been reported in referencing behaviors. Rosen, Adamson, and Bakeman (1992) found no gender differences in frequency of referencing but 12-month-old girls' behavior seemed more modulated by maternal messages than was true for boys. If girls are truly more socially interested or knowledgeable than boys by the second year of life, this might explain the relative advantage shown by girls in early language ability.

LACK OF JOINT ATTENTION IN CHILDREN WITH AUTISM

The parallels in developmental change and individual differences in the behavior of typically developing children point to some shared basis for the use of gaze in these contexts. However, there are limits to what we can understand about the functions and consequences of these different uses of joint attention from normal children. Although there may be some variation in normal groups in the rate of learning these behaviors and the frequency with which they are manifested, all normal children use gaze in all these different situations to some extent. Children with autism, however, do not use gaze across settings. Their deficits dramatically illustrate the importance of different forms of joint attention in development. Moreover, to the extent that we can postulate links between their deficits in use of gaze and subsequent communicative and adaptive problems, we may have some idea of the role that these early behaviors play in the typically developing child's language and social development.

Shared Gaze and Verbal Reference

Young autistic children are limited in their ability to share attention with other individuals for any purpose other than to obtain something that they want. In two different samples of autistic children who were functioning developmentally around 20 to 24 months of age, we have found very little joint attention behavior during a play interaction with the experimenter (Mundy, Sigman, & Kasari, 1994; Mundy, Sigman, Ungerer, & Sherman, 1986). The autistic children looked at the experimenter, alternated gaze, pointed and followed points much less than normal and mentally retarded children matched on mental age. In contrast, autistic children looked at the experimenter to receive help in obtaining a toy from a jar with the top screwed on tight or an object out of reach or to have a wind-up toy rewound. Autistic children also generally looked at the experimenter if the experimenter tickled them or if they were engaged in rolling a toy car back and forth. While there were some differences in attention even during behaviors used for requesting assistance with objects and in social interaction, these differences were small compared to those observed in joint attention with the experimenter.

Autistic children also rarely share attention with their parents (Sigman, Mundy, Sherman, & Ungerer, 1986). This was startlingly clear during a play interaction in which normal and mentally retarded children frequently held up toys for their parents to look at and carried toys to their parents to see. Very few autistic children ever brought toys to their parents' attention. Similarly, when parents were asked to observe their children's play and to refrain from initiations, the autistic children rarely looked to their parents (Kasari, Sigman, & Yirmiya, 1993b). In addition, normal and mentally retarded children looked and smiled at their parents seated to the side of them after they had completed a puzzle and looked up when praised (Kasari, Sigman, Baumgartner, & Stipek, 1993a). In contrast, few autistic children looked up for approval or in response to praise. Thus, in situations where normally developing children and their parents tend to share attention either to themselves or to objects, autistic children rarely do so.

Social Referencing of Adults in Ambiguous Situations

Autistic children rarely, if ever, look at other people's faces for information or reassurance. In the situation described previously where adults posed either fear or amusement at the entrance of a small robot, few of the autistic children looked at either the parent or the experimenter (Sigman, Kasari, Kwon, & Yirmiya, 1992). When they did look, their glances were much briefer than those of the mentally retarded or normal children who searched the faces of the adults. Thus, autistic children do not engage in either "share looks" or "reference looks."

The deficit in shared looking among autistic children might be attributed to an inability to integrate positive affect with attention to people. Dawson and her colleagues (Dawson, Hill, Spencer, Galpert, & Watson, 1990) have reported that although autistic children look and smile at their mothers as much as control children, affect and attention are not combined as they are for the children in the control groups. Because shared looking requires an integration of attention with the expression of positive affect, the deficit in shared looking could be attributed to limited capacities for affect expression-attention integration (Kasari, Sigman, Mundy, & Yirmiya, 1990). However, the evidence that autistic children do not engage in reference looks counters this interpretation. During social referencing, normal children usually show neutral or, occasionally, mildly negative affect. The fact that autistic children do not reference any more than they share attention suggests that the difficulty is not just a problem in the integration of affective expression with attention.

Response to the Distress of Others

In line with the findings regarding shared looking and social referencing, young autistic children pay very little attention when someone else is distressed (Sigman et al., 1992). In the study mentioned previously, young normal and mentally retarded children appeared to be almost spellbound when an adult, either the parent or a stranger, pretended to have hurt themselves. Although they did not show much change in facial affect or much behavioral response in this situation, they attended nearly without interruption to the face of the distressed adult. Most autistic children glanced at the distressed adult but they looked very fleetingly. Moreover, they mostly ignored the adult and, instead, played with the toy that the experimenter had been using. Similarly, when the parent or stranger pretended to feel ill and lay down on a couch, the autistic children appeared not to notice.

Social Responsiveness

One of the central questions that can be asked is whether the lack of shared attention, of social referencing, and of response to the distress of others can be attributed to lack of social responsiveness in autistic children. As we have mentioned earlier, autistic children do respond to others who initiate social interaction with them. In a social play situation where mothers were asked to interact with their autistic children with a series of different toys, two different samples of autistic children did not look any less at their mothers than did the normal children (Kasari et al., 1993b; Sigman et al., 1986). When mothers engaged in a social game, the children in all the groups looked more at their mothers and there were no group differences. The autistic children did not seem any more avoidant than the normal or mentally retarded children.

In line with these findings, autistic children do seem to form attachments to familiar caregivers and will show changes in behavior when separated from their parent and reunited (Sigman & Mundy, 1989; Sigman & Ungerer, 1984). Moreover, at least some autistic children appear to have secure attachments with their caregivers even though their behavior is more disorganized and erratic than is usually true for securely attached children (Capps, Sigman, & Mundy, 1994).

On the other hand, autistic children do not initiate social interaction with their caregivers or others when left to their own devices (Kasari et al., 1993b). Thus, they do seem as responsive as other children but appear uninterested or ill equipped to initiate social contact, at least when they are developmentally immature.

Autistic children's failure to reference and share attention has a very dramatic effect on their social interactions. One often becomes aware of a feeling of loneliness or isolation when interacting with a young autistic child even before one is aware of what is missing. Social referencing is an acknowledgement of the presence of a social partner so that a child who does not reference a partner causes the partner to feel invisible or absent. While most adults can overcome this sensation by attempting to maintain connection to the child, this is too much for most peers to attempt. Not surprisingly, autistic children have profound difficulties in relationships with peers.

What Is the Cause of the Deficit in Joint Attention in Autism?

The explanation for the deficit in autism depends on the conceptualization of joint attention in normal development. If joint attention is seen as a kind of information processing, then autistic children are thought to suffer from deficits in the ability to shift or modulate attention or to use the eye direction of others as a guide. There is some evidence that autistic individuals are less able to shift attention even with nonsocial stimuli (Courchesne et al., 1994). However, these hypotheses do not explain the failure of autistic children to look at people who are showing distress. There is little need for the child to shift attention or to read eye gaze position in these situations.

One might attribute the lack of attention to the faces of others as disinterest and lack of responsiveness except that, as discussed previously, autistic children are not so socially unresponsive. They are generally able to engage in dyadic attention. Instead, the young autistic child seems unable to read any facial expressions or signs of interest in others. Although older, more intelligent autistic children can identify emotional expressions accurately, they seem to depend on an intellectual understanding of their own and others' emotions as if they were solving cognitive problems.

The deficit, then, seems most profound at the intersection of attention and cognition with affect. This is not to say that there are no problems in attention modulation or affective responsiveness independently. However, our impression is that the greatest disorder occurs when the autistic child has to integrate attention and affect. One might think that it would be impossible to read the interests and emotions of others unless one both experienced these interests and emotions oneself and could see some sort of match between one's own experiences and emotions and those of others. There is no good evidence at this point that autistic children do not respond emotionally so it would seem that what is lacking is some way to contrast the interests and emotions of the self with those of others. Of course, this line of thinking implies that normal children are somewhat aware of their own interests and emotions and those of others when they share point of view.

The Consequences for Language Development

We have argued that joint attention may be a prerequisite for language development and have provided supporting evidence from our research and that of others with normal children. If joint attention is necessary for language acquisition, then children who do not develop joint attention should be severely impaired in language abilities. In fact, many autistic children do not develop much comprehension or productive use of language. Moreover, children with autism who do show some joint attention develop language skills that are superior to autistic children who do not show joint attention (Mundy, Sigman, & Kasari, 1990; Mundy, Sigman, Ungerer, & Sherman, 1987). Other forms of nonverbal communication, such as nonverbal requesting, do not predict language acquisition in children with autism. Thus, joint attention is uniquely important in the development of language among autistic children.

DISCUSSION

The tendency of infants to look at others in play interactions, ambiguous situations, and in response to the emotions of others seems to index their dawning social understanding. To some theorists, this understanding is seen as very primitive and involves little appreciation of the thoughts, intentions, and experiences of others. To us, the avid looking back and forth from adult to ambiguous object reflects an active process of trying to understand the reactions of others. Moreover, this process appears to include more than simply using the eyes as indicators of the mind. Affective signals from other parts of the face influence the infant's attention and behavior.

The impression one has in watching young autistic children in these situations is that they simply cannot read the facial expressions of others. There appears to be little motivation for them to look at the faces of others because these faces provide them with little information about the motives, intentions, or perceptions of others. Of course, this suggests that the normal child is able to interpret facial expression, at least at a very primitive level. It may be that the normal child is merely using the face as a marker with no thought to the mental states of others. However, it is difficult not to impute some level of social understanding to a normal 14-month-old who stares at the distressed experimenter, looks behind her at her parent, looks again at the experimenter, and repeats this sequence, each time seeming a bit more worried.

Moreover, even if one is reluctant to impute some awareness of mental states to the child engaged in these behaviors, such experiences must aggregate to help the child construct a model of other people's minds. We cannot say for sure that the autistic child in middle childhood does not understand "theory of mind" because they ignore the attention and facial expressions of others but there are certain parallels in the deficits. Several years ago, Marc Bornstein and I (Bornstein & Sigman, 1986) suggested that the most prevalent form of continuity in development was of underlying processes. We were referring to the link between different behaviors at different developmental periods that served similar functions. In line with this notion, there may be some continuity in the underlying process between joint attention in the second year of life and understanding "theory of mind" some years later.

The study of joint attention in young normal and atypical children has revealed some core processes in early social responsivenss and understanding. Even though adults are socially aware at much more intricate levels, they continue to share attention and to reference in social situations. One can learn a great deal about the social relationships of a pair or group of people by observing their social referencing patterns. The deficits in these behaviors in children with autism continue to imperil their social relationships throughout their lives.

ACKNOWLEDGMENT

The research presented in this chapter was supported by NINDS Grant 25243 and NICHD Grant 17662. Contributions to the research were made by Lisa Capps, Jung-Hye Kwon, Peter Mundy, Judy Ungerer, and Nurit Yirmiya. We appreciate the assistance provided us over the years in research design and analysis by Michael Espinosa and in administering our research projects and fathoming the ways of the university by Margie Greenwald.

REFERENCES

Adamson, L. B., & Bakeman, R. (1985). Affect and attention: Infants observed with mothers and peers. *Child Development, 56*, 582–593.

Akhtar, N., Dunham, F., & Dunham, P. J. (1991). Directive interactions and early vocabulary development: The role of joint attentional focus. *Journal of Child Language, 18*, 41–49.

Bakeman, R., & Adamson, L. B. (1984). Coordinating attention to people and objects in mother-infant and peer-infant interaction. *Child Development, 55*, 1278–1289.

Baldwin, D. A. (1991). Infants' contribution to the achievement of joint reference. *Child Development, 62*, 875–890.

Baldwin, D. A. (in press). Infants' ability to consult the speaker for clues to word reference. *Journal of Child Language.*

Bornstein, M. H., & Sigman, M. D. (1986). Continuity in mental development from infancy. *Child Development, 57*, 251–274.

Brody, L. R. (1985). Gender differences in emotional development: A review of theories and research. *Journal of Personality, 53*, 102–149.

Butterworth, G. (1991). The ontogeny and phylogeny of joint visual attention. In A. Whiten (Ed.), *Natural theories of mind* (pp. 223–232). Oxford, England: Blackwell.

Caplan, M. Z., & Hay, D. F. (1989). Preschoolers' responses to peers' distress and belief about bystander intervention. *Journal of Child Psychology and Psychiatry, 30*, 231–242.

Capps, L., Sigman, M., & Mundy, P. (1994). Attachment security in children with autism. *Development and Psychopathology, 6*, 249–261.

Collis, G. M. (1977). Visual coorientation and maternal speech. In H. R. Schaffer (Ed.), *Studies in mother-infant interaction.* London: Academic Press.

Courchesne, E., Townsend, J. P., Akshoomoff, N. A., Yeung-Courchesne, R., Press, G. A., Marakami, J. W., Lincoln, A. J., James, H. E., Saitoh, O., Egaas, B., Haas, R. H., & Schreibman, L. (1994). A new finding: Impairment in shifting attention in autistic and cerebellar patients. In S. H. Broman & J. Grafman (Eds.), *Atypical cognitive deficits in developmental disorders: Implications for brain function* (pp. 101–137). Hillsdale, NJ: Lawrence Erlbaum Associates.

Dawson, G., Hill, D., Spencer, A., Galpert, L., & Watson, L. (1990). Affective exchanges between young autistic children and their mothers. *Journal of Abnormal Child Psychology*, *18*, 335–345.

Eisenberg, N., & Lennon, R. (1983). Sex differences in empathy and related capacities. *Psychological Bulletin*, *94*, 100–131.

Feinman, M., & Lewis, M. (1983). Social referencing at 10 months: A second-order effect on infants' responses to strangers. *Child Development*, *54*, 878–887.

Gunnar, M. R., & Stone, C. (1984). The effects of positive maternal affect on infant responses to pleasant, ambiguous, and fear-provoking toys. *Child Development*, *55*, 1231–1236.

Harris, M., Jones, D., & Grant, J. (1983). The nonverbal context of mothers' speech to infants. *First Language*, *4*, 21–30.

Haviland, J. M., & Lelwica, M. (1987). The induced affect response: Ten-week-old infants' responses to three emotion expressions. *Developmental Psychology*, *23*, 97–104.

Hornik, R., & Gunnar, M. (1988). A descriptive analysis of infant social referencing. *Child Development*, *59*, 626–634.

Hornik, R., Risenhoover, N., & Gunnar, M. (1987). The effects of maternal positive, neutral, and negative affective communications on infant responses to new toys. *Child Development*, *58*, 937–944.

Jones, S. S., Collins, K., & Hong, H. W. (1991). An audience effect on smile production in 10-month-old infants. *Psychological Science*, *2*, 45–49.

Kasari, C., Sigman, M., Baumgartner, P., & Stipek, D. J. (1993a). Pride and mastery in children with autism. *Journal of Child Psychology and Psychiatry*, *34*, 353–362.

Kasari, C., Sigman, M., Mundy, P., & Yirmiya, N. (1990). Affective sharing in the context of joint attention interactions of normal, autistic, and mentally retarded children. *Journal of Autism and Developmental Disorders*, *20*, 87–100.

Kasari, C., Sigman, M., & Yirmiya, N. (1993b). Focused and social attention in interactions with familiar and unfamiliar adults: A comparison of autistic, mentally retarded, and normal children. *Development and Psychopathology*, *5*, 401–412.

Klinnert, M. D. (1984). The regulation of infant behavior by maternal facial expression. *Infant Behavior and Development*, *7*, 447–465.

Leung, E., & Rheingold, H. (1981). Development of pointing as a social gesture. *Developmental Psychology*, *17*, 215–220.

Masur, E. F. (1983). Gestural development, dual-directional signaling, and the transition to words. *Journal of Psycholinguistic Research*, *12*, 93–109.

Moore, C., & Corkum, V. (in press). Social understanding at the end of the first year of life. *Developmental Review*.

Mundy, P., Kasari, C., & Sigman, M. (1992). Nonverbal communication, affective sharing, and intersubjectivity. *Infant Behavior and Development*, *34*, 499–506.

Mundy, P., Sigman, M., & Kasari, C. (1990). A longitudinal study of joint attention and language development in autistic children. *Journal of Autism and Developmental Disorders*, *20*, 115–123.

Mundy, P., Sigman, M., & Kasari, C. (1994). Joint attention, developmental level, and symptom presentation in autism. *Development and Psychopathology*, *6*, 389–401.

Mundy, P., Sigman, M., Ungerer, J. A., & Sherman, T. (1986). Defining the social deficits in autism: The contribution of nonverbal communication measures. *Journal of Child Psychology and Psychiatry*, *27*, 657–669.

Mundy, P., Sigman, M., Ungerer, J. A., & Sherman, T. (1987). Nonverbal communication and play correlates of language development in autistic children. *Journal of Autism and Developmental Disorders*, *17*, 349–364.

Murphy, C. M. (1978). Pointing in the context of shared activity. *Child Development*, *49*, 371–380.

Murphy, C. M., & Messer, D. J. (1977). Mothers, infants, and pointing: A study of gesture. In H. R. Schaffer (Ed.), *Studies on mother–infant interaction* (pp. 325–354). London: Academic Press.

Ninio, A., & Bruner, J. S. (1978). The achievement and antecedents of labeling. *Journal of Child Language*, *5*, 1–15.

Phillips, W., Baron-Cohen, S., & Rutter, M. (1992). The role of eye contact in goal detection: Evidence from normal toddlers and children with mental handicaps or autism. *Development and Psychopathology, 4*, 375–383.

Ratner, N., & Bruner, J. (1978). Games, social exchanges, and the acquisition of language. *Journal of Child Language, 5*, 391–401.

Rosen, W. D., Adamson, L. B., & Bakeman, R. (1992). An experimental investigation of infant social referencing: Mothers' messages and gender differences. *Developmental Psychology, 28*, 1172–1178.

Scaife, M., & Bruner, J. S. (1975). The capacity for joint visual attention in the infant. *Nature, 253*, 265–266.

Seibert, J., Hogan, A. J., & Mundy, P. (1982). Assessing interactional competencies: The early social communication scales. *Infant Mental Health Journal, 3*, 244–258.

Sigman, M., & Kasari, C. (1994). *Social referencing, shared attention, and empathy in infants.* Paper presented at the Ninth International Conference on Infant Studies, Paris, France.

Sigman, M., Kasari, C., Kwon, J. H., & Yirmiya, N. (1992). Responses to the negative emotions of others in autistic, mentally retarded, and normal children. *Child Development, 63*, 796–807.

Sigman, M., & Mundy, P. (1989). Social attachments in autistic children. *Journal of the American Academy of Child and Adolescent Psychiatry, 28*, 74–81.

Sigman, M., Mundy, P., Sherman, T., & Ungerer, J. A. (1986). Social interactions of autistic, mentally retarded, and normal children with their caregivers. *Journal of Child Psychology and Psychiatry, 27*, 647–669.

Sigman, M., & Ungerer, J. A. (1984). Attachment behaviors in autistic children. *Journal of Autism and Developmental Disorders, 24*, 231–244.

Sorce, J. F., Emde, R. N., Campos, J., & Klinnert, M. D. (1985). Maternal emotional signaling: Its effect on the visual cliff behavior of 1-year-olds. *Developmental Psychology, 21*, 195–200.

Tomasello, M., Mannle, S., & Kruger, A. (1986). The linguistic environment of 1- to 2-year-old twins. *Developmental Psychology, 22*, 169–176.

Tomasello, M., & Todd, J. (1983). Joint attention and lexical acquisition style. *First Language, 4*, 297–212.

Walden, T. A., & Baxter, A. (1989). The effect of context and age on social referencing. *Child Development, 60*, 1511–1518.

Walden, T. A., & Ogan, T. (1988). The development of social referencing. *Child Development, 59*, 1230–1240.

Zahn-Waxler, C., Radke-Yarrow, M., Wagner, E., & Chapman, M. (1992). Development of concern for others. *Developmental Psychology, 28*, 126–136.

Zahn-Waxler, C., Robinson, J. L., & Emde, R. N. (1992). The development of empathy in twins. *Developmental Psychology, 28*, 1038–1047.

Chapter 10

Joint Attention, Affect, and Culture

Lauren B. Adamson
Duncan McArthur
Georgia State University

Midway through infancy, children begin to share objects with adults. Previously, the scope of their activity had been primarily interpersonal. Soon it will expand without bounds as language draws distant and imaginary events near. But for several months, infants' interests are located in an attentional sphere filled with local happenings and intimate caregivers.

In this chapter, we explore the implications of this developmental situation. Our plan is two-fold. First, we consider what it means to view joint attention developmentally. Here we argue that the temporal placement of the first episodes of joint attention provides rich soil for cultivation of the meaning of objects. Then, we illustrate this claim by drawing two sketches from our research on communication during episodes of joint attention. The first sketch displays how emotional messages about objects may vary as a function of infants' gender. The second sketch reveals a specific deficit in the receptive joint attention skills of preverbal children with autism that may impede their initiation into culture and its conventions of meaning.

THE DEVELOPMENTAL SITUATION
OF JOINT ATTENTION

By definition, joint attention involves a dynamic arrangement between infants, objects, and social partners. This is a complex arrangement that depends on the convergence of many components. One way to introduce some of these components is to present them visually, as part of an image of an episode of joint attention. This image can then be used to discuss how these components come together as joint attention emerges.

An Image of Joint Attention

In their seminal book, *Symbol Formation*, Werner and Kaplan (1963) present an image of what they call the *primordial sharing situation*. As can be seen in Figure 10.1, this image places an infant within a triadic arrangement constituted by both people and objects.

Although their diagram is sparse, it can be used to abstract four components that are integral to the process of joint attention. The first component is depicted by the three-way overlap of adult, child, and object. In Werner and Kaplan's view, this region is central to the primordial sharing situation for it provides the site for "*reference* in its initial, nonrepresentational form: child and mother are now beginning to contemplate objects together—however slightly these objects are detached from the child's self" (1963, p. 43). Moreover, in their view, the infants' activity during this shared situation is affective as well as sensory and motoric such that "the *sharing* of objects is not simply a secondary condition helpful to the learning about objects or symbols but is rather of vital significance in the child's establishment of a life space" (p. 71). The common location of both reference and affectivity has informed several recent analyses of early object-focused communication (e.g., Adamson & Bakeman, 1982, 1985; Dore, 1985).

Two additional components of joint attention are indicated by the areas of the diagram where dyadic interactions can occur. The first of these is composed

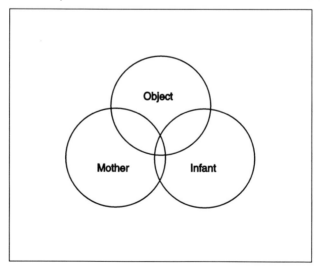

FIG. 10.1. Werner and Kaplan's (1963) primordial sharing situation.

of the infant's actions on objects. Researchers have long been fascinated by the emergence of object manipulation and its relation to cognitive development. For example, Millicent Shinn, in her classic *The Biography of a Baby*, began the chapter entitled "The Era of Handling Things" with the observation that her 5-month-old niece "sprang into this era suddenly, within four days . . . unlocking a dozen other doors of mental life" (1900, p. 141). Thirty years later, Piaget (1936/1963) centered his theory of sensorimotor development on the infant's structuring of actions on objects close at hand. However, unlike Werner and Kaplan, he tended to focus so tightly on infants' interactions with objects that his critics charge that he overlooked some of the essential qualities of the infant's environment (e.g., Gibson, 1988) and, in particular, their social environment (e.g., Bruner, 1972; Kessen, 1979; Newson & Newson, 1975).

The third component of joint attention involves the infant and the caregiver. Beginning in the 1970s, researchers (e.g., Brazelton, Koslowski, & Main, 1974; Sander, 1977; Stern, 1974; see also chapters in Bullowa, 1979; Schaffer, 1977) who drew inspiration from psychoanalytic theories such as Winnicott's (1960) view of the parent-infant relationship and from ethology (as interpreted by Bowlby, 1969; Wolff, 1969) began to describe how infants modulate expressions of affect and attention as they interact with their caregivers during the first half-year of life. By the end of the 1970s, several researchers (e.g., Adamson & Bakeman, 1982; Trevarthen & Hubley, 1978) had begun to focus on how these dyadic interactions start to ebb as the infants and caregivers begin to import objects into their social interactions.

The final component located within the primordial sharing situation is the symbol. During much of infancy, symbolic acts are only implicit. But Werner and Kaplan argued that the primordial sharing situation provides a fertile ground for their emergence because the seeds of referential communication are sowed within the overlap between partners and shared events. Symbols arise when, in accord with Werner's (1957) orthogenetic principle, the components of the primordial sharing situation gradually become increasingly differentiated and articulated. As this movement occurs, the components achieve a new level of hierarchical integration that gives rise to a new form.

Thus, from Werner and Kaplan's vantage, the emergence of symbols appears not as an individual accomplishment but as a social one that is prepared for by affective as well as sensorimotor actions. It builds upon acts of reference, of "exchanging things with the Other, by touching things and looking at them with the Other" (1963, p. 43), that are transformed so that a symbol can represent the referent. In this way, symbols emerge from a field of reference that was at first the site for the sharing of objects between caregivers and infants. This view of the developmental source of symbols has led several investigators whose primary interest is language acquisition to venture back to infancy to see what transpires during early episodes of joint attention (e.g., Bates, Benigni, Bretherton, Camaioni, & Volterra, 1979; Greenfield & Smith, 1976; Halliday, 1975).

Although Werner and Kaplan's diagram depicts components within the primordial sharing situation, it does not specify its surround. This oversight seems increasingly unfortunate in light of the recent reintroduction of Vygotsky's perspective on *Mind in Society* (1978) by scholars who are interested in the developmental relations between culture, communication, and cognition (e.g., Rogoff, 1990; Wertsch, 1985). Once the surround is acknowledged, it becomes clear that many of the "symbolic vehicles" that Werner and Kaplan discuss (1963, p. 14) are entities that reside within a culture's conventional codes such as language. Further, it is evident that the formats (Bruner, 1982) and interactional routines (Peters & Boggs, 1986) that structure joint attentional episodes are in large measure cultural constructions (Ochs, 1987).

To draw attention to the environment of episodes of joint attention, we have elaborated Werner and Kaplan's diagram in Figure 10.2 (see also Adamson, 1995; Adamson & Bakeman, 1991). Here the triadic arrangement of joint attention has been placed within the field of culture. Furthermore, a culture's conventional codes have been centered within this cultural field.

In summary, episodes of joint attention are composed of several components. These include the developing infant, his or her caregiver, and objects that are present in the immediate vicinity. Also included are implicit elements such as symbols that reside within the conventional codes of the culture in which episodes of joint attention are embedded.

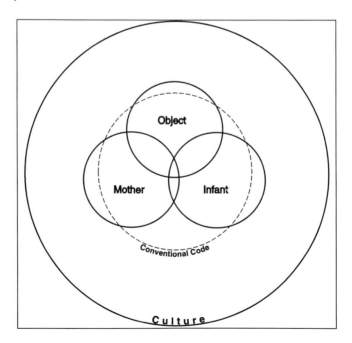

FIG. 10.2. The primordial sharing situation set in culture.

A Developmental Path Through Joint Attention

There is now sufficient evidence to specify when various components of joint attention first become apparent (Adamson, 1995; Butterworth, this volume; Butterworth & Grover, 1990; Corkum & Moore, this volume; Desrochers, Morissette, & Ricard, this volume). Although there are still skirmishes over precise dates, the order of emergence seems regular and predictable. In Table 10.1, we present an abbreviated outline of the developmental course of joint attention.

The sequence begins at birth when the newborn and caregiver share moments of attentiveness that usually do not have a sustained focus of common interest. After the biobehavioral shift at 6 to 8 weeks of age, an infant and caregiver begin to negotiate a structure for interpersonal engagement by modulating expressions of affect and attention. Subsequently, as an infant's interest becomes more absorbed by objects, episodes of interpersonal engagement become more compact and less frequent. Although infants do not yet integrate activities on objects into their dialogues with social partners, their caregivers may support shared object exploration by making objects act in interesting ways or by joining infants in their focal interest without requiring an open communication channel (Bakeman & Adamson, 1984).

The onset of joint attention proper is presented as two phases in Table 10.1. The first is designated as a phase of emergence because infants' fledgling attempts to coordinate attention to people and objects are as yet limited by object location (e.g., Butterworth & Grover, 1990) or dependent on a partner's accommodations

TABLE 10.1
Phases in the Development of Joint Attention During Infancy

Developmental Phase	Age of Onset	Characteristics*
Shared Attentiveness	Birth	Infant's alertness
		Adult's engrossment
Interpersonal Engagement	6–8 weeks	Affective reciprocity during face-to-face interactions
Object Involvement	5–6 months	Infant's object interest and manual skills
		Adult's support of object exploration
Emergence of Joint Attention	9–10 months	Infant's pointing and social referencing
		Routines involving requests for and references to objects
Consolidation of Joint Attention	13 months	Infant's first words
		Sustained and varied formats that focus on objects and symbols
Emergence of Symbols	18 months	Infant's production of decontextualized words and symbolic gestures
		Shared focus on absent events

*Characteristics were selected to describe some of the phase-typical occurrences that have been the focus of research studies that draw subjects from Western middle-class cultures.

(e.g., Bakeman & Adamson, 1984). The second is designated as a period of consolidation and begins when an infant can routinely enter and sustain episodes of joint engagement. The last phase mentioned in Table 10.1 begins as a culture's conventional codes, including language, start to surface within episodes of joint engagement. Clearly this phase overlaps with the previous one, and it is notoriously difficult to date its onset. However, by the end of an infant's second year, joint engagement has clearly taken on a new quality as language floods into interactions, transforming them into conversations about past and future, as well as present, events (see Schaffer, 1984).

The ordering of information in Table 10.1 reflects several decisions about how one might best conceptualize a complex phenomenon such as joint attention. It blends two often separated concepts of development to formulate a rather precise timeline for the onset of specific actions that are clustered into a sequence of phases. The first concept of development essentially reduces it to empirically derived timetables. For example, Charles Spiker once urged that "development" only be "used to name those changes in behavior that normally occur with an increase in the chronological age of the child" (1966, p. 41). In contrast to Spiker's emphasis on what occurs when, a second concept of development emphasizes the formal pattern of progressive organization of activity. This approach is exemplified by Werner's (1957) orthogenetic principle that calls attention to the relation between different phases of a sequence regardless of their particular behavioral content or specific ages of onset.

By blending these two concepts of development, both the timing and the sequential placement of early episodes of joint attention come into focus. Joint attention's time of special ascendancy appears to be between 9 and 15 months of age. This timing places it in a privileged developmental position. It first occurs at the height of infancy when the infant has achieved considerable control over the physiological storms of the first months of life and the complexities of interpersonal communication. It arises coincident with the advent of coordinated, intentional sensorimotor action (Piaget, 1936/1963). Further, it occurs at a time when the increasingly mobile infant begins to access an expanding territory that contains a nearly endless variety of novel objects and unfamiliar people.

Its position within the developmental course places joint object-person attentional processes upon a foundation of both interpersonal and object-related skill development. Before shared reference emerges, infants are already well schooled in many of the rudiments of affective regulation and object manipulation. Moreover, the timing of joint attention allows it to be the springboard for children's penetration of the symbolic realm. Thus, children have established ways of sharing objects with intimate caregivers before they make major strides in the acquisition of a culture's systems of conventional codes.

Table 10.1, then, specifies one normative path and a typical pace toward an important accomplishment. Such an analysis helps underscore how a new form of activity may arise upon but not be contained in miniature within an earlier constructed foundation. Moreover, it highlights some interesting developmental convergences, the expectable flowing together of component processes during development.

It is also important to note what this form of analysis does not do. It does not speak directly to the issue of what causes joint attention to emerge. It calls our attention to possible precursors and preludes, but we must be careful not to forge causal links from temporal ones. To do so courts two potential misunderstandings. First, we may end up studying earlier states only as they relate to a valued endpoint (e.g., infants' points are interesting because they precede words; see Kessen's warning about the "dragon of entelechy," 1966, p. 63). Of even more concern is the possibility that knowledge of the endpoint may lead us to view the endpoint as the cause of earlier occurring states (e.g., infants babble because they will soon speak). Such a teleological implication presents grave concern to scientists who seek efficient rather than final causes. (See Rapin, 1987, for a parallel observation concerning pathogenesis and etiology.)

In summary, joint attention's normative course is characterized by a remarkable convergence of interpersonal processes, object exploration, and cultural conventions. An object-fascinated infant shares an event with a familiar social partner who is steeped in a culture. This convergence allows an infant's understanding of the emotional meaning of objects to be cultivated within episodes of joint attention.

DEVELOPMENTAL CONVERGENCES DURING EPISODES OF JOINT ATTENTION

There are several widely regarded general models of the convergence of affect and conventions during episodes of joint attention. For example, Trevarthen (1988; Trevarthen & Hubley, 1978; see also Newson & Newson, 1975) has written cogently about secondary intersubjectivity to portray how infants are motivated to share meaning with more sophisticated culturemates. And, Dore (1985) has constructed a dialogic model of early word use that highlights the affective as well as the didactic function of an intimate adult's personalized reading of an infant's actions.

Nevertheless, the convergence of affect and cultural conventions is difficult to study systematically. The problem space is enormous, and the process under study is particularly sensitive to interference. Therefore, it is not surprising that some of the most revealing work to date has involved only one or at most a few infants and has focused primarily on how they learn to speak (e.g., Bruner, 1983; Dore, 1985). However, supplementing such close case studies with standardized procedures that adjust partner's input has begun to provide a broader view of ways in which interpersonal and cultural processes converge during episodes of joint attention (e.g., Baldwin, 1993; Tomasello & Farrar, 1986).

Here we present two glimpses of joint attention that were provided by systematic, laboratory-based observations. The first focused on normally developing infants and used the affective social referencing paradigm to spot gender differences in the way mothers and infants establish the emotional meaning of novel objects. The second drew its subjects from a developmental extreme: nonverbal preschoolers who were diagnosed either with autism or with developmental language delay. Its primary aim was to investigate what transpires when adult partners invite children to share attention to objects.

Gendered Variations in the Emotional Meaning of Objects

Central to many contemporary treatments of gender differences is the notion that the social construction of gender begins during early interpersonal engagement between mothers and infants (e.g., Chodorow, 1978, 1989). Although these accounts typically focus on the emergence of the child's sense of a gendered self and gendered modes of relationships, Keller (1985) contends that specific cultural forces intrude as well on boys' and girls' orientation toward the world around them. Within developmental psychology, Block (1984) has expressed a similar notion in her reflections on the results of the differential socialization experiences our culture affords to boys and girls. Males, she claimed, are provided with experiences that "are conducive to the development of 'wings'—which permit leaving the nest, exploring far reaches, and flying alone" whereas females are placed in a learning environment that is "more conducive to the development of 'roots'—roots that anchor, stabilize, and support growth" (pp. 137–138).

To date, there are surprisingly few studies that have focused on the social construction of gender during infancy. Available evidence is, however, consistent with the notion that gender differences in orientation to both people and objects may occur before speech. For example, by 1 year of age, girls have been found to be more socially oriented toward their mothers (Gunnar & Donahue, 1980; Wasserman & Lewis, 1985) and more wary than boys (Gunnar & Stone, 1984; Jacklin & Maccoby, 1983; however, also see Gunnar, 1980).

In a recent study, we (Rosen, Adamson, & Bakeman, 1992) sought to examine whether there might be gendered variations in the way mothers and their infants communicate about the emotional meaning of objects. This study drew both conceptually and methodologically from the burgeoning literature on *affective social referencing* (Campos & Stenberg, 1981; Feinman, 1992), one form of joint attention. During an episode of affective social referencing, an infant actively seeks another person's opinion about an object or event whose emotional significance is initially unclear. The person's message may then help resolve the infant's uncertainty and inform his subsequent actions. If the communicative partner expresses fear concerning a novel object, the infant may fret and retreat; if the partner smiles encouragingly, the infant may happily advance toward the object.

It is noteworthy that during episodes of affective social referencing the infant almost inevitably consults with a person who is more culturally sophisticated. This asymmetry of knowledge lets the infant be a cultural apprentice (Kaye, 1982; Rogoff, 1990). Well before an infant begins to acquire language, he or she is exposed to the caregiver's interpretations about how to feel about (as well as what to do with; see Rogoff, Mistry, Radziszewska, & Germond, 1992) objects.

Affective social referencing has been transported into the laboratory using a carefully controlled paradigm (e.g., Klinnert, 1984; see Feinman, Roberts, Hsieh, Sawyer, & Swanson, 1992, for a recent review of the empirical literature). The essential elements of the affective social referencing paradigm parallel the steps that can be abstracted from naturally occurring episodes of affective social referencing. First, the infant is confronted with an event such as a large robot, a live animal, or a moderate visual cliff (see, respectively, Walden & Ogan, 1988; Gunnar & Stone, 1984; Sorce, Emde, Campos, & Klinnert, 1985). Second, the partner waits for the infant's glance and then responds with a message about the event's affective significance. For example, the partner may display a trained facial expression of happiness or fear (e.g., Klinnert, 1984; Sorce et al., 1985). Finally, the infant is given time to react to the object so that the influence of the affective message can be assessed.

In the Rosen et al. (1992) study, this basic paradigm was modified in order to compare how mothers with sons and mothers with daughters negotiate the emotional meaning of objects. In this study, 37 middle-class infants who were 12 months old were observed in four 90 second trials. Each trial began with the infant equidistant from the mother and a novel animated toy such as a mooing mechanical cow or a wind up musical gazebo. In two of the trials (the "happy" conditions), the mother was asked to convey the message that the toy could be safely and happily approached. In the other two trials (the "fear" conditions), she was told to convey the message that a novel toy was dangerous and fearsome. In the first two trials (one a happy and one a fear condition with order counterbalanced across infants), the mother received no training in how to express messages. These unconstrained trials let us describe how both maternal expressions and infants' actions varied as a function of infants' sex. Then, prior to the last two trials, each mother was trained to make a fearful and a happy facial expression that she was asked to use as her exclusive means of communication. These trained trials replicate the procedure used most widely in the literature.

Gender did not affect the number of times infants sought information in any of the four conditions; infants glanced toward their mothers 3.7 times, on average ($SD = 2.8$). Nor was there evidence of gendered affective social referencing during either the unconstrained or trained happy conditions. However, an infant's gender did influence both maternal input and infants' response in the fear conditions.

Maternal displays of fear toward daughters were significantly less intense than toward sons regardless of whether mothers' expression was unconstrained or trained (Ms = 3.6 and 3.9 on a 5-point scale where 1 = *very positive* and 5 = *very negative*). Yet only girls' position relative to the mother and the toy was modulated by mothers' display of fear. Both sons and daughters were significantly more attracted to toys for which the mother conveyed a happy instead of a fear message (Ms = 3.0 vs. 2.4 on a 5-point index of infants' positive regard of the toy). But sons tended to move closer to the toy (M for average distance between son and toy during the 90-second condition = 1.42 m) than to the mother (M = 1.71 m between mother and son) in both happy and fear conditions. In contrast, daughters tended to move significantly closer to the toy in the happy conditions than in the fear conditions (Ms = 1.28 m and 1.60 m of separation, respectively) although their average distance from the mother was not affected (Ms = 1.72 m and 1.65 m).

We must wait to see if these findings are replicated before raising them in support of social-constructivist theories of gender development. Should they hold up across studies, they may contribute to recent discussions about how gender-related actions are situated in interactional contexts (Deaux & Major, 1987). Nevertheless, even in their current untested form, they help highlight the issue of how joint attention provides an occasion for objects to gain meaning through the convergence of interpersonal and cultural processes. This convergence may allow adults to provide a basis for (and even to bias; see Bretherton, 1992) a child's understanding of objects as they are defined within a specific cultural sphere (e.g., Bakeman, Adamson, Konner, & Barr, 1990; Fernald & Morikawa, 1993).

Autism and the Reception of Messages About Objects

So far, we have discussed the convergence of affect and conventions during episodes of joint attention as a normative developmental event. It seems quite reasonable to expect its timing and organization to be remarkably robust, in part because infants (as Trevarthen, 1988, has argued forcefully) may be inherently motivated to engage with other people who are inherently motivated to assist them. Nevertheless, a small percentage of infants may suffer from developmental disorders that may severely delay or impair the emergence of joint attention.

One of these disorders is autism. Since it was first described by Kanner (1943), researchers have recognized as autism's primary characteristic atypical social behavior that impairs reciprocal social relationships (see DSM–III–R, American Psychiatric Association, 1987). Consistent with this characterization, several recent studies have demonstrated that children with autism show deficits in joint attention skills (see Sigman & Kasari, this volume). For example, Mundy, Sigman, and Kasari (1990) found that children with autism initiate less gestural indicating than children in either of two comparison groups, one matched on mental age and the other matched on language ability. Moreover, Loveland and Landry (1986) reported that children with autism do not comprehend attention-directing gestures, either with or without verbal accompaniment, as skillfully as children in a developmental language delay comparison group. The impairment in joint attention processes may limit autistic children's reception of partners' messages. Richer (1978) has argued that when children with autism avoid "negotiations of shared understandings," a phrase he adopts from Newson and Newson (1975), they may fail "to acquire the skills for communication and cooperation" that are crucial for learning "the meaning of a culture's symbols, including language." This results in "the partial noncommunication of culture to autistic children," leaving them profoundly "dyscultural" (p. 48).

The possible results of an impairment of joint attentional processes are poignantly reported by Williams (1992) in her autobiography, *Nobody Nowhere*. This remarkable narrative records her experiences as a person with autism. For our current purposes, it is particularly interesting to note that she has been troubled by a lack of connection between her potent emotions and language's conventional code. She laments that "words on the wind, when they're calling you in, the words, have no meaning when the thoughts have no feelings" (p. 163). Further, she reports that:

> Although I could speak I often didn't use language in the same way as others and often got no meaning out of what was said to me. Although words are symbols, it would be misleading to say that I did not understand symbols. I had a whole system of relating that I considered "my language" . . . (p. 29)

To investigate whether nonverbal children with autism are hindered in receiving a partner's messages about objects, we recently investigated what transpired when they were invited by an adult to focus together on an object. Our primary aim was to assess the receptive joint attention skills of children with autism. We did this by observing whether or not they attend to an object highlighted by a partner while concurrently opening or maintaining a communicative channel with the partner.

For this study, we selected videotapes from the archives of the Preschool Nosology Project, a large-scale, longitudinal investigation that was designed to address a wide array of issues related to the diagnosis of autism and developmental language delay. The 30 children we observed were between 3 and 5 years old. Fifteen of the children (13 boys, 2 girls) had been diagnosed with autistic spectrum disorder and 15 (7 boys, 8 girls) with developmental language delay. All children were essentially nonverbal as indicated by a score in the first percentile on the Expressive One-Word Vocabulary Test (Gardner, 1979) relative to other same-aged children.

Each child was observed during a play session in which he or she interacted for 10 minutes with an unfamiliar adult who followed a standardized protocol. This protocol included a number of object-focused activities that the adult initiated as she tried to elicit from the child his or her highest level of language, play, and prosocial behavior.

Trained coders reviewed each videotape using an event-based coding scheme. The coding scheme was designed to describe each attempt by the adult to draw the child into an episode of joint attention. Such invitations were characterized as either *conventional* or *literal* (Adamson & Bakeman, 1984). An invitation was coded as conventional when the adult used only words and gestures to mark an object. An invitation was coded as literal when the adult attempted to draw the child's attention to the object by acting directly on it in a way that made it more perceptually salient. Thus, only a conventional marker depended solely on shared meaning to influence the child's attention.

In addition, the outcome of each invitation to joint attention was characterized as either a success or a failure. Each failure was categorized as a complete failure (the child attended to neither the object nor the partner), a failure to attend to the object, or a failure to open a channel of communication.

Consistent with earlier studies, we found that children with autism seemed to have more difficulties with joint attention than children with developmental language delay. Although the adult partners made a similar number of attempts to initiate joint attention in the two groups (approximately 2.7 attempts per minute), their invitations were far less likely to be accepted by the children in the autistic group than by children in the developmental language delay group. The mean proportions of success were .49 and .83, respectively.

Interestingly, adults did not use the same strategies when inviting children from the two groups to share attention to objects. When they interacted with a child with autism, they were far more likely to issue literal than conventional invitations; the ratio of literal to conventional attempts was 1.8 to 1. In contrast, when they interacted with a child with a developmental language delay, they issued more conventional than literal invitations; here the ratio of literal to conventional attempts was .59 to 1. This finding suggests that when adults invite nonverbal children with autism to share an object, they try to entice a common interest by drawing attention directly toward the object. This strategy may attenuate the resolution of the conventional code that overlays these objects. Thus, compared to nonverbal children with developmental language delay, nonverbal children with autism may have fewer opportunities to experience how symbols may be used exclusively to direct another person's attention toward objects.

We also found that children with autism displayed a different pattern of receptive joint attention failures than children with developmental language delay. Compared to children with developmental language delay, they were almost four times more likely to neglect the channel of communication (see Fig. 10.3). Thus, children with autism appear less likely to receive messages from adults about objects than other children with severe language delay.

Together, these findings suggest that nonverbal children with autism may have difficulty entering into adult-initiated episodes of joint attention. It is interesting

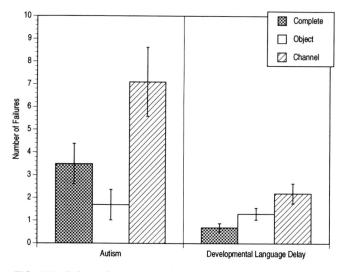

FIG. 10.3. Failures of attention by diagnostic category and type of failure.

to note how extensively these difficulties pervade their sharing situation. Children with autism often fail to attend to their partners. Moreover, their adult partners appear to accommodate their avoidance of social interaction by animating objects through literal acts rather than referring to them exclusively using conventional means. From a developmental perspective, the reduction of interpersonal processes that interferes with the establishment of episodes of joint attention appears as an ominous prelude to a restricted introduction to cultural conventions.

SUMMARY

In this chapter, we have argued that a remarkable developmental convergence of interpersonal processes, object-related skills, and culturally mediated conventional codes occurs as joint attention emerges during the second half of infancy. Typically, infants begin attending to objects intently only after they have begun consolidating ways to regulate interpersonal interactions. Thus, they are able to bring their interpersonal skills to bear on objects when, for example, they intentionally seek a partner's opinions about a novel object or they accept an adult's invitation to share an object. Adults usually couch their opinions and invitations in the terms of a specific culture's conventional codes. Thus, they inevitably convey culturally mediated knowledge and means to an infant as they lend a supportive hand during episodes of joint attention.

We have also tried to illustrate the benefits of the systematic research on variations in this complex developmental convergence. To this end, two laboratory-based studies were briefly presented, one that focused on gendered variations in affective social referencing and the other on the receptive joint attention of nonverbal preschoolers. Although these studies differ considerably, both placed children and adults in situations where the likelihood of joint attention was maximized, either because an ambiguous object pulled for adult definition or because an adult was instructed to initiate communication about objects. In both studies, these experimental manipulations proved effective in generating compact streams of joint attention episodes that could be systematically described by trained coders. Moreover, in both studies, we found evidence of interesting variations in how adults and children pattern the convergence of interpersonal and culturally mediated conventions during these events.

We think it is particularly noteworthy that the variations we found seemed to pervade the entire fabric of joint attention. Child gender qualified not only how mothers formulated fearful messages about an object but also how 1-year-old infants used these messages to inform their reaction to the object. Child diagnosis affected not only how often nonverbal preschoolers opened the interpersonal communication channel when an adult partner invited joint attention but also how often the adult relied on purely conventional means when issuing their invitations.

Such findings support the conclusion that, by dint of their normative developmental situation, joint attention episodes provide a dynamic setting in which specific objects can be shared between a developing child who passionately seeks their meaning and an adult who can tender their conventional definition. As Vygotsky stated decades ago, "the very essence of cultural development" may be contained in occasions that allow such a "collision of mature cultural forms of behavior with the primitive forms that characterize the child's behavior" (1981, p. 151).

ACKNOWLEDGMENTS

The study of gender differences in affective social referencing was supported by a grant from the National Science Foundation (BNS-8300716) awarded to Lauren B. Adamson and Roger Bakeman and is based in part on a dissertation submitted to Georgia State University by Warren D. Rosen. The Preschool Nosology Project was supported by Program Project grant #20489 from the National Institute of Neurologic and Communicative Diseases and Stroke (now National Institute of Neurologic Disorders and Stroke or NINDS); the study reported here on receptive joint attention of children with autism is based in part on a thesis submitted to Georgia State University by Duncan McArthur.

REFERENCES

Adamson, L. B. (1995). *Communication development during infancy.* Madison, WI: Brown & Benchmark.
Adamson, L. B., & Bakeman, R. (1982). Affectivity and reference: Concepts, methods, and techniques in the study of communication development of 6- to 18-month-old infants. In T. M. Field & A. Fogel (Eds.), *Emotion and interaction* (pp. 213–236). Hillsdale, NJ: Lawrence Erlbaum Associates.

Adamson, L. B., & Bakeman, R. (1984). Mothers' communicative acts: Changes during infancy. *Infant Behavior and Development, 7*, 467–478.

Adamson, L. B., & Bakeman, R. (1985). Affect and attention: Infants observed with mothers and peers. *Child Development, 56*, 582–593.

Adamson, L. B., & Bakeman, R. (1991). The development of shared attention during infancy. In R. Vasta (Ed.), *Annals of Child Development* (Vol. 8, pp. 1–41). London, England: Kingsley.

American Psychiatric Association. (1987). *Diagnostic and Statistical Manual of Mental Disorders (DSM-III-R)* (3rd ed. rev.). Washington, DC: Author.

Bakeman, R., & Adamson, L. B. (1984). Coordinating attention to people and objects in mother-infant and peer-infant interaction. *Child Development, 55*, 1278–1289.

Bakeman, R., Adamson, L. B., Konner, M., & Barr, R. G. (1990). !Kung infancy: The social context of object exploration. *Child Development, 61*, 794–809.

Baldwin, D. A. (1993). Infants' ability to consult the speaker for clues to word reference. *Journal of Child Language, 20*, 395–418.

Bates, E., Benigni, L., Bretherton, I., Camaioni, L., & Volterra, V. (1979). *The emergence of symbols: Cognition and communication in infancy.* New York: Academic Press.

Block, J. H. (1984). *Sex role identity and ego development.* San Francisco: Jossey-Bass.

Bowlby, J. (1969). *Attachment and loss: Vol. 1. Attachment.* New York: Basic Books.

Brazelton, T. B., Koslowski, B., & Main, M. (1974). The origins of reciprocity: The early mother-infant interaction. In M. Lewis & L. Rosenblum (Eds.), *The effect of the infant on its caregiver* (pp. 49–76). New York: Wiley.

Bretherton, I. (1992). Social referencing, intentional communication, and the interfacing of minds in infancy. In S. Feinman (Ed.), *Social referencing and the social construction of reality in infancy* (pp. 57–77). New York: Plenum.

Bruner, J. (1972). Nature and uses of immaturity. *American Psychologist, 27*, 687–708.

Bruner, J. (1982). The formats of language acquisition. *American Journal of Semiotics, 1*, 1–16.

Bruner, J. (1983). *Child's talk: Learning to use language.* Oxford, England: Oxford University Press.

Bullowa, M. (Ed.). (1979). *Before speech: The beginning of interpersonal communication* (pp. 1–62). Cambridge, England: Cambridge University Press.

Butterworth, G., & Grover, L. (1990). Joint visual attention, manual pointing, and preverbal communication in human infancy. In M. Jeannerod (Ed.), *Attention and performance XIII* (pp. 605–624). Hillsdale, NJ: Lawrence Erlbaum Associates.

Campos, J. J., & Stenberg, C. R. (1981). Perception, appraisal, and emotion: The onset of social referencing. In M. E. Lamb & L. R. Sherrod (Eds.), *Infant social cognition: Empirical and theoretical considerations* (pp. 273–314). Hillsdale, NJ: Lawrence Erlbaum Associates.

Chodorow, N. (1978). *The reproduction of mothering: Psychoanalysis and the sociology of gender.* Berkeley: University of California.

Chodorow, N. (1989). *Feminism and psychoanalytic theory.* New Haven: Yale.

Deaux, K., & Major, B. (1987). Putting gender in context: An interactive model of gender-related behavior. *Psychological Review, 94*, 369–389.

Dore, J. (1985). Holophrases revisited: Their 'logical' development from dialog. In M. Barrett (Ed.), *Children's single-word speech* (pp. 23–58). New York: Wiley.

Feinman, S. (Ed.). (1992). *Social referencing and the social construction of reality in infancy.* New York: Plenum.

Feinman, S., Roberts, D., Hsieh, K., Sawyer, D., & Swanson, D. (1992). A critical review of social referencing in infancy. In S. Feinman (Ed.), *Social referencing and the social construction of reality in infancy* (pp. 15–54). New York: Plenum.

Fernald, A., & Morikawa, H. (1993). Common themes and cultural variations in Japanese and American mothers' speech to infants. *Child Development, 64*, 637–656.

Gardner, M. F. (1979). *Expressive one-word picture vocabulary test.* Novato, CA: Academic Therapy.

Gibson, E. J. (1988). Exploratory behavior in the development of perceiving, acting, and the acquiring of knowledge. *Annual Review of Psychology, 19*, 1–41.

Greenfield, P. M., & Smith, J. H. (1976). The structure of communication in early language development. New York: Academic Press.

Gunnar, M. R. (1980). Control, warning signals, and distress in infancy. Developmental Psychobiology, 16, 281–289.

Gunnar, M. R., & Donahue, M. (1980). Sex differences in social responsiveness between 6 months and 12 months. Child Development, 51, 262–265.

Gunnar, M. R., & Stone, C. (1984). The effects of positive maternal affect on infant responses to pleasant, ambiguous, and fear-provoking toys. Child Development, 55, 1231–1236.

Halliday, M. A. K. (1975). Learning how to mean. London: Edwin Arnold.

Jacklin, C., & Maccoby, E. E. (1983). Neonatal sex-steroid hormones and timidity in 6–18-month-old boys and girls. Developmental Psychobiology, 16, 163–168.

Kaye, K. (1982). Organism, apprentice, and person. In E. Z. Tronick (Ed.), Social interchange in infancy: Affect, cognition, and communication (pp. 183–196). Baltimore: University Park Press.

Kanner, L. (1943). Autistic disturbances of affective contact. The Nervous Child, 2, 217–250.

Keller, E. F. (1985). Reflections on gender and science. New Haven: Yale.

Kessen, W. (1966). Questions for a theory of cognitive development. Monograph of the Society for Research in Child Development, 31(Serial No. 107).

Kessen, W. (1979). The American child and other cultural inventions. American Psychologist, 34, 815–820.

Klinnert, M. D. (1984). The regulation of infant behavior by maternal facial expression. Infant Behavior and Development, 7, 447–465.

Loveland, K. A., & Landry, S. H. (1986). Joint attention and language in autism and developmental language delay. Journal of Autism and Developmental Disorders, 16, 335–349.

Mundy, P., Sigman, M., & Kasari, C. (1990). A longitudinal study of joint attention and language development in autistic children. Journal of Autism and Developmental Disorders, 20, 115–128.

Newson, J., & Newson, E. (1975). Intersubjectivity and the transmission of culture: On the social origins of symbolic functioning. Bulletin of the British Psychological Society, 28, 437–446.

Ochs, E. (1987). Input: A sociocultural perspective. In M. Hickmann (Ed.), Social and functional approaches to language and thought (pp. 305–319). Orlando, FL: Academic Press.

Peters, A. M., & Boggs, S. T. (1986). Interactional routines as cultural influences upon language acquisition. In B. B. Schieffelin & E. Ochs (Eds.), Language socialization across cultures (pp. 80–96). Cambridge, England: Cambridge University Press.

Piaget, J. (1963). The origins of intelligence in children (M. Cook, Trans.). New York: Norton. (Original work published 1936)

Rapin, I. (1987). Searching for the cause of autism: A neurologic perspective. In D. J. Cohen & A. M. Donnellan (Eds.), Handbook of autism and pervasive developmental disorders (pp. 710–717). New York: Wiley.

Richer, J. (1978). The partial noncommunication of culture to autistic children: An application of human ethology. In M. Rutter & E. Schopler (Eds.), Autism: A reappraisal of concepts and treatment (pp. 47–61). New York: Plenum.

Rogoff, B. (1990). Apprenticeship in thinking: Cognitive development in social context. New York: Oxford University Press.

Rogoff, B., Mistry, J., Radziszewska, B., & Germond, J. (1992). Infants' instrumental social interaction with adults. In S. Feinman (Ed.), Social referencing and the social construction of reality in infancy (pp. 323–348). New York: Plenum.

Rosen, W. D., Adamson, L. B., & Bakeman, R. (1992). An experimental investigation of infant social referencing: Mothers' messages and gender differences. Developmental Psychology, 28, 1172–1178.

Sander, L. W. (1977). The regulation of exchange in the infant-caretaker system and some aspects of the context-content relationship. In M. Lewis & L. A. Rosenblum (Eds.), Interaction, conversation, and the development of language (pp. 133–156). New York: Wiley.

Schaffer, H. R. (Ed.). (1977). Studies in mother-infant interaction. London: Academic Press.

Schaffer, H. R. (1984). *The child's entry into a social world*. London: Academic Press.

Shinn, M. W. (1900). *The biography of a baby*. Boston: Houghton Mifflin.

Sorce, J. F., Emde, R. N., Campos, J., & Klinnert, M. D. (1985). Maternal emotional signaling: Its effect on the visual cliff behavior of 1-year-olds. *Developmental Psychology, 21*, 195–200.

Spiker, C. C. (1966). The concept of development: Relevant and irrelevant issues. *Monograph of the Society for Research in Child Development, 31*(Serial No. 107).

Stern, D. N. (1974). Mother and infant at play: The dyadic interaction involving facial, vocal, and gaze behaviors. In M. Lewis & L. A. Rosenblum (Eds.), *The effect of the infant on its caregiver* (pp. 187–213). New York: Wiley.

Tomasello, M., & Farrar, M. J. (1986). Joint attention and early language. *Child Development, 57*, 1454–1463.

Trevarthen, C. (1988). Universal co-operative motives: How infants begin to know the language and culture of their parents. In G. Jahoda & I. M. Lewis (Eds.), *Acquiring culture: Cross-cultural studies in child development* (pp. 37–90). London: Croom Helm.

Trevarthen, C., & Hubley, P. (1978). Secondary intersubjectivity: Confidence, confiding, and acts of meaning in the first year. In A. Lock (Ed.), *Action, gestures and symbol* (pp. 183–229). London: Academic Press.

Vygotsky, L. S. (1978). *Mind in society: The development of higher psychological processes*. Cambridge, MA: Harvard University Press.

Vygotsky, L. S. (1981). The genesis of higher mental functions. In J. V. Wertsch (Ed.), *The concept of activity in Soviet psychology* (pp. 144–188). Armonk, NY: Sharpe.

Walden, T. A., & Ogan, T. A. (1988). The development of social referencing. *Child Development, 59*, 1230–1240.

Wasserman, G. A., & Lewis, M. (1985). Infant sex differences: Ecological effects. *Sex Roles, 12*, 665–675.

Werner, H. (1957). The concept of development from a comparative and organismic point of view. In D. Harris (Ed.), *The concept of development* (pp. 125–148). Minneapolis: University of Minnesota Press.

Werner, H., & Kaplan, B. (1963). *Symbol formation*. New York: Wiley.

Wertsch, J. V. (Ed.). (1985). *Culture, communication, and cognition: Vygotskian perspectives*. Cambridge, England: Cambridge University Press.

Williams, D. (1992). *Nobody nowhere: The extraordinary autobiography of an autistic*. New York: Times Books.

Winnicott, D. W. (1960). The theory of the parent-infant relationship. *International Journal of Psychoanalysis, 41*, 585–595.

Wolff, P. H. (1969). The natural history of crying and other vocalizations in early infancy. In B. M. Foss (Ed.), *Determinants of infant behavior* (Vol. 4, pp. 81–115). London: Methuen.

Chapter 11

The Development of Joint Attention in Premature Low Birth Weight Infants: Effects of Early Medical Complications and Maternal Attention-Directing Behaviors

Susan H. Landry
University of Texas Medical School: Houston

The development of early problem solving, communication, and affective skills occurs, to a great extent, within a social context (Bruner, 1974; Schaffer, 1977). Infants develop these early skills through joint attention interactions with their caretakers. Joint attention is the ability to coordinate attention with another person to an object or topic of shared interest (Bruner, 1975). The ability to share attention to toys with another person is especially important because it signals the emergence of the skills that are precursors to more advanced cognitive and language abilities (Bakeman & Adamson, 1984; Bruner, 1977; Sugarman, 1984) and allows children the opportunity to learn about the properties and functions of objects (Lockman & McHale, 1989).

The development of joint attention skills spans most of infancy (Bakeman & Adamson, 1984). At around 6 months of age, most infants gain the ability to attend to both mothers and toys simultaneously and a new world of social interaction and shared learning opens to them (Newson & Newson, 1975). In this early stage of joint attention, infants are not able to easily shift their gaze back and forth from toys to their mothers in order to signal their interest in particular toys (Kaye & Fogel, 1980). Toward the end of the first year, infants begin to follow another's gaze and respond to gestures such as pointing and showing (Lempers, Flavell, & Flavell, 1977). Switching their gaze back and forth from caretaker to object becomes more coordinated for infants during the second year, along with the ability to signal their interest in sharing attention with another person (Bakeman & Adamson, 1984; Bates, 1979; Leung & Rheingold, 1981).

In joint attention interactions, mothers assist infants in practicing early social and exploratory skills by attending to their infants' cues, demonstrating what to do with toys, and making requests that are concordant with their infants' developmental abilities (Bruner, 1982; Kaye, 1982). Through mothers' guidance infants are able to learn how to integrate the use of eye gaze, vocalizations, gestures, and affective behaviors as well as exploratory play behaviors (Adamson & Bakeman, 1985; Ratner & Stettner, 1991). This specialized maternal assistance has been described as scaffolding because mothers control certain components of the learning task so the young child can attend to other components that are within his or her range of capability (Bakeman & Adamson, 1984; Wood, Bruner, & Ross, 1976). Studies investigating mothers' impact on development in relation to their behaviors in joint attention interactions report associations across time with children's competencies (Belsky, Goode, & Most, 1980; Ruddy & Bornstein, 1982). A number of theorists have proposed that for infants and children with developmental problems, maternal scaffolding during sociocognitive interactions may be particularly important in helping them learn (Bromwich, 1981; Girolametto, 1988; Marfo, 1990).

PRETERM SUBJECTS INCLUDED
IN JOINT ATTENTION STUDIES DESCRIBED
IN THIS CHAPTER

In the studies described in this chapter we evaluated the joint attention process for preterm low birth weight (LBW) infants and their mothers. Infants with the types of complications found in our LBW group have frequently been reported to have persistent impairments in their development of language, cognitive, and social skills, and therefore have an increased need for facilitation of their learning (Hunt, Cooper, & Tooley, 1988; Landry, Fletcher, Denson, & Chapieski, 1993; Robertson, Etches, Goldson, & Kyle, 1992; Vohr & Coll, 1985). In many studies, LBW infants have been treated as a homogeneous group, even though there are wide variations in types and severity of both prenatal and postnatal medical complications, and infants with severe complications have frequently been excluded. Evaluating LBW infants with the full range of medical complications is important because the extent and location of CNS damage is very likely to differ among these illness groups. For this reason, in the studies on preterm infants presented in this chapter we have evaluated the effects of greater degrees of neonatal illness (e.g., chronic lung disease) and medical complications (i.e., intraventricular hemorrhage) on joint attention and social communicative competence.

Over 70% of preterm infants weighing < 1600 grams have medical complications associated with prematurity (Volpe, 1981). These often lead to CNS damage, either through lack of adequate oxygenation of the brain (hypoxia) secondary to respiratory problems such as respiratory distress syndrome (RDS) or bronchopulmonary dysplasia (BPD), or from direct brain injury, as with intraventricular hemorrhage (IVH) with associated hydrocephalus. More recent studies have indicated that early medical complications associated with prematurity (i.e., IVH, RDS, and BPD) are responsible in part for differences in outcome (Bendersky & Lewis, 1990; Landry, Fletcher, Zarling, Chapieski, & Frances, 1984; Sostek, Smith, Katz, & Grant, 1987; Vohr, Bell, & Williams, 1982).

In the studies reported in this chapter, prematurity is defined as a gestational age at birth of ≤ 36 weeks and a birthweight of ≤ 1600 grams. Gestational age, defined as the time from mother's last menstrual period until birth, was always calculated by a neonatologist using Ballard's (1977) scoring system. All LBW infants included in these studies had mild to severe medical complications as defined below. The presence or absence of IVH was documented by cranial ultrasonography (or occasionally CT scans) within 7–10 days of birth. Infants with IVH received successive ultrasonograms or CT scans to detect progressive ventricular dilation (e.g., dilation present on the third week ultrasound). The degree of IVH is classified by a pediatric radiologist using the system of Papile, Munsick, Weaver, and Pecha (1979). For infants with respiratory illness the presence of BPD included ≥ 28 days of oxygen and positive x-ray findings (i.e., cystic changes, hyperinflation of the lungs) while chronic lung disease was defined as oxygen required for ≥ 28 days with cystic changes.

The Low-Risk (LR) Preterm Group

The low-risk (LR) preterm group included LBW infants who were diagnosed for either transient respiratory distress or RDS requiring intubation and oxygen support for ≥ 24 hr and/or IVH of Grades I or II, without hydrocephalus. Infants who were not intubated or did not have IVH (I or II) were not included. These complications were identified as low-risk complications because our earlier outcome studies showed that preterm infants with these complications were similar to healthy full-term infants on indices of mental and motor development by 12 to 24 months of age (Landry, Chapieski, Fletcher, & Denson, 1993).

The High-Risk (HR) Preterm Group

The high-risk (HR) preterm group included LBW infants who required supplemental oxygen therapy for over 28 days, a severe IVH, or periventricular lavcomalacia (PVL). Infants with BPD were included in the HR group if they also had Grades I–IV IVH. Infants with IVH, Grades III or IV with progressive dilatation were included with and without respiratory complications. These complications were identified as high-risk because developmental outcome as late as 3 years for infants with these complications was delayed (Landry et al., 1988, 1993).

A full-term (FT) comparison group was also included in many of the studies described in this chapter. Full-term healthy infants had gestational ages of 39 to 41 weeks, birth weight appropriate for gestational age, normal history of pregnancy and birth, Apgar scores at 5 minutes of 8 or greater, normal physical examination, and hospital discharge within 5 days of birth. Subjects were excluded if they had sensory or motor abnormalities.

The LBW and the FT groups were balanced for family socioeconomic status (SES), maternal age, and years of maternal education. The Hollingshead Four Factor Index of Social Status, based on occupation, education, and marital status was used to evaluate SES.

Children and their mothers were seen in a playroom video laboratory with a one-way mirror with age appropriate toys and child-sized table and chairs. Mother-child play sessions were videotaped and later coded by a two-person team. For all studies, 20–25% of the videotapes were coded by a second team in order to evaluate the reliability of raters. Interrater reliabilities were calculated using Cohen Kappa, percent agreements, or generalizability coefficients. The infants and children included in the joint attention studies also received standardized tests of mental, language, and motor development. The Bayley Scales of Infant Development (Mental and Motor Scales), the Sequenced Inventory of Communication Development (Expressive and Receptive Scales), and the McCarthy Scales of Children's Abilities were used to evaluate levels of developmental functioning.

PRETERM INFANTS' ATTENTION SKILLS

Premature low birth weight (LBW) infants represent one group of developmentally high-risk infants who have difficulty engaging in joint toy play with their mothers. Preterm infants are reported to have more gaze aversion and decreased joint toy play and to move their attention away from joint engagement more often than full-term infants (Brachfeld, Goldberg, & Sloman, 1980; Crawford, 1982; Landry, 1986). Several studies, however, show that for preterm infants without significant early medical complications, disruptions in joint play behaviors reported around 6 months of age may not be as evident later in the first year (Barnard, Bee, & Hammond, 1984; Brachfeld et al., 1980). In contrast, preterm infants with significant early medical problems (i.e., severe grades of IVH, BPD) show deficiencies in their development of joint attention skills throughout infancy and early childhood (Garner, Landry, & Richardson, 1991; Landry, Chapieski, Richardson, Palmer, & Hall, 1990).

In studies of interpersonal regulation of attention between mothers and preterm infants, the infant's attentional capacity has repeatedly been shown to be critical to the level of his or her response. Numerous studies have shown that measures of attention differentiate preterm and full-term infants (Kopp &

Vaughn, 1982; Rose, 1983; Sigman & Parmelee, 1974) and are associated with later intellectual functioning for both infant groups (Cohen & Parmelee, 1983; Fagan & McGrath, 1981; Lewis & Brooks-Gunn, 1981). Preterm infants have difficulty sustaining visual attention prior to 3 months of age (Cohen & Parmelee, 1983) and require longer periods of focused attention than full-term infants to process information about a stimulus (Rose, 1983). Later in the first year, they show less focused attention with active examination of objects (Ruff, McCarton, Kurtzberg, & Vaughan, 1984; Sigman, 1976) and longer latencies in organizing exploratory responses than full-term infants (Ruff, 1988). Because joint attention requires the infant to integrate a number of attentional skills such as shifting attention between a partner and a toy in order to share an awareness of objects or events, the joint attention problems reported for medically high-risk preterm infants may be attributed to deficiencies in attention regulation.

In an earlier study, we evaluated the types of early attention problems medically high-risk preterm infants showed. We measured how rapidly 7-month-old preterm LBW infants shifted their attention from a blinking light in order to attend to two different visual test patterns (Landry, Leslie, Fletcher, & Frances, 1985). We found that high-risk (HR) LBW infants took longer to inhibit their response to the light so they could turn and orient to the visual pattern, compared to low-risk (LR) LBW and full-term (FT) infants. The three groups did not differ in their ability to remember and discriminate the visual patterns, and they showed similar habituation and dishabituation, after differences in their ability to shift attention were controlled. The results of this study provided support for Cohen's hypothesis (Cohen, 1972) that infant attention involves at least two different mechanisms (attention-getting and attention-holding), and that investigation of these two separate visual attention processes may be especially important for LBW infants with severe medical complications such as IVH and BPD. The longer latencies in moving attentional focus for the HR group were attributed to delays in motor development as well as to difficulty inhibiting a response to one visual stimulus in order to attend to another.

Our next step was to extend the findings of this study by examining infants in a more naturalistic setting. Medically high- and low-risk LBW infants and full-term infants were videotaped in both independent and joint toy play with mothers, and their ability to move attentional focus and sustain attention was evaluated. In both independent and joint toy play, the high-risk infants differed from low-risk and full-term infants by showing fewer shifts of attention between toys and by noticing fewer toys, but they did not differ on measures requiring sustained looking. The high-risk infants also showed less active examination of toys compared to the other two infant groups (Landry & Chapieski, 1988). These results extended our previous findings, suggesting that LBW infants with severe intraventricular hemorrhage and/or chronic respiratory disease have particular difficulty shifting attention from one stimulus to another in independent and social learning situations that involve moving their attentional focus between objects or between their mother and objects. This type of attentional problem might make it particularly difficult for these infants to develop joint attention skills.

THE DEVELOPMENT OF JOINT ATTENTION SKILLS FOR PRETERM INFANTS

Our next series of studies were conducted to evaluate the development of joint attention in preterm infants. In a longitudinal study evaluating the development of joint attention skills for groups of medically high- and low-risk preterm infants across the first 2 years, we found persistent problems in the development of joint attention skills for the high-risk preterm infants (Garner et al., 1991). We evaluated joint attention skills for two groups of preterm LBW infants, low-risk and high-risk, and for a group of full-term infants observed in videotaped interactions at 6, 12, and 24 months with their mothers. We coded for infant and mother joint attention behaviors. For each maternal attention-directing event, observers coded the timing of mother's attention-directing behaviors in relation to the infant's already established focus of attention and the type of attention-directing strategy mothers used (i.e., pointing, showing, giving toys). The infant's response to toys that followed each maternal attempt to involve the child in joint toy play was coded according to its level of complexity, from "no response," "passive looking/holding," and "toy manipulation." The infant's communicative responses were coded as speech acts (i.e., using language and gesture to express a specific function), vocalization, or coordinated eye gaze behavior. Infants' attempts to initiate joint attention episodes were also coded.

The results of this study showed that the high-risk preterm infants had difficulties with showing higher level joint play responses and with using language and gestures to communicate their interest in toys or to direct their mothers' attention. At 6 months of age, both the full-term and preterm infant groups had few instances of coordinated joint attention (i.e., moving their attention from a toy to mother and back to the toy). Rather, at this young age, the infants were involved in what Bakeman and Adamson (1984) referred to as *passive joint engagement*. These were episodes in which the infants attended to toys the mothers touched, tapped, or manipulated. Bakeman and Adamson (1984) reported that the mothers of the normal infants in their study appeared to facilitate their infant's ability to attend to the toys. The infants, however, did not show an awareness of their mothers' presence by intermittently looking up at her and then back at the toy. We observed that the mothers' manipulations of the toys (i.e., tapping, shaking, moving them from side to side) often functioned to bring about increased attention to a toy for normal as well as for preterm infants. During these joint attention interactions at 12 months, the full-term infants began to take a slightly more active role by attempting to direct their mothers' attention to toys with eye gaze and gestures. Both preterm groups, however, showed significantly fewer attempts to actively attract their mother's attention to toys of interest.

By 24 months, the high-risk preterm infants showed less coordinated eye gaze and fewer speech acts than the full-term infants and continued to be less active in initiating directing their mothers' attention than the low-risk and full-term infants. Decreased joint play behavior involving functional toy play across all ages for the high-risk versus the low-risk and full-term infants suggests that severity of medical risk and not low birth weight per se is associated with deficits in exploratory play during joint attention episodes. By 24 months the low-risk infants also showed deficits in directing their mother's attention and in using coordinated eye gaze behaviors. This finding indicates that LBW, regardless of the severity of medical risk, is also related to problems with joint attention.

The mothers of the high-risk preterm infants provided increased input (e.g., introduction of new toys) compared to the mothers of the full-term infants, a behavior that may reflect the decreased responsiveness of these medically involved infants. Although the mothers of the high-risk infants provided more input, they were similar to the other two groups of mothers in that they also decreased their use of structured nonverbal attention-directing strategies (i.e., toy demonstrations) as their children grew older and more competent across 6 to 24 months. All three groups of mothers used significantly more attention orienting verbs (e.g., look, see) with their 6-month-old infants than they did when the infants were 12 and 24 months old. This may have occurred because the mothers were sensitive to their young infants' need for assistance in orienting their focus of attention in order for joint attention to occur. In contrast to this decrease across the three age points in verbal strategies that oriented attention, there was an increase across ages in mothers' use of verbal directives (i.e., imperatives) and questioning strategies. This finding may indicate that mothers are responsive to their infants' increased ability to understand more complex verbal language. Mothers often used directive and questioning statements to encourage their infants to become actively engaged with particular toys. An unexpected increase in maintaining children's interests in particular toys for all groups of mothers suggested that following infant cues continues to be important even after infants develop the ability to initiate these interactions on their own.

We also conducted a series of cross-sectional studies evaluating joint attention skills across the first 2 years for separate groups of medically high- and low-risk preterm infants and full-term control infants. During joint attention interactions at 6 months of age, the full-term and low-risk preterm infants showed significantly more reaching for toys during episodes of shared attention than the high-risk preterm infants, demonstrating the negative impact of delayed motor skills on joint toy play for these infants (Landry & Chapieski, 1988). Although there were no group differences in relation to how often the mothers attempted to direct their infants' attention, both high- and low-risk preterm infants withdrew their attention from episodes of shared interest in toys more often than full-term infants (Landry, 1986). This finding may indicate that the preterm infants could not stay involved in the interaction to the degree that their mothers were. These infants seemed to need to take intermittent "breaks" away from joint attention interactions followed by movement of their attention back to the interaction.

Joint Attention and Sociocommunicative Skills in Infancy. In light of language related problems frequently reported for preterm LBW infants (Landry et al., 1988; Siegel et al., 1982; Sostek et al., 1987; Taub, Goldstein, & Caputo, 1977), it may be particularly important to document preterm infants' sociocommunicative responsiveness in early joint attention. Joint attention interactions are an important social context for children to learn how to integrate the use of a broad range of communicative behaviors such as eye gaze and attention-directing gestures that signal their partner of their interests in particular toys or objects (Tomasello & Farrar, 1986). In a study evaluating sociocommunicative skills in joint attention interactions for preterm infants at 24 months of age, we found that all of the preterm infants regardless of the severity of their early medical complications showed fewer attempts to initiate directing their mothers' attention to toys and to topics of interest and used fewer verbalizations and higher level speech acts such as verbalizations and gestures that add new information to the interaction or direct mothers' attention (Landry, Schmidt, & Richardson, 1989).

Differences between the full-term and preterm groups at 24 months seemed to be specific to the particular role the children were able to take in social interactions, rather than to a more pervasive lack of social responsiveness or of understanding the rudiments of joint attention interactions. The preterm children, regardless of the type of severity of their medical complications, had more difficulty initiating exchanges in which they were required to direct their mothers' attention by requesting, commenting, or labeling toys of interest to them. Most of the preterm children's communication behaviors occurred in response to their mothers' directives.

The use of higher level communication behaviors during toy-centered play requires children to integrate a number of complex skills, including visually following their mothers' attempts to direct their attention to toys, exploring toys in response to their mothers' directives, attempting to direct their mothers' attention, and responding to mothers' social bids. By 24 months of age children should be able to initiate directing others' attention with verbalizations and gestures to objects and topics of common interest. Although the preterm children in our study were delayed in developing this aspect of the joint attention process, they were not delayed in their ability to use communication behaviors that continued interactions (verbal and gestural imitation, turn-taking vocalizations, verbalizations in response to others), and to respond to toys in relation to their mothers' attention-directing attempts.

Joint Attention and Sociocommunicative Skills at 3 Years. The development of certain joint attention abilities is important for children's development of later social competence. By the third year of life, children should be able to cooperate with parental requests as well as initiate social interactions, two important aspects of early social development (Barocas et al., 1991; Crockenberg & Litman, 1990). Participation in joint attention interactions across the first 2 years of life facilitates these later social skills by providing opportunities for children to attend to and follow mothers' attempts to direct their attention to salient aspects of the environment and to learn how to reciprocate by directing mothers' attention to objects and conversational topics of shared interest. Deficient development in early joint attention behaviors might be expected, therefore, to result in deficient social skill development.

We recently evaluated whether medically high-risk preterm children would show problems in their ability to cooperate with their mothers' requests and in initiating social exchanges. LBW children have been described to be passive and disorganized, to lack concentration, and to have poor social skills (Bjerre & Hansen, 1976), behaviors that may interfere with taking an active role in social interactions and cooperating with others. The associations among medical complications, social competence, and caretaking environment are important to evaluate in LBW children because it is hypothesized that children learn to organize their environment conceptually through active social interactions (Vygotsky, 1934/1962).

At 3 years of age when low- and high-risk prematurely born children were compared with full-term children, high-risk preterm children again showed deficits in their ability to take an active role in joint attention interactions (Landry et al., 1990). The children were observed interacting with their mothers while constructing a puzzle with each other and having a tea party. At this later age we found that high-risk preterm children showed significantly fewer attempts to initiate directing their mothers' attention to aspects of the shared experience than did low-risk preterm children. This difference was apparent even after significant effects of differences in the children's IQ and mothers' degree of directiveness were accounted for. The inability to take an active role in joint attention interactions was apparent across both social contexts (e.g., puzzle and tea party). The high-risk children were similar to the low-risk and full-term children in their ability to respond to their mothers' requests in both situations. These results demonstrate that high-risk preterm children show persistent deficits in the development of the skills necessary to initiate getting others to share interests in particular conversational topics or activities.

MATERNAL ATTENTION-DIRECTING BEHAVIORS
WITH PRETERMS

In light of persistent joint attention problems for medically high-risk preterm infants and to a lesser extent low-risk preterm infants, it is important to understand how mothers can facilitate these skills. A number of studies have reported that mothers of preterm children use increased amounts of and more highly structured stimulation with their infants than mothers of normal infants (Brachfeld et al., 1980; Field, 1980; Garner et al., 1991; Wasserman, Allen, & Solomon, 1985), but the efficacy of these strategies has received less attention.

Normal and preterm children's ability to respond in joint attention interactions has been related to mothers' responsiveness to their attentional focus and use of attention-directing strategies that are concordant with the child's abilities (Akhtar, Dunham, & Dunham, 1991; Garner, & Landry, in press; Landry, Garner, Denson, Swank, & Baldwin, 1993; Rocissano & Yatchmink, 1983; Tomasello & Farrar, 1986). Mothers who maintained the conversational topics their preterm children initiated were more likely to have children with higher levels of linguistic competence (Rocissano & Yatchmink, 1983). For normal 13-month-old infants in the early stages of language development, mothers' use of directive strategies in the context of joint focus correlated positively with the children's productive vocabulary at 22 months (Akhtar et al., 1991).

Studies of normal infants have shown that higher degrees of maternal stimulation and sensitivity are associated with increased levels of toy exploration in joint toy play interactions for 12-month-old infants (Yarrow, Morgan, Jennings, Harmon, & Gaiter, 1982). In an experimentally controlled study, Belsky and colleagues (Belsky et al., 1980) identified specific didactic strategies that facilitated toy exploration: Mothers' use of nonverbal behaviors that provide information about how to use a toy was associated with increased levels of play for normal 12-month-old infants. Responsiveness or sensitivity to infants' attention to particular tasks correlated with focused toy exploration for both preterm and full-term infants at 12 months (Lawson, Parrinello, & Ruff, 1992).

Joint Attention. Drawing on the results of some of these earlier studies and our own findings concerning the attentional deficits of high-risk preterm infants we developed a number of hypotheses that guided our investigations of the effect of mothers' attention-directing behaviors on preterm infants' joint attention skills. The hypotheses tested were based on the assumption that the greater the demands made on infants' attentional capacity, the more difficult it is for them to respond appropriately. When mothers attempt to monitor their infants' attention and encourage joint attention by following rather than redirecting the infant's focus of attention, they may reduce attentional demands for the infants and thereby facilitate the infants' ability to share attention and to actively explore toys in joint attention interactions with others. Attempts to redirect attentional focus away from a toy of interest to a different toy may require enough of the infant's attentional capacity to limit their ability to integrate the attentional, affective, and exploratory behaviors necessary to respond appropriately. For medically involved preterm infants whose attentional capacity is limited, higher level joint attention skills (e.g., active toy exploration, positive affect) can be stimulated by maternal interactive behaviors that are sensitive to the infant's needs. Specifically, mothers will enhance their infant's learning by following their infant's focus of attention rather than by encouraging redirection of attention.

We also expected that mothers' style of directing attention was important in understanding mothers' facilitation of joint attention for preterm infants. Attention-directing strategies that provide infants with information about what is expected of them (i.e., how to play with toys) rather than simply orienting their attention to toys (less structured interactive strategies) were expected to facilitate increased joint attention responsiveness for the preterm infants, especially the high-risk preterm infants. The high-risk infants whose motor and attentional skills are less well-developed may need specific information from the mother to stimulate their joint attention responses.

In Landry, Chapieski, and Schmidt (1986), we evaluated the relationship between mothers' sensitivity to infants' visual cues and their nonverbal and verbal attention-directing strategies and preterm and full-term 12-month-old infants' ability to share attention to toys and show higher levels of toy involvement while jointly attending. We expected that mothers' attempts to maintain infants' focus of interest in toys and provide more direction about how to play with toys through verbal directives and toy demonstration would be associated with increased joint attention and higher levels of exploratory play, and we also expected that these relations would be stronger for preterm infants of greater degrees of medical risk.

The infants and mothers were videotaped for 10 minutes in a toy-centered play interaction with a group of age appropriate toys. Twenty high-risk, 20 low-risk, and 20 full-term infants, and their mothers were included. The videotapes were coded for mothers' specific verbal (e.g., questions, imperatives, and attention verbs) and nonverbal attention-directing behaviors (e.g., toy demonstrations and giving, showing, and pointing to toys).

The results of this study showed that for all three infant groups maintaining infant interests was associated with increased joint attention and with a higher frequency of manipulation of toys than merely looking at toys. Redirecting attention was just as likely to produce a "no response" as a "response" and more likely to be followed by a "look" than a "manipulate." Mothers' provision of increased information about what to do with a toy through verbal directives and questions rather than words that oriented attention (e.g., look, see, this one) was also associated with increased joint attention. Directives (i.e., "get the ball") and questions (i.e., "can you throw it?") were more often followed by a manipulate than a look. In contrast, attention-orienting words were just as likely to be followed by a look as by a toy manipulation. Toy demonstrations, a nonverbal attention-directing strategy that provided infants with information about what to do with toys, were more likely to be followed by an active exploratory response than by passive looking. This was also true for handing toys to infants, a gesture that provides more structure by making toys more physically available to infants. In contrast, gestures that pointed out toys but did not make them physically available were followed by manipulations and passive looking with the same frequency.

With the exception of mothers' attempts to redirect attention, all of the maternal attention-directing strategies were effective in eliciting joint attention because they were more likely to be followed by a response than by a no response to toys. The strategies differed, however, in the extent to which they were associated with more active involvement with toys. Mothers' use of strategies that maintained interest and provided increased information about what to do with a toy, whether verbal or nonverbal, were strategies that were associated with more active toy exploration. These may be attention-directing strategies that are more important in maximizing infants' opportunities to learn about toys in joint attention interactions at least at 1 year of age.

Exploratory Play. We have evaluated the association of mothers' attention-directing behaviors with full-term and with preterm infants' exploratory play behaviors during joint attention interactions across the first 2 years of life. In general, the results of these studies demonstrate that the association of mother and child joint play behaviors vary as a function of the child's medical risk status and their age. The results of these studies also show that both mothers' responsiveness to infants' interests in particular toys and the extent to which they provide information about what type of response is expected may be important factors in understanding how preterm infants' joint attention skills can be facilitated.

In a recent study (Landry et al., in press) we attempted to identify which maternal attention-directing strategies would be most likely to facilitate 6-month-old preterm infants' learning in joint toy play interactions. The relation between specific maternal attention-directing strategies and the conditional probability of an increase in the complexity of the infants' exploratory joint play responses was evaluated for 6-month-old full-term infants ($n = 49$) and very low birth weight infants of high-risk ($n = 37$) and low-risk ($n = 42$) medical status. We evaluated two aspects of mothers' attention-directing behaviors: We observed the timing of mothers' strategies in relation to the infants' focus of attention when the exchange started and the degree of structure provided by their nonverbal or verbal strategies.

Mothers' timing was included in order to evaluate the extent to which mothers' responsiveness to their infants' interest in particular toys facilitated higher level exploratory play responses. If the infant was already looking at and/or physically engaged with the same toy to which their attention was being directed, the mother was coded as *maintaining* her infant's attention. If the infant was not attending to or engaged with any toy, the mother was coded as *introducing* a toy. If the infant was involved with a different toy from the one to which his or her attention was being directed, the mother was coded as *redirecting* her infant's attention. Mothers' attention-directing strategies were also coded. *Structured* strategies were verbal or nonverbal behaviors that provided the infant with specific information about what to do with the toy (e.g., demonstrations, imperatives). *Unstructured* strategies were behaviors like showing or pointing to a toy that did not specify how the child was to play with the toy. The joint play interactions were also coded for whether the infant jointly attended to the toy with their mothers and for the level of exploratory play response they showed during joint focus. Infants' responses were coded as "no joint attention response" or as "jointly attending" by looking at the toy, by passively holding the toy, or by actively examining or manipulating the toy.

In order to provide stronger evidence of cause and effect between these maternal and infant behaviors, we evaluated the conditional probability that a maternal attention-directing behavior would be associated with an increase in the infants' play response that immediately followed the maternal initiation. This analytical approach does not absolutely prove causation, but it provides better evidence of causation than general correlational approaches because there is a close temporal relationship between the predictor variable (maternal behavior) and the criterion variable (infant behavior), and because the analysis measures only increases in infant joint play responses, thereby controlling for the tendency of the infant to persist in a previous behavior.

Results indicated that the conditional probability of an infant increasing complexity of joint play in response to mothers' maintaining and introducing versus redirecting was greater for the HR infants than for the LR and FT infants (see Fig. 11.1). When mothers redirected the HR infants' attention, the likelihood of increasing their response decreased more dramatically than it did for the LR and FT infants. Also, structured strategies resulted in a greater probability of the infants increasing activity than unstructured strategies for all infant groups. However, a significant strategy by timing effect indicated that structured strate-

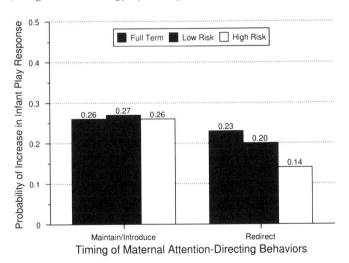

FIG. 11.1. Relation of maternal TIMING techniques to mean increases in infant exploratory play responses in high-risk, low-risk, and full-term groups.

gies resulted in increased responding more when mothers maintained or introduced than when they redirected (see Fig. 11.2). In general these results demonstrate that medically high-risk preterm infants found it harder than low-risk and full-term infants to engage in high level joint toy play when they were required to redirect their attention from one toy to another. The high-risk infants appeared to be normal in their capacity to jointly attend to objects when their attentional focus was sustained but had problems shifting the focus of their attention during a joint attention interaction. This problem may have occurred because they were required to inhibit a response to one toy in order to move their attentional focus to a different toy, an ability that appears to be delayed or deficient for these infants.

When mothers of the high-risk infants maintained rather than redirected their infants' attentional focus, and introduced new toys primarily when the infant was not already focused on another toy they provided useful scaffolding for their infants that enabled them to achieve the same level of toy exploration as that of low-risk and full-term infants. The results also showed that mothers of high-risk infants were more likely to maintain and introduce toys and were less likely to redirect infant attention than mothers of the other risk groups.

Mothers' use of structured versus unstructured attention-directing strategies were also associated with differences in infant exploratory play responses, although no differences between risk groups were demonstrated. We found that in all three infant groups, exploratory play was increased when mothers used structured attention-directing strategies to maintain their infants' attention or introduce toys, but not when they redirected attention.

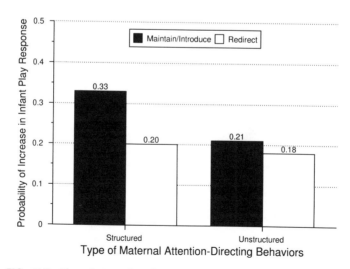

FIG. 11.2. The relation of mothers' attention-directing behaviors to mean increases in infant exploratory play responses for all risk groups combined.

The results of this study demonstrated that in joint play interactions, mothers' sensitive timing of attention-directing behaviors enhances the toy exploration of high-risk preterm infants at 6 months of age. This finding is consistent with transactional models of development suggesting that certain caretaking behaviors can compensate for the negative affects of biological risk. The use of attention-directing strategies that provide specific information about how to use a toy seemed to be facilitative of exploratory play for all of the infant groups at this young age.

Affective Responsiveness. Mothers' specialized assistance through the use of certain attention-directing strategies is also important for medically high-risk preterm infants to be able to sustain positive affective states. In a recent study evaluating affective states for preterm and full-term infants at 6 months of age in independent and joint toy play sessions, high-risk preterm infants showed more occurrences of high interest during joint toy play than during independent play (Garner & Landry, 1992). The full-term and low-risk preterm infants showed the opposite pattern. The full-term and low-risk infants also showed significantly more high interest during independent play than the high-risk infants. With their mothers' assistance, however, the high-risk infants increased their ability to share attention to toys with a sustained alert focus so that they looked comparable to the other two groups of infants on this positive affective state during joint play.

Mothers' responsiveness to their infants' visual cues as a means to promote joint attention was important in understanding the preterm infants' affective responsiveness. Mothers' attempts to maintain their infants' interest in particular toys was positively associated with high interest for the high-risk infants and with smiling for the low-risk preterm infants. We were surprised that mothers' maintaining was not associated with positive affect in the FT infant group as associations between maintaining behavior and normal infants' language development have been previously reported (e.g., Tomasello & Farrar, 1986). It may be that the FT infants' affective skills are so well organized that they do not need the same degree of maternal scaffolding as LR and HR infants to become affectively engaged in joint toy play. For instance, in a previous study we found that LR preterm infants showed less coordinated gaze behavior during joint toy play than did FT infants (Garner et al., 1991). This finding suggests that these LR infants may experience subtle affective difficulties and may require more assistance from their mothers in order to show positive affective states.

Mothers' introducing behavior was associated with increased low interest for the HR infants. When mothers were coded as introducing a toy, this meant that their infants were not attending to them or the toys. It is possible that infants use these times to take "a break" from the interaction. Periods of inactivity give infants the opportunity to process information and modulate arousal (Brazelton, Koslowski, & Main, 1974; Field, 1981). According to Fogel (1982), infants look away from objects and people so that they can reorganize their behavior "before beginning a new visual assault on the environment" (p. 55). This may be especially true for HR infants who are more behaviorally disorganized than other infant groups (Myers et al., 1992). The findings from this study indicate that medically HR infants show less positive affect during joint toy play situations than LR and FT infants. Their mothers can facilitate their affective responsiveness by using behaviors that are sensitive to their attentional capabilities. As predicted, differential patterns of associations between the infant affect variables and mothers' attention-directing behaviors were observed across the three infant groups. Maintaining behavior may facilitate increases in positive affective states for low- and high-risk preterm infants. However, none of the maternal variables we assessed predicted increases in smiling behavior for the HR preterm infants. The greater difficulty these infants have with the process of jointly attending to toys the first year may result in decreased capacity to coordinate this high level affective state even with their mothers' assistance.

Sociocommunicative Behaviors During Infancy. Mothers of prematurely born children show different types of joint attention behaviors to facilitate their children's sociocommunicative competence compared to mothers of full-term children. Also, the relation between mothers' joint attention behaviors and their children's sociocommunicative responsiveness differs between full-term versus preterm mother–infant dyads and between medically low-risk and high-risk preterm infant–mother pairs. The fact that preterm children with specific medical complications (i.e., IVH, RDS, and BPD) have poorer scores on global language measures than SES-matched full-term controls (Landry et al., 1988) suggests that functional use of language may be an important aspect of their language development to study in relation to mothers' interactive behaviors in joint attention interactions. Analyses of functional use of language (i.e., speech acts), in addition to more general measures of social interactive behavior (i.e., frequency of verbalizations, responsiveness to mothers' attempts to direct attention), have not been investigated in relation to specific medical complications such as intraventricular hemorrhage. The use of language to communicate a range of functions is an aspect of early skill development that relates to later school achievement. Language is thought to develop, in part, out of children's ability to allocate their attention to more than one aspect of the environment through joint attention (Bakeman & Adamson, 1984).

We recently evaluated the relation of mothers' verbal responsiveness to their children's interest in a particular toy or conversational topic (coded as maintaining behavior) with a range of preterm and full-term toddlers' sociocommunicative skills. In addition to coding for mothers' maintaining behavior, we coded a broad range of child sociocommunicative behaviors. These are described in Table 11.1. Of particular interest was the children's use of speech acts to communicate with their mothers in the interactions.

TABLE 11.1
Categories for Coding Functions of Children's Language and Gesture

Variables	Definition
Speech Acts:	Verbalizations and gestures that add new information to the interaction or direct mothers' attention to a toy or topic. The following five language and gesture behaviors were included in this category:
Negate	Says no or shakes head or uses other gesture to show refusal or rejection.
Affirm	Says yes or shakes head in agreement with something mother said or did.
Comment/label	Names an object or supplies information about a toy or conversational topic, e.g., "that one's red."
Request	Verbalization or gesture used to ask for information, assistance, or an object.
Direct attention	Points, shows, or indicates an object with or without a verbalization such as "this one."
Communicative acts that regulate an interaction:	Five additional interactive behaviors that could be used to respond to more general aspects of social interactions were coded. These behaviors differed from the speech acts behaviors in that they did not provide additional information to the interchange but rather merely served to continue it.
Turn-taking vocalization	The child responds to mother's questions or directives with vocalizations that serve to mark his or her turn, e.g., "uh" or "eh."
Recite/perform	Verbalizations associated with familiar social scripts, e.g., "hello," "bye bye."
Exclamatory vocalizations	The child responds to mother's attention-directing attempts with vocalization that expresses interest or surprise, e.g., "oh" or "ah."
Uninterpretable vocalizations	Vocalizations directed to mother for which the specific function was unclear.
Protest	Cries or whines that are in response to something the mother said or did.
Additional Coded Interactive Behaviors:	
Initiations	The child initiates directing the mother's behavior with a speech act or a communicative act that regulates the interaction.
Joint attention to toy	The child responds to mother's attempts to direct attention by looking at the toy or with an activity other than a communicative behavior.
No responses	Failure to use communicative behavior or to respond to the toy or event, or to mother.

Research with young normal children has described a wide range of functions that their language can serve (Dore, 1979). These communication behaviors have been investigated in terms of speech acts (Austin, 1962; Searle, 1969) and are often described according to categories such as commenting, labeling, and requesting (Bates et al., 1975; Dore, 1979). Before children are able to use language to communicate a range of functions, they use vocalizations, eye gaze, and certain gestures to regulate social interaction. These less well-developed communicative behaviors may function to mark their turn in a communicative interaction or to direct another person's attention. The children and their mothers were videotaped in a 10 minute toy-centered play interaction.

The preterm children were again subdivided into separate groups in relation to the type and severity of their early medical complications. The 37 subjects were 24-month-old toddlers. Ten full-term, 9 preterm with IVH (Grades III and IV) and RDS, 9 preterm with IVH (Grades I and II) and RDS, and 9 preterm with RDS without IVH. Because all infants with IVH had some degree of RDS associated with their prematurity, the RDS without IVH group of preterm infants was included as a comparison group to control for the effect of RDS on the communication measures. The three preterm groups were comparable on mean birth weight, amount of prematurity, and weeks of hospitalization before initial discharge, and were equated for severity of RDS.

In this study, we were interested in investigating communicative and interactive behaviors in preterm toddlers with more severe degrees of IVH, compared with full-term toddlers, preterm toddlers without IVH, and preterms with less severe degrees of IVH. We evaluated their use of language and gestures to express a range of functions (e.g., speech acts) and their use of less developmentally advanced interactive behaviors such as general responsiveness to mothers (i.e., eye gaze, turn-taking vocalizations) and attention to toys in response to mothers' attention-directing attempts. Definitions for these communicative behaviors are presented in Table 11.1. Preterm toddlers with more severe IVH were expected to differ from full-term toddlers and from preterm toddlers who had mild IVH or no IVH, on their use of speech acts but not on general responsiveness to social interaction. We were interested in determining whether mothers across the four groups of toddlers differed in their interactive behaviors. Mothers of the severe IVH group were expected to show increased attention-directing behaviors, compared with the mothers of the other infant groups, because they wished to encourage episodes of shared attention to toys. Because these children were expected to take a less active role in initiating interactions, we predicted that they would be less clear in the signals they provided for their mothers regarding their interest in a particular toy or topic. This lack of clarity was expected to be reflected in fewer maternal behaviors that served to maintain the child's interest in toys or conversational topics. Finally, we were interested in determining the association between mothers' attempts to maintain their children's interest with aspects of the children's interactive behaviors and whether this relation differed across the medical complication groups.

TABLE 11.2
Coded Behaviors

Interactive Behavior	Definitions
Mothers:	
Directives	Imperative statement that directs the child to do or say something (e.g., "Put this one here," "Say Thank you").
Suggestions	Question or suggestive statement that provides the child with a choice (e.g., "Where does this one go?", "Do you want a cookie?")
Restrictions	Imperative statement that attempts to limit the child's actions (e.g., "Don't put it there"; "Stop pouring, now").
Praise	Statement that provides positive feedback to the child about his or her behavior (e.g., "That was good").
Children:	
Self-direction	A child-initiated action with or without a verbalization to carry out a particular activity (e.g., child tries to place puzzle piece without mother's assistance, child gives mother something from the "tea party" tray). During the "tea party," self-directed behavior also included initiations of conversation with the mother (e.g., "Could I have a cookie?", "Do you want one?").
Problem behavior	Child shows any one of the following behaviors: over-activity (e.g., runs around the room), temper tantrums (whining/crying), grabbing, demanding (e.g., yells mother's name, insists that mother does what he or she wants), perseverative behavior (i.e., three or more repetitions of the same behavior), or clumsy behavior (e.g., falls off chair, drops plate on floor).
Compliance	Child attempts to carry out an action that mother has directed him or her to do. The child does not have to successfully complete what mother asks but rather has to show a response that makes it clear that he or she understood what was asked and is attempting to do it.
Noncompliance: refuse/ignore	Child indicates with a gesture (e.g., shakes head no) or a verbalization that he or she will not do what mother says to do, or continues doing what he or she was already doing, showing no attempt to follow mother's directive.
Inappropriate response	Child responds to mother's directive with an action or verbal response that shows the child either did not understand what was expected of him or her or could not show appropriate response (e.g., Mom: "Can you give me a cookie?"; child picks up cookie and puts it on his or her own plate).

Mothers' maintaining behavior was significantly associated with a number of sociocommunicative behaviors for the full-term and medically low-risk toddlers but not for the high-risk preterms. There were highly significant associations between mothers' maintaining and children's use of higher level speech acts and responsive verbalizations for full-term toddlers and for preterm toddlers with respiratory distress or mild grades of intraventricular hemorrhage. Maintaining behavior was also positively associated with children's acts that serve to regulate social interactions for the full-term toddlers with mild to moderate respiratory complications and with social initiations for both of the medically low-risk preterm groups. In contrast, mothers' maintaining behavior showed negative correlations, although not significant, with the medically high-risk preterm in-fants' social communicative behaviors. Closer inspection of mothers' maintaining behaviors with child communication behaviors for the medically high-risk pre-term group revealed that mothers of the high-risk children in this group, who seldom initiated and used few speech acts, had a large number of verbal main-taining behaviors. These may represent the mothers' responses to the children's lower level communication acts and joint attention responses to toys. This pat-tern was not apparent for the other groups. The unique relation between mothers' attempts to maintain interest and their children's reduced ability to use pragmatic language was apparent for the high-risk group, even though these mothers were comparable to the other groups in frequency of maintaining behaviors, and the children were comparable to the other preterm children in their frequency of speech acts and initiations. The high-risk children were also comparable to the other preterm toddlers on measures of mental and language development. The mothers' behavior in the high-risk group may result from the more directive and highly stimulating role they have been accustomed to playing in earlier inter-actions with these children. Bell (1979) suggests that parents' increased stimu-lation with developmentally high-risk children represents an attempt to increase the child's responsiveness.

Mothers' attempts to maintain preterm children's conversational topics have been associated with increased communicative competence in other studies. In a study conducted by Rocissano and Yatchmink (1983) medically low-risk pre-term children were divided into two linguistic groups. Children in the high group had more advanced expressive language skills, were using word combina-tions, and could express relations between objects and events. Children in the low language group produced single words with few word combinations. One objective of this study was to evaluate how dyadic interaction patterns related to linguistic competence. Synchronous turns were coded when one partner re-sponded to the other partner's attempt to initiate joint attention by maintaining the initiating partner's focus of attention. This type of responsiveness between the mother and child was significantly associated with the length of the children's utterances. When group differences for synchronous turns were evaluated, chil-dren and mothers in the high group had more synchronous turns than mother and child dyads in the low group. Mothers in the low group did not maintain their preterm children's topics as often as mothers in the high group, and the children in the low group did not pick up on mom's topic as often as children in the high group.

The findings from Rocissano and Yatchmink's study demonstrate the impor-tance of mothers' attempts to maintain preterm children's communicative efforts in social interactions. The results of our study with medically low- and high-risk preterm children suggests that mothers' attempts to maintain the focus of interest for children who are not yet developmentally ready to use functional language may be important in supporting these children's ability to use lower level communication acts and joint attention responses to toys.

Sociocommunicative Behaviors at 3 Years. In the school age years, a higher incidence of social and behavioral problems are reported in LBW children (birth weight ≤ 2,500 grams) compared to children of normal births (Bjerre & Hansen, 1976; Drillien, 1961; Pasamanick, Rogers, & Lilienfeld, 1956). In general, LBW children are reported to be passive and disorganized, to lack concentration, and to have poor social skills, behaviors that may interfere with taking an active role in social interactions and cooperating with others. The associations among medical complications, social competence, and caretaking environment are important to evaluate in LBW children because it is hypothesized that children learn to organize their environment conceptually through active social interactions (Vygotsky, 1962). Normal children's social development is facilitated by nondirective maternal behaviors, such as questioning, suggesting, and providing choices (Parpal & Maccoby, 1985). Given the high-risk preterm infants' earlier deficits in joint attention, we expected that appropriate social functioning for these children may require more structured types of maternal input, such as verbal directives, that gives them specific information about what is expected of them. Maternal warmth and sensitivity, such as praise, are also reported to facilitate social development for normal children (Lytton, 1977; Parpal & Maccoby, 1985) and may be even more vital for high-risk children. Several recent studies show that mothers of higher risk preterms respond to their children more positively than mothers of low-risk preterms and normal infants (Greenberg & Crnic, 1988; Sigman, Cohen, & Forsythe, 1981).

In light of the decreased social skills we found for high-risk preterm children compared to low-risk preterm and full-term children at 3 years of age in both social (tea party) and cognitive (Puzzle teaching) situations (see pp. 230–231 for description of these results), we evaluated the association of mothers' attention-directing style with the children's social behaviors.

Specifically, we investigated the association between children's self-directed behavior and two contrasting parenting styles—directiveness and suggestiveness—as well as maternal praise. Praise was included because maternal warmth and sensitivity, such as praise, are also reported to facilitate social development for normal children (Lytton, 1977; Parpal & Maccoby, 1985) and may be even more vital for high-risk children (Greenberg & Crnic, 1988). In light of the HR children's lower responsiveness at earlier ages (Landry & Chapieski, 1988), we predicted that the negative relation of maternal directiveness with children's self-directed behavior would be stronger for the HR compared to the FT and LR groups. Mothers' use of suggestions, however, was expected to relate positively to self-directed behaviors for the normal and LR children but not to those of the HR children. Finally, because mothers were expected to be highly responsive to their high-risk preterm children's positive involvement in the interactions, we predicted that maternal praise and children's compliance and self-directed behavior would be more strongly related for the HR than the other groups.

The study included 25 high-risk (HR) low birth weight (LBW) children, 23 low-risk (LR) LBW children, and 21 healthy full-term (FT) children. All were 3 years of age. LBW children with histories of IVH, RDS, or BPD were classified into risk groups according to the type of severity of their earlier medical complications.

The HR children had lower IQ scores (as measured by the Stanford-Binet) than the children in the LR and FT groups, and the LR children's scores were lower than the FT children although still well within average to high average levels of functioning. The children were videotaped with their mothers in a playroom equipped with a child-sized table and chairs, dolls and a crib, and a tricycle. Each mother–child dyad was videotaped in a teaching (puzzle task) and a social situation (tea party). Each mother was asked to assist her child in constructing a puzzle during a 10-minute time period. Next, the mother and child had a 10-minute "tea party" with each other, sitting at a child-sized table holding a tray that contained small plates, cups, spoons, napkins, a teapot filled with fruit juice, and a plate of cookies. Following these videotaped sessions, the children were tested with the Stanford-Binet Intelligence Test while their mothers completed the Behavioral Style Questionnaire Measure (McDevitt & Carey, 1978), a parent-reported measure of children's temperament (ages 3–7 years).

The two interaction sessions were coded by a two-person team. The team coded maternal and child behaviors related to each maternal attention-directing attempt. Each time the mother directed the child to do something or restricted the child's behavior, the child was coded for compliance or noncompliance. In addition, each time the children initiated directing their own behavior (e.g., selecting a puzzle piece, picking up a cup, or initiating conversation) they were coded for a self-directed behavior. Finally, we coded each time the child showed one of the seven problem behaviors we had identified from the Achenbach Child Behavior Checklist for ages 2–3 (Achenbach, Edelbrock, & Howell, 1987). These behaviors were coded only if they occurred at times other than in direct response to a maternal directive or restriction. Definitions for these problem behaviors and the mother and child interactive behaviors are listed in Table 11.2.

Results showed a significant negative association between maternal directiveness and children's self-directed behavior in addition to a significant contribution of children's IQ. A nonsignificant interaction term showed that the pattern of this relation was similar for the three groups. Mothers' praise was positively associated with children's social initiative and their cooperation for all groups.

For the high-risk preterm children, cognitive delay accounted for mothers' increased directiveness and this provision of structure seemed appropriate to the learning needs of these children. A number of studies show that mothers adapt their level of involvement to their children's signals of readiness to regulate their own behavior (Henderson, 1984; Wertsch, 1979).

In our study the children's cooperation and social initiative across all three groups appeared to be responsive to maternal behaviors that provided direction and positive feedback, while the mothers' use of directive or choice-providing behavior may have been influenced by their children's signals regarding their readiness to direct their own behavior.

CONCLUSION

The development of joint attention skills is important for the emergence of language, toy exploration, and social competence. Preterm LBW infants especially those with more severe neonatal medical complications have difficulty developing the full range of joint attention skills seen in most full-term children by 2 years of age. Medically high-risk preterm infants show particular problems through 3 years of age in the ability to initiate directing their mothers' attention to objects and conversational topics through the use of eye gaze behaviors, verbalizations, and gestures. Responsiveness to their mothers' efforts to direct their attention to objects or topics of shared interest does not seem to be as much of a problem.

One might question whether the high-risk preterm infants' joint attention problems observed in these studies were due to true attentional deficits or to existing motor delays. Are these infants having more difficulty making the required joint attention responses because they are actually not able to shift their focus of attention, a skill that is required frequently in joint attention situations, or because they do not have the motor skills that are necessary to show the required responses in interactions? We would argue that the high-risk infants' joint attention problems are due to attention deficits rather than motor delays. The evidence for this comes from several studies showing that they are able to show joint attention responses that are similar to those of the low-risk preterm and full-term infants under certain conditions. Their responses to mothers' attempts to direct their attention are similar to the other groups of children when their attention capacity is not exceeded, even though at these times they are still being required to show a response that requires a certain degree of motor skill. For example, when mothers noticed and followed the high-risk infants' focus of interest or when they introduced toys when the infant was not already engaged with a toy, then these high-risk preterm infants were able to show the same level of joint attention responsiveness as the other two groups of children. It was only when increased demands were placed on their attentional skills (under conditions of joint attention in which mothers attempted to redirect their attention to a different toy) that responses that involved motor skills were decreased for these infants compared to low-risk preterm and full-term infants. This same degree of support for attentional skills did not seem necessary for the low-risk and full-term infants because these infants were able to show comparable levels of joint attention responsiveness regardless of whether their attentional focus was being maintained or redirected to a new toy.

In light of these joint attention problems, it is particularly important to identify ways in which mothers can facilitate joint attention for these high-risk infants. Two aspects of mothers' attention-directing behaviors have been identified in the studies described in this chapter as possibly having facilitative effects on high-risk preterm infants' joint attention skills. Mothers' sensitive timing of attention-directing behaviors and their provision of a high degree of structure are associated with improvements in their infants' ability to jointly attend to toys with their mothers. Maintaining behaviors are thought to facilitate joint attention responsiveness because they place fewer demands on these infants' more deficient attentional skills by allowing them to maintain their attentional focus rather than shift to look at a different toy. This strategy may therefore provide support for control over attentional regulation for these infants. An important component of exploratory play competence is children's development of a sense that they can master their environment, including their own response to that environment (Lewis & Goldberg, 1969; Yarrow et al., 1982). Mothers' attempts to maintain their high-risk infants' interests may also help to support their development of a sense of autonomy in environmental exploration. Because these infants may be particularly dependent on their mothers' involvement in their learning, maternal facilitation of exploratory mastery is likely to require involvement that is finely tuned to avoid undue control. It will be important in future studies to evaluate longitudinally other aspects of mothers' joint attention behaviors in relation to their facilitative effect on preterm infants' joint attention skills.

ACKNOWLEDGMENTS

This study was supported by NIH grants HD25128 and HD23800 to the author. I am grateful to Mildred Dobson for her assistance with this manuscript and to numerous research staff who assisted in coding observations from the videotapes described in these studies.

REFERENCES

Achenbach, T., Edelbrock, C., & Howell, C. (1987). Empirically based assessment of the behavioral/emotional problems of 2–3-year-old children. *Journal of Abnormal Child Psychology, 15*, 629–650.

Adamson, L., & Bakeman, R. (1985). Affect and attention: Infants observed with mothers and peers. *Child Development, 56*, 582–593.

Akhtar, N., Dunham, F., & Dunham, P. J. (1991). Directive interactions and early vocabulary development: The role of joint attentional focus. *Journal of Child Language, 18*, 41–49.

Austin, J. L. (1962). *How to do things with words.* Oxford, England: Oxford University Press.

Bakeman, R., & Adamson, L. (1984). Coordinating attention to people and objects in mother-infant and peer-infant interaction. *Child Development, 55,* 1278–1289.

Ballard, J. L. (1977). A simplified assessment of gestational age. *Pediatric Research, 11,* 374A.

Barnard, K. E., Bee, H. L., & Hammond, M. A. (1984). Developmental changes in maternal interactions with term and preterm infants. *Infant Behavior and Development, 7,* 101–114.

Barocas, R., Seifer, R., Sameroff, A. J., Andrews, T. A., Croft, R. T., & Ustrow, E. (1991). Social and interpersonal determinants of developmental risk. *Developmental Psychology, 27,* 479–488.

Bates, E. (1979). *The emergence of symbols: Cognition and communication in infancy.* New York: Academic Press.

Bates, E., Camaioni, L., & Volterra, V. (1975). The acquisition of performatives prior to speech. *Merrill-Palmer Quarterly, 21,* 205–226.

Bell, R. Q. (1979). Parent, child, and reciprocal influences. *American Psychologist, 34,* 821–826.

Belsky, J., Goode, M. K., & Most, R. K. (1980). Maternal stimulation and infant exploratory competence: Cross-sectional, correctional, and experimental analyses. *Child Development, 51,* 1163–1178.

Bendersky, M., & Lewis, M. (1990). Early language ability as a function of ventricular dilatation associated with intraventricular hemorrhage. *Developmental and Behavioral Pediatrics, 11,* 17–21.

Bjerre, I., & Hansen, E. (1976). Psychomotor development and school adjustment of 7-year-old children with low birth weight. *Acta Paediatrica Scandinavica, 65,* 88–96.

Brachfeld, S., Goldberg, S., & Sloman, J. (1980). Parent-infant interaction in free play at 8 and 12 months: Effects of prematurity and immaturity. *Infant Behavior and Development, 3,* 289–305.

Brazelton, T. B., Koslowski, B., & Main, M. (1974). The origins of reciprocity. In M. Lewis & L. A. Rosenblum (Eds.), *The effect of the infant on its caregiver* (pp. 49–76). New York: Wiley.

Bromwich, R. (1981). *Working with parents and families: An interactional approach.* Baltimore: University Park Press.

Bruner, J. (1974). The ontogenesis of early speech acts. *Journal of Child Language, 2,* 1–19.

Bruner, J. S. (1975). From communication to language—a psychological perspective. *Cognition, 3,* 255–287.

Bruner, J. (1977). Early social interaction and language acquisition. In H. R. Schaffer (Ed.), *Studies in mother-infant interaction* (pp. 271–289). New York: Academic Press.

Bruner, J. (1982). The organization of action and the nature of the adult-infant transaction. In E. Tronick (Ed.), *Social interchange in infancy: Affect, cognition, and communication.* Baltimore: University Park Press.

Cohen, L. B. (1972). Attention-getting and attention-holding processes of infant visual preferences. *Child Development, 43,* 869–879.

Cohen, S. E., & Parmelee, A. (1983). Predictors of 5 year Stanford Binet score in preterm infants. *Child Development, 54,* 1242–1253.

Crawford, J. W. (1982). Mother-infant interaction in premature and full-term infants. *Child Development, 53,* 957–962.

Crockenberg, S., & Litman, C. (1990). Autonomy as competence in 1-year-olds: Maternal correlates of child defiance, compliance, and self-assertion. *Developmental Psychology, 26,* 961–971.

Dore, J. (1979). Conversational acts and the acquisition of language. In B. Scheiffelin & E. Ochs (Eds.), *Developmental Pragmatics* (pp. 339–361). New York: Academic Press.

Drillien, C. M. (1961). The incidence of mental and physical handicaps in school-age children of very low birth weight. *Pediatrics, 27,* 452–464.

Fagan, J. F., & McGrath, S. K. (1981). Infant recognition memory and later intelligence. *Intelligence, 5,* 121–130.

Field, T. (1980). Interactions of high-risk infants: Quantitative and qualitative differences. In D. B. Swain, R. C. Hawkins, C. D. Walker, & J. H. Penticuff (Eds.), *Exceptional infant-environmental transactions* (pp. 120–143). New York: Brunner/Mazel.

Field, T. (1981). Gaze behavior of abnormal and high-risk infants during early interactions. *Journal of the American Academy of Child Psychiatry, 20,* 308–317.

Fogel, A. (1982). Social play, positive affect, and coping skills in the first 6 months of life. *Topics in Early Childhood Special Education, 2,* 53–65.

Garner, P. W., & Landry, S. H. (1992). Preterm infants' affective responses in independent versus toy-centered play with their mothers. *Infant Mental Health Journal, 13*(3), 219–230.

Garner, P. W., & Landry, S. H. (1994). Effects of maternal attention-directing strategies on preterm infants' affective expressions during joint toy play. *Infant Behavior and Development, 17,* 15–22.

Garner, P. W., Landry, S. H., & Richardson, M. A. (1991). The development of joint attention skills in very low birth weight infants across the first two years. *Infant Behavior and Development, 14,* 489–495.

Girolametto, L. E. (1988). Developing dialogue skills: The effects of conversational model of language intervention. In K. Marfo (Ed.), *Parent-child interaction and developmental disabilities: Theory, research and intervention* (pp. 145–162). New York: Praeger.

Greenberg, M., & Crnic, R. (1988). Longitudinal predictors of developmental status and social interaction in preterm and full-term infants at age 2. *Child Development, 59,* 554–570.

Henderson, B. B. (1984). Parents and exploration: The effects of context on individual differences in exploratory behavior. *Child Development, 55,* 1237–1245.

Hunt, J. V., Cooper, B. A., & Tooley, W. H. (1988). Very low birth weight infants at 8 and 11 years of age: Role of neonatal illness and family status. *Pediatrics, 82*(4), 596–603.

Kaye, K. (1982). *Mental and social life of babies.* Chicago: University of Chicago Press.

Kaye, K., & Fogel, A. (1980). The temporal structure of face-to-face communication between mothers and infants. *Developmental Psychology, 16,* 454–464.

Kopp, C. B., & Vaughn, B. E. (1982). Sustained attention during exploratory manipulation as a predictor of cognitive competence in preterm infants. *Child Development, 53,* 174–182.

Landry, S. H. (1986). Preterm infants' responses in early joint attention interactions. *Infant Behavior and Development, 9,* 1–14.

Landry, S. H., & Chapieski, L. (1988). Visual attention during toy exploration in preterm infants: Effects of medical risk and maternal interactions. *Infant Behavior and Development, 11,* 187–204.

Landry, S. H., & Chapieski, M. L. (1989). Joint attention and infant toy exploration: Effects of Down syndrome and prematurity. *Child Development, 60,* 103–118.

Landry, S. H., Chapieski, L., Fletcher, J., & Denson, S. E. (1988). Three-year outcome for low birth weight infants: Differential effects of early medical complications. *Journal of Pediatric Psychology, 13,* 317–327.

Landry, S. H., Chapieski, L., Richardson, M., Palmer, J., & Hall, S. (1990). The effects of specific medical complications associated with low birth weight on 3-year-olds' social competence. *Child Development, 61*(5), 1605–1616.

Landry, S. H., Chapieski, L., & Schmidt, M. (1986). Effects of maternal attention-directing strategies on preterms' response to toys. *Infant Behavior and Development, 9,* 257–269.

Landry, S. H., Fletcher, J. M., Denson, S. E., & Chapieski, M. L. (1993). Longitudinal outcome for low birth weight infants: Effects of intraventricular hemorrhage and bronchopulmonary dysplasia. *Journal of Clinical and Experimental Neuropsychology, 15*(2), 205–218.

Landry, S. H., Fletcher, J., Zarling, C., Chapieski, M. L., & Francis, D. J. (1984). Differential outcomes associated with early medical complications in premature infants. *Journal of Pediatric Psychology, 9,* 384–401.

Landry, S. H., Garner, P., Denson, S., Swank, P., & Baldwin, C. (1993). Maternal attention-directing strategies and infant exploratory behaviors: Effects of intraventricular hemorrhage in low birth weight infants at 12 and 24 months. *Research in Developmental Disabilities, 14,* 237–249.

Landry, S. H., Garner, P. W., Swank, P. R., & Baldwin, C. D. (in press). Effects of maternal scaffolding during joint toy play with preterm and full-term infants. *Merrill-Palmer Quarterly.*

Landry, S. H., Leslie, N., Fletcher, J. M., & Frances, D. J. (1985). Differential effects of early medical complications on visual attention skills in premature infants. *Infant Behavior and Development, 8,* 309–321.

Landry, S. H., Schmidt, M., & Richardson, M. A. (1989). The effects of intraventricular hemorrhage on functional communication skills in preterm toddlers. *Developmental and Behavioral Pediatrics, 10*, 299–306.

Lawson, K. R., Parrinello, R., & Ruff, H. A. (1992). Maternal behavior and infant attention. *Infant Behavior and Development, 15*, 209–229.

Lempers, J., Flavell, E., & Flavell, J. (1977). The development in very young children of tacit knowledge concerning visual perception. *Genetic Psychology Monographs, 95*, 3–53.

Leung, E., & Rheingold, H. (1981). Development of point as a social gesture. *Developmental Psychology, 17*, 215–220.

Lewis, M., & Brooks-Gunn, J. (1981). Visual attention at 3 months as a predictor of cognitive functioning at 2 years of age. *Intelligence, 5*, 131–140.

Lewis, M., & Goldberg, S. (1969). Perceptual-cognitive development in infancy: A generalized expectancy model as a function of mother-infant interaction. *Merrill-Palmer Quarterly, 15*, 81–100.

Lockman, J. J., & McHale, J. P. (1989). Object manipulation in infancy: Developmental and contextual determinants. In J. J. Lock & N. L. Hazen (Eds.), *Action in social context: Perspectives on early development.* New York: Plenum.

Lytton, H. (1977). Correlates of compliance and the rudiments of conscience in 2-year-old boys. *Canadian Journal of Behavioral Sciences, 9*, 242–251.

Marfo, K. (1990). Maternal directiveness in interactions with mentally handicapped children: An analytical commentary. *Journal of Child Psychology and Psychiatry, 31*, 531–549.

McDevitt, S. C., & Carey, W. B. (1978). Measurement of temperament in 3- to 7-year-old children. *Journal of Child Psychology and Psychiatry and Allied Disciplines, 19*, 245–253.

Myers, B. J., Jarvis, F. A., Creasey, G. L., Kerkering, K.W., Markowitz, P. I., & Best, A. M. (1992). Prematurity and respiratory illness: Brazelton scale (NBAS) performance of preterm infants with bronchopulmonary dysplasia (BPD), respiratory distress syndrome (RDS), or no respiratory illness. *Infant Behavior and Development, 15*, 27–41.

Newson, J., & Newson, E. (1975). Intersubjectivity and the transmission of culture. *Bulletin of the British Psychological Society, 28*, 437–445.

Papile, L., Munsick, G., Weaver, N., & Pecha, S. (1979). Cerebral intraventricular hemorrhage in infants 1500 grams. Developmental follow-up at 1 year. *Pediatric Research, 13*, 528A.

Parpal, M., & Maccoby, E. E. (1985). Maternal responsiveness and subsequent child compliance. *Child Development, 56*, 1326–1334.

Pasamanick, B., Rogers, M. E., & Lilienfeld, A. M. (1956). Pregnancy experience and the development of behavior disorder in children. *American Journal of Psychiatry, 112*, 613–618.

Ratner, H. H., & Stettner, L. J. (1991). Thinking and feeling: Putting humpty dumpty together again. *Merrill Palmer Quarterly, 37*, 1–26.

Robertson, C. M., Etches, P. C., Goldson, E., & Kyle, J. M. (1992). Eight-year school performance, neurodevelopmental and growth outcome of neonates with bronchopulmonary dysplasia: A comparative study. *Pediatrics, 39*(3), 365–372.

Rocissano, L., & Yatchmink, Y. (1983). Language skill and interaction patterns in prematurely born toddlers. *Child Development, 54*, 1229–1241.

Rose, S. A. (1983). Differential rates of visual information processing in full-term and preterm infants. *Child Development, 54*, 1189–1198.

Ruddy, M. G., & Bornstein, M. H. (1982). Cognitive correlates of infant attention and maternal stimulation over the first year of life. *Child Development, 53*, 183–189.

Ruff, H. A. (1986). Components of attention during infants' manipulative exploration. *Child Development, 57*, 105–114.

Ruff, H. A. (1988). The measurement of attention in high-risk infants. In P. Vietze & H. G. Vaughan (Eds.), *Early identification of infants with developmental disabilities* (pp. 282–296). New York: Grune & Stratton.

Ruff, H. A., McCarton, C., Kurtzburg, D., & Vaughan, H. G. (1984). Preterm infants' manipulative exploration of objects. *Child Development, 55*, 1166–1173.

Schaffer, H. R. (1977). *Studies in mother-infant interactions*. New York: Academic Press.

Searle, J. R. (1969). *Speech Acts: An essay in the philosophy of language*. London: Cambridge University Press.

Siegel, L. S., Saigal, S., Rosenbaum, P., Morton, R., Young, A., Berenbaum, S., & Stoskopt, B. (1982). Predictors of development in preterm and full-term infants: A model for detecting the at-risk child. *Journal of Pediatric Psychology, 7*, 135–147.

Sigman, M. (1976). Early development of preterm and full-term infants: Exploratory behavior in 8-month-olds. *Child Development, 47*, 606–612.

Sigman, M., Cohen, S., & Forsythe, A. (1981). The relation of early infant measures to later development. In S. Friedman & M. Sigman (Eds.), *Preterm birth and psychological development* (pp. 313–327). New York: Academic Press.

Sigman, M., & Parmelee, A. H. (1974). Visual preference of 4-month-old premature and full-term infants. *Child Development, 45*, 959–965.

Sostek, A., Smith, Y., Katz, K., & Grant, E. (1987). Developmental outcome of preterm infants with intraventricular hemorrhage at 1 and 2 years of age. *Child Development, 58*, 779–786.

Sugarman, S. (1984). The development of preverbal communication. In R. L. Schiefellbusch & J. Pickar (Eds.), *The acquisition of communicative competence* (pp. 24–67). Baltimore: University Park Press.

Taub, H. B., Goldstein, K. M., & Caputo, D. V. (1977). Indices of neonatal prematurity as discriminators of development in middle childhood. *Child Development, 48*, 797–805.

Tomasello, M., & Farrar, M. (1986). Joint attention and early language. *Child Development, 57*, 1454–1463.

Vohr, B., Bell, E., & Williams, O. (1982). Infants with bronchopulmonary dysplasia. *American Journal of Diseases in Childhood, 136*, 443–447.

Vohr, R., & Coll, C. T. (1985). Neurodevelopmental and school performance of very low birth weight infants: A 7-year longitudinal study. *Pediatrics, 76*(3), 345–350.

Volpe, J. J. (1981). Neonatal intraventricular hemorrhage. *New England Journal of Medicine, 304*, 886–891.

Vygotsky, L. S. (1962). *Thought and language*. (E. Hanfmann & G. Vaker, Eds. & Trans.). Cambridge, MA: MIT Press. (Original work published 1934)

Wasserman, G., Allen, R., & Solomon, C. R. (1985). At-risk toddlers and their mothers: The special case of physical handicap. *Child Development, 56*, 73–83.

Wertsch, J. V. (1979). From social interaction to higher psychological processes: A clarification and application of Vygotsky's theory. *Human Development, 22*, 1–22.

Wood, D., Bruner, J. S., & Ross, G. (1976). The role of tutoring in problem solving. *Journal of Child Psychology and Psychiatry, 17*, 89–100.

Yarrow, L. J., Morgan, G. A., Jennings, K. D., Harmon, R. J., & Gaiter, J. L. (1982). Infants' persistence at tasks: Relationships to cognitive functioning and early experience. *Infant Behavior and Development, 5*, 131–141.

Chapter 12

Factors Influencing Joint Attention Between Socioeconomically Disadvantaged Adolescent Mothers and Their Infants

C. Cybele Raver
Cornell University

Bonnie J. Leadbeater
Yale University

Sharing experience in joint activity requires what Bowlby (1969) calls a "goal-corrected" partnership in which each member is "prepared, when necessary, to relinquish, or at least adjust, his or her own set goals to suit the other's" (p. 355). Infants' skills in negotiating bouts of joint visual attention may well be among the building blocks of these early social partnerships. Infants' ability to follow others' gaze to an object of interest represents a crucial transition from face-to-face engagement in early infancy to joint exploration of, and communication about, objects in the environment (Tronick, Als, & Adamson, 1979). In establishing and maintaining joint gaze on an object, mother and infant continue the mutually regulated, pleasurable process of sharing experience begun in earlier face-to-face play (Mundy, Kasari, & Sigman, 1992; Trevarthen & Hubley, 1978).

Although the establishment of joint attention in parent-child interaction requires coordinated effort on the part of both partners, research to date has focused primarily on the role of the child. Valuable work has elucidated the mechanisms that infants use to organize their spatial skills in pinpointing objects that hold others' interest (Butterworth & Grover, 1988; Butterworth & Jarrett, 1991; Corkum & Moore, 1993; Scaife & Bruner, 1975). It has been established empirically that infants 10 to 24 months have the requisite skills for following their partners' gaze. The styles used by infants to coordinate their own gaze with maternal gaze in naturalistic interaction have been less investigated (Hunter, McCarthy, MacTurk, & Vietze, 1987). Much also remains to be learned regarding mothers' roles in actively introducing objects as "topics" of joint attention. Factors that influence the ways that infants and mothers successfully coordinate their efforts to maintain the focus of their attention on the topic of nonverbal conversation during periods of free play also have not been elaborated.

In this chapter, we argue that there is a need to more fully understand both partners' participation in establishing and maintaining bouts of joint attention during naturalistic play. We suggest that reciprocity in joint attention in the second year is a developmentally advanced analogue to mutual regulation of affective expression in earlier face-to-face mother-infant play. As in face-to-face interactions, bouts of joint attention on objects may also be influenced by individual differences of mothers and infants. We also present data suggesting that maternal depressive symptoms, maternal sensitivity, and child gender, are related to patterns of establishing and maintaining joint attention when infants are 12 and 20 months of age.

THE DEVELOPMENT OF SHARED EXPERIENCE

Joint visual attention on objects can be understood by placing it within the framework of infants' development of early communicative skills with others. This framework has been advanced by theorists describing the development of intersubjectivity through infancy and early childhood, where infants develop the skills in negotiating social interactions through reciprocal, shared experience (Goncu, 1993; Stern, 1985; Trevarthen, 1979, 1989; Trevarthen & Hubley, 1978). The sharing of affect, attention, and intentions with a partner has been organized into a hierarchical, developmental sequence (Emde & Buchsbaum, 1990; Stern, 1985; Rogoff, 1990).

From 3 to 9 months of age, infants frequently participate in mutually regulated affective exchanges with parents. Each partner modifies his or her own behavior to match the affective expressions of the other (Cohn & Tronick, 1983; Stern, 1985; Tronick & Cohn, 1989). Mothers and infants utilize affect to send and receive emotional messages in an "interactive display that carries social meaning" (Gusella, Muir, & Tronick, 1988, p. 1120). When mothers are asked by an experimenter to disrupt this affective exchange by maintaining an affectively neutral "still face," infants 3 to 9 months of age first attempt to reengage the mother in play. When failing to do so, infants display signs of distress and disorganization (Carter, Mayes, & Pajer, 1990; Gianino & Tronick, 1988; Mayes & Carter, 1990).

From 9 to 24 months of age, mutual engagement in mother-infant interaction shifts to accommodate a shared focus of attention on external events and objects (Trevarthen & Hubley, 1978). During this period, infants gain skills in communicating about things in the world, utilizing nonverbal and linguistic means to refer to the focus of their attention (Tomasello, 1988). Infants become increasingly able to direct their partners' attention toward desired objects (Collis & Schaffer, 1975; Leung & Rheingold, 1981) and to understand others' attention as indicative of their interest in an object (Phillips, Baron-Cohen, & Rutter, 1992). By sharing a focus of attention, infants begin to communicate with their partners about their own and their partners' goals, expressing their own intentions and responding positively or negatively to the intentions of others (Trevarthen, 1989). In following the partner's line of gaze, the infant thus sharpens his or her understanding of the other's literal and figurative perspective (Adamson & Bakeman, 1984; Bakeman & Adamson, 1986; Baron-Cohen, this volume; Perner, 1991). While engaged in successive bouts of joint attention, both mother and infant gain practice in identifying, modifying, and responding to each other's goals in the manner described by Bowlby (1969).

DYADIC RECIPROCITY AND JOINT ATTENTION

Many investigators have advanced a dyadic approach in describing early mother-infant interactions, emphasizing their "co-regulation" (Fogel, 1990), "synchrony" (Isabella & Belsky, 1991), "attunement" (Stern, 1985), or "reciprocity" (Gianino & Tronick, 1988). In face-to-face interactions, mothers and infants can actively "bid" for each others' visual attention, match facial affect and attentional state, and enter in and out of synchronous periods of engagement (Cohn & Tronick, 1987). Their face-to-face engagement is often subject to "interactive error" and "interactive repair" (Tronick, 1989, p. 116; Tronick & Cohn, 1989): Not only is there frequent miscoordination of both partners' efforts to sustain each other's attention, but both partners can repair engagement by initiating new bouts of affective and attentional matching.

When mother and child begin to focus their visual attention on objects, the establishment and maintenance of joint attention may continue to depend on the reciprocity with which both partners offer, accept, and respond to each other's bids for engagement. During free play interactions, mothers appear to work strenuously to capture and keep children's focused attention by introducing and manipulating objects (Raver & Leadbeater, 1992). Ruff and Lawson (1990) suggest that such effort on the adult's part may be necessary because episodes of toddlers' focused attention may take time to be organized; "that is, the child orients to a toy but takes at least a few seconds to mobilize more concentrated involvement with it" (p. 90). Within those few seconds, mothers and infants subtly communicate their willingness to engage in interaction. Dyads may be differentially capable of coordinating their attention during the few second "window" of their partner's visual orientation to establish the congruent goal of playing with the same toy. For example, a mother's efforts to initiate engagement or to bid with a particular toy may be ignored or actively rejected by her infant. On the other hand, a mother may shift her gaze too quickly, or not fully face the infant so that joint visual attention is not achieved. Or, rather than following up on the baby's continued expression of interest, a mother may fail to persist with the new toy and move on to something else.

Research involving infants with organic disorders supports the hypothesis that joint attention is subject to interactive miscoordination and requires work on the part of both partners to establish and maintain. Very low birth weight infants with medical problems and infants with Down syndrome or autism show difficulty establishing joint attention with adults (Garner, Landry, & Richardson, 1991; Landry, this volume; Landry & Chapieski, 1989; Mundy, Sigman, Kasari, & Yirmiya, 1988). The mother's sensitivity to her infant's cues also plays an important part in establishing bouts of joint attention. For example, mothers of very low birth weight infants introduced objects more frequently than mothers of full-term or low-risk infants, presumably to compensate for their infants' more passive involvement (Garner et al., 1991). Mothers of Down syndrome infants redirected their child's attention less frequently than mothers of healthy infants, so as to avoid taxing the baby's limited attentional capacities (Landry & Chapiesky, 1989).

Interactive coordination and miscoordination have also been investigated in the development of children's early verbal communication with others (see Dunham & Dunham, 1992, this volume; Dunham, Dunham, Tran, & Akhtar, 1991; Tomasello, Conti-Ramsden, & Ewert, 1990; Tomasello & Farrar, 1986; Tomasello & Todd, 1983). Parental style of redirecting joint attention during the child's second year has been found to influence children's communicative development at 21 months of age. Specifically, children learn more words when mothers "join" children's gaze at an object before labelling an object than when mothers interrupt children's line of gaze by redirecting their attention and labelling a new object (Tomasello & Farrar, 1986; Tomasello & Todd, 1983). Study of conversations with a talking robot shows that 2-year-olds are particularly perturbed when the behaviors of their social partner (the robot) are frustratingly nonreciprocal (Dunham et al., 1991). Yet less is known regarding the process and variability with which mothers and healthy infants jointly coordinate their attention-getting and attention-keeping efforts during communicative bouts in everyday nonverbal interaction.

Study of mothers and infants at high-risk for difficulty in reciprocal interaction may illuminate the ways that dyads coordinate and miscoordinate their behaviors when establishing bouts of joint attention. Adolescent mothers and their infants may be at particular risk for nonsynchronous engagement during play (Levine, Garcia-Coll, & Oh, 1985). Low socioeconomic status, limited educational attainment, and family instability, all associated with adolescent motherhood, pose serious risks to responsive and reciprocal parent-infant relations. Analysis of variability across these mother-infant pairs offers to illuminate the process and the individual differences underlying dyads' capacity for joint attention. In this program of research, we first examine the process of coordinating attention by analyzing the relation between the reciprocity of the first three turns taken by both partners in establishing each bout of joint attention, and the maintenance or duration of joint attention during free play. We then go on to examine the relation between these measures of joint engagement and maternal depressive symptoms, maternal sensitivity, and child gender.

METHOD

Subjects

Data for our analyses of factors influencing the capacity for joint attention come from a sample of 120 adolescent mother-infant dyads who are part of an ongoing longitudinal investigation of the risks and protective factors affecting the development of young mothers and their children. Details of the sample are given in Leadbeater and Linares (1992). Mothers were recruited 3 to 4 weeks after delivery and were reinterviewed at 6, 12, 20, and 28 to 36 months postpartum. At delivery, the mothers were between 13 and 19 years of age ($M = 17.09$, $SD = 1.18$), and were primarily African Americans (53.1%) or Puerto Ricans (42.5%) who were born and raised on the mainland USA. Most lived in East Harlem or surrounding boroughs of New York City. All except two were primiparous. Most lived with their own mothers (71.7%) and came from families receiving public assistance (64.6%).

Procedures

Mother-infant interactions at 12 and 20 months were videotaped at a community-based adolescent health clinic. A sheet was spread on the floor, and a box of attractive toys that were developmentally appropriate (blocks) and inappropriate (rattle) was placed on the sheet. Mothers were asked to play with their babies "as they would at home." These free play interactions were videotaped using a hand-held Panasonic PV-330D camcorder that allowed the research assistant to move with the dyad in order to keep their faces and hands visible. The use of a single camera preserved the simultaneous and bidirectional quality of their joint attention. It was also hoped that the use of a single camera operated by a member of the research team familiar to the mother in a private room would be least disruptive to the ecological validity of the play interaction.

Observational Measures

Videotapes were first coded for the maintenance of joint attention, measured by the duration of time spent in joint attention. At 12 and 20 months, the onset of a bout of joint attention was coded when both mother and infant focused their gaze upon the same object for at least 10 seconds. Termination of the occurrence was coded when either partner looked away from the object for 5 seconds or more. Agreement between two coders for duration of time spent in joint attention was calculated using an intraclass R correlation and equalled .91.

By 20 months of age children have become significantly more sophisticated in their use and manipulation of objects, as well as in their ability to play symbolically (Howes, 1992; Ruff & Lawson, 1990). Hence, coding of joint attention necessarily became more sophisticated. Following Bakeman and Adamson (1984), two levels of joint attention were coded in play interactions at 20 months in contrast to simply coding onset and offset of the more passive joint gazing that was prevalent at 12 months. As shown in Table 12.1, we coded five subtypes of joint attention, collapsing the subtypes into the two levels of "noncollaborative joint attention" (e.g., one partner watched while the other manipulated an object), and "collaborative joint attention" (e.g., both partners engaged in pretend play, jointly negotiating the nature of the game). Reliability calculated by kappa across collaborative and noncollaborative categories of joint attention was .72 at 20 months.

On a separate pass through each videotape, the initiation of each bout of joint attention was assessed as a either a reciprocal or nonreciprocal bidding sequence. To code the reciprocity of these bidding sequences, we analyzed the first three turns taken by the dyad in establishing each new bout of joint attention. We first identified mother's introduction of each new object as a bid, then categorized the infant's response and the mother's subsequent reaction to the infant (see Table 12.2). Maternal bids were defined as a mother's deliberate attempt to engage the infant in interaction with an object that the infant was not already looking at by using one of the following behaviors: offering an object, vocalizing to the child, or pointing to an object.

The "infant response" to the maternal bid was then coded as either accepts or does not accept. "Accept" was coded when the infant responded positively to the bid, such as began to attend to, or to manipulate the offered object. "Does not accept" was coded when the infant ignored or rejected the bid, such as by initially reaching for the toy and then throwing it away. "Maternal reaction" to the infant's response was then coded as either persists or does not persist. "Persist" was coded when the mother continued to attempt to engage the infant in activity.

TABLE 12.1
Subtypes of Joint Attention at 20 Months of Age

Level I. Noncollaborative Joint Attention
  1. One partner watches object while the other partner plays with it.
  2. Mother and child play in parallel with the same object, but are not playing together.
  3. Mother sets up game or toy with clear agenda, child attends but does not actively play with toy. Mother does not further facilitate play.

Level II. Collaborative Joint Attention
  1. Both partners are actively engaged in play. Mother provides developmentally appropriate directives and uses several strategies to engage child.
  2. Interaction is marked by playfulness, turn-taking, and flexibility of each partner in adjusting their own agenda to accommodate the other partner's agenda, such as pretend play.

TABLE 12.2
Coding Patterns of Maternally-Initiated Bid Sequences

---

1. *Maternal bid*: a deliberate attempt to engage her infant.
2. *Infant response*
   infant accepts (a)
   infant does not accept (na)
3. *Mother reaction*
   mother persists (P)
   mother does not persist (NP)
Four types of bid sequences are possible:
1. infant accepts-mother persists (a P)
2. infant accepts-mother does not persist (a NP)
3. infant does not accept-mother persists (na P)
4. infant does not accept-mother does not persist (na NP)

"Does not persist" was coded when the mother either changed the activity or did nothing.

Mothers and infants could thus initiate joint attention using one of four bid sequences. Following a maternal bid, the infant could respond with an accept or no accept, and the mother could in turn react by persisting, or failing to persist in the activity. When a bid was followed by an infant accept and a maternal persist, that is, when both partners' goals in playing the game were congruent, the bid sequence was coded as reciprocal. Reliability across categories of maternal bid sequences was calculated; kappa equalled .67 at 12 months, .76 at 20 months.

Measures of Maternal Depressive Symptoms and Maternal Sensitivity

The chronicity of maternal depressive symptoms was assessed using the Beck Depression Inventory (BDI), a 21-item questionnaire (Beck, Steer, & Garbin, 1988). The BDI has been widely used in nonclinical samples of adolescents, and with developmentally and educationally delayed adolescents (Beck, Carlson, Russell, & Brownfield, 1987; Gibbs, 1985; Teri, 1982). The inventory has been shown to have good internal consistency ($\alpha = .73$ to .92) and stability (test-retest $r = .60$ to .83) in nonclinical populations (Beck et al., 1988).

In the present study, BDI scores at 1, 6, and 12 months postpartum were used to categorize the mothers as "not symptomatic," or having no scores at or above a cutoff of 12 on any of the three assessments (35%); "intermittently symptomatic," or having one score at or above 12 (17%); or "chronically symptomatic," or having two or more scores at or above 12 (48%). Suggested cutoff scores that have been found to be associated with, but not equivalent to, diagnostic categories of depression range from 9 to 16 (Barrera & Garrison-Jones, 1988; Beck et al., 1987). The mid-level was chosen to maximize the power in the subgroups for our analyses.

Following Field et al.'s (1991) suggestion that mothers who report no depressive symptoms on the BDI present as much risk to their children as mothers who score above a cutoff of 12, scores were inspected to identify mothers who reported no symptoms at 2 or 3 assessment points. No mothers met this criteria.

Maternal sensitivity was coded using the CARE-INDEX (Crittenden, 1981). The videotaped free-play interactions of the mothers and infants were coded by two female coders who were blind to all other data and to the hypotheses of the study. Seven aspects of maternal behavior were coded: facial expression, vocal expression, position and body contact, expression of affection, pacing of turns, control, and developmental appropriateness of choice of activity. Mothers were classified as *high* in sensitivity if they scored 1 standard deviation above the mean, *moderate* in sensitivity if they scored within 1 standard deviation above or below the mean, and *low* in sensitivity if they scored at least 1 standard deviation below the mean. We then analyzed the reciprocity of bidding sequences and duration of joint attention by gender and sensitivity level for each age group. For 20-month-olds, we chose to analyze data for collaborative joint attention with the assumption that this higher level of joint engagement was more developmentally salient and appropriate for the older age group.

THE RELATION BETWEEN DURATION OF JOINT ATTENTION AND RECIPROCITY OF BIDDING SEQUENCES

We investigated whether the duration of joint attention that was sustained by mothers and infants during 10 minutes of free play was related to reciprocity in initiating each new bout of joint attention. At 12 months of age, a strong positive correlation ($r = .64$, $p < .01$) between duration of joint attention and the occurrence of infant-accept/mother-persist bidding sequences suggests that dyads producing a higher number of reciprocal bid sequences spent a greater amount of time in joint attention (see Table 12.3). Duration of joint attention was also

TABLE 12.3
Zero-order Correlations Between Duration of Joint Attention and
Maternally-initiated Bid Sequences at 12 Months of Age ($n = 99$)

	JA	a P	a NP
1. JA			
2. a P	.64***		
3. a NP	−.13*	−.40***	
4. na P	−.38***	−.45****	−.27***

Note. JA = duration of joint attention; a P = infant accept/mother persist; a NP = infant accept/mother does not persist; na P = infant does not accept/mother persists.
*$p \le .10$. ***$p \le .01$. ****$p \le .001$.

negatively correlated ($r = -.38$, $p < .01$) with the number of infant does not accept/mother persists bidding sequences established by the dyad. While all dyads spent roughly the same amount of time in joint attention at 20 months (roughly 70% of the time), dyads differed significantly in the proportion of time spent in collaborative joint attention. Using collaborative joint attention as the developmentally appropriate measure of shared experience at 20 months, the 12 month findings were partially replicated, as shown in Table 12.4. A moderate positive correlation ($r = .28$, $p < .01$) between infant accepts/mother persists bidding sequences and duration of collaborative joint attention suggests that mothers and infants initiating engagement with higher number of reciprocal bid sequences spent more time in collaborative joint attention.

At both 12 and 20 months then, the total amount of time spent in developmentally appropriate forms of joint attention was related to the way in which both partners coordinated their efforts to initiate bouts of engagement. Either member of the dyad can make or break the success and quantity of time spent jointly attending to objects. The establishment of joint attention is not only a matter of developmental capacity of infants, but also of a willingness on the part of both the mother and infant to follow the partner's interactive lead.

Observation of the videotaped interactions also suggested that different mother-infant pairs maintained qualitatively different patterns of reciprocal or nonreciprocal engagement over the 10 minute period of play. Mothers and their infants who had more nonreciprocal engagement became frustrated, irritable, or defeated during play, while those who spent a larger proportion of their time in reciprocal engagement showed pleasure in establishing games with congruent goals. Objects served as the social "fulcrum" of their interaction (Vandell, Wilson, & Buchanan, 1980, p. 482), rather than as the locus of struggle, as it sometimes seemed for mothers and infants who engaged in a high proportion of nonreciprocal bidding sequences. We went on to investigate the relation between individual characteristics of both mothers and children and this variability in dyadic engagement.

TABLE 12.4
Zero-order Correlations Between Duration of Joint Attention and
Maternally-initiated Bid Sequences at 20 Months of Age ($n = 82$)

	JA$_{collab}$	a P	a NP
1. JA$_{collab}$			
2. a P	.28***		
3. a NP	−.21**	−.21**	
4. na P	−.05	−.61***	−.28***

Note. JA$_{collab}$ = Duration of collaborative joint attention; a P = infant accept/mother persist; a NP = infant accept/mother does not persist; na P = infant does not accept/mother persists.
**$p \leq .05$. ***$p \leq .01$.

THE IMPLICATIONS OF INDIVIDUAL DIFFERENCES
IN MATERNAL DEPRESSIVE SYMPTOMS,
MATERNAL SENSITIVITY, AND CHILD GENDER
FOR DYADIC RECIPROCITY

In this report, we chose to focus on the implications of maternal depressive symptoms, maternal sensitivity, and infant gender for joint attention between adolescent mothers and infants. In particular, maternal depressive symptoms have been extensively identified as correlates of disturbance in mother-infant interaction (for review, see Field, 1992). Mothers with depressive symptoms have been found to be less responsive, more intrusive, and more negative or affectively muted with their infants and toddlers than nondepressed mothers (Cohn, Matias, Tronick, Connell, & Lyons-Ruth, 1986; Lyons-Ruth, et al. 1986; Teti, Gelfand, & Pompa, 1990; Zeloski, O'Hara, & Wills, 1987). Infants of depressed mothers themselves demonstrate depressed mood in interaction with both their mothers and with other nondepressed adults (Field, 1992). Shared behavioral states for depressed mothers and their infants are less frequent due to decreased reciprocity of the dyad and decreased mutual attentiveness (Cohn et al., 1986; Field, Healy, Goldstein, & Guthertz, 1990). An important moderator of the effects of maternal depression on the quality of the parenting behaviors has been the chronicity of the depressive symptoms (Alpern & Lyons-Ruth, 1993; Hammen, Burge, & Adrian, 1991). Young single mothers living in poverty, especially those experiencing high levels of stressful life events, family conflict, and social isolation may be at particular risk for both depression and disturbed mother-child interactions (Downey & Coyne, 1990; Leadbeater & Bishop, 1994; Leadbeater & Linares, 1992; McLoyd, 1990). In this research, we asked what relation exists between the chronicity of maternal depressive symptoms in the first year postpartum and the initiation and maintenance of bouts of joint attention.

Maternal sensitivity may also be related to the reciprocity with which dyads establish and maintain bouts of joint attention. In face-to-face interaction in early infancy, Brazelton, Koslowski, and Main (1974) describe sensitive mothers as engaged in interaction without becoming overly intrusive. They are capable of sustaining interactions with their infants for longer periods of time than mothers who "bombard" their infants with stimulation. Mothers described as sensitive also maintain a moderate level of control, stimulation, and elaboration of their infants' behaviors while mothers who overcontrol ignore or override infant cues and fail to leave their infants "room" to initiate their own bids for social contact (Stoller & Field, 1982). Although a number of authors have argued that sensitivity be viewed as a dyadic rather than maternal characteristic (Biringen & Robinson, 1991; Crittenden, 1981), few microanalytic analyses have been conducted on joint attention or reciprocal bidding behaviors used by dyads composed of infants and mothers who have been rated as sensitive or insensitive. We expected that mothers who have been independently rated as sensitive would have more success in establishing reciprocal bid sequences with their infants, and would spend more time in joint attention than mothers rated as insensitive.

Infant gender has also been shown to play a role in the degree to which mother and infant mutually synchronize their affective and attention behaviors (Malatesta & Haviland, 1982; Robinson, Little, & Biringen, in press). Notably, research in early face-to-face engagement suggests that male infants experience more affective matching with their mothers (Tronick & Cohn, 1989). They are also more affectively negative in response to the disruption of face-to-face matching when a mother maintains a neutral "still face" than are female infants (Carter, Mayes, & Pajer, 1991). In contrast, research on the role of infant gender in toddlers' visual referencing of parents' emotional expressions when faced with frightening objects suggests that mothers encourage girls to be more interpersonally engaged, while encouraging boys to be more object focused (for review see Adamson & McArthur, this volume; Rosen, Adamson, & Bakeman, 1992). Specifically, Rosen et al. (1992) found that while mothers' facial displays of fear to daughters were significantly less intense than to sons, girls' but not boys' approaches toward a frightening object were regulated by these maternal displays. Dunham et al., (1991), and Sigman and Kasari (this volume) have also found that girls visually referenced their mothers' affective expressions more frequently than did boys when faced with a novel toy. Butterworth and Jarrett (1991) also report gender differences in infants' initial localization of an object gazed at by mothers, with girls performing better than boys at 6 and 12 months but not at 18 months of age. As Adamson and McArthur (this volume) point out, parents may "negotiate the emotional meaning of objects" differently with daughters and sons. While these studies are useful in understanding the ways in which gender may be related to affective signalling between parent and child and children's initial gaze at or approach to a toy, less is known regarding whether gender is related to dyadic reciprocity in establishing play with the toy, or to the duration of time subsequently spent by the dyad in jointly engaging with a toy.

THE RELATION OF MATERNAL DEPRESSIVE SYMPTOMS, MATERNAL SENSITIVITY, AND CHILD GENDER TO DYADIC RECIPROCITY AND JOINT ATTENTION

Our analyses suggest that maternal depression, maternal sensitivity, and infant gender are each related to differences in joint attention. At 12 months of age, no differences in joint attention were found across dyads with mothers reporting intermittent, chronic, or no depressive symptoms. At 20 months, however, mothers reporting intermittent symptoms and their infants spent significantly less time in collaborative joint attention than dyads either with no depressive symptoms or with chronic symptoms (see Table 12.5). When we examined patterns

TABLE 12.5
Mean Values of Joint Attention and Bid Sequences at 20 Months for Mothers
With History of Chronic, Intermittent, or No Depressive Symptoms ($N = 72$)

Variable	Level of Depression			
	No (n = 25)	Intermittent (n = 12)	Chronic (n = 35)	Univariate F
1. % JA$_{collab}$	.65 (.27)	.42 (.29)	.66 (.25)	3.95*
2. a P	.47 (.28)	.46 (.17)	.35 (.22)	2.37
3. a NP	.09 (.09)	.20 (.14)	.12 (.12)	3.94*
4. na P	.24 (.21)	.19 (.14)	.31 (.20)	2.02

Note. % JA$_{collab}$ = proportion of joint attention spent in collaborative engagement.
*$p \leq .05$.

of bid sequences for these dyads, it became evident that mothers with intermittent symptoms had a higher rate of infant-accept/mother-does-not-persist sequences than the nondepressed and chronic groups. This pattern of bidding is markedly passive; the child accepts the mother's effort to engage in interaction, yet the mother fails to follow up by taking the next "turn" with the offered object. Comparison of the different patterns of bid sequences displayed by the three groups of mothers also suggests that mothers with chronic depressive symptoms and their infants engage in a higher proportion of nonreciprocal bid sequences than mothers with no depressive symptoms. Mothers with chronic depressive symptoms engaged their infants in roughly equal numbers of infant-accept/mother-persists and infant-does-not-accept/mother-persists sequences. Conversely, mothers with no depressive symptoms established roughly two times more infant-accept/mother-persist bid sequences than infant-does-not-accept/mother-persists sequences with their infants. This suggests that while mothers with chronic symptoms and mothers with no depressive symptoms establish similar durations of collaborative joint attention, they achieve this type of joint attention through different means.

At both ages, the relation between maternal sensitivity and the establishment of joint attention was clear: Mothers in the high sensitivity group engaged in a significantly greater proportion of reciprocal bidding sequences and spent significantly more time in joint attention with their infants than did mothers in the moderate or low sensitivity groups (see Table 12.6).

Findings with respect to gender differed by age of the infant. At 12 months, dyads with girls established more reciprocal bidding sequences than dyads with boys (see Fig. 12.1). In interaction with sensitivity, infant gender was also related to duration of joint attention. In the low sensitivity group only, dyads with boys spent less time in joint attention than dyads with girls.

At 20 months, no gender differences were found in the amount of time spent in collaborative joint attention. Examination of reciprocity of bid sequences, however, revealed a Gender × Sensitivity interaction (see Fig. 12.2). While

TABLE 12.6
Mean Values of Joint Attention and Bid Sequences
by Maternal Sensitivity at 12 and 20 Months

	Level of Sensitivity			
	Low (n = 25)	Moderate (n = 37)	High (n = 35)	Univariate F
12 months				
1. JA	55.44 (14.7)	60.50 (13.70)	70.70 (11.05)	10.89***
2. a P	.30 (.18)	.36 (.18)	.47 (.18)	6.51**
3. a NP	.19 (.14)	.18 (.13)	.17 (.13)	.17
4. Na P	.21 (.15)	.22 (.12)	.16 (.12)	2.43+
20 months				
1. JA$_{collab}$	37.60 (21.61)	41.12 (18.62)	60.43 (24.20)	6.85**
2. a P	.35 (.19)	.38 (.23)	.54 (.24)	3.89*
3. a NP	.12 (.10)	.12 (.12)	.09 (.12)	1.40
4. na P	.30 (.20)	.28 (.20)	.20 (.19)	.40

Note. JA = Duration of joint attention at 12 months; JA$_{collab}$ = Duration of collaborative joint attention; a P = infant accept/mother persist; a NP = infant accept/mother does not persist; na P = infant does not accept/mother persists.

$^+p \leq .1$. $^*p \leq .05$. $^{**}p \leq .01$. $^{***}p \leq .001$.

mothers and girls maintained approximately equal levels of reciprocal bidding sequences across all three levels of sensitivity, mothers and boys showed different levels of reciprocity depending on whether mothers were rated as low, moderate, or high on sensitivity. Low sensitive mothers and boys engaged in fewer reciprocal bidding sequences than low sensitive mothers and girls. High sensitive mothers and boys engaged in a greater number of reciprocal bidding sequences than high

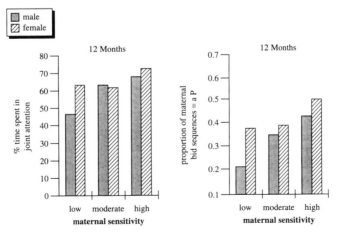

FIG. 12.1. Joint attention and reciprocity of bid sequences at 12 months by maternal sensitivity and infant gender.

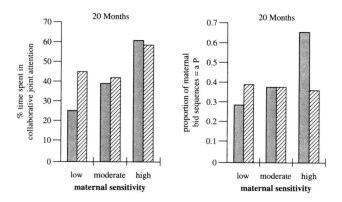

FIG. 12.2. Joint attention and reciprocity of bid sequences at 20 months by maternal sensitivity and infant gender.

sensitive mothers and girls. The reciprocity of male infants' engagement with their mothers appears to depend more on the mother's parenting style than does the reciprocal engagement of female infants. Although study of gender has not been prominent in the joint attention literature, these findings are consistent with reports of an interaction between maternal sensitivity and gender in early affect matching (Brody, 1985; Carter, Mayes, & Pajer, 1990; Robinson, Little, & Biringen, in press). These interactions between maternal characteristics and child characteristics in dyadic behavior suggest that while gender differences may indeed be found in the reciprocity of establishing bouts of joint attention, these differences may be greater or smaller depending upon maternal control and sensitivity.

In investigating the patterns of reciprocity and joint attention during an ongoing flow of dyadic interaction, we cannot specify the extent to which maternal behaviors or infant behaviors causally drive these patterns. For example, infant gender could be related to different patterns of joint attention because male and female infants exert different strengths in the context of interaction and/or because mothers treat male and female infants differently, as discussed by Adamson and McArthur (this volume). Similarly, global ratings of maternal sensitivity may reflect maternal responses to infant temperamental or cognitive differences in addition to maternal behaviors themselves. Previous research has indicated that infants of depressed mothers behave in a nonsynchronous, affectively muted manner with nondepressed adults (Cohn et al., 1986). Nevertheless, attention to individual characteristics illuminates the ways that maternal and infant characteristics are related to patterns of coordination and miscoordination in dyadic engagement.

Study of these patterns of coordination suggests that segmenting and categorizing the flow of dyadic behavior by examining bouts of joint attention provides a valid microanalytic correlate to more individually oriented constructs such as maternal sensitivity. We agree with Fogel (1993) that interacting, communicating partners engage in a continuous process of "co-regulation [defined as a] social process by which individuals dynamically alter their actions with respect to the ongoing and anticipated actions of their partners" (p. 12). Analysis of dyadic behavioral states such as joint attention facilitates our awareness of the extent to which these alterations of behavior are coordinated or miscoordinated. Moreover, we can begin to understand ways in which mothers' and infants' behaviors are not only reciprocal but recursive: Mothers who are rated as low sensitive and their infants may be caught in a "negative cycle of mutual maladjustment" (Hammen, Burge, & Stansbury, 1990, p. 25) in which a mother's sense of competence erodes as she experiences repeated failure to successfully engage in shared experiences with her infant. Mothers reporting intermittent depressive symptoms may experience similar feelings of defeat in being less able to successfully maintain bouts of collaborative play with their infants. Infants in both cases may be at-risk for developing maladaptive responses to maternal bids, demonstrating a wariness to overly intrusive or overly passive behavior on their partner's part.

Focus on joint attention offers a clear and codeable set of behaviors (e.g., head orientation, visual gaze, vocalizations coupled with a one-fingered pointing gesture, etc.) with which to track nonverbal communicative effort, and sharing of experience in later infancy. It provides a concrete behavioral ground in which to root the study of early joint engagement. Researchers have struggled with the question of where to begin an analysis of the flow of ongoing dyadic behaviors (Bakeman & Gottman, 1986; Gottman & Roy, 1992). By coding bouts of joint attention, researchers gain an ecologically sound "point of entry" into the flow of interaction (Lewis & Lee-Painter, 1974, p. 24).

DIRECTIONS FOR FUTURE RESEARCH

Our research suggests a number of directions for future studies in joint attention. Analyses of joint attention benefited from a high level of specificity in definition and coding. Our finding that dyads containing mothers with intermittent depressive symptoms differed from dyads containing no or chronic depressive symptoms only in the proportion of time spent in collaborative joint attention supports the suggestion by Bakeman and Adamson (1984) that not only quantity but quality of joint attention needs to be analyzed. Though we coded dyads' first three "turns" in establishing each bout of joint attention, questions regarding the sequencing and possible escalation of miscoordinations and coordinations in joint gazing behavior over time may best be further investigated utilizing sequential analysis (Bakeman & Gottman, 1986; Gottman & Roy, 1992).

In addition, our data suggest that the variability in a high-risk sample is itself not only extensive, but highly informative. Following a tradition in the study of "success" and "breakdown" in mother-infant interaction (Brazelton et al.,

1974; Field, 1992; Tronick & Cohn, 1989), we elucidated the mechanisms involved in establishing and maintaining joint attention in free play. In addition, we examined the implications of the heterogeneity of individual differences among mothers and infants for dyadic functioning. Comparison of group means across levels of depressive symptoms, ratings of maternal sensitivity, and infant gender suggests that different mother-infant pairs maintain qualitatively different styles of negotiating bouts of joint attention. Future research in joint attention will benefit not only from a search for a set of behavioral invariants across dyads, but also from analysis of variability within groups of dyads.

Researchers studying mother-infant communication during this age period have also considered the role of interactive context when examining infant social behavior (Bakeman & Adamson, 1986; Bretherton, O'Connell, Shore, & Bates, 1984; Dunn, Bretherton, & Munn, 1987; Fiese, 1990; Tomasello & Kruger, 1992). Mothers and infants in this study were directed to play with the box of toys "as they would at home," to elicit free play. In observing variability in joint attention across dyads, it is important to consider whether these differences would be magnified or decreased in different interactive contexts. Dyads might be differentially capable of establishing reciprocal bouts of joint attention during episodes designed to elicit conflict, such as clean-up, or designed to elicit proactive, affectively positive engagement, such as episodes of joking and teasing (Reddy, 1991), or snack time. Research is currently underway to explore the potential for differences in patterns of joint attention established by dyads across interactive contexts.

Our findings also offer a number of implications for the growing area of research on joint attention as an antecedent to later social and communicative development. As a modality used by infants and parents to nonverbally communicate, joint attention provides an important platform for a child's language development (Tomasello & Farrar, 1986). By providing a means of gauging others' interest and others' goals, joint attention is a crucial component of children's increasing comprehension of others' internal states (Phillips, Baron-Cohen, & Rutter, 1992). Affective synchrony and matching of affective states have been identified as important avenues for the development of infants' emotional self-regulation, and their sense of effectance in regulating the states of others (Tronick, 1989; Tronick & Gianino, 1986). As the visual analogue to affective matching, joint attention may play as important a role in older infants' skills in regulating their own and others' behaviors. Dyadic reciprocity in negotiating joint attention may be an important index of both partners' capacity to balance the needs of self and other in the collaborative project of having a good time together. The ability to produce social bids and to interpret the bids of others represents a developmental prerequisite for the child's participation in coherent discourse with peers (Bakeman & Adamson, 1984; Hazen & Black, 1989; Zahn-Waxler, Denham, Iannotti, & Cummings, in press). Toddlers' "working models" or representations of the strategies for the give and take commonly experienced in early social partnerships may come to underlie future expectations of other's behaviors in social exchanges (Crittenden, 1992; Goncu, 1993; Tronick, 1989). Experience in reciprocal bouts of joint attention with a parent may have powerful implications for play with peers in the preschool years.

ACKNOWLEDGMENTS

The assistance of Sandra J. Bishop in coding the data, and of L. Oriana Linares and Pam M. Kato in data collection is acknowledged with appreciation. Thanks also to Beth Shepard, Niobe Way, and Carolyn Zahn-Waxler for their comments. This research was supported in part by grants from Smith-Richardson Foundation, and a William T. Grant, Faculty Scholars Award to Bonnie Leadbeater.

REFERENCES

Adamson, L. B., & Bakeman, R. (1984). Mothers' communicative acts: Changes during infancy. *Infant Behavior and Development, 7,* 467–478.

Alpern, L., & Lyons-Ruth, K. (1993). Preschool children at social risk: Chronicity and timing of maternal depressive symptoms and child behavior problems at school and at home. *Development and Psychopathology, 5,* 371–387.

Bakeman, R., & Adamson, L. B. (1984). Coordinating attention to people and objects in mother-infant and peer-infant interaction. *Child Development, 55,* 1278–1289.

Bakeman, R., & Adamson, L. B. (1986). Infants' conventionalized acts: Gestures and words with mothers and peers. *Infant Behavior and Development, 9,* 215–230.

Bakeman, R., & Gottman, J. M. (1986). *Observing Interaction: An introduction to sequential analysis.* Cambridge, England: Cambridge University Press.

Barrera, M., & Garrison-Jones, C. V. (1988). Properties of the Beck Depression Inventory as screening instrument for adolescent depression. *Journal of Abnormal Child Psychology, 16,* 263–273.

Beck, D. C., Carlson, G. A., Russell, A. T., & Brownfield, F. E. (1987). The use of depression rating instruments in developmentally and educationally delayed adolescents. *Journal of the American Academy of Child and Adolescent Psychiatry, 26,* 97–100.

Beck, A., Steer, R., & Garbin, M. (1988). Psychometric properties of the BDI: 25 years of evaluation. *Clinical Psychology Review, 8,* 77–100.

Biringen, Z., & Robinson, J. (1991). Emotional availability in mother-child interactions: A reconceptualization for research. *American Journal of Orthopsychiatry, 61,* 258–270.

Bowlby, J. (1969). *Attachment and loss.* New York: Basic Books.

Brazelton, T. B., Koslowski, B., & Main, M. (1974). The origins of reciprocity: The early mother-infant interaction. In M. Lewis & L. Rosenblum (Eds.), *The effect of the infant on its caregiver.* New York: Wiley.

Bretherton, I., O'Connell, B., Shore, C., & Bates, E. (1984). The effect of contextual variation on symbolic play development from 20 to 28 months. In I. Bretherton (Ed.), *Symbolic play* (pp. 271–297). New York: Academic Press.

Brody, L. R. (1985). Gender differences in emotional development: A review of theories and research. *Journal of Personality, 53,* 103–137.

Butterworth, G. E., & Grover, L. (1988). The origins of referential communication in human infancy. In L. Weiskrantz (Ed.), *Thought without language* (pp. 5–24). Oxford, England: Clarendon.

Butterworth, G., & Jarrett, N. (1991). What minds have in common is space: Spatial mechanisms serving joint visual attention in infancy. British Journal of Developmental Psychology, 9, 55–72.

Carter, A. S., Mayes, L. C., & Pajer, K. A. (1990). The role of dyadic affect in play and infant sex in predicting infant response to the still-face situation. Child Development, 61, 764–773.

Cohn, J., Matias, R., Tronick, E. Z., Connell, D., & Lyons-Ruth, D. (1986). Face-to-face interactions of depressed mothers and their infants. In E. Z. Tronick & T. Field (Eds.), Maternal depression and infant disturbance (pp. 31–46). San Francisco: Jossey-Bass.

Cohn, J. F., & Tronick, E. Z. (1983). Three-month-old infants' reaction to simulated maternal depression. Child Development, 54, 185–193.

Cohn, J. F., & Tronick, E. Z. (1987). Mother-infant face-to-face interaction: The sequence of dyadic states at 3, 6, and 9 months. Developmental Psychology, 23, 68–77.

Collis, G. M., & Schaffer, H. R. (1975). Synchronization of visual attention in mother-infant pairs. Journal of Child Psychology and Psychiatry and Allied Disciplines, 16, 315–320.

Corkum, V., & Moore, C. (1993, March). The origins of joint visual attention. Paper presented at the meeting of the Society For Research in Child Development, New Orleans, LA.

Crittenden, P. M. (1981). Abusing, neglecting, problematic, and adequate dyads: Differentiating by patterns of interaction. Merrill-Palmer Quarterly, 27, 1–18.

Crittenden, P. M. (1992). Quality of attachment in the preschool years. Development and Psychopathology, 4, 209–241.

Downey, G., & Coyne, J. C. (1990). Children of depressed parents: An integrative review. Psychological Bulletin, 108, 50–76.

Dunham, P., & Dunham, F. (1992). Lexical development during middle infancy: A mutually driven infant-caregiver process. Developmental Psychology, 28, 414–420.

Dunham, P., Dunham, F., Tran, S., & Akhtar, N. (1991). The nonreciprocating robot: Effects on verbal discourse, social play, and social referencing at 2 years of age. Child Development, 62, 1489–1502.

Dunn, J., Bretherton, I., & Munn, P. (1987). Conversations about feeling states between mothers and their young children. Developmental Psychology, 23(1), 132–139.

Emde, R. N., & Buchsbaum, H. K. (1990). "Didn't you hear my mommy?" Autonomy with connectedness in moral self emergence. In D. Cicchetti & M. Beeghly (Eds.), The self in transition (pp. 35–60). Chicago: University of Chicago Press.

Field, T. (1984). Early interactions between infants and their postpartum depressed mothers. Infant Behavior and Development, 7, 527–532.

Field, T. (1992). Infants of depressed mothers. Development and Psychopathology, 4, 49–66.

Field, T., Healy, B., Goldstein, S., & Guthertz, M. (1990). Behavior-state matching and synchrony in mother-infant interactions of nondepressed versus depressed dyads. Developmental Psychology, 26, 7–14.

Field, T., Morrow, C., Healy, B., Foster, T., Adlestein, D., & Goldstein, S. (1991). Mothers with zero Beck depression scores act more "depressed" with their infants. Development and Psychopathology, 3, 253–262.

Fiese, B. H. (1990). Playful relationships: A contextual analysis of mother-toddler interaction and symbolic play. Child Development, 61, 1648–1656.

Fogel, A. (1990). The process of developmental change in infant communicative action: Using dynamic systems theory to study individual ontogenies. In J. Colombo & J. Fagen (Eds.), Individual differences in infancy: Reliability, stability and prediction (pp. 341–358). Hillsdale, NJ: Lawrence Erlbaum Associates.

Fogel, A. (in press). Two principles of communication: Co-regulation and framing. In J. Nadel & L. Camaioni (Eds.), New perspectives in early communicative development. London: Routledge & Kegan Paul.

Garner, P. W., Landry, S. H., & Richardson, M. A. (1991). The development of joint attention skills in very low birth weight infants across the first two years. Infant Behavior and Development, 14, 489–495.

Gianino, A., & Tronick, E. Z. (1988). The mutual regulation model: The infant's self and interactive regulation and coping and defensive capacities. In T. M. Field, P. M. McCabe, & N. Schneiderman (Eds.), *Stress and coping across development* (pp. 47–68). Hillsdale, NJ: Lawrence Erlbaum Associates.

Gibbs, J. T. (1985). Psychosocial factors associated with depression in urban adolescent females: Implications for assessment. *Journal of Youth and Adolescence, 14,* 47–60.

Goncu, A. (1993). Development of intersubjectivity in social pretend play. *Human Development, 36,* 185–198.

Gottman, J. M., & Roy, A. K. (1992). *Sequential analysis: A guide for behavioral researchers.* Cambridge, England: Cambridge University Press.

Gusella, J., Muir, D., & Tronick, E. Z. (1988). The effect of manipulating maternal behavior during an interaction on 3- and 6-month-olds' affect and attention. *Child Development, 59,* 1111–1124.

Hammen, C. Burge, D., & Adrian, C. (1991). Timing of mother and child depression in a longitudinal study of children at risk. *Journal of Consulting and Clinical Psychology, 59,* 341–345.

Hammen, C., Burge, D., & Stansbury, K. (1990). Relationship of mother and child variables to child outcomes in a high-risk sample: A causal modeling analysis. *Developmental Psychology, 26,* 24–30.

Hazen, N. L., & Black, B. (1989). Preschool peer communication skills: The role of social status and interaction context. *Child Development, 60,* 867–876.

Howes, C. (1992). *The collaborative construction of pretend.* New York: SUNY Press.

Hunter, F. T., McCarthy, M. E., MacTurk, R. H., & Vietze, P. M. (1987). Infants' social-constructive interactions with mothers and fathers. *Developmental Psychology, 23,* 249–254.

Isabella, R., & Belsky, J. (1991). Interactional synchrony and the origins of infant-mother attachment: A replication study. *Child Development, 62,* 373–384.

Kasari, C., Sigman, M., Mundy, P., & Yirmiya, N. (1990). Affective sharing in the context of joint attention interactions of normal, autistic, and mentally retarded children. *Journal of Autism and Developmental Disorders, 20,* 87–100.

Landry, S. H., & Chapieski, M. L. (1989). Joint attention and infant toy exploration: Effects of Down syndrome and prematurity. *Child Development, 60,* 103–118.

Leadbeater, B. J., & Bishop, S. J. (1994). Predictors of behavior problems in preschool children of inner-city, Afro-American, and Puerto Rican adolescent mothers. *Child Development.*

Leadbeater, B. J., & Linares, O. (1992). Depressive symptoms in Black and Puerto Rican adolescent mothers in the first 3 years postpartum. *Development and Psychopathology, 4,* 451–468.

Leung, E. H., & Rheingold, H. L. (1981). Development of pointing as a social gesture. *Developmental Psychology, 17,* 215–220.

Levine, L., Garcia-Coll, C. T., & Oh, W. (1985). Determinants of mother-infant interaction in adolescent mothers. *Pediatrics, 75,* 23–29.

Lewis, M., & Lee-Painter, S. (1974). An interactional approach to the mother-infant dyad. In M. Lewis & L. Rosenblum (Eds.), *The effect of the infant on its caregiver* (pp. 21–47). New York: Wiley.

Lyons-Ruth, K., Zoll, D., Connell, D., & Grunebaum, H. (1986). The depressed mother and her 1-year-old infant: Environmental context, mother-infant interaction and attachment, and infant development. In E. Tronick & T. Field (Eds.), *Maternal depression and infant disturbance* (pp. 61–82). San Francisco: Jossey-Bass.

Malatesta, C. Z., & Haviland, J. M. (1982). Learning display rules: The socialization of emotion expression in infancy. *Child Development, 53,* 991–1003.

Mayes, L. C., & Carter, A. S. (1990). Emerging social regulatory capacities as seen in the still-face situation. *Child Development, 61,* 754–763.

McLoyd, V. C. (1990). The impact of economic hardship on black families and children: Psychological distress, parenting, and socioemotional development. *Child Development, 61,* 311–346.

Mundy, P., Kasari, C., & Sigman, M. (1992). Nonverbal communication, affective sharing, and intersubjectivity. *Infant Behavior and Development, 15,* 377–381.

Mundy, P., Sigman, M., Kasari, C., & Yirmiya, N. (1988). Nonverbal communication skills in Down Syndrome children. *Child Development, 59,* 235–249.

Perner, J. (1991). *Understanding the representational mind.* Cambridge, MA: MIT Press.

Phillips, W., Baron-Cohen, S., & Rutter, M. (1992). The role of eye contact in goal-detection: Evidence from normal infants and children with autism or mental handicap. *Development and Psychopathology, 4,* 375–383.

Raver, C. C., & Leadbeater, B. J. (1992, May). *Patterns of reciprocity in the play interactions of sensitive and controlling mothers and their 12-month-old infants.* Poster presented at the International Conference on Infant Studies, Miami.

Reddy, V. (1991). Playing with others' expectations: Teasing and mucking about in the first year. In A. Whiten (Ed.), *Natural theories of mind* (pp. 143–158). Cambridge, MA: Basil Blackwell.

Robinson, J., Little, C., & Biringen, Z. (in press). Emotional communication in mother-toddler relationships: Evidence for early gender differentiation. *Merrill-Palmer Quarterly.*

Rogoff, B. (1990). *Apprenticeship in thinking: Cognitive development in a social context.* New York: Oxford University Press.

Rosen, W. D., Adamson, L. B., & Bakeman, R. (1992). An experimental investigation of infant social referencing: Mothers' messages and gender differences. *Developmental Psychology, 28,* 1172–1178.

Ruff, H. A., & Lawson, K. R. (1990). Development of sustained, focused attention in young children during free play. *Developmental Psychology, 26,* 85–93.

Scaife, M., & Bruner, J. S. (1975). The capacity for joint visual attention in the infant. *Nature, 253,* 265–266.

Stern, D. N. (1985). *The interpersonal world of the infant: A view from psychoanalysis and developmental psychology.* New York: Basic Books.

Stoller, S. A., & Field, T. (1982). Alteration of mother and infant behavior and heart rate during a still-face perturbation of face-to-face interaction. In T. Field & A. Fogel (Eds.), *Emotion and early interaction* (pp. 57–82). Hillsdale, NJ: Lawrence Erlbaum Associates.

Teri, L. (1982). The use of the Beck Depression Inventory with adolescents. *Journal of Abnormal Child Psychology, 20,* 277–284.

Teti, D., Gelfand, D., & Pompa, J. (1990). Depressed mothers' behavioral competence with their infants: Demographic and psychosocial correlates. *Development and Psychopathology, 2,* 259–270.

Tomasello, M. (1988). The role of joint attention in early language development. *Language Sciences, 11,* 69–88.

Tomasello, M., Conti-Ramsden, G., & Ewert, B. (1990). Young children's conversations with their mothers and fathers: Differences in breakdown and repair. *Journal of Child Language, 17,* 115–130.

Tomasello, M., & Farrar, M. J. (1986). Joint attention and early language. *Child Development, 57,* 1454–1463.

Tomasello, M., & Kruger, A. C. (1992). Joint attention on action: Acquiring verbs in ostensive and nonostensive contexts. *Journal of Child Development, 19,* 311–334.

Tomasello, M., Mannle, S., & Kruger, A. C. (1986). Linguistic environment of 1- to 2-year-old twins. *Developmental Psychology, 22,* 169–176.

Tomasello, M., & Todd, J. (1983). Joint attention and lexical acquisition style. *First Language, 4,* 197–212.

Trevarthen, C. (1979). Communication and cooperation in early infancy: A description of primary intersubjectivity. In M. Bullowa (Ed.), *Before speech: The beginnings of interpersonal communication* (pp. 321–349). New York: Cambridge University Press.

Trevarthen, C. (1989). Origins and directions for the concept of infant intersubjectivity. *Society for Research in Child Development Newsletter,* pp. 1–4.

Trevarthen, C., & Hubley, P. (1978). Secondary intersubjectivity: Confidence, confiding and acts of meaning in the first year. In A. Lock (Ed.), *Action, gestures and symbol* (pp. 183–230). London: Academic Press.

Tronick, E. Z. (1989). Emotions and emotional communication in infants. *American Psychologist*, 44, 112–119.

Tronick, E. Z., Als, H., & Adamson, L. (1979). Structure of early face-to-face communicative interactions. In M. Bullowa (Ed.), *Before speech: The beginnings of interpersonal communication* (pp. 349–370). Cambridge, England: Cambridge University Press.

Tronick, E. Z., & Cohn, J. F. (1989). Infant-mother face-to-face interaction: Age and gender differences in coordination and the occurrence of miscoordination. *Child Development*, 60, 85–92.

Tronick, E. Z., & Gianino, A. F. (1986). The transmission of maternal disturbances to the infant. In E. Z. Tronick & T. Field (Eds.), *Maternal depression and infant disturbance* (pp. 5–12). San Francisco: Jossey-Bass.

Vandell, D. L., Wilson, K. S., & Buchanan, N. R. (1980). Peer interaction in the first year of life: An examination of its structure, content, and sensitivity to toys. *Child Development*, 51, 481–488.

Zahn-Waxler, C., Denham, S., Iannotti, R. J., & Cummings, E. M. (in press). Peer relations in children with a depressed caregiver. In R. D. Parke & G. W. Ladd (Eds.), *Family-peer relationships: Modes of linkage*. Hillsdale, NJ: Lawrence Erlbaum Associates.

Zeloski, E. M., O'Hara, M. W., & Wills, K E. (1987). The effects of maternal mood on mother-infant interaction. *Journal of Abnormal Child Psychology*, 15, 361–378.

Author Index

Subject Index

DATE DUE
